CEYLON DAILY NEWS COOKERY BOOK

CEYLON DAILY NEWS COOKERY BOOK

HILDA DEUTROM

STAMFORD LAKE (PRIVATE) LIMITED
Book Publishers
366 High Level Road
Pannipitiya
Sri Lanka

First Edition 1929

Fifth Edition – Revised & Improved 1964
Eleventh Impression 1999

ISBN 955 – 8156 – 23 – X

National Library of Sri Lanka - Cataloguing - in - Publication Data

Deutrom, Hilda
Ceylon Daily News Cookery Book / Hilda Deutrom ..-
5th edition, 11th Impression .- Colombo : Stamford Lake, 1999
428 p. ; 22 cm.

ISBN 955 – 8156 – 23 – X   Price : Rs. 575/=

I 641.5 DDC 21   ii Title
1. Cookery

Published by
Stamford Lake (Pvt) Ltd
366 High Level Road
Pannipitiya
Sri Lanka

Printed by

Lake House Printers & Publishers Ltd
41 W.A.D. Ramanayake Mawatha
Colombo 2

Preface

To the Fifth Edition

THE 'CEYLON DAILY NEWS' COOKERY BOOK, edited by Miss H. Deutrom, might well be entitled "East meets West", for the Island's position on the highways of the World is mirrored in the variety and the range of the recipes in its pages.

The book first appeared in 1929, a slim volume (7½"×5") of 316 pages with 700 recipes. The 'revised and enlarged' second edition, issued five years later, had 300 new recipes making in all 1000— "each one of these tested by the Compiler"—and ran into 456 pages.

The 'third and enlarged edition' came out in 1942—a large-sized volume (8¾"×5½") of 440 pages—in the preparation of which the publishers had the assistance of Mrs. Marcus Rockwood. Second, third and fourth impressions of this edition followed in 1943, 1945 and 1947.

A new and revised Fourth edition was published in 1953 which set out in a more convenient manner and order the contents of previous editions. New recipes and information of value to housewives were added and the index enlarged and improved. A second impression of this followed in 1956.

The Fifth Edition now presented includes the contents of the previous edition together with additional recipes.

The Publishers wish to express their thanks to all those who helped to make the 'CEYLON DAILY NEWS' COOKERY BOOK the popular and useful publication it has proved to be through the years.

October 1964

The 'DINAMINA' COOKERY BOOK (in Sinhala), edited by Miss H. Deutrom, first appeared in 1930, and was re-issued in 1936, 1938, 1944 and 1947. A new edition was issued in 1958. A further revised edition was issued in 1968.

From the previous editions

THE 'CEYLON DAILY NEWS' COOKERY BOOK constitutes a serious attempt to aid the housewives of Ceylon to practise the art of cooking so that, like the quality of mercy, the preparation of palatable dishes will bless her that gives and him that takes.

* * * *

There is also another purpose behind the publication .... Collectors of a country's folklore are esteemed as benefactors. Why should not the collectors of a country's indigenous recipes....? Indeed a representative list of the recipes handed from generation to generation of Ceylon's housewives will reflect the march of the Island's history.

There are, first, the dishes known to many generations of Sinhalese and Tamils. Then there are other Eastern delicacies, introduced into Ceylon by the Arabs, Malays and Moors. Finally, we see in our list of Ceylon recipes the influence of the Portuguese, Dutch and British occupations to say nothing of French cookery which has revolutionized all European cooking.

* * * *

The 'CEYLON DAILY NEWS' COOKERY BOOK endeavours to preserve all the best recipes handed to the present by past generations.......No trouble has been spared to make the book as comprehensive as possible in recipes of Ceylon origin or a distinctively Ceylon interest.

A great many of these recipes are new in the sense that they have hitherto not been published, but they are all tried favourites from old 'Family Recipe Books'; while others have appeared in the columns of the *Ceylon Daily News* and *Ceylon Observer.*

* * * *

Time and thought have been given........to make it not only a Book of Recipes but also a Book of Reference for those who desire to provide variety at meals with the least possible effort, and without any of those failures which are so discouraging—and often expensive—to the amateur cook........Particular attention has been given to the instructions for making each dish, so that they may as readily be followed by beginners as by 'old hands'.

* * * *

Throughout, the intention has been to cater to the needs of the greatest number of housewives, and for this reason the majority of the recipes have been chosen for their simplicity, but more elaborate dishes have also been included to meet the requirements of those who need them.

* * * *

Good cooks thrive best in the wholesome atmosphere of good homes. Conversely, domestic felicity is usually much beholden to a refined taste in what is crudely described as 'feeding the brute' ....A country's culinary prowess is often an index of its domestic well-being.

Contents

Housewife's Guide

THE OLD ORDER CHANGETH....

Since the 'CEYLON DAILY NEWS' COOKERY BOOK made its first appearance in 1929, many changes have taken place particularly regarding the manifold household duties which in the past devolved on domestic servants. With more remunerative work available (often within easy reach of their own homes) to those who looked upon domestic service as the one avenue of employment, many homes today have fewer servants than they need and some none at all. And 'visiting servants' for regular work are not yet available in Ceylon as they are in some parts of the world. The housewife is therefore called upon to assume far greater responsibility for the home than before, and she is obliged to rely to a greater extent on the help and co-operation of all the members of her household.

While the study of Home Science in school has to some extent prepared girls to meet the changed conditions, its study has not yet been extended to boys. The intention to do so should be carried out speedily, for both girls and boys, whether they follow an academic or 'practical' education, will find few other courses in school as useful a preparation for a happy life.

However to the housewife unable to get servants or regular domestic help, many other forms of assistance are at hand. There are different kinds of power (*e.g.* oil, electricity, gas), many mechanical servants (cookers, refrigerators, food mixers, rotary coconut scrapers, etc.), prepared ingredients (*e.g.* rice and kurakkan flour, powdered curry stuffs), and time- and labour-saving devices (pressure-cooking saucepans, heat-resistant glassware for both cooking and serving in, cleaning preparations giving 'twice the shine' in half the time, etc.) to assist her in her tasks.

With the extension of electricity to the various parts of the Island, much mechanical equipment—consuming very little current for the work they do—can now be used in the home. Some of them are specially useful to those living in "rooms" owing to the housing shortage. Fluorescent lighting is very suitable for the kitchen as it is almost shadowless.

Many useful gadgets are displayed in shops, and the difficulty sometimes is to choose wisely for one's needs. One is tempted to buy many gadgets, forgetting the need to look after them. It is therefore wise to aim at a few, well-made utensils and the right tools for the various household jobs—chosen because they suit one's needs, are effective and simple to use, are sufficiently durable, and are capable of greater utility as the amount of work increases.

Periodic appraisals of the various jobs in the home, in relation to the time, labour and expense involved will help the housewife to discover what new methods are worth trying, and which of the host of gadgets available can help to meet her special needs. This may also lead to the invention of new ones to suit local demand.

The changed conditions promise great results in the future, for the methods of cooking and the choice of food are not in the hands of servants who follow the traditional pattern of rice and rice-flour meals with highly-spiced curries. The housewife is concerned with the health and the growth of the members of the family and approaches her task with vision. With the help of the many aids available, she finds in cooking an outlet for her initiative, enterprise and creativity, and much of what might have been drudgery is a source of great joy and genuine satisfaction.

THE HOUSEWIFE'S HELPERS

THE general notes in this section are intended to help the Housewife in the choice, care, and use of some of the many aids available to her—namely, cookers (oil, electric, gas, and solid fuel), steamers, pressure-cookers, minute-timers, electric hotplates, kettles, coffee percolators, waffle-irons, toasters, and food mixers, refrigerators, rotary coconut scrapers, and powdered curry stuffs. The special instructions given by the makers of each type of equipment in use should be carefully followed.

Cookers. To those who find the open hearth inconvenient or unsatisfactory, the cooking stove offers a pleasant change. Local conditions will undoubtedly influence the kind to be chosen (that is, whether solid fuel, oil, gas or electric) but it is wise not to depend entirely on one type of fuel. Cookers of all kinds are easily available and give excellent results. One with an oven door of heat-resistant glass enables the progress of the bake to be observed without having to open the door, letting out much of the heat whenever this is done.

Oil Cookers can be had in several sizes and models priced to suit the budgets of most middle-class households. The oil cooker does not depend on external connections, and kerosene oil is easily available and economical. The oil cooker which is neither smoky nor messy can be accommodated in the pantry, corridor, or even the dining-room, and with the oven, which can be bought separately, can carry out almost the entire range of cooking.

Care should be taken that the cooker is placed level, that it is not in a draught, and that liquids do not boil over into the chimneys. A simmering appliance, supplied with some cookers, is particularly useful to protect the chimneys when liquids which boil over easily (*e.g.* milk) are put on the fire.

Electric Cookers are the cleanest and most convenient form of cooking (and probably the cheapest). On the press of a button or with the turn of a dial, the electric cooker broils, grills, bakes or roasts to one's requirements. The exact temperature needed is controlled by the dial, and it stays constant where one wants it—there is no danger of over-heating.

Heavy saucepans with absolutely flat bottoms making perfect contact should be used on electric cookers with solid hotplates in order to save fuel and time. On cookers with radiant or tubular hotplates, thinner pans are an advantage.

Gas Cookers can either be bought outright or hired at a very small monthly charge. Cooking by gas is quick, clean and convenient. The cooker contains an oven and several burners of different sizes with a regulating tap for each, so that various types of cooking can be done at the same time. The consumption of gas can be reduced by using light aluminium vessels which get heated quickly and by regulating the burners so that the flame covers only the bottom of the pan. Putting as many dishes as possible in the oven at the same time, and turning off the gas the moment the food is cooked also help.

Solid Fuel Cookers (those using coal, coke, or firewood) enjoy the advantage of conserving the heat and making available at no extra cost the use of the oven for baking bread, cakes, casserole dishes, etc. and also providing a plentiful supply of hot water.

Steamers. Aluminium steamers are both convenient and economical. The simplest form of steamer consists of a perforated pan fitting into a lower pan in which water is kept boiling. While one kind of food (*e.g.* potatoes or rice) is kept boiling in the lower pan, another kind (*e.g.* a custard, pudding, or fish) can be steamed in the upper one. To cook several dishes at a time over one fire, a steamer with four pans is useful. It consists of four pans placed one over the other and resembles a tiffin-carrier. The bottoms of these are not perforated. The water is kept boiling in the lowest pan and the steam is directed into the others by a simple device.

Pressure Cookers offer remarkable benefits to the housewife. They can be used with oil, gas, or electric cookers, effecting a great saving of both time and fuel. The pressure cooker is really a saucepan designed to utilize to the full both the steam and heat usually dissipated in normal cooking and also the pressure of the steam. With gas, electric or oil stoves, the saving may be anything up to 50—65 per cent, and the saving in cooking time anything up to 75 per cent.

Fresh vegetables cooked under pressure retain their colour and flavour as well as their mineral content. Fruit cooked in a pressure cooker has a delicious flavour owing to the small quantity of water used. The cheap tougher cuts of meat become quite tender.

The Minute-Timer is a very useful time-keeper for dishes which take from 5 to 55 minutes to cook. It can be set by a single turn of the hand. One can attend to duties elsewhere while some foods are on the fire, knowing that the minute-timer will sound at the time needed. Particularly helpful for use with a pressure-cooker, the minute-timer is also useful for other purposes in the home.

The Electric Hotplate is a small portable cooker which can be used in a variety of ways wherever there is a plug. A hotplate is generally used for re-heating food, boiling water, frying an egg or omelette, or steaming small puddings—in other words to supplement the cooking done elsewhere. However, people compelled to cook in their rooms have managed to turn out all meals on one. Of the types available, those with the element covered are safer and easier to clean than the one with the coils exposed. The spilling of liquids or letting the pans to overboil on to the hotplate is dangerous—more so if the element is exposed. If it does happen, the current should be immediately switched off and the hotplate thoroughly cleaned.

The Electric Kettle boils water very quickly and economically. It is particularly useful in households with babies where small quantities of water are needed several times a day. Most kettles are now fitted with a safety device which protects the element from damage should the kettle inadvertently boil dry. Electric kettles and jugs are heat-proof and have non-drop spouts. The *Electric Coffee Percolator* can be put to the same uses as an electric kettle besides preparing coffee.

The Electric Waffle Iron enables the baking of waffles at the breakfast table. The waffle has points in common with the Ceylon hopper and is easier to prepare. *The Electric Toaster* can also be used at table and toasts easily, quickly, and evenly. Some models with a timing device toast bread to one's requirements and pop it up when done.

The Electric Food Mixer combines several functions—it is a mincing machine, egg-beater, cake-mixer, vegetable-masher, lemon-squeezer, etc. dealing with all kinds of mixtures, solid and liquid heavy and light. At the turn of a dial it can do now one thing, now another, such as beating, blending, liquidizing, mixing, creaming, whipping, juicing, slicing, mashing, mincing, chopping, grating. Thus the mixer relieves one of many irksome tasks, and makes the preparation of certain difficult dishes both possible and easy. With very little current consumed, it can do a large volume of work and a variety of things in a fraction of the time taken even by a quick worker.

Refrigerators are considered a necessity in the modern home. The "frig" is a miniature store and cool room combined, with maximum storage capacity in a minimum space. It is fitted with ice cube and dessert trays, meat-keepers and vegetable humidifiers, drawers and adjustable shelves which are detachable for easy cleaning. The "frig" enables one to keep a stock of meat, fish, vegetables, fruit, butter and cheese fresh and wholesome for a length of time, greatly easing marketing. Modern refrigerators, whether electric or oil, need no special attention. All are easily cleaned, and some have automatic defrosters.

Much food which otherwise goes to waste is easily conserved in a "frig". For those who have to manage without one, a deep shelf made of strips or slats of wood, wire-netting or open-weave rattan is suggested for the storage of vegetables. The free circulation of air will keep vegetables fresh much longer than if they are left in a box or cupboard. Sprinkling of fresh water also helps. Meat should be hung in a place where the temperature is relatively stable, and fish should be steeped in seasoning.

The Rotary Coconut Scraper. Until someone finds a way of keeping coconut milk fresh long enough to be bottled and distributed, as cow milk is, we shall have to rely on the fresh coconut, scraped as and when needed. The rotary coconut scraper is a small contrivance which can be screwed on a kitchen table, and with it scraping is easy and quick.

Powdered Curry Stuffs. Daily grinding of curry stuffs is both troublesome and wasteful. Curry stuffs for a month or a fortnight can be powdered at a time and kept in air-tight bottles. Many mills have sprung up to help those who find grinding inconvenient at home.

CATERING FOR THE FAMILY'S HEALTH

The human system requires food for the purposes of nourishment and growth, the provision of energy, and the maintenance of a healthy condition.

Some foods supply only one, others two or more of these requirements: few supply all. It is possible, however, to provide the system with all its daily needs for these purposes by a wise choice of food and a careful regulation of diet—based on, and determined by, the age of the individual concerned and the type of work he is required to perform.

It is a well-known fact that growing children and hard-working adults—particularly those who are employed in manual labour—require more food than fully-grown adults and those who lead a sedentary life.

A well-balanced diet for all persons consists of proteins, carbohydrates, fats, Mineral Salts and Vitamins.

The following lists of foods, under their respective classifications may be useful for gauging their values.

PROTEIN FOODS

All Beans, Peas, and Grams: such as Sword bean, Tonga, Soya, Green-peas, Cow-peas, Moong-ata, Dhall, Lentil, etc.
Nuts—especially Groundnuts, Cadjunuts, Coconut, Gingelly.
Milk—and its derivatives, Curd and Cheese.
Eggs—particularly the white.
Meat—particularly lean meat.
Fish.

CARBOHYDRATE FOODS

Sugars—White and brown—syrups, treacle, jaggery.
Starches—Rice, Sago, Arrowroot, Oatmeal, Macaroni, Potatoes, Yams, Nuts, Kurakkan, Meneri, Manioc, Prepared Flours.

FATTY FOODS

Milk—and its derivatives, Cream, Curds, Butter, Ghee.
Oils—particularly Gingelly and Olive oils.
Nuts—Coconut, Cadjunuts, Almonds, etc.
Eggs—Yolks only.
Meats—Pork, Bacon, etc.

MINERAL SALTS

Mineral Salts are found chiefly in Fruits and Vegetables. Of all fresh fruits the Orange is perhaps the best; for it may safely be taken by young and old alike. It is often the only kind of fruit allowed in sickness—although Grapes (and particularly the juice of grapes) come very close behind in point of value. Other fruits recommended are: Papaws, Pineapples, Apples, Mangoes, Plantains, Pomegranates, and the Citrus varieties: Grapefruit, Lemons, Limes, Pommelos.

Green vegetables, eaten in the raw state, include Lettuce, Gotukola, etc. Other vegetables, which may be eaten in the "raw" or uncooked state, are: Tomatoes, Carrots, Cabbage, Celery, Cucumber. Of these, Tomatoes and Carrots rank highest in value.

VITAMINS

It is the business of the housewife to realize the full importance of the part taken by Vitamins in the daily diet of those under her care.

It is unfortunate, however, that as civilization progresses so the demand increases for the many so-called "superior" types of food or preparation of food, now obtainable—resulting in the loss of a great deal, if not all, of the original Vitamin content of such foods. Notable examples of this are to be found in: (*a*) Rice, where the unpolished grain contains some Vitamin B; but when polished contains no Vitamin B at all; and (*b*) Cooked or Preserved Foods, where the valuable Vitamin C is lost through the process of cooking or preservation.

The following table is given to enable the housewife to see at a glance the vitamins contained in certain foods, and the part they take in promoting and maintaining good health. From this table it should be possible to provide for the daily intake of a sufficient quantity of these vitamins from foods which are available all the year round, as well as at certain seasons only.

Vitamin A—Cod and other fish-liver oils; Milk; Butter; Egg yolk; Spinach; Carrots; Sweet Potatoes; Tomatoes; Cheese; Cream; Lettuce; Prunes; Papaws; Bananas; Fish Roes; Oranges; Limes; Grapefruit; Kidney; Liver; Gotukola.

DEFICIENCY PRODUCES—Affections of the eyes; tardy growth in children; decaying teeth; glandular troubles; affections of the skin.

Vitamin B—Beans; Peas; Bran; Moong-ata; Lentils; Nuts; Onions; Leafy Vegetables; Egg Yolk; Wholemeal Wheat; Maize; Oatmeal; Barley; Unpolished Rice; Oranges; Tomatoes; Artichokes; Leeks; Cabbage; Watercress, Unpolished Gingelly.

DEFICIENCY PRODUCES—Constipation; Beri-beri; Retarded growth; Affections of the heart; Affections of the nervous system.

Vitamin C—Oranges; Grapefruit; Bananas; Tomatoes; Lemons; Limes; Mandarins; Onions; Watercress; Lettuce; Celery; Radishes; Gotukola; Carrots; Pineapple; Pepper; Apples.—All the above should be eaten raw, in a ripe fresh condition—Milk; Raw Liver. (Cooked Liver is only a fair source of Vitamin C.)

DEFICIENCY PRODUCES—Swelling and bleeding of the Gums; Anaemia; Swelling and soreness of the joints; Scurvy; Tendency to decaying teeth; Debility, especially in children.

Vitamin D—Cod-Liver Oil; Milk; Egg yolk; Fat of beef and mutton; Cream; Oily fish such as Salmon and Herrings; Butter; Liver. In addition, it should be remembered that exposure to the sun (with proper protection to the head, and particularly the eyes) does much to promote the formation of Vitamin D in the skin.

DEFICIENCY PRODUCES—Softness of the bones; Improper formation of the teeth; Muscular weakness—resulting in the condition known as "bowed-legs", "knock-knees" and affections of the spine; Affections of the nervous system, resulting in irritability.

Vitamin E—Vegetable oils; Lettuce; Watercress; Green leafy vegetables.

DEFICIENCY PRODUCES—Sterility.

Vitamin G—(B-2 Complex). Yeast; Liver; Lean Meat; Heart; Kidney; Fish; Veal; Ground-nuts; Milk; Cheese; Egg Yolks; Tomatoes.

DEFICIENCY PRODUCES—Affections of the skin; Affections of the nerves; Stomach disorders.

Vitamin K—Fish; Pig's liver; Green leafy vegetables; as Cabbage, Spinach, etc. Tomatoes.

DEFICIENCY PRODUCES—Failure of the blood to form into clots—haemorrhage, etc.

Points to Observe—Cooking, particularly of vegetables, destroys a great many of the nutritive properties of food. As little water as possible should be used in the process of boiling, and this should be served either with the vegetable or used for Soups, Sauces, etc.

Wherever possible, vegetables should be eaten in the raw state—root vegetables such as carrots, etc. being scraped rather than peeled; and grated, or very finely sliced. In all cases they must be thoroughly washed in plenty of cold water before preparation for the table.

Steaming is the best method of cooking green vegetables, as this helps to retain the mineral salts they contain.

Fruit, when fresh and ripe, should be eaten raw instead of cooked.

Dried fruit should just be well washed in plenty of cold water, and then be allowed to soak for several hours in the water in which it is to be cooked later. Certain dried fruits may, with advantage, be eaten without being cooked—as Prunes, Raisins, Dates, etc.

USEFUL TABLES AND MEASURES

TEMPERATURE CHART

For use with an oven thermometer.

250°—300° F. — Slow Oven.
300°—350° F. — Moderate Oven.
350°—400° F — Hot Oven.
400°—450° F. — Quick Oven.
450°—500° F. — Very Quick Oven.

N.B. When no oven thermometer is available the "paper test" provides a useful guide: Place a small sheet of white paper on the middle shelf of the oven, and close the door for three minutes. At the end of this time the oven is:

Slow—if the paper is of a very pale brown colour.
Moderate—if the paper is of a pale brown colour.
Quick—if the paper is of a rich brown colour.

HOMELY MEASURES

When no scales, weights, or measures are available the following homely measures may be used for:

Flour, Sugar, Rice, Sago, Currants, and other dried "cake" fruits

1 slightly rounded teaspoonful	equals ¼ oz.
1 slightly rounded dessertspoonful	equals ½ oz.
1 slightly rounded tablespoonful	equals 1 oz.
1 level teacupful	equals ¼ lb.
1 level breakfastcupful	equals ½ lb.
Powdered Curry Stuffs	
1 teaspoonful chillie powder	equals 4 dried chillies
Breadcrumbs	
2 heaped tablespoonfuls	equal 1 oz.
Golden Syrup, Treacle, Jam	
1 tablespoonful	equals 2 oz.
Butter and other Fats	
1 tablespoonful	equals 1 oz.
A piece about the size of an egg	equals 1½ oz.
Liquids	
1 teacupful	equals ¼ pint.
1 breakfastcupful	equals ½ pint.
1 tumbler	equals ½ pint.
5 tablespoonfuls	equal ½ gill.

MEASURES IN AMERICAN RECIPES

In many American recipes the measure used is the cup—a receptacle of a standardized size, marked off into quarters and thirds. When no such measuring cup is available the following table of equivalents may be used:

2½ cupfuls Castor Sugar	equal	1 lb.
3½ ,, Icing Sugar	equal	1 lb.
2 ,, Butter	equal	1 lb.
4 ,, Flour	equal	1 lb.
1 cupful each Currants, Sultanas or Raisins	equals	6 ozs.
2 cupfuls Granulated sugar	equal	1 lb.
1 cupful Syrup	equals	12 ozs.
1 cupful shelled Nuts	equals	5½ ozs.
1 square of Chocolates	equals	1 oz.

N.B. It should be noted in using any kind of weight or measure that flour and icing sugar should always be first sieved; while castor and other sugars should have lumps crushed down with the back of a spoon or a light rolling-pin. Unless otherwise stated, all measures are lightly-packed and level.

GLOSSARY OF TERMS USED IN COOKERY

A LA—In the style of. Example: a la francaise—in the French way.

AU GRATIN—Applied to a dish which is browned on top, usually coated with breadcrumbs and/or grated cheese, and served in the dish in which it is cooked.

AU NATUREL—Applied to foods which are prepared and served in a simple manner.

BABA—A very light cake, of the dough variety, usually soaked in rum.

BAIN-MARIE—An open vessel holding hot water—used for keeping sauces, etc. warm without boiling or burning.

BARDER—To cover with slices of fat bacon for the purpose of basting and flavouring. Usually employed when roasting poultry or game.

BAVAROISE—A rich, creamy mixture, usually of custard and cream.

BLANCHIR—To blanch or whiten; either by steeping in boiling water for a short time and then plunging into cold water to cool; or by placing in cold water and rapidly bringing to the boil.

Bouchees—Literally, a mouthful. A term generally applied to very small pastry cases filled with a variety of savoury creams, etc.

Bouillon—Unclarified stock made from fresh meat.

Bouquet garni—A bunch of mixed herbs (parsley, thyme, sage, etc.) used for seasoning stews, etc.

Braiser—To braise, or cook in a closely-covered pan to prevent evaporation and retain the juices of meats, vegetables, etc.

Canape—Small pieces of bread, toast, pastry, etc. topped with savoury mixtures.

Caramel—Burnt sugar; sugar boiled with a small quantity of water until of a deep brown colour. Also a kind of toffee.

Charlotte—The term used to signify the lining of a mould or basin with strips of bread, or cake, and filled up with a cream or fruit mixture.

Chaudfroid—The type of sauce used for coating pieces of meat, poultry etc. to be served cold.

Crepes—Pancakes.

Croquettes—A savoury mince of fish, meat, or poultry, moulded with sauce into various shapes dipped in egg and bread-crumbs, and fried until crisp on the outside.

Croutes—Fancy shapes of fried bread on which savoury mixtures are served.

Croutons—Small dice or fancy shapes of fried bread used for garnishing various fish and meat dishes, and for serving with soup.

Dariole—A small, cup shaped mould—usually giving its name to the mixture cooked in it.

Diable (a la)—The term often applied to a sauce or dressing highly seasoned ("devilled") with cayenne, chilli, or pepper and mustard.

Entree—A side-dish, or made-up dish, often served with a sauce—usually in the first part of a dinner when the menu is an elaborate one.

Entremet—A dainty dish served in the second part of a dinner, it may take the form of a dressed vegetable, a hot or cold sweet, a savoury, etc.

FARCE—A force-meat, or stuffing.

FLAN—An open pastry case: usually filled with fruit, or sweet or savoury mixtures.

FRICANDEAU—A piece of veal which has been larded, and is cooked by braising.

FRICASSEE—A kind of stew, usually white, made with a sauce thickened with egg-yolks and cream.

GALANTINE—Meat or poultry boned, and sometimes stuffed; served cold after being glazed, or mashed with sauce.

GLAZE—Made from stock boiled down to a jelly, well browned, and used to "glaze" or mash cold boiled meat or poultry dishes.

HORS-D'OEUVRE—Tasty "tit-bits" served at the beginning of a meal.

KABOBS, OR KABABS—Small pieces of highly seasoned meat, skewered, and grilled or braised.

LARDER—To lard, by fastening small pieces of bacon on meat etc. for purposes of seasoning and basting.

LIAISON—A mixture of eggs and cream used for thickening sauces and soups just before serving.

MASKING—To cover meat with any rich sauce.

MOUSSE—A light spongy mixture.

PANADA, OR PANADE—A mixture of flour and liquids (milk, stock etc.) usually with some butter added, cooked until thick; used for binding. Bread and liquid is sometimes used instead to form a panade.

PAPRIKA—A powder made from mild "peppers" or chillies, not as hot as cayenne.

POTAGE—Soup.

PUREE—A smooth mixture of meat, fish, vegetables or fruit reduced to a pulp by cooking, and usually pounded and/or passed through a sieve.

RAMEKIN—That which is served in a china, glass, or paper ramekin dish or case.

RAGOUT—A stew.

RECHAUFFE—A dish which is warmed-up or re-cooked.

RELEVE—The "remove" or joint course in a dinner.

ROUX—Butter and flour cooked together, and used for thickening sauces and soup—brown or white.

SALMI—A stew or hash, made of poultry or game usually.

SAUTER—To fry quickly in a small quantity of fat.

SAUTE-PAN—A thin, shallow pan or stew-pot used for quick frying.

SORBET—A half-frozen ice, of the "water-ice" variety, usually flavoured with rum, or certain liqueurs. It is served after the joint at dinner, and nowadays also as a "sweet".

SOUFFLE—A very light sweet or savoury mixture—served hot or cold, according to the variety. The lightness is usually achieved by the use of well-whisked whites of eggs.

STOCK—The liquor obtained by boiling meat, bones, vegetables, etc. Used as a foundation in the making of soups, sauces, and stews.

TIMBALE—A cup-shaped mould, which often gives its name to the various dishes cooked in it.

VOL-AU-VENT—A very light pastry case. Used for serving delicately flavoured, flaked, minced or finely-cut fish, meat, or poultry. The filling for these cases is usually prepared in a thick creamy sauce.

ZEST—Flavour—In cooking, meaning the thinly-grated or pared rind of lemon or orange used to flavour various dishes.

MENU PLANNING

IN drawing-up the Menu of a meal, whether it is one required for the family luncheon or dinner, or for an occasion on which guests will be present, there are a few points which should be remembered.

(*a*) The first and most important of these is dependent on the resources of the home:

1. The capability of the cook who is to prepare the various dishes. It is better to choose simple fare, well within the scope of the cook who prepares it, than more elaborate dishes which will so fluster him as to make it quite impossible for him to do his best with any single one of the courses ordered.

2. The utensils at his disposal. Avoid elaborate dishes which require utensils for cooking which cannot be provided. The cook is placed at a great disadvantage when he has to work under such conditions.

3. The service available for the proper presentation of the food at table. This includes both the number of servants required for

handing the respective dishes, and the table-ware in which they are served.

The choice of dishes should depend on these three points, for on them to a large extent rests the success or failure of the meal.

(*b*) Next comes the question of variety. This applies equally to the kind of food provided and to the method of cooking adopted. It is very easy to fall into the habit of presenting the same dish many times during the week or month, as the case may be, because a liking for it has been expressed by members of the family. This is a fault which the housewife should take care to avoid—monotony in food being one of the chief causes of lack of appetite, and therefore of lack of proper nourishment. Climate too, plays a definite part in the choice of food. For instance, in hot weather it is a mistake to provide rich, heavy meals. It is also *always* a mistake to provide at the same meal a number of dishes which are similar in appearance or in method of cooking. A menu consisting of fried fish, fried meat, and sweet fritters has nothing to commend it from a gastronomical point of view, and, however well each separate course may be cooked and served, such a meal cannot be termed successful.

(*c*) It is usually advisable to plan family meals several days ahead. In this way advantage can be taken of foods "in season" and therefore at their best. Forward-planning of meals also means economy—allowing for the best and most attractive use to be made of left-overs.

In the following Menus particular attention has been paid to these points in regard to the equipment and staff of the average household. More elaborate menus should only be chosen by those whose resources enable them to be successfully carried out.

In the section devoted to suggestions for Cold Buffet Suppers will be found a variety of dishes, from any group of which an attractive Supper Menu can be drawn up. Here, too, it is necessary to make a choice which will give variety in appearance as well as in the method of preparation and cooking.

For ease in reference, the index numbers of many of the recipes have been given.

SOME LUNCHEON MENUS

Chicken Mulligatawny Soup (46)
Frikkadels (814)
Liver and Bacon Puffs (259)
Pineapple Custard (568)

Mushroom Omelette (372)
Braised Chicken with Rice (303)
Chocolate Biscuit Pudding (626)

Lobster Mayonnaise (110)
Russian Steak (225)
Buttered Leeks
Fried Potatoes (426)
Fruit Shortcake (636)

Italian Vegetable Soup (67)
Chicken Vol-au-Vent (315)
Chocolate Souffle (691)

Fried Prawns (117)
Tournedos of Beef (227)
Mashed Potato Border
Butter Beans
Canary Pudding (595)
Raspberry Jam Sauce (721)

Baked Crab (83)
Lamb Salad a la Printaniere (253)
Asparagus Souffle (1465)

Scotch Mutton Broth (69)
Ham baked in milk (283)
Mashed Potatoes (427)
Green Peas
Honeycomb Mould (639)

Fried Mullet
Cheese Sauce (509)
Sausage in Onions (291)
Potato Puffs (430)
Grilled Tomatoes
Fruit Jelly (635)

Pancake Rolls (174)
Baked Cabbage with Cheese (400)
Spiced Bananas (736)
Cream

Grape Fruit
Salmon in Aspic (125)
Fried Chicken (306)
Cauliflower Fritters (410)
Parsley Potatoes
Rum Cream (658)

Buriani (771)
Liver Curry (820)
Plantain Curry (847)
Sathey Malay Curry (834)
Onion Sambol (872)
Orange Water Ice (1566)

Stringhoppers (1036)
White Mulligatawny (991)
Frikkadels (814)
Savoury Rice (778)
Chicken Curry (Badun) (982)
Ash-Plantain Pachchadi (981)
Fruit, Salad, Cream

Lampries (775)
with Lampries Curry (775)
Frikkadels (814)
Dry Plantain Curry (847)
Prawn-Blachang (874)
Cucumber Sambol (869)
Nougat Pudding (1539)

Fish Smoore (811)
Boiled Rice
Potato Chips (425)
Grilled Chicken
Buttered Cauliflower
Sweet Potatoes
Semolina Souffle (697)

Yellow Rice (780)
Chicken Curry (982)
Fried Brinjal Curry (842)
Billing Sambol (861)
Payasam (1007)

SIMPLE FOUR-COURSE DINNER MENUS

Clear Soup a la Royale (48)
Lobster Cream (108)
Roast Duck (317)
Orange and Plantain Salad (472)
Buttered Peas
Potato Puffs (430)
Rum Omelette (703)

Tomato Cream Soup (65)
Fish Souffle (103)
Beef Mignons (208)
Mashed Potato Border
Pressed Cabbage (402)
Apple Charlotte (541)
Cream

Jellied Soup (55)
Prawn Cutlets (118)
Cucumber Salad (463)
Veal and Ham Pie (237)
Parsley Potatoes
Braised Carrots
Chocolate Mousse (629)

Devilled Oysters (113)
Julienne Soup (56)
Noisettes of Lamb (251)
Creamed Spinach
Duchesse Potatoes
Chocolate Souffle (691)

Prawn Cocktail (22)
Cream Soup (49)
Roast Loin of Pork
Spiced Pineapple Sauce (528)
Baked Cabbage (400)
Roasted Potatoes (431)
Coffee Cream Mould (631)

Celery and Cheese Soup
Fried Seer (91)
Orange Sauce (as in 516)
Veal Olives (as in 211)
Creamed Potatoes
Buttered Cauliflower
Vanilla Cream Trifle (664)

Mock Turtle Soup
Rolled Mullet, with Prawn Cream filling (124)
Fillets of Veal
Lemon Sauce
Potato Balls (422)
Sprouts
Charlotte Russe (625)

Leek Soup
Red Mullet au Gratin (122)
Braised Chicken (302)
Buttered Carrots and Turnips
Fluffed Potatoes
Meringue Tartlets (567)

Dhall Soup (50)
Steamed Fillets of Sole
Tartare Sauce (531)
Savoury Beef (216)
Butter Beans
Buttered Parsnips
Ginger Creams (638)

Cabbage Cream Soup (44)
Fried Whitebait (129)
Breast of Lamb, stuffed (260)
Leeks
Fried Potatoes (426)
Savoury Asparagus Ice (1463)

Liver Soup
Seer a l' Indienne (127)
Roast Fillet of Beef (214)
Lyonnaise Potatoes
Baked Tomatoes (441)
Nut Cream (648)

Green Pea Soup
Grilled Seer, with Maitre d'Hotel Butter
Roast Guinea Fowl (319)
Orange and Watercress Salad
French Beans
Straw Potatoes
Basket Pudding, Cream (624)

TWO SPECIAL-OCCASION DINNER MENUS

Clear Soup a la Royale (48)
Steamed Sole Rolls
Tartare Sauce (531)
Jellied Lamb Rissoles (252)
Macedoine of potatoes and peas
Roast Duck (317)
Orange and Plantain Salad (472)
Dressed New Potatoes
Asparagus Tips
Surprise Pudding (661)
Cheese Bouchees (1428)

Iced Soup
Salmon Souffle (as in 103)
Chicken Vol-au-Vent (315)
Roast Shoulder of Lamb
Mint Jelly (as in 253)
Potato Puffs (430)
Green Peas
Rum Barada (657)
Devilled Roe Croutons (1441)

Please turn over

SUGGESTIONS FOR A COLD BUFFET SUPPER

Savoury Prunes, Egg Boats. Anchovy Circles (1421)

Jellied Clear Soup (55). Iced Soup. Jellied Tomato Bouillon

Salmon in Aspic. Lobster Mayonnaise (110). Mousse of Seer (128)

Chicken Galantine. Turkey and Ham in Aspic. Pate Croutons. Jellied Lamb Rissoles (252). Pate de foie gras in Aspic. Vienna Sausage Curls. Chicken Mayonnaise

---

Salad. Macedoine of Vegetables. Iced Asparagus Tips. Potato Salad (474). Mayonnaise Tomatoes. Tomato Salad (476)

Fruit Jellies (635). Creams. Fruit Creams. Wine Jellies. Iced Pudding. Coffee Bavaroise. Fruit Flans, Cream. Jellied Sponge. Basket Pudding, Cream (624). Ice Cream

---

Claret Cup (1584). Cider Cup (1583). Fresh Fruit Cup. Tinned Fruit Cup. Iced Sherry. Orangeade (1594). Grape Squash. Iced Coffee (1590). Iced Tea. Aerated Waters (1581)

Hors-d'Oeuvre

(Short Eats, Savouries and Sandwiches form a later Chapter)

Hors-d'oeuvre are small appetising morsels of a somewhat pronounced flavour served at the commencement of a meal in order to stimulate the appetite. Hors-d'œuvre are always served at hotel dinners, but they are not essential at an ordinary dinner party.

Amongst articles used as hors-d'œuvre are olives, anchovies and sardines filleted and garnished with parsley, Bologna sausage and foie gras in small thin slices, oysters, prawns, small tasty sandwiches, and caviare which is a favourite hors-d'œuvre. There are several kinds of caviare but the Russian is considered the best.

Most hors-d'œuvre are served cold, usually on small glass or china plates or on tiny dish papers which are placed on the plate of each guest before they sit down. They may also be handed round arranged on a special hors-d'œuvre dish. A few suggestions for hors-d'œuvre follow.

1 Devilled Almonds

Prepare as in Recipe, 2, using cayenne pepper or *very* finely powdered dry chillies in addition to the salt.

2 Salted Almonds

almonds **salad oil or butter** **fine salt**

Blanch the almonds, dry them and fry them a golden brown in oil or butter. Drain them carefully and turn them on to a sheet of paper and sprinkle them liberally with fine salt. When cold shake off the loose salt. They will keep crisp in a closed tin.

3 Anchovy Canapes

stale bread **butter** **hard-boiled egg**
filleted anchovies **anchovy paste** **chopped parsley**

Cut some neat rounds of bread and fry them a nice golden brown in butter or salad oil, and allow them to cool. Mix a little anchovy paste and butter together and spread the mixture over the bread. Then curl two fillets upon each round, and fill the centre with finely-chopped white and the powdered yolk of egg, and garnish with chopped parsley. (See Recipe 20.)

N.B.—The decoration may be varied according to taste.

4 Anchovy and Gherkin Circles

Proceed as directed in Recipe 3 or Recipe 1421, and instead of the anchovy fillets arrange small rounds of pickled midget gherkins round the top of the bread circles. In the centre of each round of gherkin pipe a small "flower" of anchovy butter. Leave in the refrigerator to harden the butter, then arrange as above.

N.B.—This recipe will suggest other savoury ways of serving these small circles. The tiny inner rounds left over may be fried as above, and served as a garnish for many soups. If perfectly fresh coconut oil is used for frying, and if the rounds are afterwards thoroughly drained on white paper, they will keep fresh for at least a week when stored between layers of white paper in an air-tight tin.

5 Angels on Horseback

1 dozen oysters
a few thin slices of bacon
chopped parsley
strips of fried or toasted bread
lime juice
pepper and salt

Beard the oysters and season each one with pepper and lime juice. Then roll them in thin slices of bacon which must be cut in squares large enough to roll round an oyster. Fix the rolls with a tiny wooden skewer, and fry or grill them until the bacon is cooked a nice brown colour. Place one on each strip of fried or toasted bread, garnish with chopped parsley and slices of lime, and serve hot.

6 Bacon and Mushrooms

rashers of streaky bacon
a tin of button mushrooms

Drain the mushrooms from their liquid, and wrap half a slice of bacon around each one, tying with a piece of thread. Fry till the bacon is crisp. Remove the thread and serve at once.

7 Devilled Cadjunuts I

200 cadjunuts
salt
a pinch of ground saffron
1 dessertspoonful finely ground dry chillies
butter or dripping

Skin the cadjunuts and rub them over with the salt, saffron and chillies mixed together and let them remain for an hour or two. Heat the butter or dripping in a frying pan and when very hot put in the cadjunuts and fry them until they are nice and crisp. Drain them carefully and wipe them dry in a soft cloth. They will keep crisp in a closed tin.

8 Devilled Cadjunuts II

Skin the cadjunuts and fry them in hot butter or dripping. Drain them carefully. Mix on a sheet of paper some fine salt and cayenne pepper or *very* finely-powdered dry chillies and toss the cadjunuts about in this mixture. When cold shake off the loose powder.

9 Beef Canapes

lightly-grilled fillet of beef or underdone roast beef
horse-radish sauce
butter
fried croutons of bread
parsley
seasonings

Cut the meat into thin slices, chop into fine pieces, and season with a little salt and some freshly-ground black pepper, with a trace of made mustard, if liked. Mix well. Spread each crouton with a paste made by mixing horse-radish sauce with butter, cover with the prepared meat, and put a tiny sprig of fresh parsley in the centre of each mound of beef. Chill in a covered dish, and serve cold on a small plate or dish with a paper d'oyley underneath, putting small sprigs of parsley here and there as a garnish.

10 Cabbage and Bacon Rolls

boiled cabbage
very thin rashers of streaky bacon
a little made mustard
black pepper
dripping

Boil the cabbage, and drain well, then press between two plates to extract all surplus moisture. Chop up very finely adding black pepper to season highly. Press again, and leave to get cold, then cut into wedges the same size as the width of the bacon. If the bacon is very narrow, the wedges may be the size of cocktail sausages but no larger. Smear one side of each rasher with a little mustard. Wrap each wedge of cabbage round with a rasher of bacon, and skewer firmly with small wooden picks. Melt a little dripping in a baking dish, place the rolls in it, and bake in a fairly hot oven, turning occasionally to brown the bacon evenly. Drain on white paper, remove picks, and replace with clean ones, as these are likely to be discoloured after cooking. Serve very hot.

11 Canapes au Caviare

small squares of fried or toasted bread and butter
Russian caviare
cayenne
lime juice

Season some caviare with cayenne and lime juice, pile some up neatly on each square of bread, and decorate with a little plain or anchovy butter. To make the latter mix a little anchovy paste and butter together.

N.B.—Caviare must never be touched with a steel knife or any other metal. Use a silver knife or spoon or a wooden skewer for mixing the caviare.

12 Chicken Liver Canapes

small rounds of toasted bread and butter
3 chicken livers (cooked)
1 hard-boiled egg
pepper and salt
parsley

Chop the livers very finely and mix with the egg also finely chopped. Add a seasoning of pepper and salt. Pile this on the rounds of toast and garnish with parsley.

13 Stuffed Eggs

6 eggs
2 oz. grated cheese
4 oz. butter
one tablespoonful tomato sauce
pepper and salt
one stick celery cut into slices
colouring

Hardboil the eggs, boiling them for at least fifteen minutes to make sure the whites get really hard and the yolks floury. For the first five minutes of boiling, stir them gently so that they get turned around. This prevents the whites from hardening entirely on one side, leaving the other side with a very thin covering, and spoiling the look of the completed hors-d'œuvre. When the eggs are boiled, shell them and cut them in half lengthwise when cool, using a sharp knife. Sieve the yolks through a wire sieve, and discard any lumps. Mix them with the butter, cheese, pepper, salt and sauce, and colour one third of the mixture pink and another third green, and leave the rest as it is or intensify the yellow colour with vegetable colouring. Pipe through a fancy icing nozzle, rose or shell pattern, into the whites of the eggs. Place a crisp slice of celery on top of each, and chill thoroughly. Serve on a bed of shredded lettuce. The eggs may be decorated with flowers cut from red chillies, carrot or cucumber, and with "leaves" of green chillies.

14 Grapefruit Maraschino

½ a grapefruit for each person
sugar and salt
a small bottle of Maraschino cherries

Halve the grapefruits and loosen the sections of pulp with a sharp pointed knife for easy removal. Remove all seeds. Sprinkle each half with two teaspoonfuls white sugar, and a tiny pinch of salt. Pour a dessertspoonful of Maraschino liquid over each prepared fruit, and stand on ice or keep in the refrigerator till required. Top each half with a Maraschino cherry and serve, standing each in an individual dessert dish or glass packed with crushed ice. This is a very popular first course.

N.B.—The addition of a spoonful of cherry brandy is an improvement.

15 Devilled Mushrooms

1 small tin black mushrooms
¼ pint thick brown sauce
a good pinch of powdered red chillies
black pepper
2 red onions chopped finely
1 scant dessertspoonful butter
rounds of fried bread

Melt the butter, and fry the onions in it until just browned, then add the finely-chopped mushrooms and heat over a low flame, Season strongly with the chillies and pepper, and add a little salt, if necessary then stir into the warm sauce and simmer for a few minutes. Pile up on the fried bread, and place under a red-hot grill for about two minutes. Serve immediately.

16 Olive Farcies

Stone the olives and fill them with any fish paste, such as sardine or anchovy, or any nice savoury butter. They may then be served as they are, or stand each olive on a buttered round of fried bread and garnish with parsley.

N.B.—Olives can be bought ready stuffed.

17 Oyster Canapes

brown bread and butter
sliced cucumber
cayenne
salt
oysters
lime juice

Cut some thin slices of bread and stamp them out into rounds 1½ inches in diameter. Spread the rounds with butter, and lay a thin slice of cucumber on the top of each. Then place a fresh and bearded oyster on the top of the cucumber and season with salt, lime juice and pepper. Serve two or three to each person.

18 Oysters au Naturel

Oysters served raw in their shells make a favourite though simple hors-d'œuvre. When oysters are served raw they must be very fresh. Wash the oysters well before opening them, and do not open them until a very short time before they are needed. Serve the oysters in their deeper shell, and allow three or four oysters for each person. Garnish with tiny sprigs of parsley, and hand slices of lime, thin brown bread and butter, and pepper separately.

19 Peach and Cream Cheese

tinned peach halves
cream cheese
mayonnaise
pepper
salt
one head cabbage lettuce

Place peach halves on large lettuce leaves, cut side uppermost. Make a mixture of cream cheese, mayonnaise, pepper and salt, tasting as you go to get a piquant but not too acid flavour. Fill the peach halves with this, piping it through a nozzle in a decorative pattern. Top with a Maraschino cherry, and serve iced.

20 Mixed Pickles

a bottle of sweet mixed pickles
OR a bottle each of pickled onions, gherkins, cauliflower

On toothpicks arrange a selection of the pickles, for instance, an onion, a slice of gherkin, a sprig of cauliflower, and another onion. Try to obtain coloured onions, as a different coloured onion at each end of the toothpick will add to the decorative effect. Serve as an accompaniment to Anchovy Canapes (Recipe 3).

21 Prawn Canapes

brown bread
butter
boiled prawns
anchovy essence
pickled gherkins
powdered dry chillies
salad oil or butter

Cut out some thin slices of bread, stamp them out in ovals or rounds and fry them in salad oil or butter. Allow to cool and then spread them with butter mixed with a few drops of anchovy essence. Place a prawn on each and sprinkle over with chopped gherkins and powdered chillies.

22 Prawn Cocktail

For Each Serving:
6—8 very small boiled prawns
1 tablespoonful each of thick mayonnaise and chopped lettuce
1 teaspoonful each diced cucumber, diced cooked beetroot & shredded heart of cabbage
1 small teaspoonful thick tomato sauce
cayenne pepper
1 stuffed olive and a slice of red onion

Choose the very small prawns which will measure about ¾ of an inch across when boiled.

Rub the inside of the glass in which the cocktail is to be served with the cut onion. Mix lettuce and cabbage together, add a teaspoonful of the mayonnaise, and the cucumber and beetroot, and mix well with a fork so that all are thinly coated with the sauce. Put half of the mixture in the glass, place four prawns on top leaveing a space between each. Mix the rest of the mayonnaise with the tomato sauce, and coat each prawn with some of it. Pile up the balance of the salad mixture on top, and put the rest of the prawns round it, standing them up on their sides. Pour the remaining sauce over, dust with cayenne, and place the olive in the centre.

In making prawn cocktail it is essential that all ingredients be well chilled before mixing. The lettuce should be crisp and quite dry, and mixing should be done just before serving. It is advisable to chill the glasses by standing them in the refrigerator for about ten minutes—usually while the mixing is being done.

23 Radish and Onions

small red radishes **spring onions** **salt**

Cut a slice off the top of each radish after washing well. Cut each across into about six sections, not quite severing them. Put into icy cold water and leave them till the sections separate slightly and open up to look like flowers. Serve packed in crushed ice with well-washed spring onions alongside.

24 Sardine Canapes

strips of fried or toasted bread and butter
tinned sardines
beetroot
pickled gherkin
hard-boiled white of egg

Bone the sardines, if not already done, place one on each strip of bread, and garnish with chopped beetroot, pickled gherkin and hard-boiled white of egg, using just a little of each.

Soups

(For Rasam, see Tamil Recipes)

SOUPS form an important part of the daily culinary routine. The making of a good soup is quite an art, but it is an art which can be acquired by anyone who spends some time and care in learning it. Soups, apart from being wholesome and digestible, are economical as well, for they afford opportunities of utilizing such materials as bones, trimmings, etc., that would otherwise be wasted.

Soups can be made of anything—fish, flesh or vegetables. Stock of course, is the basis of all meat soups, but both tasty and nourishing soups can be turned out without any meat or stock.

Take care to season all soups sufficiently before sending them to table, but at the same time remember that salt should be added with care, as too much salt will spoil any soup.

In making soups it is well to remember that quality is more important than quantity, "little and good" rather than "much and bad."

There are a great many different kinds of soups, but the foundations are usually the same, the names varying according to the different flavours and garnishes used. From the recipes for soups given here, anyone with a little knowledge of cooking should be able to turn out a great many more.

Stock

STOCK is the liquor in which meat, bones, vegetables, etc., have been boiled. It serves as a foundation for most soups, and also for sauces, gravies and the like.

Stock can be made from various materials, such as meat and bones, cooked and uncooked, and flavoured with vegetables; the bones, neck and feet of poultry and game. Fish bones and trimmings also make good stock, and even vegetables alone can be utilized for the purpose.

Stock made from left-overs, etc., will do very well for ordinary soups, but for a good strong soup such as Clear Soup, fresh meat and bones must be used.

Carrot, turnip, onion, and celery are the vegetables generally used for flavouring stock. Take the vegetables in the proportion of a carrot, an onion, half a turnip, and a strip of celery to three quarts of water, together with a teaspoonful of salt and 12 peppercorns.

Always allow 1 quart of water to each pound of meat and bones.

In making stock remember that stock should never be allowed to boil, but only to simmer. Gentle stewing is necessary so as to extract all the goodness from the bones, etc.

41 Asparagus Soup

the liquid from a tin of asparagus
4 or 5 stalks of asparagus
1 pint of white stock
1 gill milk
1 dessertspoonful butter
1 dessertspoonful cornflour
white pepper and salt

Pour the liquid from a tin of asparagus into a saucepan and add the stock to it. Cut off the tips from the asparagus stalks, reserving them for serving in the soup. Mash down the remainder, and add it to the liquid in the saucepan. Simmer slowly for about 20 minutes, and, if desired, sieve the soup through a medium sieve. Mix the cornflour with a little milk, add it and the remainder of the milk, butter, salt and pepper. Keep stirring till it boils. Add the asparagus tips and serve the soup hot.

42 Bone Soup

2 lb. brisket bones
2 quarts cold water
2 carrots
1 turnip
1 desertspoonful of sliced onions
2 leeks
2 strips of celery
1 dessertspoon dripping
salt
8 peppercorns

Break the bones into pieces and put them into a saucepan with the water. Bring to the boil, skim well and add the salt and pepper. Allow the soup to simmer slowly from 4 to 5 hours. If the water boils down, more must be added. When ready, strain through a sieve or towel, and set aside to cool and, when quite cold, remove the fat. Put the soup back into the pan, add the vegetables cut in dice or cubes and boil slowly until the vegetables are tender. Remove the meat from the bones, cut into small pieces and add to the soup. Heat the dripping in a pan and fry the sliced onions till well browned, then turn in the soup, make it thoroughly hot and serve.

43 Brown Soup

2 lb. beef
2 quarts boiling water
1 large Bombay onion
1 carrot
1 turnip
2 strips of celery
1½ oz. flour
2 oz. dripping

Cut the meat in pieces, dredge well with flour and fry in dripping until brown; then slice and fry the onions. Put the meat and onions into a pan, pour in the water, add pepper and salt and boil gently for 3 hours. Strain off the stock, and when cold, remove the fat. Now add the vegetables cut up small and simmer slowly until the vegetables are tender. Serve with squares of fried or toasted bread.

N.B.—A little browning (Recipe 508) may be added, if required.

44 Cabbage Cream Soup

1 level tablespoonful cornflour
1 pint milk
3 tablespoonfuls finely shredded white heart of cabbage
2 red onions
salt and white pepper to taste
1 tablespoonful shredded cabbage for garnishing

Boil the 3 tablespoonfuls cabbage with the onions and as little water as possible to prevent burning. When tender, turn into the warmed milk, and simmer over boiling water until the milk is nicely flavoured with the cabbage. Strain. Meanwhile, keep the other tablespoonful of cabbage in a covered dish in the refrigerator, as dry as possible after washing, to retain its crispness. Mix the cornflour with a few spoonfuls of the strained milk, and stir into the rest of the milk. Re-heat over a very low flame, stirring all the time, until the mixture thickens slightly and the cornflour is cooked. Serve very hot, in warm soup plates or cups, with a little of the shredded cabbage sprinkled on top. The pepper and salt used for flavouring may be added just before serving, and the addition of 2 tablespoonfuls cream is an improvement although it is not necessary.

45 Cheese Soup

2 pints light stock
¼ lb. cheese
salt
pepper
2 slices of bread
a little butter
2 yolks of eggs
1 teacup milk

Cut the bread in small pieces, melt the butter in a saucepan and fry the bread until it begins to take colour. Then add the stock, and the cheese cut in thin slices. Stir well and boil for about half an hour. Beat up the yolks of the eggs with the milk and add to the soup stirring all the time. Season to taste and make the soup thoroughly hot, but do not boil again after the egg is added.

46 Chicken Mulligatawny

1 large chicken
1½ pints cold water
½ pint thick coconut milk
¼ oz. coriander seed and ⅛ oz. each sweet cummin seed and white cummin seed ground together
⅛ oz. white cummin seed ground separately
a pinch of ground saffron
4 medium-sized ripe tomatoes (sliced)
1 tablespoonful sliced red onions
2 cloves of garlic (chopped)
2 slices green ginger (chopped)
2 inch piece cinnamon
¼ teaspoon fenugreek
a small sprig curry leaves
1 dessertspoonful dripping
lime juice
salt

Cut the chicken into joints and put it into a saucepan, add the water and let it simmer for half an hour, then add the coriander, sweet cummin and white cummin ground together, the saffron, fenugreek, half the onions, the garlic and ginger, cinnamon, curry-leaves, tomatoes and salt; boil until the chicken is tender. Strain off the stock and put back the best pieces of chicken into the stock. Mix the remaining white cummin with the coconut milk and add to the stock. Heat the dripping in a pan and fry the remainder of the onions. When browned, turn in the prepared stock add salt and lime juice to taste, and let it boil up once. Serve boiled rice with the mulligatawny.

47 Clear Soup

2 lb. shin of beef
2 quarts cold water
2 carrots
6 oz. red onions
the whites and shells of 2 eggs
2 bandakkas (ladies' fingers)
2 strips of celery
1 dessertspoonful dripping
salt

Cut up the shin into pieces, put into a saucepan with the water, bring slowly to the boil, and skim well, add now the vegetables (cut up), and the salt, and simmer slowly for 4 hours or until the meat is quite tender. Strain off the stock, let it cool, then remove the fat. Beat up the whites of the eggs and the shells with a little cold water, add to the stock, and whisk well for about 5 minutes. Slice the onions finely, without peeling, heat the dripping in a pan and fry the onions a dark brown, being careful not to let them burn, turn in the stock and let it simmer slowly without stirring, until it boils up once. Set it aside to cool, and, when cold, strain through a towel which should be previously rinsed out in cold water. If the soup is not clear, strain twice or three times until it becomes clear. Re-heat the soup and put in a few pieces of the meat and, if liked, flavour with a glass of sherry. Serve very hot. A variety of vegetables cut in fancy shapes and cooked separately in salted water, may be used for garnishing.

48 Clear Soup a la Royale

1 quart clear soup
1 gill stock
2 eggs
salt

Whisk 2 yolks and one white of egg and add the stock and a small pinch of salt; butter a mould or cup, pour in the mixture and steam until firm. Turn it out and when cold, cut it up in small dice. Boil up the soup put in the custard and serve hot.

49 Cream Soup

½ lb. boiled potatoes
the white part of 3 small leeks
1½ pints good white stock
1 oz. butter
1 dessertspoonful flour
½ pint milk
chopped parsley or cress to garnish

Cut the leeks into very thin slices, add to the stock, and simmer until very tender. Turn in the potatoes cut in thin slices, and simmer until they break up well. Pass through a sieve, rubbing the potatoes down well to form a thin puree of the mixture.

Mix the flour with the cold milk, a little at a time, until quite smooth, stir over a low flame until slightly thickened, and add the butter. Add the stock, and stir until almost boiling.

Garnish with cress, if available.

50 Dhall Soup

½ measure dhall	**1 teacup milk**
1½ pints water	**salt**
1 strip celery	**pepper**
1 carrot	**a pinch of sugar**
1 Bombay onion	**dripping**

Wash the dhall well several times removing any discoloured ones which float on top of the water. Put the dhall into a bowl, pour in the 1½ pints of water and allow to soak for an hour or two. Prepare the vegetables and cut them in thin slices. Melt a dessertspoon of dripping in a saucepan and fry the vegetables for a few minutes; then add the dhall and the water in which it was soaked. Stir for a few minutes and let all come to boiling point; then simmer slowly for about two hours or until the dhall and the vegetables are quite soft. Stir the soup occasionally while it is cooking and, should it become too thick, more water must be added. When ready rub the soup through a wire sieve into a basin, have the saucepan rinsed out and return the soup to it to re-heat. Add the milk and the sugar and season to taste with salt and pepper. Bring to the boil and simmer a few minutes longer. Serve with dice of fried bread or toast.

51 Egg and Milk Soup

2 pints milk	**1 oz. butter**
2 oz. cheese	**1 oz. flour**
salt and pepper	**3 yolks of eggs**

Grate the cheese and put it into a small saucepan and melt it over the fire, adding a little of the milk. Put the remainder of the milk into another saucepan, make it very hot and add the butter and flour mixed together. Stir until the mixture thickens and is quite smooth. Then add the melted cheese and season to taste. Beat up the yolks of the eggs and add to the soup, stirring all the time. Make the soup thoroughly hot but do not boil again after the egg is added. Serve with toast.

52 Fish Mulligatawny

½ lb. fish	**1 medium-sized ripe tomato sliced**
2 teacups water	**½ a saltspoon fenugreek**
½ teacup thick coconut milk	**4 red onions (sliced)**
a level dessertspoonful of coriander seed and ½ teaspoon sweet cummin seed ground together	**2 cloves of garlic and 2 slices green ginger (chopped)**
1 teaspoonful white cummin seed ground	**1-inch piece of cinnamon**
a pinch of ground saffron	**a small sprig of curry-leaves**
	½ a strip of celery
	a squeeze of lime juice
	salt
	1 teaspoonful ghee

Any small fish may be used for making mulligatawny. Wash and prepare the fish and put it into a saucepan with the water and let it boil for five minutes. Then add the coriander and the sweet cummin ground together, the saffron, tomato, garlic, ginger, cinnamon, celery, salt and half each of the onions and curry-leaves. Let all simmer slowly until the fish and the other ingredients are cooked. Then mix the white cummin with the coconut milk and add to the fish stock. Heat the ghee in a saucepan and fry the remainder of the onions and curry-leaves together with the fenugreek; when the onions are browned, turn in the prepared stock. Season with lime juice and let it boil up once, then serve hot.

53 Fish Soup

1 lb. fish
1½ pints cold water
1 tablespoonful flour
6 peppercorns
1 pint milk
1 Bombay onion
½ oz. dripping
3 cloves
salt

Wash the fish well and cut it into small pieces, put it into a saucepan with the water, add a little salt, and bring to the boil. Skim well, add the pepper and cloves and let it simmer gently for half-an-hour, then remove a few pieces of fish from the bone and reserve them for serving in the soup. Return the bones, etc., to the pan and boil for about an hour. Then strain, being careful that none of the bones slip through. Melt the dripping in a pan, put in the onions finely minced and fry them a light brown; add the stock and let it boil for 5 minutes. Mix the flour smoothly with the milk, add to the soup and stir until boiling. Then put in the pieces of fish and serve the soup very hot.

54 Haricot Bean Soup

½ lb. Haricot beans
3 pints water
1 Bombay onion
1 carrot
half a turnip
a strip of celery
a sprig of parsley
½ pint milk
1 teaspoonful butter
pepper and salt

Wash the beans and let them soak overnight in cold water. Next day put them into a saucepan and add the water and the vegetables cut in small pieces. Boil until the beans and the vegetables are quite soft, adding more water if the soup becomes too thick. It must be stirred occasionally. When ready, rub through a wire sieve into a basin. Rinse out the saucepan and return the soup to it. Add the milk and the butter, season to taste with pepper and salt and cook about ten minutes longer. Serve with fried or toasted bread.

55 Jellied Soup

For the STOCK:
1 lb. each shin of beef and lean beef
1 quart water
1 small carrot, turnip and Bombay onion
1 stick of celery with a few of the smaller leaves

For CLEARING:
½ lb. lean beef
1 medium-size leek
2 cloves
1 teaspoonful salt
6 peppercorns
a small sprig of parsley
the white and shell of 1 large egg
sherry to taste

Wash the shin and beef quickly under the tap, and dry well. Cut up the meat into small pieces, removing all fat, and break the bones into small pieces so that the marrow can be readily extracted—for if this is left in, the soup becomes cloudy and greasy. Put meat and bones into a saucepan with the water and salt, and leave to soak for about an hour. Bring to the boil slowly, then simmer gently until the scum rises to the surface. Remove this carefully after about an hour's simmering, then put in all the vegetables, peeled or scraped and cut into small pieces, with the peppercorns and cloves tied in a small piece of coarse muslin. Simmer very gently for at least 3 hours, removing the scum as it rises. Strain through a cloth wrung out of boiling water, and leave to cool. The stock thus made should set into a rather firm jelly when quite cold, and should be entirely free from congealed fat. If there is a thin film of hard fat on top, it is best removed with spoons heated by dipping in boiling water, after which the surface may be lightly wiped over with a cloth wrung out of boiling water to ensure that every particle of it has been removed.

Turn the stock into a saucepan, and heat up, then put in the ½ lb. beef, which must be wiped over with a wet cloth and passed through the mincing machine. Wash the shell of the egg thoroughly, separate the white from the yolk, and put the crushed shell and the white into the pan. Whisk briskly over a good flame until the soup comes to the boil, then allow it to boil up well. Reduce the heat to a minimum, cover the pan, and let it stand for ten minutes or so, then strain carefully through a cloth wrung out of boiling water. When quite cold, set the basin on ice or in the refrigerator until thoroughly chilled. Sherry may be added when the soup has cooled, before chilling.

56 Julienne Soup

1 quart clear soup
1 carrot
1 turnip
1 Bombay onion
a strip of celery
1 oz. fresh butter or dripping
sugar
salt

Prepare the vegetables and cut them into fine strips an inch in length and an eighth of an inch thick. Heat the butter in a pan, put in the vegetables and a pinch of sugar and stir over the fire until brown. Drain, add to the soup and simmer slowly for 15 minutes.

57 Milk Soup

2 lb. brisket bones
1 quart cold water
2 pints milk
2 carrots
1 turnip
4 sliced red onions
2 potatoes
2 leeks
2 sticks of celery
1 dessertspoon dripping
12 peppercorns
salt

Break the bones into pieces and put them into a saucepan with the water. Bring to the boil, skim well and add the salt and the pepper. Allow the soup to simmer slowly from four to five hours. If the water boils down more must be added. When ready, strain through a sieve or towel, set aside to cool, and when quite cold remove the fat. Put the soup back into the pan, add the vegetables cut in cubes, and boil until they are tender. Remove the meat from the bones, cut into small pieces and add to the soup. Add the milk and boil for a few minutes longer. Heat the dripping in a pan and fry the sliced onions brown, then turn in the soup, make it thoroughly hot and serve.

58 Mulligatawny

Mulligatawny can be made with any kind of meat or fish. See Chicken Mulligatawny (46), Fish Mulligatawny (52), and Mulligatawny (White), 991.

59 Scotch Mutton Broth

1 lb. mutton
3 pints boiling water
1 carrot
1 turnip
1 Bombay onion
2 oz. pearl barley
2 oz. dried green peas
2 strips of celery
1 leek
1 dessertspoonful minced parsley
10 peppercorns
salt

Cut the meat into small pieces and put into boiling water with the barley previously washed, and the peas which should be soaked overnight in cold water. Bring these to the boil, skim well, add pepper and salt, and let it simmer for 2 hours. Now add the vegetables cut in dice and boil with the lid off the pan for 5 minutes, then cover and boil gently until the vegetables are tender but not broken. If the soup becomes too much reduced by boiling, more water must be added.

60 Ox-tail Soup

1 ox-tail
2 quarts water
1 carrot
1 turnip
1 Bombay onion
1 strip celery
1 oz. dripping
$\frac{1}{2}$ oz. flour
8 peppercorns
salt
a glass of sherry

Cut the tail separating it at the joints and wash the pieces well. Put them into a saucepan with cold water to cover, bring to the boil and pour off the water. Rinse and dry the pieces of tail and rinse out the saucepan. Melt half the dripping in the saucepan, put in the pieces of tail and the vegetables prepared and cut small and fry for about ten minutes. Then add the water, pepper and salt. Let all come slowly to the boil and then simmer gently for about four hours or until the pieces of tail are tender. Take out the pieces of tail and strain the soup through a fine sieve and set aside to cool. When cold, remove all fat from the top of the soup and reserve some of the best pieces of tail for serving in the soup. Melt the remainder of the dripping in a saucepan, add the flour and stir until browned. Then add the strained stock and stir over the fire until boiling. Put in the pieces of tail and any seasoning required and simmer a few minutes longer. Add the wine and, if desired, some small rounds of carrot and turnip previously cooked.

61 Pea Soup

2 lb. shin of beef
1 ham bone
3 quarts cold water
½ oz. dripping
1 dessertspoonful sliced red onion
4 oz. green-gram

Cut the shin into pieces and put it into a saucepan with the water. Bring to the boil and skim well; add the ham bone broken into pieces, and let it simmer slowly for about 4 hours. Strain off the stock, and, when cold, remove the fat. Roast slightly, peel, and grind finely the green-gram and mix it smoothly with the stock. Fry the onions in the dripping and, when browned, turn in the stock and let it boil gently until thickened, stirring occasionally. Have some ham and bread cut in small dice, fry the ham slightly and the bread a golden brown, and serve with the soup.

62 Potato Soup

1 lb. potatoes
1 quart cold water
½ pint milk
1 Bombay onion
2 strips of celery
1 oz. crushed tapioca or sago
12 peppercorns
1 oz. dripping
salt

Slice the potatoes, onions and celery and fry them in the dripping, but do not brown them. Add the water, pepper and salt and simmer gently from 1½ to 2 hours or until the potatoes are quite soft. Rub the pulp through a sieve, return to the saucepan and add the milk, let it come to the boil, then stir in the tapioca or sago and let it simmer for another 10 minutes. Stir occasionally.

N.B.—If liked, stock or meat-boilings could be used instead of water.

63 Prawn Soup

25 small prawns
2 pints fish stock
½ oz. butter
1 tablespoonful flour
1 teaspoon anchovy essence
½ teacup milk
a squeeze of lime juice

Wash and shell the prawns and remove the heads and tails. Put the shells, heads and tails into a saucepan with the stock and simmer slowly for 15 minutes to extract the flavour. Strain the stock and throw away the prawn trimmings. Return the stock to the saucepan, add the picked prawns and simmer slowly until the prawns are cooked. Mix the flour to a smooth paste with the milk and add it and also the butter, salt and anchovy essence to the soup and stir until boiling. Add a squeeze of lime juice just before serving.

64 Tomato Soup

1 lb. tomatoes
¼ lb. Bombay onions
pepper
½ oz. butter
1 dessertspoonful flour
1 teaspoonful sugar
1 pint water
1 gill milk

Melt the butter or dripping in a saucepan, put into it the tomatoes and onions chopped and cook them for five minutes, then add the water, salt and pepper to taste, put the lid on the pan and simmer slowly for one hour. Rub the soup through a sieve into a basin, rinse out the saucepan and return the soup to it. Mix the flour to a smooth paste with a little of the milk and add it to the soup. Stir well, add the sugar, return the saucepan to the fire and boil for five minutes. Now add the milk and make the soup thoroughly hot but do not bring it to the boil again.

65 Tomato Cream Soup

1 oz. cornflour
1 pint milk
1 tablespoonful butter
2 teacups tomato puree
¼ pint cream

For the puree, quarter 1½ lbs. small, ripe tomatoes, after washing well in cold water, and put into a saucepan with 2 cups cold water, 4 shredded red onions, 3 cloves, 6 peppercorns, a thin inch-strip of cinnamon, 1 level teaspoonful salt, and an inch or two of celery with some of its tender leaves. Bring to the boil rapidly, then reduce the heat and simmer until the tomatoes are reduced to a soft pulp. Strain through a piece of net, pressing out as much of the pulp as possible with the back of a wooden spoon. Keep hot.

Mix the cornflour with a little of the milk, and heat the rest in a saucepan. When almost boiling, pour in the cornflour, and stir over a moderate flame until cooked. Allow to cool slightly, then very gradually stir the tomato puree into the milk. Mix well, add the cream, and serve hot. If not stirred sufficiently, the mixture will curdle. If prepared some time before serving, stand the pan in another of hot water, and cover with a damp cloth.

66 Vegetable Soup

2 carrots
1 turnip
2 leeks
1 Bombay onion
2 strips of celery
1½ pints boiling water
1 pint milk
1 oz. sago
1½ oz. dripping
1 dessertspoonful minced parsley
salt

Prepare the vegetables and cut them into small cubes. Melt the dripping in a saucepan, put in the vegetables, and let this cook gently for 10 minutes without browning. Add the water and salt and simmer slowly until the vegetables are tender. If the water boils down more must be added, then add the milk, parsley and the sago, and boil for another 10 minutes or until the sago becomes clear.

67 Vegetable Soup (Italian)

4 medium-sized tomatoes
3 tablespoonfuls melted butter
2 large sticks of celery with some of the leaves
1 Bombay onion
3 small carrots thinly sliced
1 teaspoonful mixed dried herbs
1 quart white stock
6-8 strips of macaroni or spaghetti broken into inch lengths
salt and pepper to taste
grated cheese
2 lumps sugar

Peel and slice the tomatoes, cut the celery into short lengths, slice the onion and carrots, and put all together in a saucepan with the butter. Cover the pan, and allow to cook slowly, without browning, for about 15 minutes. Add the herbs and a little salt and pepper, and cook for a few minutes longer.

Pour in the stock, and bring to the boil, then add the spaghetti and simmer gently until the vegetables are well cooked and the spaghetti tender. Drop in the sugar, stir well to dissolve it, and, if needed, add a little more salt and pepper.

Hand grated cheese when serving.

Fish

(For Fish Curries, see Rice—Curries—Sambols and Kandyan-Sinhalese and Tamil Recipes.)

Fish is both a nutritious and tasty food, and is more easily digested than meat.

In selecting fish care should be taken to see that it is quite fresh. In fresh fish the flesh is stiff and firm, the eyes are bright, and the gills red. In choosing cut fish such as Seer, Para, etc., see that the flesh is firm and close grained; if it looks coarse and watery it is not good.

By way of large fish we have the Seer and Para, both equally good. Amongst other fish we have the Red Mullet, Cotton Fish, Skate and Sole. Amongst denizens of the sea which, though generally classed for culinary purposes as Shell-fish, are really not fish, are Oysters, Lobsters and Prawns. Oysters, as perhaps everyone in Ceylon knows, are found most plentifully at Bentota. Crabs, too, are generally regarded as Shell-fish. The only varieties of crabs that are edible are those found in lagoons, *e.g.*, those in Negombo, the most famous crab-district in Ceylon. Sea crabs are not generally eaten.

Preparation of Fish for Cooking—Washing is a very important item in preparing fish for cooking and water should not be spared. A lime skin or two put into the water in which fish is washed will take away the fishy smell. All slime on fish should be removed by scrapping with a knife. To remove scales from fish, lightly scrape them off with a knife from tail to head. Skate and Sole require to be skinned. In all fish the inside must be taken out and the cavity well washed. Some fish have to be cut open to be emptied, others have the inside drawn out by the gills.

81 Baked Cod Roe

1 tin cod roes	**grated cheese**
¼ lb. Bombay onions	**breadcrumbs**
white sauce	**butter**

Cut the roe in slices half an inch thick. Peel the onions, slice them thinly and put them into a saucepan of fast boiling salted water. Cook them from 15 to 20 minutes and drain. Grease a pie-dish and put in a layer of sliced cod roes, arrange a layer of onions on it, pour over a little white sauce and sprinkle a little grated cheese. Repeat the layers and finish with a layer of white sauce sprinkled with cheese and breadcrumbs. Put a few small pieces of butter on the top and brown in the oven.

82 Cod's Roe Cutlets

Cut the roe into slices half an inch thick. Dip the slices in egg, cover with breadcrumbs and fry in hot dripping to a golden brown. Drain on paper. Serve with toast spread with anchovy paste.

83 Baked Crab

4 medium-size crabs
1 dessertspoon Worcester sauce
1 teaspoonful mustard
1 teaspoonful chopped fennel
1 tablespoonful chopped red onions
1 oz. dripping
1 egg
1 teaspoonful flour
egg and breadcrumbs
cloves
cinnamon
pepper and salt

Boil the crabs, pick out all the flesh, season with pepper, salt powdered cloves and cinnamon, add the mustard, sauce, fennel, and one-third of the onions. Heat ½ oz. dripping in a saucepan and fry the remaining onions, then turn in the crab mixture, add a little of the liquor in which the crabs have been boiled and dredge in the flour. Let it cook for about 10 minutes but do not allow the mixture to dry. Take it off the fire, and when cool mix in the egg well beaten. Wash and clean the large body shells of the crabs, fill with the mixture, brush over the tops with beaten egg and spread over with powdered breadcrumbs. Put small pieces of dripping on the top and bake in a moderate oven until the breadcrumbs are nicely browned.

84 Baked Tinned Crab

1 tin crabs
1 dessertspoon Worcester sauce
1 teaspoon mustard
1 teaspoonful chopped fennel
1 teaspoonful chopped red onions
1 oz. dripping
1 egg
1 teaspoon flour
cloves
cinnamon
pepper
salt
fish stock or milk
egg and breadcrumbs

Chop the crab meat but not too finely, season with pepper and salt, powdered cloves and cinnamon, add the mustard, sauce, fennel, and one-third of the onions. Heat half the dripping in a saucepan and fry the remainder of the onions, then turn in the crab mixture, add a little fish stock and dredge in the flour. Let it cook for about 5 minutes but do not allow the mixture to become dry. Take it off the fire, and when cool mix in the egg well beaten. Put the mixture into a greased pie-dish, beat up an egg and pour it evenly on the top and spread over with powdered breadcrumbs. Put some pieces of dripping on the top and bake in a moderate oven until the breadcrumbs are nicely browned.

85 Baked Fish

1 lb. seer or any kind of fish **juice of half a lime**
pepper and salt **1 oz. dripping**

Baking is a good way of cooking fish as in this way none of the goodness of the fish is lost. Wash the fish well, then dry thoroughly and cut into convenient-sized pieces. Small fish should be baked whole. Place the fish in a buttered fire-proof dish, sprinkle with pepper and salt, moisten with lime juice, and put the dripping in small pieces on the top. Bake in a moderate oven, basting frequently: brown it nicely and serve hot.

86 Fish Baked in Batter

½ lb. boiled fish **1 oz. butter**
2 hard-boiled eggs **pepper and salt**

For the BATTER :
¼ lb. flour **2 eggs** **½ pint milk** **salt**

Remove all skin and bone from the fish and break it into pieces. Shell the eggs and cut them in slices. Put the fish into a greased pie-dish, arrange the slices of egg on it, sprinkle with pepper and salt and pour the melted butter over.

To Make the Batter—Sieve the flour into a basin, break one egg into it, add a little milk and mix the flour into it. Add the other egg and more milk. Beat the batter well until it is perfectly smooth, then add the rest of the milk. Add salt to taste and pour the batter over the fish. Bake in a moderate oven until nicely browned and firm to the touch. Serve hot.

87 Boiled Fish

Seer and Para are both good for boiling, and so are Red Mullet and Cotton Fish. Small fish should never be boiled, nor thin slices of fish. Clean the fish, wash well and wrap it in a fine piece of muslin and put it into a stewpan with salted hot water. Place an old plate at the bottom of the pan. Bring to the boil and simmer very gently. When one side is boiled turn over to the other side. Fish should be allowed to simmer very slowly, It takes much less time to cook fish than meat. No regulated time can be given, as much depends on the size and shape of the fish. A 2-lb. piece of Seer will take from 20 to 30 minutes to cook. As the scum rises it must be taken off the surface or it will settle on the fish and spoil its appearance. A teaspoonful of vinegar added to every pint of water will whiten the fish and keep it firm.

Boiled fish should never be allowed to remain in the liquid in which it has been cooked. When the fish is boiled, drain it well and put on a dish. Serve with any suitable sauce, e.g. Egg (Recipe 513), White (534), Anchovy (502).

88 Creamed Fish and Eggs

Flake sufficient boiled fish to fill a breakfast cup, and leave to get cold
1 cupful white sauce
salt and pepper to taste
4 eggs
2 teaspoonfuls each of finely chopped red onions and green chillies
½ teaspoonful Worcester sauce
½ teaspoonful salt and a dash of black pepper
2 tablespoonfuls butter

Season the sauce with pepper and salt, add the fish, and mix all well together. Pile up on a lightly buttered glass baking dish, and heat in a moderate oven.

Meanwhile, melt the butter in a frying-pan, and cook the onions and chillies in it until tender without being browned. Beat the eggs very well, add all the rest of the seasonings, and turn into the frying-pan. Cook over a brisk flame for a minute, stirring all the time to loosen the mixture as it sets, then reduce the heat and stir constantly until the whole is beginning to form into large, shiny-looking clusters of partly-cooked egg. Hold the pan away from the flame, and stir well to break into smaller pieces. If an aluminium pan is used, the heat retained in it is sufficient to finish the cooking while the final stirring is being done, but if the mixture still looks somewhat uncooked, the pan may be replaced over the low flame to cook through. When done, the eggs should be shiny and well broken up, but not dry. Arrange in small mounds round the prepared fish, and decorate with fingers of dry toast and small tufts of parsley. Serve very hot. This is a quickly prepared breakfast or light luncheon dish, and an excellent way of using up left-over fish and sauce. If the sauce has already had parsley added to it, it may still be used. In fact, this addition is considered by some to be an improvement.

89 Fish Cutlets

1 lb. boiled fish
¼ lb. boiled potatoes
1 tablespoonful chopped red onions
1 teaspoonful chopped fennel
pepper and salt
powdered cloves and cinnamon
yolk of 1 egg
1 dessertspoon Worcester sauce
dripping
egg and breadcrumbs

The remains of any cold boiled fish may be used for cutlets. Free the fish from all skin and bone and mix with the potatoes which must be mashed; add the onions, fennel, sauce and seasonings and moisten with the yolk of the egg. Then shape the mixture into small oblong cakes about ¼ inch thick, dip in beaten egg and breadcrumbs, and fry to a nice brown colour in boiling dripping.

90 Devilled Fish

1 lb. boiled fish
¼ lb. Bombay onions
1 oz. mustard seed (ground)
¾ oz. dry chillies (ground)
½ oz. dripping
salt
1 tablespoon Worcester sauce
2 tablespoons vinegar
1 dessertspoonful sugar
¼ stem lemon-grass
2- inch piece rampa
½ teacup or a little more of thick coconut milk

Any kind of cold, cooked fish or a tin of salmon may be used for this. Mix the mustard and chilli smoothly with the coconut milk, and add the vinegar, sauce, sugar, lemon-grass and rampa. Cut the onions in quarters and fry them in dripping, then turn in the mixed ingredients and cook until the gravy is thick. Lastly, add the fish which should be broken up in pieces not too small, and cook for a few minutes longer.

91 Fried Fish

To fry fish properly, it is necessary to have in the frying-pan as much dripping or oil as will cover the fish. The dripping must be very hot and it should smoke faintly. All kinds of fish may be fried. Small fish should be fried whole, bigger ones could be cut in slices or filleted. Fish to be fried must be well dried after it is washed. Then season with pepper and salt, dip in beaten egg, then in breadcrumbs and fry a nice golden brown in dripping. Drain on paper and serve hot.

N.B.—Instead of coating the fish with egg and breadcrumbs, if liked, it could be rubbed over with dry flour and fried.

92 Fish Kedgeree

½ lb. boiled fish
1 breakfastcupful boiled rice
2 hard-boiled eggs
1 oz. butter
pepper
salt

Melt the butter in a saucepan, add the fish broken up in flakes, the eggs which should be chopped up finely, and pepper and salt to taste. Stir over the fire till very hot. Any cold cooked fish may be prepared in this way, salmon kedgeree being specially good.

93 Fish Mayonnaise

Prepare in the same way as Lobster Mayonnaise (Recipe 110) using 6 oz. cold cooked fish instead of lobsters.

94 Fish Mayonnaise in Capsicums

large green capsicums
flaked boiled fish (seer or mullet being the best)
mayonnaise sauce
grated red onions
a little finely chopped parsley and finely chopped gherkin or olives
small sprigs of parsley to garnish and thin slices of stuffed olive

Choose the very large capsicums, wash well and dry, picking off the stalk and removing the small hard piece at this end. Cut in halves, and remove seeds and strings, then chill until very crisp.

Mix the coarsely-flaked fish with the sauce and all the seasonings to taste. Chill.

Just before sending to table, wipe the skin of the capsicums, arrange them neatly on a cold dish and garnish round the edge with a slice of olive in which a very tiny sprig of parsley has been stuck. Fill up the cases with the prepared fish, and put a small sprig of parsley in the centre of each.

This is a good way of using up remains of boiled or steamed fish, and a mixture of seer, mullet, and prawns may be used. As it is a harder fish, the mullet must be flaked finer than seer.

95 Fish Mouille

boiled fish (Recipe 87) or steamed fish (Recipe 105)
1 gill fish stock
1 gill thick coconut milk
1 dessertspoonful butter
1 level teaspoonful cornflour
2 chillies (1 ripe and 1 green)
a small sprig of curry-leaves
a good pinch of ground saffron
a small piece of cinnamon
pepper
salt

To Make the Sauce—Melt the butter in a small saucepan, put into it the curry-leaves and cinnamon and fry for a few minutes. Then add the stock seasoned with pepper and salt. Bring to the boil and add the chillies cut in strips and the coconut milk in which has been mixed the cornflour and saffron sufficient to colour the sauce a nice yellow. Stir until it thickens. Once the coconut milk has been added the sauce must be stirred continuously or it will curdle. Arrange a border of boiled rice round a dish, put the fish in the centre and pour the sauce over. Serve hot.

96 Fish Pie

1 lb. boiled fish
1 lb. mashed potatoes
2 or 3 tomatoes
2 oz. boiled macaroni
2 oz. grated cheese
1 oz. dripping
2 eggs
½ teacup fish stock or milk
breadcrumbs
pepper and salt

Free the fish from all skin and bone and break it in little flakes. Butter a pie-dish, put in a layer of potatoes, then a layer of fish seasoned with pepper and salt, then a layer of macaroni which sprinkle over with cheese and put a few pieces of dripping on top. Now put in a layer of sliced tomatoes seasoned with pepper and salt. Another layer of fish, then macaroni and cheese. Fill up the dish in this way. Beat up the eggs, mix with the fish stock, add seasonings and pour over the fish. Now cover with a layer of potatoes, scatter over with breadcrumbs and cheese, put a few pieces of dripping on the top, and bake until nicely browned.

97 Fish and Prawn Pie

½ lb. boiled fish
50 small prawns
1 tablespoonful chopped red onions
1 dessertspoon Worcester sauce
1 teaspoon mustard
powdered cloves
cinnamon, pepper and salt
2 eggs
powdered breadcrumbs
dripping

Free the fish from all skin and bone and break it into little flakes. Shell the prawns, remove the heads and tails and boil them, then chop them. Mix the fish and the prawns together, add the onions, sauce and mustard and season with the powdered ingredients and salt. Stir in the eggs well beaten and, if the mixture is not sufficiently moist, add a little fish stock or milk. Pour the mixture into a greased pie-dish, scatter over with breadcrumbs and put a few pieces of dripping on the top. Bake until nicely browned. Serve either hot or cold.

98 Fish Pudding

1 lb. boiled fish or a tin of salmon
¼ lb. grated bread
2 oz. butter
pepper and salt
1 teaspoonful anchovy essence
1 teacup milk
3 eggs

Free the fish from all skin and bone and mix with the bread, beat in the eggs and the butter and add the rest of the ingredients. Mix well together, put into a buttered mould, and steam from 1 to 1½ hours. Turn out on to a dish and serve either hot or cold, with any nice sauce poured over it.

99 Fish Roe Fried

fish roe
pepper and salt
egg and breadcrumbs
dripping

Wash the roe well, tie it in a piece of muslin to prevent it breaking and boil in salted water for half an hour. When ready, drain off the water and let the roe become quite cold. Then cut it in convenient-sized pieces, season with pepper and salt, dip in beaten egg and then in breadcrumbs, and fry a nice brown in hot dripping.

100 Fish Roll

½ lb. cooked fish
½ lb. cold potatoes
1 oz. butter
1 teaspoonful chopped fennel
1 teaspoon anchovy essence
pepper and salt
yolk of 1 egg
a little milk or fish stock, if necessary
egg and breadcrumbs

The remains of any cold cooked fish may be used or tinned salmon. Free the fish from all skin and bone and chop it finely. Mash the potatoes and mix together with the fish, season with pepper and salt, add the fennel and anchovy and the butter, stir into it the yolk of egg well beaten and, if not sufficiently moist, add a little milk or fish stock. When well mixed form into a roll using a little flour, brush over with beaten egg, roll in bread-crumbs, place on a greased tin and bake in a quick oven for half an hour. Serve with anchovy sauce.

101 Fish Salad

½ lb. boiled fish or half tin salmon
salad dressing (Recipe 494) or Mayonnaise sauce (Recipe 492)
lettuce
cucumber
tomatoes
pepper and salt

Remove all skin and bone from the fish, break into neat flakes and season with pepper and salt. Line a salad dish with some lettuce leaves, pile the fish in the centre and pour the dressing over it. Garnish with thinly sliced cucumber and tomato.

102 Fish Souffle I

½ lb. boiled white fish
1 oz. butter
1 oz. flour
½ teaspoon anchovy essence
2 eggs
¼ pint milk
pepper
salt

Free the fish from all skin and bone and break it up very finely. Melt the butter in a saucepan, stir in the flour and anchovy essence and season to taste, then add the yolks of the eggs beaten up in the milk and stir over the fire until the mixture is thick. Take it off the fire and mix in the fish, and lastly stir in the whites of eggs beaten to a stiff froth. Pour the mixture into a buttered pie-dish or souffle dish and bake for half an hour. Serve at once.

103 Fish Souffle II

1 thick slice of seer
a small sprig of fennel leaves
1 small Bombay onion
2 oz. sieved flour
2 oz. butter
3 eggs
¼ pint milk (or fish stock from the boiling of fish used)
salt and pepper to taste
a dash of cayenne
4 tablespoonfuls cream

Boil the fish in slightly salted water, with the onion and fennel added to it. Remove the skin and bones, and the dark-coloured fat. Allow it to get cold, then flake very finely. Strain the stock. Melt the butter in a saucepan, stir in the flour, and cook for a few minutes over a low flame. Stir in the stock or milk (half milk and half stock may be used, if liked) and cook, while stirring, until the mixture thickens. It should, when beaten, form into a soft ball and leave the sides of the pan almost clean. Beat in the yolks of the eggs, very thoroughly, and leave to get cold.

Mix the flaked fish and cream with the paste, or "panada" as it is called, and press it through a coarse sieve or a piece of coarse net stretched over a basin. Well butter a souffle dish, beat the whites of the eggs to a very stiff froth and fold them gently into the fish mixture, adding seasoning to taste. Turn into the prepared dish, and bake in a hot oven until well risen and delicately browned on top.

104 Soused Fish

½ lb. boiled fish
4 cloves
12 peppercorns
a blade of mace
2 ripe chillies
¼ pint vinegar
cucumber
Bombay onions
boiled beetroot
salt

Put the vinegar into a saucepan, add the cloves, peppercorns, mace, salt and the chillies cut in rings and boil for a few minutes. Put the fish into a pie-dish, pour the spiced vinegar (hot) over it and leave for about 12 hours. To serve, place the fish in the centre of a dish, arrange some slices of cucumber, Bombay onions and boiled beetroot round and strain the vinegar over it.

105 Steamed Fish

Steaming is a better way of cooking fish than boiling.

Take slices of fish or fillets of fish. Wash the fish well and rub it over with pepper, salt and a little lime juice. Place the fish on a buttered deep plate, put a few pieces of butter on the top and cover over with another plate. Have ready a saucepan nearly full of boiling water, place the plates on it and cook from 10 to 15 minutes. Then turn the fish and cook about the same length of time on the other side. The water must be kept boiling all the time. The fish should have a creamy appearance and break easily when done. Serve with the liquid left on the plate or any nice sauce.

106 Fish Stew

1 lb. seer or para
1 Bombay onion
1 teaspoonful chopped parsley
½ oz. flour
1 oz. dripping
12 peppercorns
6 cloves
salt
¾ pint fish stock or water

Wash the fish and cut into neat pieces. Melt the butter in a stewpan and fry in it the onion, sliced also the flour, until browned, then pour in the stock, stir well and add the rest of the ingredients. Simmer gently for half an hour or until the fish is quite done.

107 Baked Lobster

1 lobster
2 tablespoons white sauce
1 teaspoonful chopped fennel
1 teaspoon anchovy essence
pepper and salt
2 tablespoonfuls powdered breadcrumbs
lime juice
1 yolk of egg
a little butter

Boil the lobster, break it up, remove all the meat and chop it into small pieces. Put the chopped meat, the white sauce, anchovy essence, and half of the breadcrumbs into a saucepan, mix well, and season to taste with pepper, salt and lime juice. Then mix in the yolk of egg and make all thoroughly hot over the fire. Put the mixture into a greased pie-dish, sprinkle the remainder of the breadcrumbs over the top, lay on some small pieces of butter and bake in a moderate oven from 20 to 30 minutes.

108 Lobster Cream

2 level tablespoonfuls butter
2 large or 3 small lobsters
2 level tablespoonfuls flour
1 pint milk
yolks of 3 eggs
¼ pint thin cream
salt and pepper
cayenne, and a little lime juice
½ wineglass pale sherry

Melt the butter in a pan, add the lobster-meat cut into dice, and fry for a few minutes, being careful not to let the butter brown. Mix the flour with a little of the cold milk until smooth, then add the rest of the milk and stir well. Turn this into the pan with the lobster, and cook over a low flame for a few minutes, stirring all the time. Beat the yolks of the eggs in a basin, stir in the cream and mix well, and then add to the mixture in the pan. Continue stirring over a very low flame until the mixture thickens and the flour is quite cooked. Season to taste, with salt, pepper, and a good sprinkling of cayenne (or sifted, powdered red chillies), and add a few drops of lime juice. Just before serving, add the sherry, stir well and turn into a hot dish, garnish with neat triangles of dry toast.

If the cream has to be made some time before it is required, it should be kept hot by standing the pan in another of warm water, with a wet cloth placed over. This prevents a "crust" from forming.

109 Lobster Cutlets

1 lobster
1 oz. butter
1 oz. flour
¼ pint milk or fish stock
1 teaspoonful lime juice
a little mustard
egg and breadcrumbs
pepper and salt

Remove all the flesh from a boiled lobster and chop it finely. Put the butter into a saucepan and when it is melted mix in the flour smoothly, add the milk and boil for five minutes, then add the lobster and seasoning and mix well together. Spread out the mixture on a flat plate to cool. When cold divide into 12 equal portions, which form into cutlets. Egg and breadcrumb them and fry in hot dripping till a golden colour.

110 Lobster Mayonnaise

2 or 3 lobsters, according to size
6 small, round tomatoes of an even size
the heart of fresh lettuce
2 scant teaspoonfuls capers
1 gill thick mayonnaise sauce, well iced
parsley

Boil the lobsters, and remove carefully from the shell. Split into halves when doing this so that the large pieces of fish may preserve a good shape. The meat from the claws should also be removed very carefully to avoid breaking up into untidy pieces. When thoroughly cleaned wipe over with a damp cloth, and chill.

Wash the lettuce, leaf by leaf, and shake in a cloth until dry. Put in a covered dish, and chill until very crisp. Peel the tomatoes (by plunging into boiling water and then carefully paring away the skin with a sharp knife), and chill. Particular emphasis is laid on the chilling of all ingredients before mixing, because on this depends the success of the dish.

Cut the lettuce into fine shreds, and cover the bottom of the serving dish with it. Place the halves of lobster on it in a neat row, and coat each piece with mayonnaise. Sprinkle capers over. Arrange the tomatoes round the dish, and between each place a small mound of the chopped claw-meat dipped in mayonnaise. Put a tiny sprig of parsley on top of each tomato and serve immediately.

111 Lobster Salad

lobster
salad lettuce
salad dressing (Recipe 494) or Mayonnaise sauce (Recipe 492)
hard-boiled egg

Boil the lobster, break it up, pick out all the meat and cut in neat pieces. Arrange some lettuce leaves in a salad bowl, place the lobster on it and pour over the dressing. Garnish with slices of hard-boiled egg.

112 Maldive Fish Cutlets

¼ lb. Maldive fish
2 oz. red onions
½ teaspoon ground dry chillies
1 tablespoonful scraped coconut and 1 dessertspoonful raw rice (ground)
powdered cloves
cinnamon and pepper
salt
lime juice
1 egg
egg and breadcrumbs
oil for frying

Pound the Maldive fish very finely and add to it the onions finely chopped, the ground chilli, the coconut and ground rice and season to taste with cloves, cinnamon, pepper, salt and lime juice. Mix well together and moisten the mixture with the egg lightly beaten. Shape into small flat rounds about quarter of an inch thick, dip in egg and breadcrumbs and fry a nice brown in hot oil.

113 Devilled Oysters

1 tin oysters
2 tablespoonfuls melted butter
1 saltspoonful powdered dried chillies finely sieved
1 small teaspoonful Tabasco sauce
lime juice to taste
black pepper
beaten egg, and fine browned breadcrumbs
lard and butter for frying

Drain the liquor from the oysters, and place them in an earthenware or glass dish. Pour the butter over, and sprinkle them with all the seasoning ingredients. Leave to marinate in this mixture for 15 minutes, turning them over occasionally so that they become evenly seasoned.

Life out one at a time, and roll in the breadcrumbs, then in the beaten egg, and again in the crumbs. Fry in equal quantities of lard and butter. Serve very hot.

114 Oyster Fritters I

For the BATTER:

4 oz. sieved flour
whites of 2 large eggs
1 gill tepid water
1 tablespoonful salad oil (or melted butter)
1 heaped saltspoonful salt
fat for frying

Sieve the flour again with the salt, put into a basin and make a well in the centre. Using a wooden spoon for stirring, add the water very gradually and mix thoroughly until a perfectly smooth paste is formed, then add the rest of the water and beat well. Stir in the oil, beat again for a few minutes, cover, and set aside for at least one hour. When ready to use, stir the mixture in the basin and then fold in the stiffly-whisked whites of eggs. The above quantity of batter is sufficient for 12 fritters. Drain 12 bearded oysters, dust liberally with powdered dry chillies or cayenne pepper, and sprinkle a few drops of lime juice on each. Have ready 24 rounds of thinly-sliced fat bacon. Press an oyster between each pair of bacon rounds so that the edges adhere together well, dip into the prepared batter, and fry in deep fat until a good golden brown colour and well puffed out. Drain on a double sheet of kitchen paper, and serve very hot, with a dusting of finely minced parsley on top.

In frying fritters it must always be remembered that the best results are obtained by frying only a few at a time,, and the fat must be allowed to boil level with a faint blue smoke rising from it in between each lot of frying. The fritters should be allowed to brown on one side before turning over, and should be lifted out with a perforated spoon and placed directly on the draining-paper.

115 Oyster Fritters II

Using the same batter as in Recipe 114, with the addition of cayenne pepper to taste, take up a dessertspoonful of the mixture, drop a bearded oyster into the centre of it, and with another spoon slide the batter-covered oyster into a deep pan of boiling fat. Cook on both sides until lightly browned, drain well, and serve very hot. Slices of lime and rolls of thin brown bread and butter should be handed with this dish.

116 Oyster Stew

1 pint oysters
1 pint milk
1 oz. butter
12 peppercorns
2-inch piece cinnamon
salt

Open the oysters and strain the liquor into a stewpan. Heat the liquor until it boils, then add the milk which must be previously heated, the butter, and the seasonings. Beard the oysters, add them to the rest of the ingredients and cook until the oysters are done.

117 Prawn Cutlets I

prawns
red onions
fennel
pepper and salt
egg and breadcrumbs
dripping

Choose large prawns for cutlets. Wash and trim the prawns but do not take off the heads and tails. Chop one side of the prawn very lightly using a table-knife taking care that the flesh does not separate. Season with pepper and salt and rub over with finely chopped fennel and onions. Dip the prawns in beaten egg and then in breadcrumbs and fry them a nice golden brown in hot dripping.

118 Prawn Cutlets II

1 breakfastcupful of minced prawns
3 oz. grated bread
1 dessertspoonful chopped red onions
1 teaspoonful chopped fennel
1 teaspoon anchovy essence
1 dessertspoon Worcester sauce
1 egg
pepper and salt
egg and breadcrumbs
dripping

Shell the prawns, remove the heads and tails and mince them but not too finely. Mix the minced prawns with the grated bread and add the onions, fennel, anchovy essence, sauce, pepper and salt. Mix well together and bind with the egg slightly beaten. Form the mixture into cutlet shapes or round cakes, dip in egg and bread-crumbs and fry them in dripping until nicely browned.

119 Prawn Mayonnaise in Capsicums

large green capsicums
boiled prawns
thick mayonnaise sauce
a suspicion of grated red onion for each serving

Choose the medium-large, shiny green capsicums. Wash well and dry, cut a thin piece off the stalk end and then cut into slices about $\frac{1}{4}$-$\frac{1}{2}$ inch thick. Remove seeds and strings, and chill in a covered dish to keep them crisp.

Cut the prawns into small pieces and add just enough mayonnaise to coat them well, and onion to give a delicate flavour.

Arrange the sections of capsicum, three to each individual serving, clover-wise on a plate, with a tiny slice of capsicum to represent the stalk. Fill up each section with the prepared prawns, and serve very cold.

120 Prawn Salad

boiled prawns
Mayonnaise sauce
lettuce
radish
hard-boiled eggs

Shell the prawns, remove the heads and tails and boil them. Arrange some lettuce leaves in a salad bowl, place the prawns on it and pour the Mayonnaise sauce over. Garnish with sections of hard-boiled egg and thinly sliced radishes.

121 Stewed Prawns

50 medium size prawns
1 teaspoonful flour
1 oz. dripping
¼ lb. Bombay onions
1 gill milk
1 gill water
12 peppercorns
4 cloves
a blade of mace
salt

Wash and shell the prawns and remove the heads. Melt the dripping in a stewpan and fry in it the onions sliced, then sprinkle in the flour and allow it to brown. Pour in the milk and water, stir well and add the prawns, peppercorns, cloves, mace and salt and simmer slowly until the prawns are cooked.

122 Red Mullet au Gratin

1 medium size red mullet
4 red onions
6—8 tinned "button" mushrooms
1 level teaspoonful chopped parsley
a good pinch grated rind of lime
pepper and salt to taste
1 heaped tablespoonful powdered browned breadcrumbs
butter

For the DRESSING:
½ gill white wine
1 scant dessertspoonful tomato ketchup
1 teaspoonful anchovy essence
some small pats of butter

Wash and clean the fish thoroughly. Chop the onions and mushrooms into small pieces, and mix them with the parsley, rind of lime, and seasonings. Butter a fire-proof baking dish liberally, sprinkle half of the prepared seasonings on the bottom, place the fish on top and score it across in two or three places with a sharp knife. Sprinkle the balance of the seasonings on top, and cover with the breadcrumbs. Mix the three dressing ingredients together thoroughly, pour over the fish, and put small pats of butter on top. Bake in a moderate oven until the fish is cooked through, basting several times, with the dressing during the first twenty minutes, and then leaving undisturbed until cooked

123 Red Mullet Baked

red mullet salt pepper butter

Clean and prepare the fish. The inside must be emptied, the fins cut off and the skin scraped well from tail to head. Season the fish with pepper and salt and place it on a greased pie-dish. Lay some butter in small pieces on the top and bake the fish in a moderate oven until ready.

124 Rolled Mullet

8 slices of mullet each about 2 inches square and $\frac{1}{8}$th of an inch thick
25 very small prawns boiled and shelled
1 level teaspoonful each flour and butter
$\frac{1}{2}$ gill milk
salt and pepper
a good pinch of powdered red chillies
the yolk of 1 egg and 1 whole egg
fine browned breadcrumbs
thin slices of lime and parsley to garnish
oil for frying

Wash and dry the slices of fish, and rub in salt and pepper on both sides. Chop the prawns into very small pieces.

Melt the butter in a small saucepan, stir in the flour and stir over a very low flame until the mixture bubbles. Add the milk, a little at a time, and cook gently for 5 minutes, taking care not to let the sauce brown. Remove from the fire, add the yolk of egg, and beat well, then add salt, pepper, and cayenne or chilli to taste. Leave to get cold. Mix the prawns with the sauce, and spread over two-thirds of each of the prepared slices of fish, roll over to a neat shape and brush the plain end of each roll with a little beaten egg. Fold over completely, and fasten with small wooden picks. Brush over with the beaten egg, roll in breadcrumbs, and fry in deep, very hot oil. Lift out very carefully, and drain for a few minutes. Place a very small sprig of parsley in the opening at each end of the rolls, and arrange on a dish paper placed on a hot dish. Garnish with the lime, and small sprigs of parsley.

N.B—An unusual method of arranging lime garnish is to cut each thin slice of lime in half almost to the centre core, bend up one side—pinching the rind between the fingers so that it will stand up in a curved fan-shape resting on the other half. Place a tiny sprig of parsley inside the curve, and arrange at intervals round the dish. This garnish should be prepared before it is needed, as it takes a little time to do, and holds the shape better when allowed to stand for some time before use.

125 Salmon in Aspic

1 lb. tin of any good brand of salmon
1 square tin of asparagus tips
$\frac{1}{2}$-$\frac{3}{4}$ gill thick mayonnaise
1 pint liquid aspic jelly
1 teaspoonful finely chopped parsley
a little salt and white pepper
a plain round mould about 6 in. diameter and 3 in. deep will be needed for these quantities and a smaller mould for shaping the centre cavity.

Put a thin layer of the liquid jelly at the bottom of the larger mould, and set firm.

Drain off the liquid from the asparagus, and spread the spears carefully on a folded cloth to dry, turning them over on to a fresh fold of the cloth to dry the other side as well.

Remove skin and bones from the salmon, turn into a bowl with its own liquor, and flake finely with a fork. Season with parsley, salt and pepper.

As soon as the first layer of jelly has set firm, line the sides of the mould with a thin layer of jelly, as directed for Charlotte Russe (Recipe 625) and when it is all evenly coated, and very firm, line the sides of the mould with the spears of asparagus set fairly close together with the "flower-tip" downwards. Each spear must be dipped in liquid jelly, when this is done, and all must set quite firmly. It is usually possible to place two spears at a time. When all are firmly placed in position go all over again, pouring in liquid jelly to come almost level with the asparagus, and letting each set before turning the mould round to set the next spoonful. When quite firm pour in just sufficient liquid jelly to cover the flower-tips at the bottom, the mould now being restored to its upright position. Set this layer of jelly very firmly, because it has to support a weight.

Half fill the smaller mould with iced water and a spoonful or two of crushed ice, and place it right in the centre of the larger mould, then pour round enough jelly to make a deep enough cavity for filling in later with the salmon mixture. Set very firmly.

Meanwhile, mix the mayonnaise with the salmon and add some of the liquid jelly to it, then chill until the mould is ready for it.

Holding the two moulds firmly together, quickly tip out the water and ice, and pour in some warm water. Test the inner mould, and as soon as it works loose by itself lift it out carefully, and at once pack the cavity with the prepared salmon. Leave this to set firmly, then cover the whole with liquid jelly, and leave until firm enough to turn out. Serve on an ice-cold dish, suitably garnished.

For very special occasions the dish may be garnished with flower-tips of asparagus, dipped in jelly and set in position round the edge, with thin slices of stuffed olives similarly set in between. Care must be taken when garnishing in this manner to leave sufficient room for the mould to be inverted exactly in the centre.

126 Timbale of Salmon

½ pint thick rich white sauce
1 heaped teaspoonful minced parsley
a pinch of mixed herbs
½ lb. tinned salmon
the yolks of 2 eggs
salt and pepper to taste
a pinch of cayenne
about 4 oz. macaroni cooked in its full length in salted water
butter
onion sauce

Remove skin and bones from fish, and break up with a fork, retaining the liquor. Season to taste with pepper, salt, and cayenne, and add the parsley. Break the yolks of the eggs into the sauce, and stir well to mix, then add to the prepared fish.

Butter a pudding basin, and after draining all moisture from the cooked macaroni coil the strips round and round inside the basin to form a complete lining. Turn the fish mixture in very carefully, cover with buttered paper, and steam for an hour.

Turn out carefully on to a hot dish, and hand the onion sauce separately.

127 Seer a l'Indienne

1 lb. seer cut in a slice about ¾ inch thick
6 red onions
½ pint fish stock
2 tablespoonfuls mango chutney
1 teaspoonful powdered mustard
1 tablespoonful tomato sauce
1 scant teaspoonful chilli vinegar
a few drops lime juice
1 rounded teaspoonful dripping
1 level tablespoonful cornflour
a little salt
a little butter

Boil the fish, and remove bones and skin while hot. Separate into four sections. Save ½ pint of the water in which it was boiled, straining it to remove onion, fennel, or other flavourings boiled with it.

Chop the onion finely and fry a golden brown in the dripping. Stir in the mustard, the fish stock, and a little salt. Boil up, and pour on to the cornflour mixed with a little cold water. Return to the pan, and stir over gentle heat for a few minutes to thicken. Add all the other ingredients, one at a time, mixing well. Butter a china baking dish, pour a little of the sauce on the bottom, and place the pieces of fish neatly over it. Pour the rest of the sauce over, and bake in a moderately hot oven for ten minutes, basting with the sauce twice. Serve in the same dish, as hot as possible.

128 Mousse of Seer

½ pint white sauce
¾ lb. boiled seer free from skin and bone
½ pint thick cream
¾ oz. leaf gelatine
1 tablespoonful water
salt
white pepper, and cayenne to taste

The sauce must be made with well-seasoned milk, and the fish should also be cooked with onion, peppercorns, a little fennel, and some celery leaves to impart a good flavour. If this is not done the mousse is inclined to be insipid.

Flake the fish very finely and mix with half of the sauce. Pass through a sieve, using the rest of the sauce a little at a time to force the mixture easily through the mesh, otherwise it is inclined to stick. Add a good seasoning of salt and pepper, and enough cayenne to give a fairly hot taste to the mixture. Chill thoroughly.

Dissolve the gelatine in the water, and stir it gently into the cream. When all streaks have disappeared leave it to chill until it is just beginning to set, then add the fish mixture to it, add a little more salt, if needed, and stir well but very gently, then pour into a mould rinsed with iced water, and leave to set.

Turn out on to an ice-cold dish, and garnish with stuffed olive sliced very thinly, rounds of gherkin, and small tufts of parsley.

129 Fried Whitebait

whitebait
flour
salt and pepper
cayenne
sections of sliced lime
parsley for garnishing
frying fat

Choose the very small fish, as these are more tasty than the larger kind. Wash thoroughly until free from all particles of sand, and leave wrapped in a cloth for ten minutes. Have very hot fat ready for frying and a fine-meshed wire frying basket.

Sprinkle flour seasoned liberally with pepper and salt on to a sheet of kitchen paper, and drop the fish on it. Shake well until coated, then shake through a coarse sieve to remove surplus flour. Place in the basket and fry for three or four minutes, until very crisp. Dust with cayenne pepper, and serve piled up on a dish paper placed in a hot dish. Garnish with the lime and a few tufts of fresh parsley, and hand rolls of very thin brown bread and butter with the fish.

Meat

For convenience, recipes which can be prepared out of different kinds of meat (*e.g.* beef, mutton, chicken, etc.) are grouped together here.

For other meat recipes, please see under Beef, Veal—Lamb—Mutton, Pork, Poultry and Game, Eggs.

For meat Curries, see under Rice—Curries—Sambols and Tamil Recipes.

Hints on Choosing Meat

Beef should be of a rich colour with yellowish fat.

Mutton should be of a rich red colour, but darker than beef; the fat whitish and firm.

The flesh of pork should be finely grained and the fat white.

The flesh of good meat is firm to the touch, and it must not be moist and clammy.

Different Methods of Cooking Meat

The methods most frequently employed are:

Roasting or Baking, Boiling, Frying and Grilling.

Roasting or Baking—Roasting, properly speaking, is cooking in front of an open fire, and baking means cooking in an oven, but both methods of cooking are commonly referred to as roasting. Baking or roasting in the oven has quite taken the place of the old-fashioned method of roasting in front of the fire.

Trim the piece of meat to be roasted, wash it, and remove all superfluous fat. Rub it over with pepper and salt and place it on a baking tin, pour in a little cold water and set it in the oven. After the fat melts a little, lift it up with a spoon from the tin and pour it over the meat—this is *basting*—and should be done at intervals of 15 minutes to prevent the meat from getting dry. If the meat is lean, rub it over with a little dripping before putting it into the oven, or there will not be sufficient fat for basting.

The time allowed for roasting meat is 15 minutes to the pound and fifteen minutes over, but the shape of the joint must be taken into consideration as well as its weight. Experience will be found to be the best guide. If the joint is large and thick it should be turned over once or twice during the cooking.

Roasting in a Pan or Chatty—Another, and a more convenient method of roasting meat is cooking it in a pan or chatty. Wash and trim the meat, rub over with pepper and salt, and if necessary tie into shape with a piece of string. Put the meat into a saucepan or chatty, pour in just a little boiling water and let it cook slowly until the water is absorbed. Then allow the meat to fry, turning it over so that the whole is nicely browned. No fat need be added unless the meat is lean, in which case a little dripping may be necessary.

This method of cooking will be found convenient for roasting small joints and birds.

Boiling—This, although one of the easiest methods of cooking meat, is not always done successfully. Boiled meat should be tender and juicy but it is usually served tough and tasteless. Small joints should never be boiled—do not boil anything under 3 lbs.

Wash the meat, trim it, and, if necessary, fasten with a wooden skewer or tie into shape with a piece of string or tape. Plunge it into a saucepan of boiling salted water sufficient to cover the joint, and allow the water to boil rapidly for 5 minutes, then let it simmer slowly until sufficiently cooked. Remove all the scum that rises on the surface, or it will settle on the meat and spoil its appearance.

The usual time allowed for boiling meat is 20 minutes to the pound, but it will vary according to the size and shape of the meat.

The liquor in which the meat has been cooked can be used for making soup.

Frying—This important method of cooking meat is not so generally understood as it ought to be, and that is the reason why frying is often a failure. Frying is one of the quickest methods of cooking meat. There are two different methods of frying.

1. *Dry or Shallow Frying* is cooking in a frying-pan using a small quantity of fat, dripping or oil. The fat must be made quite hot, then the meat placed on it, and cooked slowly, first on one side then on the other until browned. This method is suitable for cooking chops, steaks, kidneys, etc.

2. *Wet or Deep Frying* is cooking in a large quantity of fat, dripping or oil sufficient to cover the article to be fried. This method is suitable for frying fritters, rissoles, etc. The articles to be fried are usually protected with a coating of egg and breadcrumbs or batter.

To fry properly, it is necessary that the fat should be smoking hot before the article to be fried is put in. The fat must be heated until all bubbling has ceased and a thin bluish smoke is seen to rise from the surface. A good way of testing the heat is to put a small crust of bread or a drop of batter into the fat; if it frizzles at once, the fat is ready for use. Do not put too many articles into the pan at the same time as they will cool the fat; and always allow time for the fat to re-boil before the second and other articles are added. Let them fry a nice brown colour, then lift them out carefully with a perforated spoon and let the fat drip through. When well drained, turn the articles on to a paper to absorb any superfluous fat.

Grilling—This is cooking on a gridiron over hot coals. This method of cooking is only suitable for small pieces of meat which will cook quickly, such as chops, steaks, kidneys, small birds, etc. The fire should be clear and bright consisting of glowing red embers, without any smoke or flame. A little salt sprinkled over the fire will help to disperse any smoke. Place the gridiron about 3 or 4 inches above the coals, and when hot, grease it well with a piece of suet or any other fat. Lay the meat on the gridiron and turn the meat at intervals of 2 minutes repeating the process until it is cooked.

Frozen Meat

Frozen meat must always be thawed before cooking. Let the meat hang in a cool place for at least 10 hours before using it. Once the meat is thawed it must be cooked, otherwise it will not keep.

Meat Recipes

151 Brain Cutlets

1 brain	**egg and breadcrumbs**
pepper and salt	**dripping**

Wash the brain well and boil it for about 15 minutes. Allow it to cool, then cut into rather thick slices, rub over with pepper and salt, dip each slice first in beaten egg, and then in breadcrumbs and fry a golden brown colour in dripping.

152 Brain Fritters

1 brain	**1 gill milk**
2 tablespoonfuls flour	**salt**
1 egg	**dripping**

Wash the brain well in warm water and boil it for about 15 minutes. Make a batter with the flour, egg and milk, add salt to taste. Cut the brain in slices, season with pepper and salt, dip each slice in the batter and fry in hot dripping till brown and crisp.

153 Brain Omelette

cooked brain
4 eggs
pepper
salt
a little chopped fennel
dripping

Take some cooked brain, mash it free of lumps, season with pepper and salt and add the fennel. Separate the yolks from the whites of the eggs. Beat the yolks until thick and creamy and season with pepper and salt. Beat the whites until stiff and dry and mix lightly with the yolks. Melt a little dripping in a frying pan and when very hot pour in the egg mixture, spread evenly, and as soon as it commences to set, put the brain in the centre and fold the edges over to make it oval. When nicely browned on one side turn over and brown the other side. An omelette should be served immediately it is cooked or it will become leathery.

154 Brain Pudding

1 brain
½ lb. Bombay onions
1 stick celery
1 small bunch of fennel
2 eggs
½ cup milk
2 oz. butter or ghee
a little grated cheese
lime juice to season
pepper and salt

Soak the brain in cold water for about an hour, wash well and boil with a little salt. Mash with a fork, mix with the well beaten eggs and the milk. Season with salt, pepper and lime juice and add the fennel and celery chopped very fine.

Heat the fat, fry the onions, add the brain mixture, and fry for a few minutes, mixing all well together. Turn into a greased baking dish, put dabs of butter and a grating of cheese on top, sprinkle with breadcrumbs, and bake in a moderate oven till brown. An improvement on this is to have a crust of potatoes boiled and mashed with butter on top of the brain mixture.

155 Scrambled Brain

1 brain
2 eggs
pepper and salt
1 teaspoonful chopped fennel
1 dessertspoon Worcester sauce
1 tablespoon butter
hot buttered toast

Wash the brain well in warm water, add salt and boil it for about 15 or 20 minutes. Then drain off the water. Mash the brain free of lumps, add the eggs well beaten and mix both lightly together. Season with pepper and salt and add the sauce and fennel. Heat the butter in a frying pan, put in the brain and egg mixture and cook for a couple of minutes, stirring all the time. Arrange the mixture neatly on rounds of hot buttered toast and serve very hot.

156 Braised Beef or Mutton

Small joints of the cheaper cuts of beef or mutton may be braised in the same manner as chicken (see Recipe 302), the only difference being that brown stock should be used instead of white stock, and sherry or Marsala instead of white wine.

This method of cooking renders the meat tender and tasty, and is particularly useful when freshly killed or very tough meat only is available.

157 Cold Meat Mince

1 lb. cold roast meat
¼ lb. Bombay onions
1 dessertspoonful dripping
powdered cloves
cinnamon and pepper
1 tablespoon Worcester sauce
salt and mustard
1 teacup stock
1 hard-boiled egg
potatoes

Remove all skin and gristle from the meat and mince it finely or pass it through the mincing machine. Chop the onions and fry a dessertspoonful of it in the dripping; when browned put in the meat and the remaining onions, season to taste, add the sauce, and stir for a few minutes. Then pour in the stock and let the mince get quite hot. If necessary, thicken with a little flour. Arrange a wall of mashed potatoes round a dish, put the mince in the centre, and place a few pieces of hard-boiled egg on the mince.

N.B.—A little chopped ham or bacon added to the meat is a great improvement. Chicken and mutton can also be prepared in the same way. A border of boiled macaroni or rice may be used instead of the potatoes.

158 Cold Meat Souffle

½ lb. cooked meat
1 tablespoonful minced onions
1 oz. dripping
1 tablespoonful flour
¼ pint milk
¼ pint stock
1 teaspoonful chopped fennel
pepper and salt
a grate of nutmeg
2 eggs

Use a mixture of meats such as mutton and tongue or veal and ham. Trim the meat and chop it very finely or pass it through the mincing machine. Melt the dripping in a saucepan, mix in the flour, add the milk and stock and stir until it thickens. Now put in the meat, the minced onion and the fennel, and season to taste. Remove the saucepan from the fire and add the yolks of eggs, beating them well in. Whisk the whites of eggs to a stiff froth and stir them in lightly at the last. Pour mixture into a greased souffle dish or pie-dish and bake in a quick oven for 20 minutes or until well risen and firm to the touch.

159 Fried Kidneys

kidneys
1 tablespoonful flour
pepper and salt
dripping

Skin the kidneys and cut them the round way, into thin slices. Season the flour with pepper and salt, dip the slices of kidney in it, and fry them in dripping. They must be cooked very gently and will take about 20 minutes. When ready, place the kidneys on a dish, season the gravy left over in the pan and pour over. Serve while very hot.

N.B.—The kidneys may be grilled instead of being fried. Brush the slices of kidney with salad oil or melted butter, season with pepper and salt, and grill (see *Grilling* under *Different Methods of Cooking Meat*).

160 Kidneys on Toast

3 sheep's kidneys
½ oz. butter
½ teaspoon flour
pepper
salt
1 dessertspoon Worcester sauce
1 yolk of egg
hot buttered toast

Remove the skin from the kidneys and mince them rather finely. Heat the butter in a saucepan, put in the minced kidney and stir for about ten minutes. Then dredge in the flour and add the sauce and seasonings. Beat the yolk of egg, add it to the mixture and stir all together for a few minutes. Arrange the mixture on squares of buttered toast.

161 Stewed Kidney

1 ox kidney
1 oz. dripping
1 oz. flour
pepper
salt
1 Bombay onion
2 tomatoes
½ pint stock or water

Wash the kidney well, dry it and cut it in thin slices. Season with pepper and salt and coat the slices well with flour. Heat the dripping in a stewpan, put in the sliced kidney and the onion (minced) and keep turning them over and over until well browned on all sides. Add the stock and the tomatoes cut in pieces, cover the pan and allow to simmer very gently until the kidney is tender. When ready, remove any grease from the top of the gravy and serve at once with a border of mashed potatoes.

162 Liver and Bacon

1 lb. liver
½ lb. bacon
1 oz. flour
½ teacup stock or warm water
pepper
salt

Slice the liver ¼ inch thick, wash thoroughly and dry in a towel. Fry the bacon which should be sliced. Season the slices of liver with pepper and salt, coat them well with flour, and fry in the bacon fat left in the pan. A little dripping must be added, if necessary. When ready, arrange the slices of liver on a dish and place the bacon on the top. To make the gravy, pour in the stock or water into the pan, season with pepper and salt, dredge in a little flour, and, if necessary, colour with a little browning (Recipe 508). Stir until it boils and pour round the liver.

If liked, serve with tomatoes sliced and fried.

163 Liver and Bacon Pie

1 lb. liver
½ lb. sliced bacon
1 teaspoon flour
½ teacup stock or boiling water
pepper and salt
short crust

Wash the liver well, dry in a cloth and cut in slices about ¼ inch in thickness. Remove the rind from the bacon, cook it a few minutes in a hot frying pan and then lift it on to a plate. Season the slices of liver with pepper and salt and coat them well with flour, now fry them in the fat left from the bacon adding a little dripping if necessary. The liver must not be fried too much. When ready, place the liver and bacon in a pie-dish in layers. Pour the stock or boiling water into the pan in which the bacon and liver have been fried, add pepper and salt and stir until it boils. Pour this stock over the liver and bacon and cover the dish with short crust (Recipe 1353) or any other suitable pastry.

164 Liver Cutlets

1 lb. liver
¼ lb. mashed potatoes
1 tablespoonful chopped red onions
1 teaspoonful chopped fennel or parsley
1 teaspoon lime juice
1 tablespoon Worcester sauce
1 yolk of egg
powdered cloves
cinnamon and pepper
salt
egg and breadcrumbs
dripping

Boil the liver, let it cool, then grind it to a paste. Add to it the mashed potatoes, onions, fennel, lime juice, and sauce and season to taste with pepper, cloves, cinnamon and salt. Mix well together and moisten with the yolk of egg. Then shape the mixture into small oblong cakes about quarter of an inch thick, dip in beaten egg, then in breadcrumbs and fry to a nice brown colour in boiling dripping. When ready arrange the cutlets on a dish, pour a little brown gravy round and garnish the dish with Baked Tomatoes (Recipe 441) nd Potato Balls (Recipe 422).

165 Liver Pudding

1 lb. liver
2 oz. lean ham or bacon
4 oz. grated bread
1 teaspoonful chopped fennel or parsley
1 teaspoon lime juice
3 eggs
1 tablespoon Worcester sauce
powdered cloves
cinnamon, pepper and salt

Cut the liver in slices and boil it. Let it cool, then put it and the ham through the mincing machine. Add to it the grated bread, fennel, lime juice and sauce, and season to taste with pepper, cloves, cinnamon and salt. Mix well together and moisten with the eggs well beaten, and, if necessary, add a little of the water in which the liver was boiled. Pour the mixture into a well-greased mould and steam for one hour. When ready, turn out and serve hot or cold with Tomato Sauce (Recipe 532) poured round.

166 Stewed Liver

½ lb. liver
¼ lb. sliced bacon
1 Bombay onion
1 oz. flour
2 teacups light stock or boiling water
pepper
salt

Fry the bacon, and when fried remove and keep warm. Fry the onion (sliced) in the bacon fat left over in the pan. Add the flour and the stock or boiling water, season to taste and boil up. Then add the liver sliced thinly and simmer slowly for about three-quarters of an hour. Put the liver in the centre of a dish, arrange the fried bacon round it and pour the gravy over. Serve hot.

167 Frikkadels

(Dutch: FORCED-MEAT BALLS)

½ lb. each of lean beef and fat pork
8 red onions
2 teaspoonfuls each of ginger and garlic finely chopped
1 level teaspoonful black pepper
the strained juice of 1 lime
4 cloves and an inch of cinnamon pounded together and sieved
a pinch of grated nutmeg
1 teaspoonful salt
a sprig of fennel
2 large eggs
fine browned breadcrumbs
coconut oil for frying

Mince the meat, chop the onions and fennel finely, and mix well together, then add the rest of the seasonings and mix all thoroughly with the yolks of the eggs. Form into balls the size of a small marble. Beat the whites of the eggs with a fork, just enough to break them up but without frothing. Dip the balls in this, and then roll them in the crumbs so that they are well coated all over. Have ready a fairly deep pan of boiling oil, and fry the frikkadels in it about 6-8 at a time, taking care that they do not cling together. When cooked through they should be crisp on the outside and juicy inside. Use fresh oil, or the frikkadels will have an unpleasant flavour. Keep hot, draining on a piece of kitchen paper, until all are fried, then pile up on a hot dish and serve with a garnish of sections of cut lime.

168 Meat Cake

1 lb. cold roast meat
2 oz. ham or bacon
¼ lb. grated bread
1 tablespoonful chopped parsley or fennel
1 tablespoon Worcester sauce
2 eggs
pepper
salt
½ teacup stock

Chop the meat and ham very finely, or pass them through the mincing machine. Season the minced meat with pepper and salt, add to it the grated bread, sauce and parsley, and moisten with the eggs slightly beaten, and the stock. Grease a cake tin, pour in the mixture, and bake in a moderately hot oven for one hour. Turn out and serve with White or Brown Sauce.

N.B.—Beef, cold mutton or chicken can be used.

169 Meat Cutlets

1 lb. meat
¼ lb. grated bread or ¼ lb. mashed potatoes
1 tablespoonful chopped onions
1 egg
juice of one lime
1 teaspoonful chopped fennel
powdered cloves
cinnamon, pepper and salt
egg and breadcrumbs
dripping

Remove all skin and gristle from the meat, and chop it finely or put it through the mincing machine. Put the minced meat into a basin and add to it the grated bread or mashed potatoes, the onion and fennel and season to taste with pepper, salt, cloves and cinnamon. Mix well together, add the lime juice and bind with the egg slightly beaten. Divide the mixture into twelve equal portions and form them into cutlet shapes or round cakes. Dip them in egg and breadcrumbs, and fry them in dripping until they are nicely browned. Drain well and serve with Brown Gravy (Recipe 506) poured over.

(For Rolled Cutlets, see Recipe 177).

170 Meat Hot-Pot

1½ lb. beef or mutton
1 lb. potatoes
½ lb. Bombay onions
½ pint stock or water
1 oz. flour
pepper
salt
½ oz. butter or dripping

Wash and wipe the meat and cut it in small square pieces removing any gristly parts. Season the meat with pepper and salt and coat with flour. Prepare the potatoes and onions, slicing the potatoes rather thickly and the onions thinly. Take a deep earthenware jar with a cover. Arrange a layer of meat at the bottom of the jar, then a layer of vegetables with a sprinkling of seasoning. Repeat the layers until the ingredients are all in, potatoes forming the top layer. Pour in the stock or water and put the butter or dripping in small pieces on the top. Put on the lid and stand the jar in a tin half full of water and bake in a moderate oven for about 3 hours. The water in the tin must be replenished as it boils away.

171 Meat Kedgeree

½ lb. cooked meat
1 breakfastcupful boiled rice
2 oz. butter or dripping
2 hard boiled eggs
1 raw yolk of egg
pepper and salt

Trim the meat and chop it rather finely, chop also the hard-boiled eggs. Melt the butter in a saucepan, add the meat, the boiled rice, and the hard-boiled eggs. Season with pepper and salt and add the raw yolk of egg. Stir over the fire till very hot. Pile in the centre of a dish making a neat pyramid and serve very hot.

172 Meat Loaf

2 lb. beef
½ lb. ham or bacon
2 cups soft breadcrumbs loosely packed
2 eggs beaten
milk
Worcester sauce
pepper and salt

Mince the beef and ham or bacon, and mix with the breadcrumbs. Bind together with the egg and sufficient milk to form a moist mixture which sticks together. Season well with Worcester sauce, salt, pepper, and a little fennel. One minced onion may be added if liked, but it must be minced very finely indeed. Bake in a loaf tin in a moderate oven for one and a half hours or till brown on top. Chill before serving. This may also be boiled. To do this, shape the meat mixture into a roll and wrap it in a scalded, floured cloth. Then plunge into boiling water and boil for about two hours.

The loaf may be jellied when cool by making a jelly from two tablespoons of gelatine dissolved in one large cup of boiling water. A cup of tomato sauce is then added, and a little extra vinegar if necessary. When the jelly is almost setting, pour it in spoonfuls over the chilled loaf. Repeat till the loaf has a coating of jelly about ¼ inch thick.

173 Meat and Macaroni Timbale

¼ lb. cooked meat
2 oz. ham or bacon
¼ lb. macaroni
2 oz. grated bread
1 teaspoonful chopped fennel
2 eggs
salt
dripping
1 tablespoon Worcester sauce
½ teacup stock or milk
brown gravy

Mince the meat and ham very finely and put it into a basin with the grated bread and seasonings. Mix well together and moisten with the eggs well beaten and the stock or milk. Boil the macaroni in salted water until tender and drain well. Butter a pudding mould or basin, arrange the macaroni round the bottom and sides, fill up with the meat mixture, cover with macaroni, put a plate on the top and steam for one hour. Then turn out carefully and serve with a nice brown gravy.

174 Minced Meat Pancake Rolls

4 oz. flour
¼ pint milk
½ teaspoonful salt
a pinch of white pepper
the yolks of 2 eggs and the white of one
soft well-seasoned mince for filling (chicken, beef, or mutton may be used for this, and it should be soft enough to roll up well but not what is usually known as a wet mince)
parsley to garnish
dripping for frying

Sieve the flour and salt together three times to make the flour as light as possible. Put into a bowl, and break in the yolks of the eggs. Mix with a wooden spoon, drawing down the flour from the sides, then add the milk a small spoonful at a time until half has been used up. Now beat with a rotary beater until perfectly smooth and full of air-bubbles. Add the rest of the milk, stir well, cover, and leave to stand for an hour before using.

When ready to cook, beat the white of the egg to a very stiff froth and fold into the batter, which must be stirred first to mix the ingredients thoroughly again.

Melt the dripping and use just enough each time to fry one pancake. Pour the batter into the frying pan, about 2 tablespoonfuls at a time according to the size required—the smaller the pan the better, as these pancakes should be not more than 3½ to 4 inches in diameter. As each one is fried, lightly browned on both sides, slip it on to a piece of waxed paper, put a generous spoonful of the mince at one side, in a long roll, and curl the pancake over it, making it as neat as possible. When all are thus finished, place them two by two, crosswise, on a hot dish with a paper d'oyley underneath, garnish with tufts of parsley, and serve.

175 Minced Meat Pancake Sachets

¼ lb. flour
½ teaspoon baking powder
¾ pint milk
1 egg
salt
dripping
egg and breadcrumbs
cold meat mince (Recipe 157)

Mix the flour, baking powder, milk and egg into a smooth batter, adding a pinch of salt. It should be a little thicker than the ordinary pancake batter. Melt a little dripping in a frying pan and pour in enough batter to make a pancake. Do not cook both sides of it. When cooked underneath, turn on to a plate, place a spoonful of mince in the centre, and fold it neatly into an oblong parcel, using white of egg to paste it with. The parcels should be made as soon as each pancake is taken off the fire (once they get cold they will break in folding). After all the parcels have been made brush them over with beaten egg, coat with breadcrumbs and fry a golden brown in dripping. They could be served as liked, either hot or cold.

176 Minced Meat Potato Pie

2 lb. potatoes
1 tablespoonful dripping
1 egg
salt
breadcrumbs
cold meat mince

Boil the potatoes, mash them and make into a paste with the dripping and yolk of egg, add salt to taste. Butter a pie-dish and put alternate layers of potato and mince, potato forming the bottom and top layers. Scatter some breadcrumbs on the top and put a few pieces of dripping here and there. Put in the oven and bake until the top layer of potatoes is nicely browned. Serve hot in the dish.

177 Meat Rissoles (Rolled Cutlets)

1 lb. boiled, mashed potatoes
cold meat mince (Recipe 157)
1 egg
crisp bread or toast crumbs
fat for frying

Have the mince simmered till rather dry, and form into roll shapes. Take sufficient mashed potato to cover the meat, flatten till about $\frac{3}{4}$ inch in thickness, and place the meat in the middle. Mould the potato round the meat, keeping the long roll shape the rissole should be. Dip the rissole in the beaten egg, then coat it thickly with the toast crumbs. Fry in boiling fat till a golden brown.

178 Savoury Mould

$\frac{1}{2}$ lb. cooked meat
$\frac{1}{4}$ lb. bread
1 oz. butter
3 tablespoonfuls grated cheese
pepper
salt
2 eggs
a little milk
stock
slices of cooked or uncooked bacon
hard-boiled eggs

Trim the meat and mince it very finely. Cut off the crumbs and soak the bread in a little milk for 10 minutes, then beat it with a fork until free from lumps. Melt the butter in a saucepan, add the minced meat, the bread, cheese and seasonings and mix all together. Moisten with the eggs well beaten and a little stock, if necessary. Butter a plain mould and line it with thin slices of bacon and slices of hard-boiled egg. Fill up the mould with the meat mixture and steam for an hour. Turn it out and serve hot with gravy.

179 Savoury Roly Poly

cold meat mince **pastry**

Make the pastry according to the directions given in Beef Steak and Kidney Pudding (Recipe 224) and the mince according to Recipe 157. Roll out the paste into an oblong shape about $\frac{1}{6}$ inch in thickness, and spread the mince evenly on it. Keep the mince about an inch from the edge all round. Wet round the edges of the pastry with white of egg or cold water, and roll up as you would a roly-poly pudding, pinching the edges well together. Rinse out a pudding cloth in boiling water, dredge it well with flour, and wrap up the pudding in it, tying up the two ends firmly. Have ready a saucepan of boiling water, put a plate at the bottom of the pan, and place the roll on it. There must be sufficient water to cover the roll well, and as the water lessens more boiling water must be added. Boil for 2 hours. When ready, lift it out and let it stand for a couple of minutes. Then remove the cloth carefully, and cut the roll into slices which arrange on a dish. Serve Brown Sauce (Recipe 505) or Brown Gravy (Recipe 506) separately. A salad should accompany the dish.

180 Shepherd's Pie

½ lb. cooked or tinned meat
¼ lb. Bombay onions
½ oz. dripping
1 teacup stock
1 dessertspoon Worcester sauce
seasoning
mashed potatoes
a little milk or beaten egg

The remains of cold roast beef or mutton could be used for this. Trim the meat removing all skin and gristle and chop it finely or put it through the mincing machine. Heat the dripping in a stew-pan, put in the onions (chopped) and brown them lightly, then add the meat and the stock, season to taste with powdered cinnamon, cloves, pepper and salt, add the sauce and cook slowly for about 15 minutes. Put the meat into a greased pie-dish, prepare some mashed potatoes and pile them on the top. Smooth over neatly with a knife and roughen the top with a fork. Brush over with a little milk or beaten egg and bake in a moderate oven for about three-quarters of an hour or until browned.

181 Steak Rolls

slices of steak
white breadcrumbs
minced onion
centre leaves of cabbage
finely-chopped fat bacon
a little chopped parsley
a pinch of mixed herbs
crisply-fried Bombay onions cut in thin rings
well-seasoned brown stock
pepper and salt

Cut the steak into thin slices about 2 inches wide and 3 inches long. Rub over one side with a little pepper and salt, and turn over to the other side.

Mix the minced onion, bacon, parsley, and herbs, and add a little crumbed white bread to give about a third of the bulk of the other ingredients. Moisten with a little stock, and shape into rolls a little shorter than the width of the meat and the size of a thick pencil. Roll these up in the unseasoned side of the meat, then roll each in a leaf of cabbage split down the centre and with the thick rib removed. Tie round with cotton.

Cover the bottom of a stew pan with the fried onions, place the meat rolls on top, and almost cover with stock. Bring to the boil, then reduce heat and simmer very gently for about 1 hour. Arrange the rolls on a hot dish, mix the stock well, and pour over. Or, the stock may be strained and thickened with a little flour, and then poured over. To thicken the stock, mix 1 heaped teaspoonful flour with a rounded teaspoonful butter melted in a small saucepan. Stir until well browned, then add the strained stock and cook for about 5 minutes.

182 Tinned Meat and Potato Pie

½ lb. tinned meat
2 or 3 tomatoes
3 oz. cooked macaroni
1 teaspoon made mustard
pepper and salt
potato pastry

Any kind of tinned meat may be used. Mince it or cut it in small pieces and mix together with the macaroni, add the mustard and season with pepper and salt. If the meat is dry, a little stock may be added. Slice the tomatoes thinly. Make some potato pastry, roll it out about half an inch in thickness and line a greased pie-dish with it. Fill up with the meat mixture and tomatoes in layers. Cover the pie with more of the pastry. Brush over with beaten egg and bake for about three-quarters of an hour or until nicely browned.

183 Baked Tongue

1 tongue
1 dessertspoonful flour
1 tablespoon Worcester sauce
½ teaspoon mustard
powdered cloves
cinnamon and pepper
salt
egg and breadcrumbs

Wash the tongue and boil it. When it is half done, take it off the fire, skin it, and boil again until soft, and when ready split it in two lengthwise. Add the spices, mustard and sauce into the stock left in the pan, dredge in the flour and rub the tongue well with this mixture Then brush the tongue over with beaten egg, cover with breadcrumbs and bake in a moderate oven for about half an hour, or until the breadcrumbs are browned.

184 Boiled Tongue

Wash the tongue thoroughly and put it into a saucepan with sufficient hot water to cover it, add a little salt, and let it simmer slowly until partially boiled. Then lift the tongue out of the water, skin it whilst hot, trim it and return to the saucepan, and let it cook slowly until the tongue is tender.

185 Tongue Fritters

cooked tongue
mustard
pepper
1 tablespoon olive oil
1 tablespoon Worcester sauce
salt

For the BATTER:

3 tablespoonfuls flour	**½ pint milk**
¼ teaspoon baking powder	**1 egg and salt**

Cut the tongue in slices and place them on a plate. Sprinkle each slice with a little dry mustard, pepper and salt and pour over them the olive oil and sauce. Allow the tongue to lie in this marinade for about half an hour, turning the slices occasionally. Make a smooth batter with the flour, baking powder, milk and egg adding salt to taste. Dip each slice of tongue in the batter and fry till brown in dripping. Drain well and serve hot. Tomato or any other suitable sauce may be served separately.

186 Tongue Salad

cold tongue	**a few thin slices of cucumber**
1 lettuce	**salad oil**
2 or 3 cooked potatoes	**a heaped-up teaspoonful of mustard**
pepper and salt	**¼ teaspoon sugar**
2 tomatoes	**3 tablespoons vinegar**
2 hard-boiled eggs	

Mince the tongue or cut it in dice. Wash and dry the lettuce, cut it in shreds and mix with the tongue and the potatoes also cut in shreds. Season with pepper and salt. Put the mixture into a salad dish and garnish with the tomatoes cut in slices and the cucumber and the whites of eggs cut in rings. Then make the dressing. Mash the yolks of eggs and mix to a smooth paste with a few drops of salad oil, add the mustard, pepper, salt and sugar, mix well and stir in the vinegar. Pour the dressing over the salad.

Beef and Veal

(For other recipes, see under Meat)

201 Boiled Beef

6 lb. beef	**6 cloves**
boiling water	**2-inch piece cinnamon**
12 peppercorns	**salt**

Trim the piece of meat, wash it, and, if necessary, bind it into shape with a piece of string or tape. Put the meat into a saucepan with sufficient boiling water to cover it; let it boil up, then add a dessertspoonful of salt and skim well. Add the seasoning and let it boil gently until the meat is tender. When ready, lift the meat on to a dish, remove the tape, and serve either hot or cold. Any vegetable or salad may accompany it.

If liked, the vegetables could be cooked with the meat, in which case put them in after the meat has been skimmed the first time.

202 Beef Cannelon

1 lb. cooked beef	**pepper and salt**
¼ lb. ham or bacon	**a grate of nutmeg**
¼ lb. powdered breadcrumbs	**1 teaspoonful chopped fennel or parsley**
1 egg	**melted butter**
stock	

The remains of either roast or boiled beef may be used for this dish. Trim the meat and put it and the ham or bacon through the mincing machine or chop them very finely. Then put them into a basin, add the breadcrumbs and fennel and season with pepper, salt and nutmeg. Mix well together, add the egg well beaten and sufficient stock to make it moist enough to work into a roll. Sprinkle some flour on a board, turn out the meat mixture and form into a neat roll. Place it on a greased baking tin, sprinkle with powdered breadcrumbs and pour some melted butter over it. Bake for about 30 minutes. When ready, lift the roll on to a dish and pour some brown sauce (Recipe 505) over. Garnish the roll with stewed tomatoes (Recipe 442).

203 Corned Beef

6 lb. beef	**¼ oz. cinnamon**
½ lb. ham	**a blade of mace**
salt	**1 tablespoonful sugar**
1 oz. saltpetre	**½ oz. pepper**
¼ oz. cloves	**half a nutmeg**
	half a lime

Any fleshy piece of meat may be corned, but a piece from the round is generally used. The meat must be as fresh as possible, and it is usually boned. Wipe and trim it, but on no account wash it. Pound finely and mix together the pepper, cloves, cinnamon, nutmeg, and mace; also pound the saltpetre. Slice the lime finely. Lay the meat on a mincing board, and prick it well all over with a steel skewer for 15 minutes. Then rub into it gradually the salt, saltpetre, spices and the lime, and knead well for another 15 minutes. Tie the meat into a neat shape with a piece of string and put it into a deep basin or pan, place a weight on the meat, sufficiently heavy to press it down, and cover the basin closely. Turn the meat every day for three days. Then lift the meat out and wash it well and cook according to direction given in Recipe 233.

Serve with Country Mustard (Recipe 523) and boiled carrots.

204 Corned Beef in Batter

1 pint Yorkshire pudding batter
1 lb. tinned corned beef
pepper
butter
parsley
salt

Make the batter at least an hour before it is wanted, adding a little more salt than usual and seasoning with a good dash of pepper. All batters are improved by standing, but they must be well stirred before use.

Butter a glass baking dish, and cut the meat into fairly thick slices, then again into strips about 1 inch wide.

Pour the batter into the dish, and drop in the sliced meat so that it is evenly distributed. Bake until the pudding is cooked through and nicely browned on top. Serve straight from the oven, or the pudding will sink and harden.

205 Corned Beef and Cabbage

cold corned beef
cooked cabbage (red cabbage for preference)
salt
pepper
nutmeg
Worcester sauce
butter or dripping

Cut the meat into thin slices and trim away all skin and gristle. Chop the cabbage and season with pepper, salt and nutmeg. Melt a little butter or dripping in a frying pan and fry the slices of meat very lightly on both sides. Keep them warm and fry the cabbage also lightly in the fat left over in the pan. Stir in a little sauce, and, if not moist enough add some gravy or stock. Arrange the cabbage neatly on a dish and place the slices of meat round it. Serve hot.

206 Beef a la Danda

cold roast beef
½ lb. potatoes
2 hard-boiled eggs
1 teaspoon vinegar
1 teaspoonful mustard
1 tablespoonful sliced red onions
½ teacup thick coconut milk
salt

Boil and mash the potatoes, and add to it the yolks of the eggs, the mustard and salt, and mix into a smooth batter with the vinegar and coconut milk. Arrange some slices of cold beef or mutton on a dish and pour the potato dressing over it. Garnish the top with the whites of the eggs cut in rings and the sliced onions.

207 Devilled Beef

1 lb. cold roast beef
½ lb. potatoes
½ lb. Bombay onions
1½ oz. mustard seed (ground)
1 oz. dry chillies (ground)
¼ stem lemon grass
4 cloves of garlic (sliced)
4 slices green ginger
1 teacup boiling water
1 teaspoonful mustard
1 tablespoon Worcester sauce
2 tablespoons vinegar
1 dessertspoonful sugar
1 dessertspoonful sliced red onions
salt
dripping

Cut the meat in rather thickish slices and put them into a stewpan. Add the water, chillies, ground mustard, lemon-grass, garlic, ginger, vinegar, salt, and the Bombay onions cut in quarters. Let it cook slowly for 15 minutes, then add the sauce, mustard and sugar and stir for a couple of minutes. Heat the dripping, fry the sliced onions in it, and turn in the whole mixture and add the potatoes which should be previously boiled and cut in halves or quarters according to size. If necessary, thicken the gravy with a little flour or with breadcrumbs.

208 Beef Mignons

fillet, or undercut of beef
olive oil
parsley
butter
rounds of fried bread
seasoning of salt and pepper
a little mustard
mashed potatoes

Cut the beef into slices about ½ inch thick, and as nearly round as possible to fit the rounds of bread. Wipe over with a damp cloth, rub in a mixture of salt, pepper, and mustard powder on both sides, lay on a flat dish, and pour a small teaspoonful olive oil on each piece. Cover, and leave to stand for half an hour, then turn on to the other side, repeat the oil, cover, and allow to stand for at least one hour. Meanwhile, fry the rounds of bread until crisp and browned and drain on white paper. Mash the boiled potatoes with butter, milk, and seasoning of salt, pepper, and a little finely-chopped parsley. Keep hot, by standing the bowl in a saucepan of boiling water. Place the mignons on a grid, and grill quickly on both sides, then reduce the flames and cook for 5 minutes, turning once, and basting with warm olive oil or melted butter.

Put the rounds of fried bread on a hot dish, and pour over the "drippings" collected at the bottom of the grid-pan, place a piece of the meat on each, and pipe the prepared potato at intervals round the dish in neat mounds. Have ready some butter mixed with a little finely-chopped parsley. Put a small teaspoonful on top of each round, place under the grill again for two minutes, and serve immediately.

209 Beef a la Mode

4 lb. round of beef
a few slices of bacon
½ teacup vinegar
1 dessertspoonful chopped fennel or parsley
boiling water
a glass of port wine
powdered cloves
cinnamon and pepper
salt
dripping

Mince the parsley or fennel and mix with the cloves, cinnamon, pepper (about half a teaspoon of each) and salt. Cut the bacon in long thin slices, dip them in vinegar and then in the seasoning and roll them up. With a sharp knife make holes in the piece of meat and push in the rolls of bacon. Then rub the meat over with the remainder of the spices and bind into shape with a piece of tape or string. Melt the dripping in a stewpan, put in the piece of meat and brown it on all sides. Then pour in just sufficient boiling water to cover the meat, and let it cook very gently for about 3 hours, or until the meat is very tender. Turn the meat once or twice during the cooking. When ready, lift the meat on to a dish and remove the tape. Skim the gravy, add the port wine and let it boil for a few minutes, then pour it over the meat.

210 Beef and Macaroni Pie

½ lb. finely minced cold meat
seasoning
3 oz. cooked macaroni
tomatoes
cheese
breadcrumbs
butter or dripping

Butter a pie-dish and put in first a layer of minced meat well seasoned, then a layer of macaroni, next a layer of sliced tomatoes sprinkled with pepper and salt, then one of grated cheese. Repeat these layers. Spread a thick layer of breadcrumbs on the top and place a few pieces of butter or dripping on the top of it. Bake for half an hour.

211 Beef Rolls

2 lb. beef
pepper and salt
1 teaspoonful mustard
1 oz. flour
1 oz. dripping
1 pint boiling water
1 tablespoon Worcester sauce
1 teaspoonful sugar
hard-boiled eggs

For the FORCEMEAT:

2 oz. ham or bacon
1 tablespoonful grated bread
1 tablespoonful chopped onions
1 egg
1 tablespoonful chopped fennel or parsley
1 dessertspoon Worcester sauce
seasoning

Cut the meat into pieces 4 inches long and 2½ inches wide—the meat should be in thin slices. Beat them out slightly and season each piece with pepper and salt. Prepare the forcemeat and spread a layer of it on each slice of meat on which place a hard-boiled egg; roll them up, tie round with a piece of coarse thread and coat with the flour. Melt the dripping in a stewpan and when very hot put in the rolls and keep turning them over and over until browned on all sides. Then add the water and allow to simmer very slowly until the meat is tender. Lift the rolls and remove the thread and carefully cut each into 3 or 4 slices. Arrange neatly on a dish. Add the mustard, sauce and sugar to the gravy in the pan, let it boil up, then pour round the dish.

To Prepare the Forcemeat—Chop the ham or bacon very finely or put it through a mincing machine, add to it the grated bread, the onions and fennel; season with pepper, sauce and salt and moisten with beaten egg.

212 Roast Beef

The sirloin and the ribs are the two best joints for roasting. Follow the general directions given for roasting. When the meat is ready, lift it on to a dish and serve with gravy poured round. To make the gravy see Recipe 506. Yorkshire pudding and mashed potatoes usually accompany roast beef.

213 Yorkshire Pudding to serve with Roast Beef

½ lb. flour
1 pint milk
3 eggs
a pinch of salt

Sieve the flour, put it into a basin with the salt, and stir in gradually enough milk to make it into a stiff batter. Rub down all the lumps, then pour in the remaining milk and the eggs which should be well beaten. Beat the batter well until it is full of air-bubbles, then pour into a shallow baking tin which should be previously well greased with dripping. Bake in a quick oven for about one hour. Cut the pudding in pieces and serve.

214 Roast Fillet of Beef

1½-2 lb. undercut or fillet of beef cut in one thick piece
2 oz. dripping
salt and pepper to season
1 tablespoonful butter

Cut away the shiny white skin as close to the meat as possible, and remove any untidy ends. Wipe over with a damp cloth, and dry well. Rub in a little salt on both sides of the meat, sprinkle with a very little pepper, and place on a grid in a baking dish in which the dripping has been melted. Put into a very hot oven for five minutes, then baste well with the dripping, and reduce the heat so that the oven will maintain a temperature of about 350-400 degrees. Let the meat cook for about twenty minutes longer, basting it three or four times. Just after the last basting put the butter on top of the meat and finish cooking for the specified time. Serve on a hot dish, with baked tomatoes arranged round, and the fat from cooking poured over the meat.

Cooked in this way, fillet of beef should be browned on the outside and underdone in the middle. If liked, a mustard-spoonful of made mustard may be mixed in with the baking fat, stirred well, and then poured over the meat.

215 Pan or Chatty Roast

3 lb. beef
pepper
salt
½ pint boiling water

Wash and trim the meat, season with pepper and salt, and bind into shape with a piece of string or tape. Put the meat into a saucepan or chatty, add the water and boil slowly until the water is all absorbed. Then let the meat fry until it is nicely browned. If the meat is not sufficiently fat in itself, add a little dripping. Make the gravy (Recipe 506) and pour it round the meat.

216 Savoury Beef

2 lb. beef steak, cut in a thick slice
5-6 thin rashers of fat bacon
6 anchovy fillets
1 carrot
1 turnip
8 red onions
four small sprigs of parsley
pepper and salt (the latter according to the saltiness of the bacon)
brown stock
1 wineglassful sherry or Marsala
butter
a good pinch of grated nutmeg

Butter a casserole dish, and cover the bottom with the chopped carrot and turnip and the peeled onions, a sprinkling of pepper and salt and the nutmeg and tufts of parsley. Place the beef on top, and lay the bacon over with the uncurled anchovies placed lengthwise on top. Pour in just enough stock to come about half-way up the side of the meat, cover, and bake in a slow oven for 2 hours, basting with the liquid frequently to prevent drying on top.

Half an hour before the meat is ready pour in the sherry or Marsala, stir well and baste two or three times during the last period of cooking.

Lift the meat out on to a hot dish, and keep hot while thickening the strained stock with a little flour. Boil up, and strain again over the meat. Serve at once.

217 Spiced Beef

4 lb. brisket of beef
½ oz. saltpetre
8 cloves
10 peppercorns
2-inch piece cinnamon
a blade of mace
salt to taste

Wash the piece of meat, trim it and rub it over with the pounded saltpetre. Then put it into a saucepan, add the spices and salt and pour in sufficient cold water to cover. Bring to the boil and then simmer for about 4 hours. A few pieces of flavouring vegetables such as carrot and onion may be added. Lift out the meat when tender, remove the bone and press between two dishes with a weight on the top until cold.

218 Stewed Beef

4 lb. beef
½ lb. Bombay onions
½ lb. potatoes
3 carrots
1 tablespoon Worcester sauce
2-inch piece cinnamon
8 cloves
20 peppercorns
salt
1 tablespoonful dripping
boiling water

Melt the dripping in a stewpan and when very hot put in the piece of meat and brown it on all sides; when nicely browned, pour in a sufficient quantity of boiling water to cover it, add the seasonings, and let it simmer slowly for one hour. Then add the vegetables prepared and cut into convenient-sized pieces, and continue to cook slowly until the meat is tender. Lift the meat on to a dish, add the sauce, mustard and sugar to the gravy and vegetables, thicken with a little flour, if necessary, let it boil for a couple of minutes and then pour over the meat.

219 Steak in Batter

1½ lb. beef
pepper
salt
dripping
¼ lb. flour
½ teaspoon baking powder
2 eggs
½ pint milk

Beat down the meat with a rolling pin, cut it into 2-inch squares and season with pepper and salt. Heat some dripping in a frying pan and fry the meat. When ready place the steak in a greased pie-dish. Make a smooth batter with the flour, baking powder, milk and eggs, add salt to taste and pour the batter over the steak. Put it into the oven and bake for about 30 minutes or until the batter is nicely risen and browned.

220 Fried Steak

1½ lb. beef
½ lb. Bombay onions
pepper and salt
dripping

Procure a nice slice of beef rather thinly cut. Wash and trim it and beat it out with a rolling-pin; season with pepper and salt. Heat a little dripping in a frying pan, put in the meat, and keep turning constantly until sufficiently cooked. When ready, place the steak on a dish, put a little more dripping into the pan and fry the onions which should be sliced. Put the onions over the steak, and, if there is no gravy left over in the pan, pour in a little stock or hot water, add seasonings, and pour over the steak. Serve at once as steak should be sent very hot to table.

221 Grilled Steak

1½ lb. beef
pepper and salt
1 tablespoon salad oil or melted butter

The meat should be of an equal thickness, about three-quarters of an inch. Wash the meat, trim it, and beat out slightly with a rolling-pin. If liked, the meat can be cut in slices. Brush the meat with a little salad oil or melted butter and grill according to directions given for grilling. The time for cooking will depend on the thickness of the meat, and whether it is liked underdone or well cooked. When ready, rub the steak over with butter, season with pepper and salt, and serve at once.

222 Piquant Steak

1½ lb. beef
½ lb. Bombay onions
1 teaspoonful mustard
1 tablespoon Worcester sauce
1 tablespoon vinegar
1 teaspoonful sugar
pepper and salt to taste
dripping

Take a nice slice of beef about three-quarters of an inch in thickness. Wash and trim it and beat it out slightly with a rolling-pin. Mix together the mustard, sauce, vinegar, sugar, pepper and salt and pour over the meat and let it remain for half an hour. Then pour it off and squeeze the meat as dry as possible. Heat some dripping in a frying pan, put in the meat and keep turning constantly until sufficiently cooked. The time for cooking will depend on the thickness of the meat and whether it is liked underdone or well cooked. When ready place the steak on a dish, put a little more dripping into the pan and fry the onions which should be sliced. Put the fried onions on the steak, and into the pan pour in the dressing in which the meat was soaked. Let it boil up, then pour over the steak and serve very hot.

223 Beef Steak with Poached Eggs

2 lb. beef
a few slices of bacon
½ lb. potatoes
2 Bombay onions
4 tomatoes
1 dessertspoon Worcester sauce
½ teaspoon mustard
1 teaspoonful sugar
1 teacup stock
1 teaspoonful flour
pepper and salt
dripping
6 poached eggs

Fry the slices of bacon and into the same pan, after the bacon has been taken out, put in some dripping. When very hot, put in the meat which should be prepared as in the previous recipes.

When nicely browned, lift the meat on to a dish. Put a little more dripping into the pan and fry the potatoes which should be previously boiled and sliced rather thick. Arrange the bacon and potatoes on the steak and the poached eggs round it. Cut the onions and tomatoes in slices, dredge with flour, sauce, mustard, sugar and stock, and season with pepper and salt. Let it simmer for a few minutes, stirring all the time, then pour over the steak and serve hot.

224 Beef Steak and Kidney Pudding

1½ lb. beef
½ lb. ox-kidney
a few slices of bacon
¼ lb. Bombay onions
¼ lb. potatoes
2 hard-boiled eggs
1 dessertspoonful dripping
1 dessertspoon Worcester sauce
1 teaspoonful flour
½ teaspoon mustard
½ teaspoon sugar
8 peppercorns
4 cloves
1 inch piece cinnamon
1 teacup stock or boiling water
salt

PASTRY:

10 oz. flour
½ teaspoon baking powder
1 oz. dripping
1 egg
salt
stock or milk

Beat down the meat with a rolling-pin, cut it into 2-inch squares, and the kidney into thin slices. Season with pepper and salt. Fry the bacon, and in the fat left over in the pan fry the meat and kidney. If the bacon fat is not sufficient, add a little dripping. Next fry the onions slightly. They should be cut in quarters as also the potatoes, which should be previously boiled and may be fried together with the onions. Now make the gravy. Pour the stock into the same pan in which the ingredients have been fried, add the peppercorns, cloves, cinnamon, mustard, sauce, salt and sugar, stir until it boils, and thicken with the flour. Then put in the steak, bacon, potatoes and onions and mix well together. Meanwhile, prepare the pastry. Sieve the flour and mix in lightly the baking powder and a pinch of salt, rub in the dripping, add the egg beaten, and as much stock or milk as required to make it into a nice firm paste. Roll it into a round piece and line a pudding basin with it, leaving the paste on the sides hanging out, which after the stew has been put in, turn up, so that the whole is covered. Fill up the lined basin with the prepared meat, shell the hardboiled eggs, cut each into six pieces lengthwise and arrange on top of the meat, and cover with the paste. Tie over with a scalded and floured cloth, plunge the pudding into a saucepan of boiling water,—there must be sufficient water to cover it—and boil from 2 to 2½ hours. More boiling water must be added as required. When ready, lift it out of the saucepan, remove the cloth, and turn out the pudding.

N.B.—The pudding may be baked instead of boiled. Almost any kind of meat or mixture of meats may be used for filling.

225 Russian Steak (Vienna Steak)

1 lb. undercut of beef
3 sausages
1 Bombay onion
½ teaspoonful mixed herbs (dried)
pepper and salt to taste
a little made mustard
finely-chopped parsley
1 tablespoonful olive oil
a little butter

Cut the beef, after removing the whitish skin, into pieces about ½ inch thick. Rub in pepper and salt, mix the mustard with the oil, and brush over each piece with it, then leave it to stand in what remains of the oil, turning once, until the rest of the ingredients are prepared.

Prick the sausages with a fork to prevent splitting, plunge in boiling water, and boil up for five minutes. When cool enough to handle split the skin and remove it. Mince the onion and fry it in just enough butter to prevent burning, then mix it into the sausage meat with the herbs and a little more mustard.

Grill the slices of beef quickly on one side, then slowly on the other, adding a little butter to each piece to prevent drying. As soon as the second side is lightly browned spread a thick layer of the sausage on it, flattening it down with the blade of a knife. Return to a hot grill, and cook until well browned on top. Sprinkle with chopped parsley, pouring the drippings from the pan over first. There will be very little of this, and a few drops on each will be quite sufficient. Serve very hot.

This dish is sometimes called Vienna steak or Vienna cutlets, but for these the meat should, properly speaking, be minced, mixed with the sausage meat, herbs, etc., and dipped in beaten egg, rolled in breadcrumbs, and fried crisp on both sides. Egg is usually used for binding the ingredients.

226 Stuffed Steak

2 lb. beef
¼ lb. potatoes
¼ lb. Bombay onions
4 tomatoes
½ teaspoon mustard
1 dessertspoon Worcester sauce
1 tablespoonful dripping
pepper and salt
stock or boiling water

The meat should be cut in one slice, and about half an inch or less in thickness. Wash the meat, trim it, and beat it out slightly with a rolling-pin. Rub it over with a little dripping, and season with pepper and salt. Boil and mash the potatoes, chop the onions and tomatoes and mix together with the potatoes, add the sauce and mustard, and season with pepper and salt. Mix well together and spread this over the meat, roll it up, and tie it round with a piece of string or tape. Melt the dripping in a stewpan and fry the roll a nice brown. Then pour in a pint or a little more of stock or boiling water, and let it simmer on a slow fire until the meat is tender. The meat should be turned once or twice during the cooking. When ready, lift the meat on to a dish and remove the string. Thicken the gravy with a little flour, add more seasoning, if necessary, and pour over the roll.

N.B.—The stuffing could be varied, sausage meat or bacon added to the potatoes and onions or any other forcemeat being used.

227 Tournedos of Beef

1 lb. fillet, or "undercut" of beef
croutons of fried bread
1 rounded tablespoonful butter
¼ pint thick brown sauce well-flavoured with onion and a dessertspoonful Marsala
mashed potatoes, with milk, butter, and a good seasoning of salt and white pepper
parsley

Cut the meat into neat round pieces, about ¾ inch thick and 3 inches in diameter, removing all skin and fat. Wipe over carefully with a damp cloth, and season with pepper and salt. Melt the butter in a frying pan, and quickly sear the outside of the meat, then cook until browned well, leaving the inside underdone.

Pipe a double line of the mashed potato down the centre of the hot dish in which the meat is to be served, place the croutons round this, and pipe a "rose" of the potato mixture between each, with a small tuft of parsley on top of each. Place a piece of meat on each crouton and pour the hot sauce over, allowing some of it to soak into the fried bread, but do not let the sauce overflow the bread.

Serve very hot.

228 Bullock's Heart Stuffed

1 bullock's heart
pepper
salt
a little dripping

STUFFING:

the meat cut from the heart
1 Bombay onion
2 oz. potatoes
1 dessertspoonful dripping
2 oz. grated bread
teaspoonful chopped fennel
1 tablespoon Worcester sauce
½ teaspoon mustard
powdered cloves
cinnamon
pepper and salt

Wash the heart well and boil it. Slit it open on one side and carefully cut away some of the meat from the inside. Season the inside with pepper and salt and fill it with the stuffing. Sew up the opening, rub the heart over with pepper, salt and dripping, and bake in a moderate oven. Baste it frequently. If preferred, the heart may be fried instead of being baked. Serve very hot on a hot-water dish. Make the gravy (Recipe 507) and pour over it.

To Make the Stuffing—Mince finely the meat cut from the heart and add to it the Bombay onions chopped finely, the potatoes boiled and mashed, the grated bread, the spices, salt, fennel, mustard and sauce. Heat the dripping in a pan, put in the mixture and stir for 5 minutes. If the stuffing is dry, moisten with a little stock.

229 Calf's Feet Stewed

2 calf's feet
1 teaspoonful mustard
½ lb. potatoes
½ lb. Bombay onions
1 teaspoon Worcester sauce
1-inch piece cinnamon
6 cloves
10 peppercorns
salt
dripping

You can buy the feet cleaned. Wash them thoroughly, put them into a saucepan with sufficient water to cover, and cook slowly until they are quite tender and the gelatinous part will slip away easily from the bones. When the feet are cooked, lift them out, bone them, and cut the meat in pieces. Strain the stock and return to the saucepan together with the meat. Add the potatoes which should be previously boiled, the onions cut in halves or quarters according to size, and the seasonings, and let it simmer slowly for about half an hour, then add the sauce and mustard, and, if necessary, thicken with a little flour.

230 Crumb Chops

1 lb. beef
1 tablespoonful minced red onions
1 teaspoonful chopped fennel
juice of one lime
powdered cloves
cinnamon and pepper
salt
egg and breadcrumbs
dripping

Cut the beef in nicely-shaped cutlets and flatten them. Mix together the onions, fennel, spices, salt and lime juice. Rub the cutlets over with this, then dip in beaten egg and breadcrumbs, and fry a nice brown in hot dripping.

231 Ox-tail Hot-Pot

1 ox-tail
¼ lb. bacon
1 Bombay onion
2 carrots
1 oz. flour
1 oz. dripping
pepper and salt
1 pint stock or water

Cut up the tail, separating it at the joints, and wash the pieces well. Put them into a saucepan with cold water to cover, bring to the boil and pour off the water. Rinse the pieces of tail, dry them and coat them with the flour. Melt the dripping in a stew-pan, put in the pieces of tail, the bacon sliced and the vegetables prepared and cut in dice and fry for ten minutes. Then turn the contents of the pan into a casserole or an earthenware jar with a cover, add the stock or water and the seasoning, put on the lid and bake in a good oven for about three hours or until the pieces of tail are quite tender. Serve in the dish.

232 Stewed Ox-tail

1 ox-tail
¼ lb. potatoes
¼ lb. Bombay onions
3 carrots
1 oz. flour
3 cloves
1 oz. dripping
¼ teaspoon peppercorns
1 tablespoon Worcester sauce
1 teaspoonful mustard
1 teaspoonful sugar

Cut the tail at the joints and wash the pieces well. Put the pieces into a saucepan with cold water to cover, add a little salt, bring to the boil and pour off the water. Rinse the pieces of tail, dry them and coat with the flour. Melt the dripping in a stewpan, and when smoking hot put in the pieces of tail and brown them well on all sides. Then pour in sufficient warm water to cover them and add the seasonings. Cover the stewpan and let the pieces of tail simmer very gently until tender. This will take from three to four hours. Prepare the vegetables, cut the potatoes and carrots in slices and the onions in quarters. About three-quarters of an hour before the stew is ready put in the vegetables. If the liquid dries up, a little more warm water may be added but the stew must not be made watery. Just before taking it off the fire, add the sauce, mustard and sugar mixed together. Serve the stew very hot.

233 Boiled Salt Beef

Salt beef should be well washed and soaked overnight, or for a few hours in cold water, before putting it on to boil. Then tie it into shape with a piece of tape and put it into a saucepan with cold water to cover it. Bring it quickly to the boil, and then simmer gently until tender, skimming when necessary. It takes longer boiling than fresh meat. The time will vary from 20 to 30 minutes to the pound.

234 Fried Tripe

tripe
pepper and salt
egg
breadcrumbs
dripping

Prepare the tripe as in Recipe 235. When it has boiled tender, drain well and when cold, season with pepper and salt. Dip in beaten egg, then in fine breadcrumbs and fry in boiling dripping until nicely browned. Drain and serve quickly.

235 Tripe and Onions

1 lb. tripe
½ lb. Bombay onions
1 pint milk
1 teaspoonful flour
pepper
salt

Wash the tripe well in warm water and put it into a stewpan, cover with cold water, and let it simmer for some time. Then take it off the fire and scrape the tripe quite clean. Cut it into 2-inch squares and return to the pan which should be well washed. Pour in sufficient cold water to cover the tripe, and let it boil from 2 to 3 hours. Then pour off the water and put in the milk, and the onions cut into pieces, season to taste, and let it simmer for about 30 minutes stirring occasionally. Now add the flour mixed smooth with a little milk or water, boil for another 10 minutes and it will be ready.

236 Veal en Casserole

2 lb. chump of veal
½ lb. sausages (pork)
the grated rind of 1 lime and its juice
pepper and salt
8 red onions
butter
1 teaspoonful minced parsley
1 level teaspoonful mixed dried herbs

Bone and trim the veal, wipe over with a damp cloth, and season on both sides with a little salt and pepper and about half of the lime juice. Put into a buttered casserole dish, and add water to almost cover. Cook in a moderate oven for one hour, covering the dish. Lift out and turn the meat over, sprinkle the top with the grated rind of lime, and spread with the sausage meat mixed with the parsley and herbs, and the chopped onions. Pour the rest of the lime juice into the liquor, and mix well. Cover, and cook for another hour, basting frequently with the liquor.

Serve on a hot dish, with the liquor poured over. If liked, this may be thickened with a little flour, but if it has been reduced to about half, it is better left plain.

237 Veal and Ham Pie

¾ lb. flaky pastry made by using half the quantities given in Recipes 1355
6 oz. lean ham cut fairly thick
grated rind of half a lime
a few drops of lime juice
1 level dessertspoonful finely chopped parsley
2 hard-boiled eggs
a little beaten egg for brushing over the top
1 lb. chump of veal
¾ pint veal stock
flour
salt
pepper
2 rounded tablespoonfuls dripping

Melt half the dripping in a saucepan, stir in 1 tablespoonful flour, and cook, while stirring, until it bubbles and turns a deep brown colour, then add the stock a little at a time, and mix well.

Return to the fire, and simmer until it begins to thicken and takes on a good colour.

Cut the veal and ham into small pieces, wipe over with a damp cloth and dredge with flour seasoned with pepper and salt. Fry in the rest of the dripping until lightly browned on both sides. Place in layers in a small pie-dish, with a sprinkling of grated rind of lime and parsley and a few drops of the juice over each layer. Cut the eggs into halves and place on top, then pour the thickened gravy over all. Cook very slowly in a moderate oven for twenty minutes, then cover with the paste, rolled out to the required thickness. Decorate with snippets of paste, brush over with beaten egg, and bake in a rather quick oven until the pastry is cooked and nicely browned on top.

Lamb and Mutton

(For other recipes, see under Meat)

251 Noisettes of Lamb

6 lamb chops cut about 5/8ths of an inch thick, the same number of narrow rashers of streaky bacon cut thinly, and rounds of crisply fried bread
salt and pepper to taste
melted butter
¼ pint brown sauce
1 teaspoonful sherry
1 dessertspoonful chopped olives
small sprigs of fresh parsley to garnish

Cut away the lean round of meat from the chops, leaving the thinnest possible rim of fat the full length of the bone. Curl the fat round each piece of meat, and over this wind the strip of bacon, fixing it in place with cotton or a small wooden pick. Keep the meat as neat and round as possible. Rub salt and pepper into each side, and brush over liberally with melted butter.

Place under a very hot grill, turning frequently until the meat is nicely browned and the bacon cooked through. Noisettes should always be underdone, rather than over-cooked, and from 7 to 8 minutes is usually sufficient for meat of this thickness.

Meanwhile, sprinkle each round of bread with a thin layer of chopped olives, add the sherry to the hot sauce, and pour about two teaspoonfuls over each round, allowing it to soak in. Arrange on a hot dish, and put a noisette on each piece. Remove the pick or cotton. Pour a little of the sauce over the meat, place a sprig of parsley on each, serve immediately.

252 Jellied Lamb Rissoles

Rissoles made with raw minced lamb
Mint Jelly

Season the meat very well with onions, pepper and salt, lime juice, and finely-chopped green chillies, adding a little mixed spice, if this flavour is liked. To every pound of lamb allow 3 oz. very fine white breadcrumbs and 1 beaten egg to bind. Mix all well together, and shape into small, flat cakes. Dip in beaten egg and then in fine browned breadcrumbs, and fry in dripping until nicely browned. When quite cold coat with the mint jelly, as described in Recipe 253. To get a nice clear effect with the jelly it may be necessary to give three coatings, but each must be thin and allowed to set very firmly before the next is applied.

253 Lamb Salad a la Printaniere

6 lamb chops
salt
pepper and olive oil
2 tablespoonfuls finely-chopped mint
2 rounded dessertspoonfuls castor sugar
4 tablespoonfuls mild vinegar
2 tablespoonfuls water
2 leaves gelatine
2 heads lettuce
4 tablespoonfuls cooked green peas
1 small boiled carrot
3 spring onions
½ gill thick mayonnaise
2 small eggs hard-boiled
small sprigs of fresh parsley

Remove the meat from the bones, and cut away the rim of fat leaving a neat round of lean meat. Rub in the salt and pepper, dip in olive, and grill quickly to brown on the outside leaving the inside underdone and juicy. Drain on white paper, and allow to become quite cold.

Mix the mint with the sugar and vinegar, cover, and allow to steep stirring occasionally until the sugar is dissolved. Melt the gelatine in the water, and strain into the mint sauce after allowing it to steep for at least an hour to extract the full flavour of the mint. Chill, and when just on the point of setting dip the cold meat in it, and place on a sheet of waxed or grease-proof paper in the ice-compartment of the refrigerator. When the jelly coating has set firm pour over a very thin layer of the liquid jelly on top of each piece to give a thicker coating. Let this set, then place on a fresh piece of paper, turning the meat the other side up, and coat in the same manner. Allow to set very firm. The jelly left over after the first dipping may be softened by removing from the refrigerator and standing in a warm room to become almost liquid again, and it must be well stirred to ensure an even distribution of the mint.

Break the lettuce leaves from the heart of each head into fairly small pieces, first washing and chilling well, mix in the peas, diced carrot, and quartered bulbs of the onions, with a little of the tender green stalk chopped small, and pour the mayonnaise over, using two forks to mix all well together until the salad is nicely coated. Arrange the salad in the centre of an ice-cold dish, placing the jellied cutlets round, with a garnish of quartered eggs. Put a tiny sprig of parsley on each cutlet, and serve at once.

To remove the cutlets from the paper wet the underside with a little warm water, when they may be lifted off with the prongs of two forks held at opposite sides. In this way the jelly is not damaged at all. If liked, as an added improvement to the appearance of this dish, the yolks of the eggs may be removed, passed through a fine sieve, and mixed to a cream with softened butter and a seasoning of white pepper and salt then piped back into the quartered whites with a fancy tube.

254 Mutton and Beans

1½ lb. mutton
½ lb. Bombay onions
1 oz. dripping
2 teacups stock or boiling water
boiled haricot beans
pepper
salt
minced parsley

Melt the dripping in a stewpan and fry the onions (minced), then add the meat cut in 2-inch pieces and brown them. Pour in the stock or boiling water, add seasonings, cover the pan and cook slowly until the meat is tender. Arrange the beans round a dish, place the meat in the centre and sprinkle a little minced parsley over it.

255 Boiled Mutton

mutton
boiling water
cloves
cinnamon
peppercorns
salt

The leg and breast are the pieces usually chosen for boiling. Trim the piece of meat, wash it, and put it into a saucepan containing as much boiling water as will cover the joint. Add salt, a piece of cinnamon, a few cloves and peppercorns, and boil according to directions given under *Different Methods of Cooking Meat.* When the meat is tender lift it on to a dish, mask it with White Sauce (Recipe 534) and serve with boiled carrots and mashed potatoes.

256 Mutton Chops

as many chops as wanted
pepper
salt
dripping

Trim the chops and flatten them with a rolling-pin. Rub over with pepper and salt and let them remain for about an hour. Then melt a little dripping in a frying pan, and when very hot put in the chops and fry them a nice brown. Turn occasionally until the chops are sufficiently cooked. When ready, place the chops on a dish and make the gravy. Remove any fat left in the pan, pour in a little stock or hot water, season to taste, and let it boil up. Pour over the chops and serve very hot. Garnish the dish with Fried Potatoes (Recipe 426).

257 Devilled Mutton

1 lb. cold mutton
½ lb. potatoes
¼ lb. Bombay onions
a few tender cabbage leaves
1 oz. mustard seed (ground)
½ oz. dry chillies (ground)
1 oz. dripping
salt
1 tablespoon Worcester sauce
2 tablespoons vinegar
1 dessertspoonful sugar
½ stem lemon-grass
2-inch piece rampa
1 teacup thick coconut milk

Mix the mustard and chilli smoothly with the coconut milk and add the vinegar, sauce, sugar, salt, lemon-grass, rampa, cabbage leaves, which must be previously boiled, and the potatoes boiled and cut in halves, or quarters according to size. Cut the onions in quarters and fry them in the dripping, then turn in the mixed ingredients and cook until the gravy is thick. Lastly add the mutton cut in slices and allow to become thoroughly hot.

258 Mutton Fried in Batter

slices of cold roast mutton
pepper and salt
dripping
3 tablespoonfuls flour
½ pint milk
1 egg

Mix the flour, egg, and milk into a smooth batter, and add a pinch of salt. Trim the slices of mutton and season with pepper and salt. Dip each slice in the batter and fry a nice golden brown colour in dripping. Drain well and serve hot.

259 Liver and Bacon Puffs

potato puff mixture (430)
¼ lb. sheep's liver
4 oz. streaky bacon cut in thick rashers
seasoned flour for dusting
½ cupful soup stock or water
1 dessertspoonful tomato sauce
a few drops Worcester sauce
1 teaspoonful flour
rounds of fried bread

Wash the liver carefully in slightly salted water, wipe dry, and cut into strips and then into small dice—leaving it to the cloth to drain well. Cut the bacon into dice, and fry in a hot pan until crisp. Drain and keep hot. Sprinkle a sheet of grease-proof paper with a very thin layer of seasoned flour, turn the diced liver on it, and shake until very lightly coated. Fry in the bacon fat as quickly as possible, turning it carefully so that it browns evenly, adding a little more fat, if needed, to prevent sticking. Mix the liver and bacon together, and keep hot. Stir a teaspoonful of flour into the hot bacon fat in the frying-pan, and cook for a few minutes until nicely browned, then add the stock or water, the sauces, and a little more pepper and salt, if needed. Stir until it boils, and when of a good colour strain into the bowl with the liver and bacon. Mix thoroughly.

Prepare the potato puff mixture, and with a fancy pipe in a paper cornucopia force out a border all round the edge of each slice of crisply-fried bread. Bake in a quick oven until the potato border is quite firm and set, then fill up the centre with the liver and bacon mixture, return to the oven for a few minutes to make piping hot, and serve at once.

260 Stuffed Loin of Mutton

2½ lb. loin of mutton
4 oz. lean veal
3 oz. fat bacon
3 heaped tablespoonfuls grated white breadcrumbs
1 dessertspoonful minced onion
1 level teaspoonful minced parsley
mixed dried herbs to taste
a squeeze of lime juice and a good pinch of the grated rind
pepper and salt to taste, and beaten egg to bind
1 dessertspoonful butter

Prepare the stuffing by moistening the breadcrumbs with a little water until quite soft. Fry the onion, without browning, in the butter, then turn in the soaked bread and stir until the mixture begins to leave the sides of the pan. When cold, add the rest of the ingredients, the veal and bacon first being minced, and bind all with beaten egg.

Remove the bones from the meat, scraping off any small pieces of meat which cling to them, and pressing these back into the fleshy part of the loin. Season with pepper and salt, having regard to the quantity of these seasonings already added to the stuffing. Pack the fleshy part with the stuffing, shaped into a roll to fit well, spreading any surplus a little way down towards the edge of the meat. Roll up as evenly and firmly as possible, to make a good shape, and tie round with a strip of cloth, so that it holds the shape while being cooked. If string is used this leaves ugly ridges, but a strip of cloth or tape wound round and round keep the roll quite even. Roast in a baking tin on a grid, with dripping in the tin which must be used for basting. Remove cloth, and serve on a hot dish, with a good gravy handed separately.

N.B. Breast of lamb may be prepared in the same manner, the only difference being that the stuffing is spread evenly over the surface of the meat—leaving about an inch at the end quite clear to make a neat finish to the roll.

261 Mutton Miroton

cold roast mutton or lamb
pepper
salt
chopped parsley
thick well-seasoned brown sauce
the same quantity of tomato sauce
finely chopped mint
mashed potato

Cut the meat into rather thick slices, trimming off skin and fat. Dredge lightly with pepper and salt, sprinkle with the parsley, and arrange them overlapping on a buttered fire-proof dish. Pipe a border of mashed potato all round, and pour enough sauce (the two kinds mixed together) to cover the meat. Bake in a fairly quick oven, and dust the top of the sauce with the freshly-chopped mint just before sending to table.

262 Roast Mutton

The leg and loin are the best joints for roasting. Follow the general directions given for roasting meat. When the meat is ready, lift it on to a dish and strain the gravy (Recipe 506) over it. Serve with Red Current Jelly or Mint Sauce (Recipe 519), and any nice vegetable may accompany it.

N.B. Guava or Lovi-lovi Jelly (1103, 1108) go just as well with mutton as Red Current.

263 Mutton Stew

1½ lb. mutton
2 carrots
2 turnips
2 leeks
2 Bombay onions
1 tablespoon Worcester sauce
1 tablespoonful dripping
1 teaspoonful mustard
1 teaspoonful sugar
1-inch piece cinnamon
4 cloves
10 peppercorns
salt
boiling water

Cut the meat in pieces about 1½-inch square. Melt the dripping in a stewpan and brown the pieces of meat, then pour in sufficient boiling water to cover, and let it simmer very gently for about an hour. Now add the vegetables and seasoning and boil until the vegetables are cooked. Mix in the mustard, sauce and sugar, and, if necessary, thicken the gravy with a little flour. (If liked, boiled macaroni may be added to the stew and simmered for about 20 minutes).

264 Mutton and Tomatoes

cold mutton
tomatoes
butter
pepper
salt
breadcrumbs

Slice the mutton thinly and also slice the tomatoes. Grease a pie-dish and coat it with finely powdered breadcrumbs. Put in a layer of mutton, then a layer of tomatoes seasoned with pepper and salt and place a few pieces of butter on the top. Repeat these two layers and finish with a layer of tomatoes. Spread the top with breadcrumbs, place a few pieces of butter on the top and brown in the oven. Serve hot.

265 Sheep's Head and Trotters Baked

1 sheep's head and 4 trotters
¼ lb. red onions
1 dessertspoonful chopped fennel or parsley
1 tablespoon Worcester sauce
1 teaspoonful mustard
powdered cloves
cinnamon and pepper
salt
1 dessertspoonful dripping
egg and breadcrumbs

You can buy the head and trotters cleaned. Wash them thoroughly and put them into a deep saucepan, cover with cold water and let it simmer slowly until the meat slips away easily from the bones. Then remove all the meat from the bones and cut it in neat pieces; skin the tongue and cut it in slices. Chop the onions and fry a dessertspoonful of it in the dripping, then add the meat, the liquid left over in the pan, the remainder of the onions, the fennel, spices, salt, mustard and sauce, and let it cook gently for a few minutes. Turn the mixture on to a flat dish, beat up 2 or 3 eggs and pour evenly on the top, scatter thickly with breadcrumbs, and bake until the breadcrumbs are nicely browned.

Pork

(For other recipes, see under Meat)

281 Bacon and Potato Scramble

4 eggs
½ teaspoonful Worcester sauce
a saltspoonful black pepper
2 tablespoonfuls butter
3 small boiled potatoes
4 rashers streaky bacon
salt to taste
2 red onions chopped very finely

Beat the eggs well and add pepper and sauce. Fry the bacon until almost cooked, then remove from the pan, put in the potatoes cut into fairly small pieces, and fry until just browned in the bacon fat. Meanwhile, cut the bacon into strips about ½ inch wide, return to the pan with the potatoes and the onions, and fry all together until the bacon and onions are cooked and the potatoes well browned and crisp on the outside.

In another pan melt the butter, and cook the prepared eggs in it as described in Recipe 88.

Turn into the pan with the other ingredients; warm through, mixing well, and pile up on a hot dish.

282 Boiled Bacon

Soak the bacon for an hour or two before boiling it. Then wash well, put it into a saucepan with sufficient cold water to cover it and bring to the boil. Let it simmer very gently until it is thoroughly done; then take it up and remove the rind. A 2-lb. piece of bacon will take about 1 hour to cook.

283 Ham Baked in Milk

1 slice of ham, cut about ½-¾ inch thick
butter
a little less than 1 pint milk
1 saltspoonful mustard powder
1 heaped teaspoonful cornflour
white pepper and salt to taste
chopped parsley
2 teaspoonfuls cold milk
mashed potatoes

Soak the ham in cold water for about 3 hours, or according to its saltiness, changing the water a few times. Dry well, and cut away the rind and any discoloured parts. Lightly butter a fireproof baking dish, put the ham in, and cover with the milk. Bake until it is tender, in a moderate oven, pouring the milk over the ham when it is reduced to below the level of the slice. If baked very slowly this is seldom necessary.

Have ready about ½ lb. boiled potatoes, mashed with a little butter. When the ham is cooked, turn out the gas and take a spoonful of the milk at a time to mix with the potatoes until they are quite smooth and soft enough to pipe through a forcing tube. Leave the dish in the oven to keep warm meanwhile.

Mix the cornflour with the cold milk, in a small saucepan, and pour in about $\frac{1}{4}$ pint of the milk. Stir over a low flame until it thickens and is cooked, add the mustard, and season to taste with white pepper and salt, if required. Place the ham in a hot dish, and pipe a border of potato all round, then pour the sauce over and sprinkle with parsley. Serve immediately.

284 Boiled Ham

ham
water
breadcrumbs
cloves

Soak the ham overnight, then wash it well and scrap it, removing the rusty and discoloured parts. Put the ham into a saucepan with sufficient cold water to cover it, bring to the boil and then allow to simmer slowly until the ham is cooked. It is ready when the skin will peel off easily. Allow from 25 to 30 minutes to the pound. If the ham is to be served cold, let it cool in the water in which it has been boiled. Then lift it out, strip off the skin, strew thickly with finely powdered breadcrumbs and stud it over with cloves.

N.B. A bottle of beer added to the water will improve the flavour of the ham.

285 Roast Pig

1 sucking pig
pepper and salt
a little ground saffron
a little flour

STUFFING

the pig's liver
1 lb. grated bread
$\frac{1}{2}$ lb. Bombay onions
$\frac{1}{4}$ lb. potatoes
1 dessertspoonful chopped fennel or parsley
1 dessertspoonful chopped celery
1 tablespoon Worcester sauce
1 teaspoonful mustard
powdered cloves
cinnamon and pepper
grated nutmeg
salt
$\frac{1}{2}$ teacup stock
2 hard boiled eggs
dripping

For roasting, the pig should not be more than four weeks old, and it should be cooked the same day that it is killed. Wash it and clean it thoroughly inside and out, and season the inside with pepper and salt. Put the stuffing into the pig and sew it up. Then truss it, with its forelegs skewed back and the hind legs forward, and put a raw potato in its mouth. The ears should be covered with oil paper to prevent them from burning. Mix together a little pepper, salt, and saffron. Rub the pig over first with this and then with dripping and dredge over with flour. Then place the pig on a baking tin and put it into a hot oven, and baste every 20 minutes or so. It will take from 2 to 3 hours to cook. The skin should be brown and crisp. When ready, place it on a dish, remove the trussing thread and skewers, take off the paper from the ears, and remove the potato from the mouth and substitute a lime. Send very hot to table. Serve with Baked Sweet Potatoes (Recipe 437), Cucumber Salad (Recipe 463) and Lime Sauce (Recipe 516)

To Make the Stuffing: Parboil and chop the liver, and add to it the potatoes boiled and mashed, the grated bread, the fennel, celery, sauce, and mustard, and season highly with pepper, salt, cloves, cinnamon and nutmeg; mix well together. Chop the onions, heat a little dripping in a stewpan, put in the onions and let them cook for a few minutes—do not let them brown—then put in the mixed ingredients and the stock and stir over the fire for about five minutes. Take it off the fire and mix in the hard-boiled eggs finely chopped.

N.B. If liked, a little minced bacon can be added to the stuffing.

286 Pork en Casserole

6 small pork chops
4 medium size Bombay onions
1 teaspoonful dried sago
1 lb. potatoes
3 thick slices pineapple
salt
pepper and mustard powder to season
good brown stock
butter (or dripping)

Grease the casserole dish with butter or dripping, lightly fry the onions in a little more of the same fat. Rub salt, pepper, and mustard into the chops on both sides, and just brown them in the pan with the onions. Cut the pineapple into small chunks, removing the core.

Place the chops, pineapple, potatoes, and onions in the dish in this order, sprinkling the sage over the chops. This quantity makes two layers of each—three chops at the bottom and the other three in the middle. Pour in the stock to come to the level of the last layer of onions. Cover, and cook in a moderate oven for at least 2 hours, basting with the stock frequently to prevent drying, and also to ensure even seasoning all the way through.

This may be served in the same dish, or with the potatoes, pineapple, and onions piled in the centre of a hot dish, the chops arranged round the mound, and the sauce poured over all.

287 Pork Chops

as many chops as wanted
pepper and salt

Cut the chops from the loin or the best end of the neck, trim them neatly and season with pepper and salt. Heat a frying pan over the fire and when very hot put in the chops and fry them a nice brown, turning them several times. No dripping need be added as the pork fat should be sufficient for frying the chops. Be careful to cook the chops thoroughly or they will not be wholesome. When ready, place the chops on a dish, season the gravy in the pan and pour over the chops. Serve with mashed or plain boiled potatoes.

288 Roast Pork

When preparing pork for roasting, score the skin across with a sharp knife at intervals of ¼ inch. Wash and trim the meat, season it well with pepper and salt, and follow the general directions given for roasting meat. Serve with Brown Gravy (Recipe 506 or 507), Lime Sauce (Recipe 516), Cucumber Salad (Recipe 463) and boiled potatoes.

N.B. Pork should be thoroughly cooked. Never serve under-done pork.

289 Pork Stew

2 lb. pork
boiling water
2 Bombay onions
½ lb. potatoes
½ teaspoon peppercorns
3 cloves
1 tablespoon Worcester sauce
1 teaspoonful mustard
½ teaspoon sugar

The pork must not be too fat for stewing. Trim the meat and cut it in pieces about 1½ inches square. Place the pieces in a stewpan, pour in sufficient boiling water to cover them and add the seasoning. Put the lid on the pan and stew slowly for one hour until the meat is nearly tender. Then add the onions and potatoes peeled and cut in slices and stew half an hour longer. If the liquid dries up, a little more boiling water must be added. When nearly ready, mix the sauce, mustard and sugar together and add it to the stew.

290 Sausages

1 lb. lean pork
½ lb. fat pork
¼ oz. coriander seed
powdered cinnamon
cloves and pepper
grated nutmeg
salt
vinegar

Remove all skin and gristle from the meat and chop it very finely or pass it through the mincing machine. Cut the fat into small pieces and mix with the lean. Add to it the coriander slightly roasted and powdered, and season to taste with pepper, salt, cloves, cinnamon and nutmeg. Mix the ingredients well together with the hand and moisten with a little vinegar. Then fill into prepared skins. Do not fill the skins too full or they will burst, and they must be twisted at intervals of 6 inches so as to divide off the sausages. When the sausages are ready, smoke them for 24 hours.

N.B. Sausage skins can be bought ready prepared from the butcher and they only require a little more washing.

291 Sausage in Onions

6 large Bombay onions boiled in salted water until tender but not soft
½ lb. pork sausages
1 teaspoonful chopped parsley
1 saltspoonful dried mixed herbs
salt and black pepper to season
dripping
½ gill white sauce
minced parsley

Remove the centres from the onions very carefully, leaving as large a cavity as possible without breaking the case.

Mix the par-boiled sausages (removing the skin first) with the seasonings, and fill up the onions with this. Melt about 2 tablespoonfuls dripping in a casserole, put in the onions, cover, and bake in a moderate oven, basting with the dripping occasionally. Have the sauce ready, as hot as possible.

Place the onions on a hot dish, pour a spoonful of the sauce over each, and sprinkle with parsley. Serve very hot.

292 Sausages and Macaroni

1 lb. sausages (tinned)
¼ lb. macaroni
2 oz. grated cheese
½ oz. butter
pepper and salt
½ pint stock

Slice the sausages and remove the skin. Break the macaroni in short lengths, put it into a saucepan of slightly salted boiling water and cook until tender, then drain. Grease a pie-dish and put in a layer of macaroni, then a layer of sausages, sprinkle with cheese and dot with a few pieces of butter. Continue these layers until the dish is full. Then pour in the stock and bake in a moderate oven for half an hour. Serve hot.

293 Fried Sausages

Put the sausages into a pan, add just a little vinegar and water, and let them boil slowly for 10 minutes or so until the vinegar and water are absorbed. Then prick the sausages with a stout pin—this prevents them from bursting—and fry them in a little dripping. Keep turning the sausages over and over until they are cooked on all sides.

294 Sausage Rissoles

1 lb. sausages
1½ lb. potatoes
1 dessertspoonful butter
pepper and salt
egg and breadcrumbs
dripping

Boil and mash the potatoes, season with pepper and salt, add the butter and mix into a smooth paste. Blanch the sausages by putting them into a saucepan with cold water and bringing them to the boil. Then drain, remove the skins, and break up the meat. Divide the potato paste and form into 12 balls, flatten out each ball, place a little sausage meat in the centre and close up the paste, neatly, forming them into oblong rolls. Egg and bread-crumb them, and fry a golden brown colour in dripping.

N.B. Any sort of minced meat or boned sardines, etc., may be used instead of sausage meat.

295 Toad in the Hole

1 lb. sausages

BATTER :

½ lb. flour
2 eggs
¼ teaspoon baking powder
1 pint milk
salt

Fry the sausages, remove the skins, and cut them in rather thick slices. Butter a pie-dish and put in the sausages. Make a smooth batter with the flour, baking powder, eggs, and milk, add a pinch of salt, and pour the batter over the sausages. Put it into the oven and bake for about an hour. Turn it out on a dish and serve.

N.B. Steak and kidney or bacon may be used instead of sausage, and instead of being baked it may be steamed.

Poultry and Game

[For curries, see under Rice—Curries—Sambols and Tamil Recipes]

Poultry

In choosing poultry for cooking always select young and fat birds. Home-reared birds are always the best. Those bought are usually very lean and should be fattened for at least a fortnight before they are fit for the table.

Poultry should always be plucked dry. Ceylonese cooks are very fond of using hot water for the purpose as it is the quicker way, but this method is not to be recommended except in a case of emergency.

Poultry should always be hung from 8 to 12 hours before being cooked. Pluck and draw the bird, tie the two feet together and hang on a hook.

301 Boiled Chicken

Prepare the fowl and truss it for boiling. Then put it into a stew-pan with slightly salted warm water, a small piece of cinnamon, 4 cloves, and 8 peppercorns, and let it simmer very gently until the fowl is tender. The time will depend on the age and size of the bird, from 1½ to 3 hours. When ready, lift it on to a dish, remove the trussing string, and serve with White or Parsley Sauce (Recipes 534, 527).

A piece of boiled ham or bacon may be served separately.

302 Braised Chicken

1 pint white stock (strained and with all fat removed)
2 tablespoonfuls dripping
1 chicken, trussed as for roasting
2 carrots
3 small Bombay onions
2 outside sticks of celery with a few of the leaves
½ teaspoonful dried thyme
salt and pepper to season
½ wineglass sherry or white wine (Graves)

Melt the dripping in a saucepan or deep stew-pan and fry the bird in this until it is lightly browned all over. Add the stock, and all the vegetables quartered, and the celery cut into inch lengths. Bring to the boil, then reduce the heat and simmer for an hour, turning the chicken over several times during cooking, and removing scum as it rises. Put in the thyme and wine, stir well, and simmer very gently for about half an hour longer, pouring the stock over the bird so that the full flavour is absorbed. Add salt and pepper to taste during the last part of the cooking. When ready, lift the chicken out very carefully to avoid splitting, mash the softened vegetables against the side of the pan, stir to mix well, then pour through a strainer on to the bird, which should be placed on a hot dish. Serve at once.

303 Braised Chicken with Rice

1 medium size chicken
1 large Bombay onion
2 thick rashers of streaky bacon
1 cupful well-washed rice
1½ cupfuls white stock
3 oz. butter
4 thin rashers of bacon
2 ripe tomatoes
a clove of garlic
a small sprig of parsley
pepper and salt to taste
a little grated nutmeg
2 wineglasses white wine or a teacup white stock

Cut the thick rashers into dice, and fry in a saucepan with a dessertspoonful of the butter, the finely-chopped onion, and a little pepper. Add the washed rice and the first lot of stock. Boil together until the rice is cooked and has absorbed the liquid.

Stuff the bird with this mixture, and truss for boiling.

Put the rest of the butter into a fire-proof baking dish, cover the breast with the thin rashers, and put the lid on. Cook in a moderate oven until the chicken is nicely browned all over, basting it from time to time to prevent drying. Now add all the rest of the ingredients, cover, and allow to cook slowly until the bird is very tender. Lift out the chicken, and put on a hot dish, strain the liquid through a piece of coarse net, and pour over.

304 Chicken Croquettes

¼ lb. cooked chicken
2 oz. cooked ham
1 dessertspoonful finely chopped red onions
1 dessertspoon Worcester sauce
1 teaspoon chopped fennel
pepper
salt
about 2 tablespoons white sauce
egg and breadcrumbs
dripping

Chop the chicken and ham finely removing all skin and gristle. Add the onions and the seasoning and mix well. Then add enough white sauce to bind the mixture together without making it too moist. Form the mixture into cork-shaped pieces, the desired size, roll in beaten egg and breadcrumbs and fry to a nice golden brown in hot dripping.

305 Chicken Cutlets

1 chicken
2 tablespoonfuls grated bread
1 tablespoonful finely chopped red onions
1 dessertspoon Worcester sauce
1 teaspoonful chopped fennel
1 egg
powdered cinnamon
cloves and pepper
salt
dripping
juice of half a lime
about half a teacup or a little less of stock
egg and breadcrumbs

Cut up the chicken and remove all the flesh from the bones. Mince the meat finely or pass it through a mincing machine. Season the minced meat with pepper, salt, cloves and cinnamon, and add the fennel and two-thirds of the onions and mix well together. Fry the remainder of the onions in a little dripping, add the chicken mixture and stir for a few minutes, then pour in the stock, add the lime juice and sauce and cook until it is a fairly thick paste. Then set it aside to cool. When cold, mix in the grated bread and the egg slightly beaten, and divide the mixture into seven or eight equal sized portions and form them into cutlet shapes. Stick a piece of chicken bone at the narrow end, dip in beaten egg and breadcrumbs, and fry to a nice brown colour in hot dripping.

N.B. For a richer cutlet a couple of slices of ham or bacon could be minced together with the chicken. Stock may be made by stewing the chicken bones and trimmings.

306 Chicken Fried in Batter

1 chicken
pepper and salt
dripping
3 tablespoonfuls flour
½ pint milk
1 egg

Cut the chicken into small neat joints, season with pepper and salt, and boil for about 10 minutes. Mix the flour, egg and milk into a smooth batter, and add a pinch of salt. Dip each piece of chicken in the batter, and fry to a nice golden brown colour in dripping. Drain well and serve hot.

307 Grilled Chicken

Split the chicken in half, season with pepper and salt, brush it over with melted butter, and grill slowly turning and basting with the butter several times. Serve very hot with Tomato Sauce. (Recipe 532).

308 Chicken Hot-Pot

1 chicken
¼ lb. Bombay onions
1 cupful carrot and turnip
a strip of celery
½ pint stock or water
pepper and salt

Clean and wash the chicken and cut it in small neat joints, keeping back any trimmings for making the stock. Prepare the vegetables—slice the onions thinly, cut the carrot and turnip in dice and shred the celery. Take a casserole dish or an earthenware jar with a cover. Butter the dish and put in a layer of the prepared vegetables, arrange a layer of chicken on it, and sprinkle over with pepper and salt. Repeat these layers until the ingredients are all in. Pour in the stock or water and put on the lid. Stand the jar in a tin half full of water and bake in a very moderate oven from 1½ to 2 hours. The water in the tin must be replenished from time to time.

309 Indian Fried Chicken

1 plump chicken
1 large Bombay onion
4 oz. dripping
1 saltspoonful each of ground turmeric and coriander
2 small green chillies sliced thinly
black pepper and salt to taste
6 red onions

Remove the meat from the chicken, and cut up into small pieces. Slice the Bombay onion very finely, and fry in the dripping until a light brown in colour. Drain, and allow to crisp in the oven just before it is required. Add the spices to the dripping in the pan, the chillies (with seeds removed before slicing), and fry for a few minutes, then add the chicken lightly sprinkled with salt and pepper, the finely-chopped red onions and fry all together over a low flame until the meat is cooked and tender. If required, a little more dripping may be added.

Serve in a hot dish, with the crisped onions on top.

310 Chicken Pie

2 chickens
a few slices of ham or bacon (fried)
3 or 4 parboiled potatoes
½ lb. Bombay onions
1 tablespoon Worcester sauce
½ teaspoon mustard
1½ teaspoonfuls sugar
1 teaspoon vinegar
powdered cinnamon
cloves and pepper
salt
dripping
½ pint stock
2 hard-boiled eggs

PASTRY:
1 lb. flour
3 oz. dripping
1 teaspoonful baking powder
1 teaspoonful sugar
a pinch of salt
4 eggs
stock or milk

Cut the chicken in small neat joints, keeping back any trimmings for making the stock. Break up the bones and trimmings and put them into a saucepan with cold water to cover, a couple of onions, and a little salt, and allow to simmer until the goodness is extracted. Then strain. Melt some dripping in a frying pan, and when very hot put in the pieces of chicken and fry them a nice brown colour. Then lift them out and drain well. Now fry the parboiled potatoes and the onions cut in halves or quarters according to size. Pour the stock into a stew-pan, add the mustard, sauce, vinegar, sugar and the seasonings, and allow to boil; then add the chicken, the potatoes and the onions, and, if necessary, thicken the gravy with a little flour or breadcrumbs. Take a pie-dish just large enough to hold the stew, put in the stew, place the fried ham and the hard-boiled eggs cut in pieces on the top, and cover the pie with pastry.

To Make the Pastry—Sieve the flour on to a pastry board, keeping aside ¼ lb. for rolling out, mix in the baking powder and sugar, add salt to taste and rub in lightly, using the fingers, 2 oz. dripping.

Then add the eggs (the 3 yolks and one white beaten together) and a sufficient quantity of stock or milk to form it into a soft dough. Work the paste lightly with the hands until free from cracks. Then flour the board and roll the pastry out thinly. Divide the remainder of the dripping into four equal portions, put one portion on the pastry in little pieces, flour the surface lightly, and fold the pastry in two. Roll out the pastry again, and proceed as before until the three remaining portions of dripping have thus been used. The last time roll out the pastry to the required thickness.

To Cover the Pie—Roll out the pastry about ¼ inch thick, and cut a strip about 1½ inches in width. Wet the rim of the dish with white of egg, lay on the strip neatly, and press down lightly. Then wet the strip of pastry with white of egg, roll out the remaining pastry thinner, take up a piece large enough to cover the dish, and lay it carefully over the entire top of the dish. Press this piece of pastry well on, and with a sharp knife cut off any surplus pieces overlapping the edge. Then decorate the pie neatly. Roll out the trimmings of pastry and cut out leaves, and a flower or two. These look attractive placed in the centre. Beat up an egg lightly and brush over the top of the pie before putting it into the oven. Bake in a slow oven for about 2½ hours or until the pastry is nicely coloured.

311 Roast Chicken

Have the fowl drawn and trussed for roasting. Rub it over with pepper and salt and then with dripping, place it on a baking tin and roast in a moderately hot oven, basting frequently. It will take from 1½ to 2½ hours according to the age and size of the bird. A short time before the fowl is to be taken from the oven dredge it with flour and let it brown nicely. When the fowl is ready, lift it on to a dish, remove the trussing string, and pour the gravy round, but not over the fowl. To make the gravy see Recipe 507. Boiled Bacon and Bread Sauce are the usual accompaniments to roast fowl.

312 Roast Chicken Stuffed

It is not usual to stuff a fowl for roasting, but of course it is a matter of choice. Stuff and roast according to directions given for Roast Turkey (Recipe 324).

313 Chicken Salad

cold cooked chicken
1 lettuce
2 tomatoes
a few slices of cucumber
1 hard-boiled egg
Mayonnaise sauce (Recipe 492)

Cut all the meat off the fowl, remove the skin, and cut the meat in small square pieces. Wash, dry, and shred the lettuce and put round a salad bowl. Mix the chicken with a little Mayonnaise and put this mixture into the middle of the salad bowl. Pour some more Mayonnaise over the top, and garnish with slices of cucumber, tomato, and hard-boiled egg.

314 Chicken Souffle

6 oz. cooked chicken
2 oz. cooked ham
1 oz. flour
1 oz. butter
½ pint milk
3 eggs
pepper
salt

Mince the chicken and ham very finely or pass them through the mincing machine. Put the butter into a stew-pan, add the flour and cook for 3 minutes, stirring well all the time. Then stir in gradually the milk, and when quite smooth and thick, put in the chicken, season with pepper and salt and remove from the fire. Now stir in the yolks of the eggs well beaten. Let it cool for a few minutes, then mix in lightly the whites of the eggs beaten to a stiff froth. Pour the mixture into a well-greased souffle dish or pie-dish, leaving space for it to rise, and bake in a moderate oven until well risen and firm to the touch. It will take about 15 to 20 minutes. Serve at once in the dish it was baked in.

315 Chicken Vol-au-Vent

vol-au-vent case (Recipe 1359)
1 large chicken boiled with good seasoning to make a well-flavoured stock, and to flavour the bird nicely
1 small tin "button" mushrooms
yolks of 2 eggs
2 tablespoonfuls butter
2 tablespoonfuls sieved flour
a teaspoonful finely chopped green chillies
½ pint chicken stock
a few drops lime juice
¼ pint thick cream
1 small teaspoonful minced parsley
salt and pepper to season well
a tablespoonful white wine or sherry added to the stock improves the flavour

Remove the skin from the chicken, and cut the meat into ¾ inch cubes, using as much of the white meat as possible.

Melt the butter until it bubbles, stir in the flour, and stir over a low flame until well mixed and somewhat grainy in appearance.

Remove the pan from the fire and mix in the stock a little at a time, beating until quite smooth. Add the yolks of the eggs, and cook over a very low flame again, still stirring, until the flour is quite cooked. Do not let the mixture brown or colour at all.

Add the chicken, halved mushrooms, chillies, and lime juice, and season to taste, then add the cream and parsley. Warm up, and add a little more salt, if needed. If the sauce is too thick it may be thinned down with a little more stock or cream, but for a vol-au-vent the sauce must be fairly thick. Put the mixture, very hot, into the hot case, cover with the pastry lid, and serve immediately.

316 Salmi of Duck

2 ducks
a few slices of ham
1 tin of green peas
1½ glasses of sherry or claret
1 tablespoon Worcester sauce
1 dessertspoonful sliced red onions
½ oz. flour
2 oz. dripping
2-inch piece cinnamon
pepper and salt

Prepare and wash the ducks and put them into a saucepan with a pint of water and allow to boil slowly for about half an hour. Then lift the ducks out, rub them over with pepper and salt, and half the dripping, and roast them in the oven or pan. Or the ducks may be cut into joints and fried. Melt the remainder of the dripping in a saucepan and fry the onions; then add the flour and when browned, add the stock in which the ducks have been cooked, the sauce and cinnamon, and season with pepper and salt. Bring to the boil, skim off the fat, and add the sherry just before taking it off the fire. Cut the roast ducks into neat joints, arrange on a dish together with the ham which must be fried, and the green peas, and pour over the gravy.

317 Roast Duck

Singe and draw the duck, wash it in warm water and dry it. Cut off the feet and wings at the first joint, and season the bird with pepper and salt inside and outside. If liked, the duck may be stuffed (see Recipe 324) or only trussed and roasted. Roast and serve the duck in the same way as Roast Chicken (Recipe 311). Green peas usually accompany Roast Duck.

318 Roast Goose

Prepare and truss the goose as directed for Roast Duck (Recipe 317). It may be simply roasted or filled with stuffing as preferred.

319 Roast Guinea Fowl

guinea fowl
8 slices very fat bacon
flour seasoned with pepper
a good pinch of mustard and a little salt
3 rounded tablespoonfuls dripping
1 cupful brown stock
a little flour
buttered paper

Truss the bird, and cover entirely with the bacon. Place on a grid in a baking tin with the dripping, and put into a very hot oven for five minutes. Reduce the flame, and baste the bird well, and continue basting every five minutes for the first half hour. The flesh of the guinea fowl is very dry, and unless it is basted frequently it is unpalatable, the fat from the bacon not being sufficient by itself. If the bird is small to medium-sized, allow about 50 minutes for the cooking, in a moderately hot oven after the first 5 minutes. At the end of the first half hour cover over with a piece of buttered paper, leave for ten minutes longer, then remove paper and bacon, dredge the breast with the seasoned flour, baste once more, and finish off by allowing it to brown nicely.

Remove trussing strings, and stand on a hot dish in the oven, with the door open. Pour off some of the fat from the baking tin, mix some flour with the rest, brown over a moderate flame, then add the stock and boil up. Strain, and pour just a little over the breast of the bird, sending the rest of the gravy to table separately. Garnish the dish with tufts of watercress.

320 Grilled Pigeons

Pigeons should be plucked and drawn as soon as killed. Wash them and split them open, rub over with butter, and season with pepper and salt. Then grill them over a moderate fire, turning them from side to side until nicely browned. Serve very hot with Brown Gravy (Recipe 507).

N.B. Only young and tender pigeons are used for cooking.

321 Pigeon Pie

6 pigeons
a few slices of ham or bacon
1 tablespoonful dripping
1 or 2 hard-boiled eggs
pepper
salt
a little stock
pastry

Clean and prepare the pigeons, remove the head and neck and split them in two. Season with pepper and salt, dredge lightly with flour and brown them in dripping. Take a pie-dish just large enough to hold the ingredients, put in the pieces of pigeon, with the slices of ham or bacon between, and arrange the hard-boiled egg cut in pieces on the top. Pour in some well-seasoned stock, cover with pastry as directed in Recipe 310, and bake in a good oven.

322 Devilled Turkey

The remains of cold roast turkey are nice devilled. Prepare in the same way as Devilled Mutton (Recipe 257).

323 Devilled Turkey Legs

the legs of a turkey
2 teaspoons mustard
2 teaspoons chutney
white pepper
cayenne
salt
melted butter

With a sharp knife score the legs round in deep regular gashes and brush them over with melted butter. Mix together the mustard, chutney (chopped if there are pieces) and a good dash of pepper, cayenne and salt. Spread this paste over the legs. Grease the grid, place the legs on it and broil them quickly under the grill of a gas stove for about 10 minutes. During the process baste the pieces with melted butter and turn them frequently. Serve hot with Mashed Potatoes (Recipe 427) and Baked Tomatoes (Recipe 441).

324 Roast Turkey

1 turkey
pepper
salt
dripping

STUFFING:

the liver, heart and gizzard of the turkey
¼ lb. Bombay onions
2 oz. mashed potatoes
1 tablespoon Worcester sauce
1 tablespoonful chopped fennel
salt
powdered cinnamon
cloves and pepper
1 dessertspoonful dripping
2 hard-boiled eggs
4 oz. grated bread
½ teaspoon mustard
half a teacup or a little less of stock

Have the turkey plucked, singed, drawn and washed. Make the stuffing and put some of it into the crop of the bird and the remainder into the body. Sew up the openings and truss the bird for roasting. Sprinkle with pepper and salt, place it on a baking tin, and put it into the oven. Baste frequently until the turkey is done, turning often. 15 minutes to each pound for roasting is the usual allowance. A medium-sized bird will require from 2 to 3 hours. About 15 minutes before the turkey is taken from the oven, dredge it lightly with flour and let it brown nicely. When the turkey is ready, lift it on to a dish, remove the trussing strings, and pour some gravy (see Recipe 311) round the dish. Serve a piece of boiled ham separately, and Bread Sauce (Recipe 504).

To Make the Stuffing—Boil and mince finely the liver, heart and gizzard, and mix together with the potatoes and the grated bread, add the fennel and sauce, and season with pepper, salt, cloves, and cinnamon. Chop the onions, heat the dripping in a stewpan, put in the onions and let them cook for a few minutes, then put in the mixed ingredients and the stock and stir over the fire for about 15 minutes. Take it off the fire and mix in the hard-boiled eggs finely chopped.

Game

331 Doves

Pluck, singe and draw the birds, season with pepper and salt, and roast them in a pan or before a clear fire. Doves are also nice curried (see Recipe 798).

332 Pea Fowl

Prepare and cook in the same way as Turkey.

333 Grilled Snipe

Snipe, though generally liked high, is preferred fresh by some people. Pluck the snipe carefully as the skin is very tender, but do not draw them. The head, too, is kept on. Skin it and use the beak for trussing the bird instead of a skewer. Rub well with butter, season with pepper and salt, and grill according to directions given for Grilling under *Different Methods of Cooking Meat.* The time will depend upon how they are liked, underdone or well cooked—from 15 to 20 minutes. Serve hot with pieces of fresh lime. Make a good gravy and serve it separately.

334 Roast Teal

Pluck and draw the teal, wash it in warm water and dry it in a cloth. Cut off the feet and wings at the first joint and truss it for roasting. Season the bird with pepper and salt inside and outside, and rub it over with dripping. Place it on a baking tin, pour in a little cold water and bake in a moderately hot oven, basting frequently until it is cooked. When it is ready lift it on to a dish, remove the trussing string and pour the gravy round the bird.

Another Method—Place the teal in a stewpan, pour in a little cold water and allow to cook slowly until the bird is tender. The bird should be turned once or twice during the process, then lifted out of the pan and fried to a nice brown in dripping, or browned it in the oven.

To Make the Gravy—Pour away the fat from the baking tin, retaining the brown sediment, to which add a small quantity of boiling water or stock and a seasoning of pepper and salt. Cook for 2 or 3 minutes.

An acid accompaniment should be handed with roast teal such as an orange salad, apple or tomato sauce or guava jelly.

335 Salmi of Teal

Prepare in the same way as Salmi of Duck (Recipe 316).

336 Wild Duck

Wild Duck can be prepared and cooked in the same way as ordinary duck.

337 Wild Fowl

Prepare and cook in the same way as ordinary fowl, but the flesh of wild fowl is tough and requires longer boiling unless the bird is young.

338 Jugged Hare

1 hare	**1 glass port wine**
½ lb. Bombay onions	**1-inch piece cinnamon**
¼ lb. bacon	**3 cloves**
1½ oz. dripping	**2 strips of lime-peel**
1½ oz. flour	**pepper and salt**
stock or water	

Skin and paunch the hare and cut it in small neat joints. Wash and dry the pieces and coat them with the flour. Peel the onions and cut them in quarters and cut the bacon in small thick strips. Melt the dripping in a stewpan, put in the pieces of hare, the onions and the bacon and fry for 10 minutes. Then turn the contents of the pan into a jar or deep earthenware dish with a cover, add the port wine, cinnamon, cloves, lime-peel, pepper and salt and sufficient stock or water to cover the hare. Cover the jar tightly, place it in a saucepan of boiling water and steam from 3 to 4 hours. When ready, arrange the hare on a dish, thicken the gravy with a little flour, if necessary, and pour over the hare. Serve guava or red currant jelly separately.

339 Roast Hare

Skin and clean the hare, wash it well, and if the whole hare is to be roasted it may be stuffed or not as preferred. Make the stuffing as for Roast Pig (Recipe 285), stuff the hare, sew it up, and truss and roast in the same way as directed for Roast Pig.

It is more usual to roast only a portion of the hare. Follow general instructions for roasting. Red currant or any other acid jelly should always be served with Roast Hare.

340 Venison

Venison is the flesh of deer. It is usually served roasted. Venison can also be cooked according to any of the recipes given for cooking beef.

341 Wild Pork

Prepare and cook in the same way as ordinary pork. The skin is usually tough and requires long boiling.

Egg Dishes

(For egg curries, see under Rice—Curries—Sambols)

Eggs are one of our most useful and necessary foods. They are also very nourishing, and provide an excellent emergency dish. Many and varied are the dishes that could be turned out with eggs. Below are some suggestions for different ways of cooking and utilizing them generally.

The nutritive quality of an egg depends greatly on its freshness, and in purchasing eggs, always make sure that they are fresh. Eggs, if fresh, are clear when held up to the light; if there is a cloudy part or black spot attached to the shell, they are stale. You can also test an egg by shaking it. When shaken, the inside of a fresh egg does not move about.

Eggs are most easily digested when eaten uncooked. Hard-boiled eggs must be avoided by those who have a weak digestion.

351 Bacon and Eggs

Cut the bacon in thin slices, trim off the rind and remove any little pieces of gristle or bone. Heat a frying pan, put in the slices of bacon and cook until the fat is transparent. Turn the slices once or twice whilst cooking. When sufficiently cooked, place them on a dish and serve with fried or poached eggs laid on the top of the bacon.

352 Egg and Bacon Pie

eggs
cooked bacon
pepper and salt
potatoes
butter
milk

Boil and mash the potatoes, mix with a little butter and milk and add salt to taste. Grease a pie-dish and put in a layer of potatoes, then a few slices of bacon, and over it an egg beaten with a little pepper and salt. Then another layer of potatoes and some more bacon and egg over it. Cover with a layer of potatoes, brush over with beaten egg, and bake for about half an hour or until nicely browned.

353 Boiled Eggs

Eggs for boiling cannot be too fresh. Have ready a saucepan of boiling water and slip the eggs gently into it with a spoon. There must be enough water in the pan to cover the eggs well. Keep the water boiling all the time and allow 3 minutes, if a lightly boiled egg is desired, and one minute more, if it is wanted firm.

ANOTHER METHOD—Place the eggs in a saucepan with cold water, put it over the fire and remove the eggs as soon as the water boils. The white of an egg cooked this way will be found very digestible.

354 Hard-Boiled Eggs

Put the eggs into a saucepan of boiling water, allow the water to come to boiling point again, and then boil the eggs exactly 10 minutes. Then lift them out and put them into a basin of cold water so that they may shell more easily.

355 Egg Cutlets

6 hard-boiled eggs
1 chicken (boiled) or
½ lb. cold beef
2 oz. ham or bacon
1 tablespoonful chopped red onions
1 teaspoonful chopped fennel
1 tablespoon Worcester sauce
½ teaspoon mustard
yolk of one egg
powdered cinnamon
cloves and pepper
salt
dripping
beaten egg
breadcrumbs

Shell the eggs and cut them in halves lengthwise. Remove the yolks and mix them with the chicken and ham very finely minced; season with pepper, salt, cloves and cinnamon, and add the onions, fennel, sauce, and mustard. Mix well together and moisten with the yolk of egg. Fill up the whites with this mixture, piling it rather high, and form each half into its original whole egg shape. Dip in beaten egg and breadcrumbs and fry them a golden brown colour in hot dripping. Serve hot with Brown Gravy (Recipe 507) poured over.

356 Fried Eggs

One egg must be fried at a time. Put a little dripping into a small frying pan, and when the dripping is very hot, break an egg into a teacup and slip it carefully into the hot fat; with a spoon gather the white quickly together to give the egg a round shape, and while frying, ladle a little dripping over it. Three or four minutes will be sufficient to cook it, but the time will depend on how the egg is liked, soft or hard. When ready lift out carefully, drain well, and proceed with the other eggs in the same way, adding more dripping to the pan as required.

357 Egg and Macaroni Pie

4 hard-boiled eggs
2 oz. macaroni
pepper
salt
½ pint thick white sauce
3 tablespoonfuls grated cheese
a little made mustard
butter

Shell the eggs and cut them in halves lengthwise and season with pepper and salt. Break the macaroni into short lengths and boil in slightly salted water until tender. Make the sauce and add to it the mustard and the grated cheese reserving a little of the cheese to sprinkle on top of the pie. Grease a pie-dish and put in a layer of the sauce, place the macaroni over it and arrange the halves of egg on top of the macaroni. Pour the remainder of the sauce over it, scatter the top with grated cheese and put some small pieces of butter here and there on the top. Bake in a moderate oven for 20 minutes or until nicely browned.

358 Poached Eggs

Pour some boiling water into a deep frying pan, and add vinegar in the proportion of one teaspoon to one pint of water. Break one egg at a time into a cup and slip it carefully into the pan without, in any way, hurting the yolk, and gather the white quickly together with a spoon to keep it in form. Proceed with the rest of the eggs in the same way, and let them cook for about 4 minutes or until the whites seem to be properly set. Be careful not to let them be overdone. When ready, lift them out, allow to drain, and cut away any uneven edges. Serve on hot buttered toast or in any other way desired.

359 Poached Eggs with Mince

4 eggs
4 rounds of hot buttered toast
¼ lb. cooked meat
2 tablespoons stock or gravy
1 dessertspoon Worcester sauce
seasoning

Any cooked meat may be used or a mixture of two different kinds of meat together such as chicken and ham or veal and tongue. Trim the meat and mince it very finely or put it through the mincing machine. Then put it into a saucepan with the stock or gravy and sauce and make all thoroughly hot. Season to taste and spread this neatly on the rounds of toast. Place a poached egg on the top of each and serve very hot.

360 Egg Ruloung

8 eggs
1 dessertspoonful sliced red onions
pepper and salt
1 teaspoonful chopped fennel
1 dessertspoonful ghee or dripping

Beat the whites of the eggs, then add the yolks and beat together season with pepper and salt, and add the fennel. Heat the ghee, put in the onions and let them boil—they must not brown; then turn in the beaten egg and stir briskly for a minute or two.

361 Egg Salad

3 hard-boiled eggs
1 tomato
1 beetroot (boiled)
1 lettuce
Mayonnaise sauce (Recipe 492)
a little chopped parsley

Slice the eggs, tomato and beetroot and shred the lettuce. Arrange these ingredients in layers in a salad bowl or glass dish, sprinkle with chopped parsley, and pour over some Mayonnaise sauce.

362 Scrambled or Buttered Eggs

4 eggs
3 tablespoons milk
1 oz. butter
1 teaspoonful chopped fennel
pepper
salt

Beat the eggs slightly together, add the milk and fennel, and season with pepper and salt. Melt the butter in a saucepan, add the egg mixture and stir over a moderate fire until the eggs just begin to set and the mixture is of a nice creamy consistency. Have ready some squares of hot buttered toast, pour the mixture carefully on the toast and serve at once.

N.B. Scrambled eggs may be varied by mixing them with a little minced ham or chicken, boned sardines, etc.

363 Scrambled Eggs with Tomatoes

2 eggs
2 tomatoes
½ oz. butter
1 oz. chopped ham
½ teaspoonful chopped fennel
pepper
salt
buttered toast

Peel the tomatoes and cut them in small pieces. Melt the butter in a saucepan, add the tomatoes and ham, season to taste and cook for about 10 minutes. Remove the pan from the fire and add the eggs, well beaten, and the fennel. Return the pan to the fire and stir until the mixture becomes thick. Have ready some squares of hot buttered toast, put a little of the mixture on each and serve at once.

364 Eggs with Cheese Sauce

4 hard-boiled eggs
pepper and salt
½ pint thick white sauce
3 tablespoonfuls grated cheese
a little made mustard
1 tablespoonful finely powdered breadcrumbs
a little butter

Shell the egg, cut them in slices and season with pepper and salt. Add the grated cheese and mustard to the white sauce. Grease a pie-dish and put in a layer of the sauce and over this some slices of egg. Repeat these layers and finish with a layer of sauce. Scatter the top with the breadcrumbs and a little grated cheese if liked. Put on a few small pieces of butter and bake in a moderate oven for about 15 minutes. Serve hot.

365 Eggs with Salmon

6 hard-boiled eggs	**breadcrumbs**
1 oz. butter	**pepper**
2 tablespoonfuls chopped salmon	**salt**
	¼ pint white sauce

Shell the eggs and cut them in two crosswise. Remove the yolks and cut a small piece off the whites to enable them to stand. Put the yolks into a basin and add to them the butter, salmon, pepper and salt and mix well together until smooth. Fill the whites of eggs with this mixture and sprinkle them lightly with breadcrumbs. Pour the sauce at the bottom of a dish and stand the prepared eggs on it. Bake in a moderate oven for about 10 minutes.

366 Eggs in Tomatoes

eggs	**minced onion**
tomatoes	**chopped fennel**
pepper	**breadcrumbs**
salt	**butter**

Take as many tomatoes as required; they must be of a medium size, round and not over-ripe. Cut a slice off the stalk end of each and scoop out the seeds and watery centre with a small teaspoon. Sprinkle the inside of each with a little pepper and salt and the onion and fennel mixed together. Break an egg into a cup and pour it carefully into the centre of each tomato. (If the eggs are large, a little of the white should be kept back.) Place them in a fire-proof dish, sprinkle over with breadcrumbs, and pour a little melted butter over each. Bake in a moderate oven from 10 to 15 minutes.

367 Ham and Eggs

Cut the ham into slices being careful to make them of equal thickness. Trim off the rind, and if the ham is very saltish, soak the slices for about 10 minutes in hot water and then dry them in a cloth. Heat a frying pan over the fire, lay in the slices of ham, and cook them quickly first on one side then on the other. If the ham is lean, it will be necessary to melt a little butter or dripping in the pan before the ham is put in. When ready, place the ham on a dish, which should be kept very hot while the eggs are being cooked. Fry the eggs in the ham fat in the same frying, pan, slip them on to the slices of ham, and serve quickly.

368 Asparagus Omelette

asparagus	**pepper**
grated cheese	**salt**
4 eggs	**butter**

Take some asparagus and chop up the tender part. Make the omelette as in Recipe 373 and before folding it over, put the asparagus in the centre and sprinkle over with a little grated cheese.

369 Cheese Omelette

4 eggs
1 tablespoonful grated cheese
pepper and salt
butter

Make in the same way as Plain Omelette (Recipe 373) and sprinkle the cheese in the centre before folding it over.

370 Fish Omelette

3 oz. boiled fish
6 eggs
1 tablespoon milk
pepper
salt
1 dessertspoonful chopped parsley or fennel
dripping

Any white fish, salmon or boned sardines may be used for this. Free the fish from all skin and bone and break it in small flakes. Separate the yolks from the whites of the eggs. Add to the yolks the parsley, pepper, salt and milk and mix well together. Beat up the whites of the eggs to a stiff froth and lightly stir into the other mixture. Put some dripping into a frying pan, and when very hot, pour in the egg mixture, and as soon as it commences to set, put the fish in the centre and fold the edges over to make it oval. When nicely browned on one side, turn it over and brown the other side. Serve very hot.

371 Ham Omelette

4 eggs
2 tablespoonfuls minced ham
butter or dripping
1 teaspoonful chopped fennel or parsley
pepper and salt

Mince the ham very finely and fry it for 2 minutes in a little butter. Make the omelette as in the previous recipe, and sprinkle the ham in the centre before folding it over. Serve very hot.

372 Mushroom Omelette

1 small tin "button" mushrooms
2 red onions
1 small teaspoonful chopped parsley
1 dessertspoonful butter
a little salt and black pepper for the filling
3 large eggs
1 oz. butter and a little salt and white pepper to season

Prepare the filling first, by chopping the mushrooms fairly small. Melt the butter in a small saucepan, fry the finely-chopped onions in it for a minute or two, then add the mushrooms, salt, pepper and parsley, and cook over gentle heat for about five minutes, stirring all the time. Keep hot.

Whisk the whites of the eggs to a very stiff froth, add the yolks one at a time, and stir until well mixed, add salt and pepper to taste. Melt the butter in the omelette pan, but do not let it brown. Turn the eggs into it, and place over a moderate flame, cutting into the base of the mixture here and there with a knife to let some of the soft mixture run out on to the pan. This helps in the quick cooking of the egg, and should not be continued after the bottom begins to set and brown lightly, as the inside of this omelette must be creamy. Test the sides with a knife, and as soon as the mixture is firm enough to be turned over place the mushrooms on one half and quickly turn over the other half to cover them and make a neat fold. Loosen the underneath with the knife, and slide off on to a hot dish. Serve at once.

373 Plain Omelette

4 eggs	**a little butter or dripping**
1 tablespoonful chopped fennel	**pepper and salt**

Separate the yolks from the whites of the eggs. Beat the yolks until thick and creamy, mix in the fennel, and season with pepper and salt. Beat the whites until stiff and dry and stir in lightly into the other mixture. Melt the butter in a frying pan (the pan must be perfectly clean and not burnt or worn in any part) and when very hot, put in the mixture, spread evenly and cook slowly until it begins to set; then slip a knife under it and double over first from one side then from the other, towards the centre to make it oval. When ready it should be soft and creamy inside and a golden yellow outside. It will probably take some practice to turn out an omelette as light as it ought to be, and to give it the correct bolster-like shape. An omelette must be served immediately it is cooked or it will become leathery.

N.B. In making omelettes the size of the pan must be taken into consideration. The omelette should not be too thin or too thick, so that the pan should be in proportion to the number of eggs used.

374 Sausage Omelette

¼ lb. sausages	**pepper and salt**
4 eggs	**butter or dripping**

The sausage should be put into a saucepan with cold water and brought to boiling point and then boiled for 5 minutes. Then drain, remove the skin and cut up the sausage meat finely. Make the omelette as in the previous recipe and place the sausage meat in the centre.

375 Savoury Omelettes

A great variety of omelettes can be produced by adding different flavourings to the plain omelettes. Savoury omelettes can be made by the addition of a small quantity of herbs finely minced or powdered, grated cheese, shellfish, ham, bacon, or anything in the way of cold meat or fish. Whatever is used must be very finely minced, and can either be mixed with the egg mixture or used as a filling.

376 Sardine Eggs

4 hard-boiled eggs
1 oz. butter
½ doz. sardines
pepper and salt
lettuce, cucumber
tomatoes

Shell the eggs and cut them in halves across. Remove the yolks and cut a small piece off the whites to make them stand like little cups. Put the yolks into a basin with the butter and the sardines which have been scraped and boned, season with pepper and salt and work all together until smooth and thoroughly mixed. Fill the whites of eggs with this mixture, piling it high in the centre. Line a dish with some crisp lettuce leaves, arrange the eggs on it, and garnish round the sides with slices of cucumber and tomato.

377 Scotch Eggs

4 hard-boiled eggs
½ lb. sausage meat
dripping
a little flour
egg and breadcrumbs

Shell the eggs and roll them in a little flour, keeping them whole Divide the sausage meat into four equal portions. Wrap one portion round each egg, covering it smoothly, and using a little flour to prevent it sticking to the hands Then brush over with beaten egg, roll in breadcrumbs, and fry to a light brown colour in dripping. When ready, cut the eggs in halves crosswise and arrange neatly on a dish. Serve hot, with or without a gravy.

Vegetables

[For vegetable curries, see Rice—Curries—Sambols and Kandyan-Sinhalese and Tamil Recipes]

All green vegetables should be procured as freshly gathered as possible. Cabbage, cauliflower, lettuce and all other vegetables of this class should be steeped in salt water before being cooked, as this brings out any insects that may be between the leaves. Green vegetables should be cooked in boiling salted water with the lid off the saucepan. This improves both the colour and flavour.

Root vegetables can be cooked with the lid on. They should be well scrubbed and washed in cold water before peeling. Potatoes, artichokes, turnips and yams must be put into cold water as they are peeled to prevent discoloration.

391 Jerusalem Artichokes, Boiled

artichokes **salt** **white sauce (Recipe 534)**

Wash the artichokes well, scrape them and at once drop into a bowl of cold water or they will become discoloured. Then cook in boiling salted water until tender. Serve with White Sauce poured over them.

392 Butter Beans, Boiled

butter beans **pepper** **salt**

Boil the beans as in the following recipe, but boil them whole.

393 French Beans, Boiled

French beans **pepper** **salt**

Choose, young, fresh beans. Break off the heads and tails drawing away with them the strings on either side of the bean. You could either boil the beans whole or cut them into fine strips in a slanting direction. As they are cut drop them into a bowl of cold water. Have a saucepan of boiling water ready into which add a pinch of bicarbonate of soda and a little salt; put in the beans and boil quickly until tender with the lid off the saucepan. Drain well, sprinkle with pepper and serve.

394 Haricot Beans, Boiled

½ lb. haricot beans **pepper**
½ oz. butter **salt**

Put the beans into cold water and let them soak for 12 hours; then put them to boil in salted water, bring quickly to boiling point and simmer very slowly for about 3 hours or until tender.

Drain off the water, place the saucepan by the side of the fire with the lid partially off, and dry the beans. Add the butter, season with pepper and salt, and shake the beans over the fire for a couple of minutes. Serve them hot.

395 Beetroot, Boiled

Wash the beets carefully, taking care not to prick or break the skins or fibres before they are cooked, or they will bleed and lose their beautiful colour in boiling. Put the beets into a saucepan of boiling water, with water sufficient to cover them, and let them boil until tender, keeping the saucepan covered. When ready, drain and skin them with the fingers while hot. Beetroot is usually served in salad form.

396 Beetroot, Spiced

2 boiled beetroots
1 oz. butter
2 tablespoons vinegar
½ teaspoon mustard
pepper and salt
½ teacup water

Peel the beets, cut them into thin slices while hot and arrange them in a vegetable dish. Put the butter, vinegar, mustard, pepper, salt and water into a small saucepan, bring to the boil and pour over the beets.

397 Breadfruit Cutlets

half a large-sized breadfruit
1 oz. Maldive fish
2 oz. red onions
½ teaspoon ground chillies
a pinch of ground saffron
powdered cloves
cinnamon and pepper
salt
1 egg and breadcrumbs
oil for frying

Cut the breadfruit in pieces, remove the core and wash it well in cold water. Put the pieces into a saucepan, cover with water, add a little salt and boil until it is cooked. Drain off the water, mash the boiled breadfruit and add to it the Maldive fish finely powdered, the onions chopped, the ground chillies and saffron, and season to taste. Mix well together and moisten the mixture with the egg, lightly beatèn. Shape into small flat rounds, dip in egg and breadcrumbs and fry to a golden brown in hot oil.

398 Stuffed Breadfruit

1 breadfruit
pepper and salt
a pinch of ground saffron
dripping

For the STUFFING:

2 or 3 oz. cooked meat
a slice of ham or bacon
1 dessertspoonful grated bread
1 dessertspoonful chopped onions
1 dessertspoon Worcester sauce
1 egg
pepper
salt

Peel the breadfruit, cut off the stem and cut a round piece neatly out of the top. Reserve this round for filling up the hole later on. Then with a sharp knife remove the core and as much of the inside as possible without damaging the shape of the fruit. Rub the fruit over outside and inside with dripping, pepper, salt and saffron. Fill up the breadfruit with the stuffing and replace the round that was cut off from the top. Place the breadfruit on a well-greased baking tin, put a few small pieces of dripping on the top and bake in a moderate oven until the breadfruit is cooked and the outside nicely browned, basting frequently with the dripping. Serve hot.

To Prepare the Stuffing—Mince the meat and ham finely, put it into a basin and add to it the bread, onions and sauce. Season with pepper and salt and moisten with the egg lightly beaten and a little stock, if necessary.

399 Brinjal Cutlets

6 medium sized brinjals
½ lb. cooked meat
2 oz. ham or bacon
1 tablespoonful chopped red onions
1 teaspoonful chopped fennel
1 egg
1 tablespoon Worcester sauce
powdered cinnamon
cloves, pepper and salt
dripping
egg and breadcrumbs

Choose nice round brinjals of equal size—the thin long-shaped ones will not do. Cut the brinjals in halves lengthwise and boil them. When boiled, with a teaspoon scoop out the seeds and some of the pulp from the inside, taking care not to break the skins. Then make the stuffing. Chop up half the pulp and mix it with the meat and bacon both finely minced. Melt a little dripping in a saucepan and fry one-third of the onions, then add the meat mixture, the remainder of the onions, the fennel and the sauce, and season with pepper, salt, cloves and cinnamon. Let it cook slowly for a few minutes, then take it off the fire and mix in the egg slightly beaten. Fill the brinjals with the stuffing, piling it rather high, brush the tops with beaten egg, strew over with bread-crumbs, and bake in rather a hot oven for about half an hour.

N. B.—If liked, the cutlets may be fried in dripping instead of being baked.

400 Cabbage, Baked

2 cupfuls boiled cabbage
1 oz. butter
½ oz. flour
1 egg
1 gill milk
pepper
salt
breadcrumbs

Take the remains of cooked cabbage and chop them finely, removing any hard portions. Put the chopped cabbage into a saucepan, add the butter and stir over the fire until hot. Season with pepper and salt, dredge in the flour and add the milk. Stir for a few minutes, take it off the fire and stir in the egg, beaten.

Grease a pie-dish, put in the cabbage mixture, sprinkle the breadcrumbs over the top, place some small pieces of butter over and bake quickly in the oven or under the grill.

401 Cabbage, Boiled

cabbage **pepper** **salt**

Pick out all the withered outside leaves and if the cabbage is a large one cut it across in two or quarter it according to size. A small cabbage should be boiled whole. Wash the cabbage well and soak it in salted water for half an hour; then drain off all the water, and put the cabbage into a saucepan of fast boiling salted water; boil quickly until tender, with the saucepan uncovered. When ready, take it up and while hot drain well by pressing the cabbage between two plates. Cut it into small pieces, sprinkle with pepper and serve hot.

402 Cabbage, Pressed

the heart of a firm young cabbage
butter
salt
pepper
2 red onions

After picking off all the coarse outer leaves of the cabbage, cut it in quarters and remove the centre stalk. Wash thoroughly in several lots of cold water, then drop into boiling salted water and add the onions. Boil with the lid off the pan, until tender. Lift out carefully, and drain through a colander, pressing out all the water. Turn on to a large plate, and chop very finely, adding a little more salt, if needed, pepper and a large pat of butter. Mix all well together, and shape into a flat square. Press down with the back of another plate, tilting both so that surplus water runs off. Stand over a pan of boiling water to heat through, then cut into small squares. Lift off carefully, and serve in a hot dish.

403 Cabbage Rolls

1 cabbage
a little butter
grated cheese or breadcrumbs

For the STUFFING:

¼ lb. cooked meat
2 oz. ham or bacon
1 dessertspoonful chopped onions
1 dessertspoon Worcester sauce
pepper
salt
1 egg

Choose some nice tender leaves from a cabbage. Wash them and cook them for about 5 minutes in boiling, salted water. Then drain them and spread out the leaves. Meanwhile, prepare the stuffing as in Recipe 398. Put some of the stuffing on each leaf of cabbage and fold up in neat parcels. Arrange them in a well-greased pie-dish sprinkle with a little grated cheese or breadcrumbs and place a few small pieces of butter on the top. Bake in a moderate oven.

404 Cabbage, Stewed

1 cabbage
1 oz. butter
1 oz. flour
½ pint milk
pepper
salt

Wash and prepare the cabbage as in Recipe 401. Remove the hard piece of stalk in the centre and boil as directed until nearly tender. Then drain and cut into fine shreds. Melt the butter in a saucepan, put in the cabbage and add the flour gradually, stirring all the time. Add the milk, stir until boiling and season to taste. Serve very hot.

405 Cabbage, Stuffed

1 cabbage
1 pint stock

For the STUFFING:
¼ lb. cooked meat
2 oz. ham or bacon
1 dessertspoonful grated bread
1 dessertspoonful chopped onions
1 tablespoonful chopped fennel
pepper
salt
1 egg

Choose a firm, round cabbage of medium size. Wash it well, remove any discoloured leaves, and cut off the stalk. Then put the cabbage into a basin of boiling water, cover it and allow to soak for half an hour. Prepare the stuffing as directed in Recipe 398. Pull the leaves of the cabbage apart, put some of the stuffing in the centre and the remainder between the leaves. Tie the cabbage with a string, put it into a stewpan, pour in the stock and allow to simmer slowly for about half an hour or until the cabbage is quite tender. When ready, lift the cabbage on to a dish and remove the string. Boil down the stock in the pan and pour it round the cabbage. Serve very hot.

406 Carrots, Boiled

carrots
salt

Cut off the green tops from the carrots, scrape them and wash them well. If the carrots are large, divide them in two or four lengthwise. Put them into a saucepan of boiling water slightly salted, and boil them quickly with the lid on the saucepan, until tender. Drain well and serve hot.

407 Carrots, Stewed

2 large carrots
1 pint light stock or boiling water
pepper
salt
1 oz. butter
1 teaspoonful cornflour
2 tablespoons milk

Scrape the carrots, cut them in slices and put them into a saucepan with the stock, salt and pepper. Put the lid on the pan and let them simmer slowly until tender—be careful that the carrots are not broken. Then mix the cornflour with the butter, add them and the milk to the carrots, and stir carefully until thoroughly mixed.

408 Cauliflower, Baked

2 cauliflowers
½ pint milk
1 oz. flour
½ oz. butter
pepper and salt
1 yolk egg
3 tablespoonfuls grated cheese
1 tablespoon grated bread

Boil the cauliflowers as directed in Recipe 409. Drain them and place them in a shallow pie-dish. Melt the butter in a saucepan, mix in the flour, then the milk, and stir over the fire until it thickens; season to taste. Take the pan off the fire and add the yolk of egg and half the cheese. Pour this over the cauliflowers, coating them well, sprinkle the remainder of the cheese and the grated bread over the top and bake in a moderate oven until nicely browned. Serve hot.

409 Cauliflower, Boiled

cauliflower **salt** **White Sauce (Recipe 534)**

Pick out the leaves, wash the flower carefully and soak it in salted water for half an hour. Then tie it up in a muslin cloth to prevent the flower from breaking and put it into a saucepan of boiling water, slightly salted, and boil from 20 to 30 minutes, with the saucepan uncovered. Serve with the White Sauce poured over it.

410 Cauliflower Fritters

1 small or half a large cauliflower
vinegar, salt and pepper

For the BATTER:

1 egg
2 tablespoonfuls sieved flour
a pinch of salt
¼ pint milk
2 teaspoonfuls olive oil
hot oil for frying

Wash the cauliflower well and parboil it in salted water. Drain and divide into neat sprigs. Mix salt and pepper with a little mild vinegar, dip each piece into it and then allow to drain again. Make the batter by beating the egg slightly in a basin, stir in 2 heaped tablespoonfuls flour and a pinch of salt. Mix in the milk gradually until a very smooth batter is formed. Beat with a rotary beater, stir in the oil and allow to stand for an hour. When ready to cook prepare a pan with very hot oil about 2 inches deep, stir the batter mixture, and dip the cauliflower in it one piece at a time until well coated, drop into the oil and fry golden brown. Drain, and serve piled up on a folded napkin in a hot dish.

The best way of dipping the cauliflower is to pick up each sprig with a fruit fork, and hold it firmly with another so that it does not slip off with the weight of the batter. In this way it can be held over the bowl until surplus batter drains off.

411 Sweet Corn, Baked

1 tin sweet corn
1 level dessertspoonful cornflour
a little cold milk
1 tablespoonful butter
salt and pepper to taste

Mix the cornflour with a little cold milk, then add the liquid from the tin of corn and a little more milk, if necessary. (Some brands of corn have less liquor than others, and it is thicker. When this is the case the extra milk is required, to make a thick but not quite firm sauce). Cook, while stirring constantly, over a low flame until the mixture is like a thick custard. Add the corn and butter, and a little pepper and salt to bring out the flavour nicely.

Turn the mixture into a buttered pie-dish and bake in a quick oven for 10—15 minutes.

When fresh corn is used instead of the tinned variety, the cobs should be boiled in slightly salted water until the grains are very tender. These are removed from the cob, put into a double-saucepan with milk to cover, enough sugar to sweeten, and allowed to cook for half an hour. A little butter is then added. They are then ready to use as directed above.

To prepare the cobs for boiling, remove the green leaves, and pull away the silky brown fibre. Wash well, and wash enough of the inner leaves to cover each cob well. Tie these round the cobs top and bottom, and drop into the boiling water.

412 Stuffed Cucumber I

1 cucumber
½ pint stock

For the STUFFING:

2 oz. cooked meat
a slice or two of ham or bacon
1 dessertspoon grated bread
1 teaspoon chopped fennel
1 dessertspoon Worcester sauce
pepper
salt
1 yolk of egg

Choose a thick, straight cucumber, cut it in two lengthwise and scoop out the seeds. Fill the space with the stuffing prepared as in Recipe 398 and place the halves together. Bind round with tape, place the cucumber in a baking dish and pour in the stock. Cook in a moderate oven until tender, basting occasionally with the stock. When ready, lift the cucumber on to a dish and remove the tape. Thicken the gravy in the pan and pour round the cucumber.

413 Stuffed Cucumber II

1 cucumber
3 oz. cooked fish
2 oz. grated cheese
pepper and salt
2 yolks of eggs
breadcrumbs
butter
½ pint milk

Choose a thick, straight cucumber, cut it in two lengthwise and scoop out the seeds. Sprinkle the inside with salt and turn it cut side down to drain. Meanwhile make the stuffing. Any cooked fish or tinned salmon may be used for this. Free the fish from all skin and bone and break it up in small flakes. Put it into a basin and add the cheese and seasoning. Mix well and add the yolks of eggs and enough milk to form it into a stiffish mixture. Place the pieces of cucumber on a greased dish and fill up the hollows with the stuffing. Sprinkle over with breadcrumbs, put a few small pieces of butter on the top, pour the milk round and bake in a moderate oven until the cucumber is cooked and the breadcrumbs nicely browned.

414 Dhall Cutlets

¼ measure dhall
1 oz. dried prawns
1 oz. Maldive fish
2 oz. red onions
½ teaspoon ground dry chillies
a pinch of ground saffron
powdered cloves
cinnamon and pepper
salt
a squeeze of lime juice
egg and breadcrumbs
oil for frying

Wash the dhall well in several changes of water removing any discoloured ones which float on the surface of the water. Put the dhall into a saucepan with cold water to cover and cook slowly until it is tender. Then drain and mash it well with a spoon. Roast and pound the dried prawns and also pound the Maldive fish finely. Mix these three ingredients together and add to them the onions chopped, the ground chilly and the saffron. Add seasoning to taste. Mix well together and shape into small flat rounds about a quarter of an inch thick, dip in egg and breadcrumbs and fry a nice brown in hot oil.

415 Green Peas, Boiled

green peas **butter** **salt**

Shell the peas and drop them into a bowl of cold water. Then drain well and put into a saucepan with sufficient boiling salted water to cover them and simmer slowly, with the saucepan uncovered, until the peas are tender. Drain, and toss in a little butter.

416 Leeks, Boiled

leeks **salt** **White Sauce (Recipe 534)**

Wash the leeks well in cold water, trim off the roots, the green ends, and the outside skin. Then split them open lengthwise and cut them in convenient-sized pieces. Wash well, put into boiling water, add a pinch of salt and boil slowly. When tender, dish carefully and serve with White Sauce.

417 Onions, Baked

Bombay onions
breadcrumbs
grated cheese
butter
pepper
salt

Cut off the roots and tops of the onions, peel them, and put them into a saucepan of boiling salted water. Boil for half an hour and drain. Then place the onions in a buttered dish, season with pepper and salt, sprinkle over with breadcrumbs and cheese, put a few pieces of butter on the top and bake in the oven until brown.

418 Onions, Boiled

Bombay onions **salt** **White Sauce (Recipe 534)**

Cut the root and top off the onions and peel them; then put them into a saucepan of cold water, bring to the boil and strain. Have ready a saucepan of boiling salted water, put in the onions and cook until tender from 1½ to 2 hours. Drain well, arrange the onions on a dish and pour the sauce over them.

419 Onions, Stewed

4 Bombay onions
½ pint light stock
1 oz. butter or dripping
½ teaspoon cornflour
1 tablespoon Worcester sauce
salt

Cut the root and top off the onions and remove the outside skin. Put them into a stewpan with cold water to cover them, add a little salt, bring to the boil and boil for 5 minutes. Drain the onions and rinse with cold water. Then put them back into the stewpan, add the stock and butter and simmer gently until the onions are tender. Mix the cornflour to a smooth paste with the sauce, add it to the onions, stir well and cook a few minutes longer. Dish the onions and pour the gravy over.

420 Onions, Stuffed

6 medium-sized Bombay onions
2 tablespoonfuls cooked meat
1 tablespoonful grated bread
pepper and salt
1 tablespoonful chopped fennel or parsley
1 dessertspoon Worcester sauce
dripping
a little stock

Choose onions of equal size, cut off the roots and tops and peel the onions. Put them into a saucepan of boiling salted water and boil for 10 minutes, drain, and, when cold, carefully scoop out the centres, making a hole large enough to receive a dessertspoonful of stuffing.

For the stuffing chop up three of the centres and mix with the meat which should be finely chopped (chicken and ham or any other cooked meat), add the grated bread, sauce and fennel, and season to taste with pepper and salt. Moisten with a little stock or beaten egg. Fill the onions with this mixture, sprinkle the tops with breadcrumbs, and put a piece of dripping on each. Arrange on a well-greased baking dish and bake for about half an hour. Serve with Brown Gravy (Recipe 507).

421 Peas, Buttered

2 cupfuls shelled green peas
2 oz. butter
2 red onions
1 level teaspoonful sugar
a small sprig of fresh mint
pepper and salt
boiling water

Choose fresh young peas, shell and measure them. Wash well in cold water, and drain. Put them in a wide shallow basin or earthenware cooking vessel, and stand in a pan with sufficient boiling water to come half-way up the sides. Pour on just sufficient boiling water to nearly cover the peas, add the sugar, salt, mint, and onions, peeled and sliced in halves, and allow to simmer for about 25-30 minutes. Do not cover the pan. When the peas are quite tender and nearly all the water has been absorbed, or evaporated, add the butter and a dash of white pepper. Cook for another five or ten minutes. Remove the mint and onion, and turn on to a hot dish.

Peas cooked in this way retain all their flavour and goodness. Care should be taken not to stir or otherwise disturb them while they are cooking, or they become mushy; but after the butter has been added the bowl may be lifted out occasionally and shaken to allow the butter to coat them evenly.

An important point in preparing peas is that they should not be shelled until just before they are to be cooked. If this is done too early, and the peas are left soaking in water, they lose much of their delicate flavour and may even lose their crisp tenderness. It is also inadvisable to cook them in a metal saucepan, as this too, impairs their flavour.

422 Potato Balls

½ lb. boiled potatoes
1 dessertspoonful butter
pepper
salt
1 yolk of egg
a little flour
egg and breadcrumbs
dripping

Mash the potatoes smoothly or put them through a patent masher. Season with pepper and salt and mix in the yolk of egg. Heat the butter in a saucepan and put in the potato mixture. Stir well together and turn the mixture on to a plate to cool. Then form into small balls of equal size, using a little flour. Egg-and-breadcrumb them and fry in boiling dripping to a golden brown colour.

423 Potatoes, Boiled

potatoes
salt

First wash the potatoes well in cold water, then pare them as thinly as possible, and with the point of the knife remove the "eyes". As the potatoes are peeled drop them into cold water. Choose potatoes of an equal size for boiling, if some are larger than others, cut them in halves or quarters according to size. Put them into a saucepan with sufficient cold water to cover them, put the lid on the saucepan, bring quickly to the boil and then simmer gently until cooked. The time will vary from 20 to 30 minutes, according to age and size. When done, drain off the water, sprinkle in some salt, and place the saucepan by the side of the fire for about 5 minutes longer, with the lid half on the pan. Shake the pan occasionally until the potatoes are quite dry and floury. Serve at once.

424 Potatoes Boiled in their Skins

Wash the potatoes well in cold water, pare out the "eyes", and put them into a saucepan with just enough cold water to cover them. Boil until soft, then drain off the water, peel the potatoes and sprinkle a little salt over them.

425 Potato Chips

Pare the potatoes and cut them into thin slices, then across into chips or strips. Wipe them very dry in a towel and then fry as directed in Recipe 426.

426 Potatoes, Fried

potatoes **dripping** **salt**

Pare the potatoes and cut them into slices as thin as possible. Wash the sliced potatoes, drain them well, and dry in a towel. Make the dripping quite hot in a frying pan, put in the potatoes, a few at a time, and fry them a nice golden colour, shaking them so as to cook them equally. When they are crisp and done, drain them on paper, dredge with salt and serve very hot.

427 Potatoes, Mashed

1 lb. potatoes **salt**
pepper **1 oz. butter**

For mashing, the potatoes may either be peeled and boiled, or boiled in their skins and afterwards peeled. Mash the potatoes well with a fork or put them through a patent masher. Add the butter and season to taste. If the potatoes appear dry, a little milk may be added.

428 Potato Mould

potatoes **pepper and salt**
milk **parsley**
butter **grated cheese**

Peel and boil as many potatoes as required. Drain well and mash them smoothly, adding a little milk and also some butter, but do not make it too moist. Season to taste with pepper and salt and mix in a little chopped parsley. Put into a buttered mould and bake for half an hour. Turn out of the mould and dust over with grated cheese.

429 Potato Nests

1 lb. cold mashed potatoes	**1 small tin green peas**
1 dessertspoon butter	**12 boiled prawns**
2 dessertspoons grated cheese	**pepper and salt**

Mix the potato with the butter, cheese, pepper and salt, and pipe the mixture through an icing nozzle into nest shapes. Choose a nozzle like the small rose nozzle, or the shell nozzle. These make markings which give the effect of twigs. Build the sides of the nests up rather high. Bake in a hot oven till brown. Fill each nest with green peas, and perch a boiled prawn on top. Leave the red tail on the prawn so that it looks like a brightly-coloured bird.

To make these more substantial, put a layer of flaked chicken, fish, or minced prawns under the peas.

430 Potato Puffs

½ lb. boiled potatoes	**about 3 tablespoonfuls milk**
yolk of 1 egg	**salt and pepper to taste**
1 oz. butter	**a little beaten egg**

Pass the potatoes through a potato masher, and turn into a large basin or pudding bowl. Pour on the melted butter, and mix with a fork. Now add the yolk of egg mixed with half the milk, and beat thoroughly with a fork until light and fluffy. Season to taste, and add the rest of the milk gradually until the mixture is soft enough to pass through a fancy rose pipe or plain meringue pipe. Place the pipe in a double cornucopia of grease-proof paper, put in the potato mixture, and pipe on to a buttered tin in small fancy-shaped mounds. Brush very lightly (so as not to spoil the shape) with the beaten egg, and bake in a quick oven until tipped with brown. Lift off very carefully and serve on a hot dish with a paper d'oyley, garnishing here and there with small tufts of fresh parsley, or a tiny sprig of parsley stuck on the top of each puff.

431 Potatoes, Roasted

1 lb. potatoes	**salt**
1 oz. dripping	**pepper**

Choose round, equal-sized potatoes. Wash and pare the potatoes as directed in Recipe 423. Put them into a saucepan with sufficient boiling water to cover them and add a little salt. Boil for 10 minutes and then drain. Sprinkle them over with a little flour and place them in a baking tin with the dripping. Bake in a moderate oven until they are cooked and nicely browned, adding salt to taste. Turn the potatoes occasionally during the cooking. Drain them from the dripping before serving.

N.B. If a joint of meat is being roasted the potatoes can be cooked in the same pan.

432 Potato Salad

1 lb. boiled potatoes
1 tablespoon ground red onions
1 teaspoon ground garlic
1 tablespoon finely chopped parsley
1 tablespoon butter
2 tablespoons mayonnaise
pepper and salt

Peel and slice the potatoes into thick slices. Melt the butter in a saucepan, add the ground onions and garlic, chopped parsley and mayonnaise. Turn in the potatoes and toss them in the mixture till all the pieces are well coated with the seasoning. Take off the fire, sprinkle with salt and pepper and serve hot.

433 Potatoes, Steamed

Steaming is one of the best ways of cooking potatoes. Pare the potatoes as for boiling, sprinkle with salt, and put them into a steamer. Place the steamer over a pan of boiling water and put on the lid. The time for cooking will depend on the size and age of the potatoes. When sufficiently cooked remove the steamer from the water and stand it in a warm place until the potatoes are dry.

434 Potatoes, Stewed

4 or 5 potatoes
1 Bombay onion
2 oz. dripping
$\frac{1}{2}$ pint stock or hot water
pepper
salt

Peel and cut the potatoes in quarters or thick slices. Skin and slice the onion thinly. Melt the dripping in a stewpan, put in the potatoes and onion and cook them for a few minutes without allowing them to brown. Then pour in the stock or hot water, season to taste and stew very slowly until the potato is cooked but not broken . Serve very hot.

435 Purple Yam, Boiled

purple yam **salt**

Pare the yam rather thickly, cut into $1\frac{1}{2}$-inch squares and drop at once into cold water. Then wash well and put into a saucepan with sufficient water to cover them. Boil until soft, then drain, sprinkle a little salt over them, shake the pan for a couple of minutes and serve the yams very hot.

Nearly all yams are boiled in the same way.

436 Spinach Boiled

3 lb. spinach
pepper
salt
a tablespoonful butter

Pick the spinach carefully and wash it well in plenty of cold water. Then put it into a saucepan with a teaspoonful of salt, adding no water. Boil quickly, with the lid off from 15 to 20 minutes, stirring occasionally with a wooden spoon. When done, drain the spinach and rub it through a sieve or chop it very finely. Melt the butter in a stewpan, add the spinach, season with pepper and salt and set it on the fire until it is hot.

437 Sweet Potatoes, Baked

sweet potatoes salt pepper

Boil the potatoes as in Recipe 438, but keeping them whole. When boiled cut them in halves lengthwise, sprinkle over the tops with pepper and salt and put into the oven. Bake until the tops are nicely browned.

438 Sweet Potatoes, Boiled

sweet potatoes salt

Scrape the potatoes and wash them well. If the potatoes are large cut them in halves or quarters according to size. Put the potatoes into a saucepan with enough water to cover them and boil until tender; then drain, sprinkle a little salt over them, toss over the fire for a couple of minutes and serve hot.

439 Sweet Pumpkin, Boiled

sweet pumpkin pepper salt

Peel the pumpkin, cut into 1 or 1½-inch squares and remove the seeds. Wash the pumpkin well and put to boil in slightly salted water. When tender, drain well, sprinkle over with pepper and serve hot.

440 Stuffed Snake-gourd

1 snake-gourd
1 teacupful minced prawns
1 dessertspoonful chopped red onions
1 dessertspoonful grated bread
1 teaspoon chopped fennel
1 dessertspoon Worcester sauce
pepper
salt
1 egg
egg and breadcrumbs
dripping

Choose a thick, straight snake-gourd, trim off the ends and cut it in pieces about 2½ inches long. Scoop out the seeds and scald the pieces in slightly salted boiling water for 10 minutes. Then rinse in cold water and drain. Meanwhile prepare the stuffing. Melt a little dripping in a saucepan and fry half the onions, then add the minced prawns, the remainder of the onions, the fennel and the sauce and season with pepper and salt. Let it cook for a few minutes. Then take it off the fire, mix in the grated bread and moisten with the egg lightly beaten. Fill up the pieces of snakegourd with this filling, dip in egg and breadcrumbs and fry a nice brown in hot dripping. Serve hot with a brown gravy poured over it.

441 Tomatoes, Baked

tomatoes **pepper**
butter **salt**

Choose small tomatoes of equal size. Wipe them, take off the stalks and place them in a pie-dish. Put a small piece of butter on each, sprinkle with pepper and salt and bake in the oven for about 10 minutes or until tender.

442 Tomatoes, Stewed

½ lb. tomatoes **1 oz. butter**
½ teaspoon sugar **pepper and salt to taste**

Remove the stalks and put the tomatoes into a basin of boiling water and let them remain for a couple of minutes. Then lift them out and remove the skins. Cut them in slices or quarters, place in a stewpan with the butter, sugar, pepper and salt, and stew slowly until tender. Serve hot.

443 Tomatoes with Salmon

large ripe tomatoes **1 egg**
1 tin salmon **salt**
2 tablespoons butter **pepper**
breadcrumbs **sauce**

Flake the salmon, after removing all skin and bones. Mix with 1 tablespoon butter, pepper, salt, sauce, and the beaten egg. Cut a slice off the top of each tomato, scoop out the pulp and mix it with the salmon. Pile the salmon back into the tomatoes, cover the top with breadcrumbs, dot with the remaining butter, and bake in a moderate oven for about half an hour.

444 Turnips, Boiled

turnips **salt**

Pare the turnips thickly, wash them and cut them in halves or quarters according to size or leave them whole, if they are small, put them into a saucepan of boiling water, slightly salted, and boil slowly until tender. Drain and serve.

445 Turnips, Mashed

turnips **salt**
pepper **butter**

Boil the turnips as in the preceding recipe, drain well, and return them to the saucepan. Mash them with a fork, add a little butter or dripping, season with pepper and salt and serve hot.

446 Vegetable Cutlets

½ lb. mixed cooked vegetables
1 dessertspoonful finely sliced red onions
pepper
salt
1 teaspoonful dripping
2 teacups milk
½ oz. flour
egg and breadcrumbs
dripping for frying

This is a nice way of using up left over vegetables. Chop the vegetables finely. Melt the dripping in a saucepan and fry the onions, sprinkle in the flour and stir for a few minutes. Take the pan off the fire, add the milk and cook again stirring constantly until the mixture boils. Then add the chopped vegetables, make hot, season to taste and spread on a plate to cool. Shape into cutlets with the aid of a little flour. Brush them over with beaten egg, coat with breadcrumbs and fry in hot dripping. Drain on paper and serve hot.

See also Recipes 397, 399, 414.

447 Vegetable Hot-Pot

2 carrots
1 turnip
2 Bombay onions
2 tomatoes
2 or 3 potatoes
pepper and salt
butter
sugar
powdered breadcrumbs
light stock or water

Wash and prepare the vegetables and cut them in slices. Cook the carrots, turnips and onions in boiling salted water for 20 minutes and the potatoes for 5 minutes. Grease a deep baking dish and dust it with powdered breadcrumbs. Arrange the carrots, turnips and onions in the dish in layers, season with pepper and salt and put a few pieces of butter on the top, then a layer of tomatoes and sprinkle over with sugar. Lastly, a layer of potatoes seasoned with pepper and salt with a few pieces of butter on the top. Half-fill the dish with light stock or water, cover the dish and bake in a moderate oven until the potatoes are soft and browned.

448 Vegetable Marrow Boiled

vegetable marrow salt White Sauce (Recipe 534)

Peel the marrow, cut it in pieces and take out the seeds. Cook in boiling salted water until tender. Serve with white sauce.

449 Stuffed Vegetable Marrow

1 small vegetable marrow 1 teacup stock

For the STUFFING:

3 tablespoonfuls minced meat
1 tablespoonful grated bread
1 teaspoon chopped fennel
1 dessertspoon Worcester sauce
pepper and salt
a little beaten egg

Wash and peel the marrow, cut it in two pieces from end to end and scoop out all the seeds and the soft pulpy part from the centre. Prepare the stuffing as in Recipe 398 and put it into the marrow, place the halves together and bind it round with tape. Place the marrow in a baking tin and pour in the stock. Cook in a moderate oven until tender, basting frequently with the stock. When ready, lift the marrow on to a dish and remove the tape. Thicken the gravy in the pan and pour round the marrow.

450 Vegetable Puree

4 large tomatoes
10 spring onions
4 or 5 cloves of garlic
2 teaspoons sugar
pepper and salt
1 tablespoon Worcester sauce
3 tablespoons salad oil
a small piece of green ginger
3 green chillies
a few coriander leaves

Scald the tomatoes and remove the skins, and chop them finely. Mince separately the spring onions, leaves and all, garlic, ginger, chillies, and coriander leaves. Heat the salad oil in a saucepan, and when quite hot put in the minced onion and fry for a few minutes. Add all the other ingredients excepting the coriander leaves, and cook for 25 minutes. Now add the coriander leaves, 2 teaspoons sugar and 1 tablespoon sauce, and cook for ten minutes longer. Add pepper and salt to taste. Serve spread thickly on fingers of crisp fried bread, or on buttered toast.

Salads and Salad Dressings

(For Fruit Salads, see a later Chapter)

Nearly all vegetables may be served as salads, and in a variety of ways. The most essential thing is to have the vegetables fresh, and, if green, to have the leaves crisp and dry. All greens, lettuces in particular, should be carefully washed in cold water to free them from dust and insects; then dry well, for if there is any moisture left on the leaves, the oil or dressing will not adhere to them. Lettuce leaves should not be cut but torn with the fingers. Tomato and cucumber, together with or without lettuce, form quite a nice salad, as do tomato and onion. Cold cooked vegetables could be turned into nice salads, the exact mixture being a matter of individual taste. Carrots and potatoes go well together, mashed with mayonnaise, and garnished with sliced tomatoes and minced parsley Turnips could be cut into strips, a dressing poured over them, and the salad garnished with beetroot. Peas, French beans, and cauliflower together with tomatoes, cucumber, radish, lettuce and cress go towards the making of very successful salads.

Salads should be served cold, and as a rule, the dressing should not be added until just before serving.

One must be very particular about the oil used for the dressings. None but the best olive oil should be used.

Salads

461 Bandakka Salad (Ladies' Fingers)

bandakkas — **salt**
pepper — **vinegar**

The bandakkas must be quite fresh and tender. Wash them and boil in salted water until soft. Then drain, split them open lengthwise, sprinkle with pepper and salt and moisten with vinegar.

462 Beetroot and Onion Salad

1 beetroot — **1 tablespoon vinegar**
1 Bombay onion — **salt**
1 tablespoon salad oil — **pepper**

Boil the beet and the onion separately and when cold cut them in thin slices and arrange neatly on a salad dish. Mix the salad oil and vinegar together, add pepper and salt and pour over the vegetables.

463 Cucumber Salad

1 cucumber — **red onions**
salad dressing (Recipe 496) — **pepper and salt**

Peel and slice the cucumber very thinly, sprinkle it with salt, let it remain for half an hour and then drain off the water. Arrange the cucumber in a dish and pour the dressing over it. Garnish the salad with whites of eggs cut in rings and sliced red onions. If liked, a Bombay onion or two, thinly sliced, could be mixed with the cucumber, in which case, red onions need not be used for garnishing.

464 Cucumber and Tomato Salad

cucumber **pepper and salt**
tomatoes **vinegar**

Peel and slice the cucumber very thinly and slice the tomatoes too rather thinly. Arrange the cucumber and tomatoes in a dish, sprinkle over with salt and pepper and moisten with a little vinegar. It can be served as it is, if liked, pour over it a salad dressing a short time before serving.

465 French Bean Salad

cooked French beans **salad oil**
pepper and salt **vinegar**

If the beans are young and tender, they may be left whole, if not, cut them in fine shreds. Arrange them on a salad bowl, sprinkle with pepper and salt and moisten with a little salad oil and vinegar.

466 Haricot Bean Salad

cooked haricot beans **tomatoes**
hard-boiled eggs **salad dressing (Recipe 494)**

Have the beans well boiled. Arrange them on a salad dish and pour the dressing over. Garnish with sections of hard-boiled egg and slices of tomatoes.

467 Hot Salad

4 or 5 cooked potatoes **a wineglass of vinegar**
2 cooked beetroots **pepper and salt**

Remove the skins and cut the potatoes in slices, also peel and slice the beets. Arrange alternate layers of the sliced potatoes and beets in a dish, sprinkle with pepper and salt and pour the vinegar carefully over the top. Place the dish in the oven until very hot.

468 Lettuce Salad

red onions **lettuce** **salad dressing (Recipe 492 or 496)**

Prepare the lettuce as in the preceding recipe, arrange it in a salad bowl and pour the dressing over it. Garnish with whites of eggs cut in rings and salted red onions.

469 Mixed Vegetable Salad

equal quantities of cold cooked
potatoes
carrots
turnips
beetroot and cauliflower
pepper and salt
ripe tomatoes
lettuce
Mayonnaise sauce or salad dressing (**Recipe 494**)

Cut the potatoes, carrots, turnips and beetroots into strips or dice, and divide the cauliflower into small tufts. Arrange the vegetables in layers in a salad bowl or glass dish, and season each layer with pepper and salt. Pour over the salad dressing and garnish with sliced tomatoes and a border of lettuce.

470 Onion Salad I

Bombay onions
pepper and salt
salad dressing (**Recipe 494 or 496**)

Peel the onions and boil them in salted water until tender; then drain and break into pieces. Arrange in a glass dish, sprinkle with pepper, and pour the dressing over.

471 Onion Salad II

Bombay onions
vinegar
pepper
salt

Peel the onions and slice them very thinly, sprinkle with salt, let it remain for about 10 minutes, and then drain off the water. Season with pepper and salt and moisten with vinegar.

472 Orange and Plantain Salad

2 oranges
2 or 3 ripe sour plantains
lettuce
cayenne pepper
salt
salad dressing (**Recipe 494**)

Arrange some crisp lettuce leaves on a salad dish. Peel and slice the plantains using a silver knife to prevent discoloration. Dust with cayenne pepper. Peel the oranges and remove every trace of the white pith. Split each section down the length with a sharp knife and remove the edible portion, keeping it as whole and undamaged as possible. Toss the orange in pepper and salt and sprinkle with the salad dressing. Mix well. Arrange the sliced bananas and the seasoned oranges on the lettuce and serve with more salad dressing poured over.

473 Pineapple and Prune Salad

one large ripe soft pineapple
½ lb. prunes
a little chutney
lettuce
chilli powder
vinegar
pepper and salt
mayonnaise

Skin the pineapple, remove all traces of the "eyes", and cut it into ¾ inch thick slices, breadthwise. Remove the hard stalk from the centre. Rub the slices with vinegar to which a dash each of chilli powder, pepper and salt, has been added. Pour the rest of the mixture over the slices, and let them stand for a while. Wash and prepare some crisp leaves of lettuce, and arrange a few on each plate. On the leaves, place a slice of pineapple, drained from the vinegar. Fill the hollow in the centre with mayonnaise. Stone the prunes and put a dab of chutney in the centre of each. Place three prunes around the centre of each slice of pineapple. Serve chilled.

474 Potato Salad

4 cups cold boiled potato, diced
2 hard-boiled eggs
1 cup fresh green peas, boiled
mayonnaise
pepper
salt
butter

Melt about 3 oz. of butter in a saucepan and when it is hot, put in the peas and stir well. Then turn in the diced potatoes, and stir gently so as not to break the pieces. Season with pepper and salt to taste, transfer to a deep bowl and toss carefully in four tablespoons of mayonnaise. Garnish with wedges of hard-boiled egg.

475 Spinach Salad

spinach
hard-boiled eggs
pepper and salt
salad dressing (Recipe 496)

Boil the spinach according to directions given in Recipe 436, and mince it finely. Season with pepper and salt and mix with a little of the dressing. Pile the spinach in the centre of a salad dish and pour the dressing over. Garnish with slices of hard-boiled egg and a border of lettuce.

476 Tomato Salad

four large red tomatoes
1 cup cold cooked fish, shell-fish or chicken
2 hard-boiled eggs
salad cream
lettuce

Wash the tomatoes well, and, using a sharp knife dipped in hot water, make five cuts in each tomato, at the blossom end. Cut three-quarters of the way down the tomato, but do not sever the pieces. Open them gently with the fingers so that each tomato resembles a flower. Fill the centre with the cooked fish or chicken. Boiled crab meat is particularly good in this, and so is boiled lobster, minced roughly. Whatever filling is used, it should first be well seasoned. Take the yolks of the hard cooked eggs, and rub them through a sieve on to the centre of the tomato "flower". Arrange the tomatoes on a bed of lettuce, cut the whites of eggs into rings and use for garnishing, and serve with salad cream.

Salad Dressings

491 French Dressing (Sauce Vinaigrette)

½ teaspoon made mustard
2 tablespoons salad oil
2 tablespoons vinegar
pepper and salt

Mix the mustard, pepper and salt together, and add the oil gradually. When well mixed add the vinegar a little at a time. Stir well till all the ingredients are blended.

492 Mayonnaise Sauce

2 yolks of eggs
¼ pint salad oil
½ teaspoon made mustard
½ teaspoon salt
a pinch of pepper
2 tablespoons vinegar
2 tablespoons lime juice
a pinch of sugar

Mix the mustard, pepper and salt together, add to the eggs and mix well with a wooden spoon, stirring always in the same direction. When well mixed add the oil, drop by drop, and stir continually. As the mixture thickens, thin with vinegar or lime juice alternately with the oil, until all is used, stirring all the while. It must be thick and creamy when ready.

493 Potato Dressing for Cold Meats

½ lb. boiled potatoes
2 hard-boiled eggs
1 tablespoon vinegar
1 teaspoonful mustard
½ teacup thick coconut milk
white pepper and salt

Mash the potatoes smoothly and add to it the yolks of the eggs, the mustard salt and pepper and mix into a smooth batter with the vinegar and coconut milk.

494 Salad Dressing

2 hard-boiled eggs
1 teaspoon made mustard
1 tablespoon salad oil
pepper and salt
2 tablespoons Worcester sauce
2 tablespoons vinegar
¼ teaspoon sugar

Mash the yolks and mix with the mustard, pepper, salt and sugar. Pour in the oil slowly, stirring briskly all the time; lastly, add the sauce and vinegar in the same manner. Stir until the dressing is perfectly smooth, and it is then ready for use.

N.B. The whites of the eggs, cut in slices, could be used for garnishing the salad.

495 Salad Dressing for Fish

2 hard-boiled eggs
1 teaspoonful made mustard
pepper and salt
1 dessertspoonful anchovy sauce
3 tablespoons vinegar
¼ teaspoon sugar

Mash the yolks of the eggs, add the mustard, pepper, salt and sugar, stir it well, add the anchovy sauce and mix to a smooth liquid paste with the vinegar. Chop the whites of the eggs and add them to the sauce.

496 A Simple Dressing

1 teaspoonful made mustard	**salt**
1 tablespoon vinegar	**2 tablespoons thick coconut milk**
pepper	**1 hard-boiled egg**

Mash the yolk and mix it smoothly with the milk, add pepper and salt, and lastly stir in the vinegar. Mix well together.

Sauces and Gravies

SAUCE-MAKING is an important branch of cookery. It is most essential that suitable sauce or gravy should accompany each dish. Almost all dishes are improved by a well-made sauce, while with others the success of the dish depends upon the sauce. Sauces containing flour must be mixed smoothly, stirred constantly, and allowed to boil until the flour with which they are thickened is cooked.

Sauces and gravies should be sent to table very hot.

501 American Sauce

2 tablespoonfuls butter
2 tablespoonfuls sieved flour
1 cupful fish stock
2 brimming tablespoonfuls tomato sauce
1 teaspoonful onion juice
salt and pepper to taste
a dash of cayenne
1 tablespoonful white wine

Melt the butter, add the flour, and stir over moderate heat until cooked and just beginning to brown lightly. Add the stock, a little at a time, and stir until smooth, then return to the fire and stir until it boils. Put in the onion juice and tomato sauce, and season to taste with salt and pepper. Bring to the boil again, and strain into a clean saucepan. Stir in the wine and keep hot by standing in a pan of boiling water, with a wet cloth to cover.

This is a nice sauce to serve with boiled or steamed fish. Arrange the slices of fish in a hot dish, and pour the hot sauce over. The bone and skin should be removed from the fish first.

If brown stock is substituted for the fish stock, and the butter and flour allowed to brown well, other directions being the same, this makes a good sauce for fried meat dishes, with or without the addition of a little mixed herbs.

502 Anchovy Sauce

½ oz. butter
1 oz. flour
pepper
salt
½ pint milk or stock
a teaspoonful anchovy essence

Make the sauce as directed in Recipe 534 and just before taking it off the fire mix in the anchovy essence.

503 Apple Sauce

½ lb. apples
½ teacup water
1 tablespoonful soft sugar
1 oz. butter

Choose sharp, greenish apples for making sauce. Pare, core and slice the apples using a silver knife to prevent discoloration. Put them into a saucepan with the water and stew slowly until reduced to a pulp, stirring frequently with a wooden spoon. Add the butter and sugar and mash until smooth. Serve hot. This sauce is a nice accompaniment to roast pork, roast duck, and roast goose.

504 Bread Sauce

½ pint milk
2 oz. bread
½ oz. butter
1 Bombay onion
pepper
salt

Mince the onion and boil it in the milk for 15 minutes, strain the milk over the bread and beat it up with a fork, add the seasonings and butter and simmer slowly for 10 minutes. This sauce is specially good with roast birds of any kind.

505 Brown Sauce

1 tablespoonful each of butter and sieved flour
1 teaspoonful finely-chopped onion
½ pint brown stock
salt
pepper

Melt the butter, fry the onion in it quickly until browned, then stir in the flour and cook over a low flame until it bubbles well. Remove from the fire and stir in the stock a little at a time, mixing until quite smooth. Return to gentle heat and cook slowly, stirring all the time, until it thickens well. Strain before use, and season to taste.

Brown sauce is the basis of many savoury sauces, although it may be used plain for less elaborate dishes. It is important that the butter, onion and flour should all brown well in their turn, or the finished sauce will be pale in colour, and will look and taste insipid. On the quality of the stock used depends the richness or otherwise of the flavour. Stock prepared without the proper addition of flavouring vegetables—onion, carrot and turnip, celery, parsley, etc.—has no flavour to recommend it. Certain spices may be added with advantage, especially when the sauce is to be further enriched with wine.

506 Brown Gravy I—for Roast Meat, etc.

Pour away the fat from the baking tin, retaining the brown sediment, to which add a small quantity of boiling water or stock, and a seasoning of pepper and salt. Boil up and strain over the joint.

507 Brown Gravy II —for Roast Game, Poultry, etc.

Pour away the fat from the baking tin, add a teaspoonful of flour, half a pint of stock, pepper and salt. Let it boil for about 10 minutes, strain, add a dessertspoon of Worcester sauce and serve.

508 Browning for Soups, Gravies, etc.

¼ sugar **½ pint water**

Put the sugar with just a little water into a small saucepan and stir until the sugar melts and turns brown, then add the remaining water, let it boil, and bottle when cold.

509 Cheese Sauce

½ pint white sauce
½ oz. butter
2 tablespoonfuls grated cheese

Make half a pint of white sauce (Recipe 534), and just before taking it off the fire stir in the cheese and butter.

510 Chilli Sauce

1 teaspoonful butter
1 teaspoonful finely-chopped green chillies
¼ pint brown sauce
1 small red onion finely chopped
strips of green chilli

Melt the butter, and fry the chopped chillies and onion in it until browned, taking care not to let them burn. Now add the sauce and stir over a low flame until very hot but not boiling. Strain, and pour over the meat or boiled fish, for which this sauce is particularly recommended, garnishing with strips of green chilli.

N.B. For dry **beef** or **mutton** mince, beef croquettes, thick slices of meat cut from a cold joint and lightly fried in butter or dripping, and boiled or steamed **fish**.

511 Chilli Vinegar

25 ripe chillies or dry chillies
garlic and green ginger to taste
¼ pint vinegar
sugar
salt

Grind the chillies, garlic and ginger finely in vinegar, mix with the remaining vinegar and add sugar and salt to taste.

512 Devilled Paste

2 teaspoons mustard
2 teaspoons chutney
½ oz. butter
1 teaspoon chilli vinegar
cayenne
salt
a squeeze of lime juice

Chop the chutney finely, if there are pieces, and then mix all the ingredients together to a smooth paste. Serve with grilled steak, kidney, etc.

513 Egg Sauce

4 eggs
1 oz. dripping
2 ripe chillies (sliced)
salt
1 tablespoonful sliced red onions
2 teaspoons vinegar

Beat up the eggs and add the vinegar and salt. Fry the onions and chillies in dripping, turn in the egg, and stir well for a few minutes.

514 Fennel Sauce

2 oz. butter
1 dessertspoonful flour
½ pint boiling water
salt
1 dessertspoonful chopped fennel

Mix the flour to a smooth paste with a little cold water, and stir into it the boiling water. Add a pinch of salt and stir the sauce over the fire until it boils, then add the butter and fennel and stir for another minute or two. This sauce is specially good with **fish**.

515 Lemon Butter

butter **cayenne pepper** **strained lime juice**

Put the butter on a plate, and work well with the blade of a knife until soft, then add lime juice to give a pronounced flavour. Tilt the plate to allow surplus juice to run off, add the cayenne and mix in well, then shape into a flat square. Put to chill until very firm, then take off in curls with a butter-curler. Arrange on a small block of ice as soon as each curl is made, to keep firm, and hand separately with any grilled **fish** or put a couple of curls on top of each section of the fish and serve at once.

516 Lime Sauce

juice of 2 limes
1 dessertspoonful of sliced red onions
2 or 3 ripe chillies (sliced)
1 dessertspoon Worcester sauce
salt

Mix all the ingredients together. Serve with roast pork, roast beef, etc.

517 Mayonnaise Sauce

1 teaspoonful each
mustard (powder)
fine salt
icing sugar
the yolks of 2 fresh eggs
2 scant tablespoonfuls each of malt vinegar and strained lime juice
a good pinch of powdered red chillies sieved to remove the coarse grains
¾ pint olive oil
crushed ice

Stand a bowl in a larger bowl of crushed ice, mix the mustard and sugar in the bowl, and stir in the yolks of eggs and half of the vinegar. Mix well with a wooden spoon until quite smooth, then add the olive oil—which should be ice-cold—drop by drop, stirring all the time. When about 2 tablespoonfuls of the oil have been added the mixture should be thickening nicely, and at this stage a rotary egg-beater should be used, and the oil may be added a teaspoonful at a time until half of it has been used up. Whisking must be continuous. Add the lime juice and vinegar alternately with the oil, a teaspoonful at a time, until both have been used up, then continue with the oil until finished. Shake off surplus sauce from the beater, and stir in the salt and chilli, using a clean wooden spoon for this final mixing, and stirring with a gentle movement. Turn into a clean, dry jar, cover with waxed paper, and then close down securely with the lid. Packed thus, this mayonnaise will keep for ten days in the refrigerator, requiring only to be stirred gently before use.

518 Melted Butter Sauce

2 oz. fresh butter
salt
pepper
1 teaspoonful lime juice

Put the butter into a saucepan with a pinch of salt and pepper, and stir it over a slow fire until melted. Add the lime juice and serve hot in a sauce-boat.

This is served with fish, asparagus, etc.

519 Mint Sauce

1 tablespoonful chopped mint
¼ pint vinegar
pepper and salt
sugar

Wash the mint well, strip the leaves from the stalks, and mince them finely. Put into a sauce-boat or tureen, add the vinegar, sugar, pepper and salt to taste, and stir until the sugar is dissolved. Make about an hour before it is wanted.

520 Mushroom Sauce I

1 medium sized tin black mushrooms
2 level teaspoonfuls each of sieved flour and butter
black pepper and salt to taste
1 saltspoonful mustard powder
3 red onions
½ wineglassful white wine

Drain the liquor from the tin and cut the mushrooms into quarters. Chop the onions very small, and fry in the butter until cooked but not browned, lifting the pan off the flame occasionally to prevent burning the butter. Strain, and return the butter to the pan, stir in the flour and cook for a few minutes until of a nice colour, then add the mushroom liquor and stir until smooth, allowing to come to the boil slowly. Mix in the mushrooms and onions, the seasonings to taste—pepper and mustard should be rather pronounced, and, if liked, a good pinch of powdered dried chillies may be added at the same time—and allow to simmer gently for about five minutes, or until the flour is quite cooked.

Keep hot until ready to serve, and add the wine just before turning into the hot sauce-boat.

This sauce is usually served with boiled or steamed fish, but it is an excellent accompaniment to grilled chops, steak and sausages.

521 Mushroom Sauce II

1 small tin black mushrooms
1 teaspoonful melted butter
½ pint brown sauce

Chop the mushrooms into rather coarse pieces, and fry until heated through in the butter. Add the sauce, and thin down slightly with a little of the liquor from the tin.

522 Mustard

Put a dessertspoonful of dry mustard into a cup and mix it into a smooth paste with a little cold water. Add a teaspoon of vinegar, and a pinch each of sugar and salt. Or, if preferred, the vinegar and sugar may be omitted.

523 Country Mustard

1 tablespoonful mustard seed
¾ teacup vinegar
2 cloves garlic
a thick slice of green ginger
1 teaspoonful sugar
a pinch of salt

Grind the mustard seed, garlic and ginger with a little of the vinegar. Put the ground ingredients into a cup, add the sugar and salt and mix in the remaining vinegar.

N.B. A couple of dry chillies can be ground with the other ingredients if liked.

524 Mustard Sauce

1 oz. butter
½ oz. flour
1 teaspoonful mustard
1 teaspoon vinegar
½ pint boiling water

Melt the butter, stir in the flour smoothly, add the water and bring it to the boil, stirring it well to keep it smooth, then add the mustard and vinegar and mix well together.

Serve with fish.

525 Onion Sauce for Fish

½ lb. Bombay onions
1 oz. dripping
¼ pint vinegar
pepper and salt

Peel and slice the onions, heat the dripping, put in the onions and let them cook for a few minutes—the onions must not fry—then add the vinegar and seasonings and let it simmer slowly until the vinegar boils.

526 Papaw Sauce

½ lb. papaw
½ teacup vinegar
½ teacup water
1 dessertspoonful soft sugar
salt

The papaw must be ripe but not too ripe. Peel it, cut it in pieces and remove the seeds. Then weigh the fruit and put it into a saucepan with the vinegar and water and boil slowly until reduced to a pulp, stirring frequently with a wooden spoon. Add the sugar and a pinch of salt and mash until smooth.

527 Parsley Sauce

½ pint white sauce
1 dessertspoonful chopped parsley

Make half a pint of White Sauce (Recipe 534) and just before taking it off the fire add the parsley.

528 Spiced Pineapple

Cut 3 slices from a large pineapple, each about ¼ inch thick. Remove the core, and dice the fruit very small. Put into a saucepan with just enough water, or the juice which runs out when cutting up, to prevent it from burning, and add brown sugar to taste. Simmer until the fruit is soft and pulpy, then add an inch of cinnamon, 4 cloves, a few strips of thinly peeled rind of lime, and a good pinch of grated nutmeg. Boil up rapidly, stirring all the time, then allow to simmer gently again until nicely flavoured. Remove the rind, cinnamon, and cloves, stir well, and serve as an accompaniment to Roast Pork, Pork Chops, or Fillet of Beef.

529 Sauce a la Diable

1 teaspoonful each of made mustard, chilli vinegar, mango chutney and thick tomato sauce
1 dessertspoonful each of mushroom ketchup and sherry
¼ pint thick brown sauce

Put the sauce into a small pan, and stand in a larger pan of boiling water. Add the rest of the ingredients one at a time, stirring well between each addition. Stir over a low flame until almost boiling then strain and use as required.

530 Sauce Robert

1 wineglassful white wine
1 teaspoonful made mustard
the juice extracted from 1 large onion
½ pint brown sauce

Mix the mustard with the sauce, warming it slightly first by standing in a pan of boiling water. Add the onion juice (about 1 scant teaspoonful) and then the wine. Stir over a low flame until heated through.

This is an excellent accompaniment to grilled cutlets, roast duck, fried or boiled fish, and fried chicken. Used sparingly, just enough to coat them, it is also a tasty sauce for serving with a macedoine of vegetables—peas, carrots, turnips and potatoes—the garnish being finely-chopped parsley sprinkled over.

531 Tartare Sauce

to every ½ pint mayonnaise sauce allow 1 tablespoonful finely chopped red onion
1 dessertspoonful each of finely chopped pickled gherkins and olives
1 tablespoonful halved capers
a pinch of cayenne pepper or powdered red chillies
a dash of white pepper
1 teaspoonful of the liquid from the gherkins

Mix all the ingredients together in a small bowl, and chill thoroughly before serving.

Tartare Sauce is an excellent accompaniment to fried or grilled fish. It may also be used as a topping for grilled fillet of beef fried or grilled sausages, and Viennese steak. For meat dishes omit the gherkin liquor, and chill the mixture until firm, then put a good teaspoonful on top of each piece of meat or sausage and serve at once before the heat causes the sauce to melt.

532 Tomato Sauce

½ lb. ripe tomatoes
1 teaspoon lime juice
1 tablespoon chilli vinegar
salt

Scald the tomatoes and cut them in slices, add a little water and boil until the fruit is soft. Then add the chilli vinegar, lime juice and a little salt. Stir well together, and, if the sauce is too thick, mix in a little vinegar.

533 Tomato Sauce for Fish

½ lb. tomatoes
1 Bombay onion
½ oz. butter
1 teacup water
pepper and salt
1½ oz. cornflour

Melt the butter in a stewpan, chop the onion and fry it. Then add the tomatoes peeled and cut in slices, and the water. Season to taste with pepper and salt and simmer slowly until the tomatoes are quite soft, stirring occasionally. Mix the cornflour to a smooth paste with a little cold water, add it to the rest of the ingredients and cook for a couple of minutes stirring all the time.

534 White Sauce

½ oz. butter
1 oz. flour
½ pint milk or stock
pepper and salt

Mix the flour to a smooth paste with a little of the milk. Bring the rest of the milk to the boil, mix in the flour, add the butter and seasonings and let it cook gently for a few minutes until the flour is boiled, stirring all the time.

N.B. If liked, cornflour could be used instead of ordinary flour. This sauce is the foundation of many kinds of sauces.

Puddings and Cold Sweets

PUDDINGS play an important part in the daily menu, for no dinner is complete without a pudding. This Chapter includes a representative selection of recipes for various kinds of puddings, cold sweets and jellies arranged as follows:

- Baked Puddings
- Boiled and Steamed Puddings
- Cold Sweets
- Fritters
- Souffles and Sweet Omelettes
- Sweet Sauces

Baked Puddings

General Hints

Before beginning to mix the pudding see that the oven will be sufficiently hot by the time the pudding is ready for it.

Then get ready the pie-dish or baking tin in which the pudding is to be baked. The dish should be well greased with butter or dripping, or it is sometimes lined with pastry. To line a dish with pastry see under *Sweet Dishes with Pastry* in Chapter on Pastry and Pastry Cakes.

Puddings which are baked require more liquid than puddings which are boiled or steamed.

Custard Puddings require a very moderate oven. The dish should be placed in a baking tin with a little cold water round it. The water in the tin will prevent the custard becoming too hot and the eggs curdling.

Puddings with pastry will require a hot oven. If the pastry should brown before the pudding is sufficiently cooked, cover with a piece of white paper.

Puddings containing baking powder should be put into the oven directly they are ready and not allowed to stand.

If the pudding has to be sent to table in the dish in which it has been baked, a pie-dish collar or paper frill should be put round it.

541 Apple Charlotte

6 large, firm, green-skinned apples
1 inch cinnamon
the grated rind of 1 small lime
a few drops of lime juice
3 oz. fine brown sugar
1 oz. butter
little water
thin slices of bread dipped in melted butter to line the bottom and sides of the baking dish
if a very crisp covering is preferred, the bread should first be fried in hot oil, drained and then lightly buttered on both sides

Peel and core the apples, and slice them thinly. Put into a saucepan with the sugar and two scant tablespoonfuls water. Cook until the fruit is tender, then add the grated rind of the lime and the cinnamon, and finish cooking until reduced to a soft pulp. Prepare the dish by buttering lightly and fixing the bread all round the sides and at the bottom so that it is entirely covered. Remove the cinnamon from the apples, stir in the ounce of butter, and mix well. Turn into the prepared dish, cover with a round of buttered greaseproof paper, and bake in a quick oven for ten minutes, then reduce the heat and cook for another fifteen or twenty minutes. Turn out on to a hot dish, and hand cream separately.

542 Baked Chocolate Pudding

2 tablespoonfuls cornflour
4 oz. grated chocolate
3 tablespoonfuls sugar
1 pint milk
3 eggs
vanilla flavouring

Mix the cornflour to a smooth paste with a little of the milk. Put the remainder of the milk into a saucepan and bring to boiling point. Remove the saucepan from the fire and pour the mixed cornflour into it, stirring vigorously. Return the saucepan to the fire and let it boil for 5 minutes, stirring all the time. Then add the chocolate and sugar and stir until it is perfectly smooth. Let the mixture cool a little, then stir in the eggs well beaten and the flavouring. Pour into a greased pie-dish and bake in a moderate oven for about half an hour. Turn out and serve with Raspberry or Custard Sauce.

543 Baked Cornflour Pudding

2 oz. cornflour
2 breakfastcups milk
3 oz. sugar
1 oz. butter
3 eggs
lemon flavouring
a pinch of salt

Mix the cornflour smoothly with a little of the milk. Boil the remainder of the milk, remove the saucepan from the fire and pour the mixed cornflour into it, stirring all the time. Add the butter and flavouring. Return the saucepan to the fire, bring to the boil, stirring well, and boil for 3 or 4 mintues. Let the mixture cool a little, then stir in the yolks of eggs and sugar well beaten together.

Lastly, stir in the whites of eggs beaten to a stiff froth with a pinch of salt. Pour the mixture into a greased pie-dish and bake in a moderate oven until nicely browned. Sprinkle with sugar and serve hot.

544 Baked Custard Pudding

4 or 5 eggs
flavouring to taste
¾ pint milk
1 tablespoonful sugar
a pinch of salt

Beat the eggs and sugar together, add the salt, and flavour with nutmeg, chopped lime-rind, or any flavouring which may be preferred. Heat the milk and pour it slowly on the egg mixture, stirring all the time. Pour into a buttered pie-dish and bake in a moderate oven for about 40 minutes or until the custard sets and becomes a light brown colour.

545 Baked Ice Cream Pudding

1 tray ice cream
1 plain cake, similar in shape and size to the block of ice cream
4 or 5 egg whites
¾ cup sugar
salt
vanilla

The ice cream must be frozen really hard, else this will not be a success. The cake should be just a little larger all round than the block of ice cream. If the ice cream is home-made, it is advisable to line the tray with greaseproof paper, so that it will be easy to lift the ice cream out without delay.

Get a wooden board at least 1½ inches thick, pad it with two pieces of corrugated cardboard, and cover the top with greaseproof paper, in two or three thicknesses. Place the cake on this. Beat up the whites of the eggs till stiff with a pinch of salt, add the sugar and beat again till smooth. Place the ice cream on the cake, cover thickly with the meringue, making sure it is at least an inch thick all over, and leaving no space uncovered. Bake in a very hot oven till the meringue is slightly browned. Serve at once.

546 Baked Jam Pudding

6 oz. flour
2 oz. soft sugar
2 oz. butter
about a teacup of milk
yolks of 2 eggs
white of 1 egg
½ teaspoon baking powder
a pinch of salt
2 tablespoonfuls jam

Sieve the flour into a basin, mix in the baking powder and salt and rub in the butter until free from lumps. Then make a well in the centre and add the eggs well beaten and enough milk to make a thick batter. Beat well for a few minutes. Grease a pie-dish or pudding mould and put the jam at the bottom. Pour the batter over the jam and bake in a moderate oven for about one hour or until well risen and firm to the touch. When ready, turn out on a dish and serve hot.

N.B. This pudding may be steamed instead of baked.

547 Baked Plum Pudding

½ lb. flour
¼ lb. sugar
3 eggs
1 teaspoonful baking powder
3 oz. suet
2 oz. currants
2 oz. raisins
2 oz. sultanas
1 oz. ginger preserve
1 oz. candied peel
a grate of nutmeg
a pinch each of powdered cinnamon, cloves and cardamoms
a little milk

Prepare the fruit as directed in Recipe 600, and mix them in a basin with the dry ingredients. Moisten with the eggs well beaten and add enough milk to make the pudding of the consistency of a very thick batter. Put into a well-greased baking tin and bake in a moderate oven from 1 to 1¼ hours. When ready, turn it out, cut into pieces, sprinkle with sugar and serve.

548 Baked Sago Pudding

2 tablespoonfuls sago
2 tablespoonfuls sugar
1 pint milk
2 or 3 eggs
lemon flavouring
a pinch of salt

Wash the sago, put it into a saucepan with the milk and boil until it is very thick, stirring all the time. Just before taking it off the fire mix in the sugar and salt. Remove the saucepan from the fire and when the contents have cooled a little, add the yolks of eggs well beaten and the flavouring. Lastly stir in the whites of eggs beaten to a stiff froth. Pour the mixture into a greased pie-dish and bake in a moderate oven for about one hour or until the pudding is browned and set.

549 Bakewell Pudding

pastry
jam
2 oz. soft sugar
1 oz. butter
yolks of 4 eggs
white of 1 egg
1 teaspoon lime juice
vanilla flavouring

Line a pie-dish with pastry and cover the bottom of the paste with a generous layer of some nice jam. Beat the butter and sugar to a cream, then add the eggs well beaten, the lime juice and the flavouring. Stir all together until thoroughly mixed; pour this over the jam and bake in rather a quick oven for half an hour, or until the mixture is set. Dust with sugar and serve hot or cold.

N.B. Small patty pans may be used instead of a pie-dish.

550 Bread Pudding de Luxe

stale bread
1 cup thick coconut milk
3 cups thin coconut milk
4 eggs
3 oz. butter
6 oz. sugar
50 cadjunuts
¼ lb. raisins
2 oz. cherries
2 oz. ginger preserve
½ oz. candied peel
almond essence
salt

Beat the eggs well and add to the coconut milk. Soak a sufficient amount of stale bread in it to absorb the milk. Break up the soaked bread till there are no lumps, then add most of the sugar, reserving about two tablespoons for the top of the pudding. Wash and pick the raisins, and chop the candied peel, cherries, ginger preserve and cadjunuts rather coarsely. Keep half the nuts and a few raisins for the top of the pudding, and mix in the rest of the fruits and nuts. Flavour well with almond essence, mix in two ounces of the butter, a pinch of salt, and pour the mixture into a buttered dish. Sprinkle the remaining sugar, nuts and raisins on top of the pudding, and dot the remaining butter over the surface. Bake in a moderate oven for about 1½ hours, or till the pudding is a deep brown on top.

551 Bread and Butter Pudding

slices of bread and butter
sugar to taste
2 oz. sultanas
1 pint milk
2 or 3 eggs
vanilla or almond flavouring

Butter a pie-dish, put in a layer of thin bread and butter, sprinkle it with sugar and sultanas, then another layer of bread and butter, sugar and sultanas and so on until the dish is about half full. Beat up the eggs, add the milk, a little sugar or flavouring, mix well together and pour over the bread in the pie-dish. Allow the pudding to stand for about one hour until the bread is thoroughly soaked, press down the top slices so that they may get soaked too. Put into a moderate oven and bake for about 40 minutes or until nicely browned.

552 Bread and Cheese Pudding

slices of bread and butter
a breakfast cup of milk
2 or 3 eggs
sugar to taste
2 oz. grated cheese
a grate of nutmeg, if liked

Make in the same way as Bread and Butter Pudding, sprinkling the cheese between the slices of bread and butter.

553 Bread and Chocolate Pudding

6 oz. stale bread
2 or 3 oz. chocolate
¼ lb. sugar
1 pint milk
3 eggs
vanilla flavouring

Grate the chocolate and dissolve it with the milk. Bring the milk to the boil and pour it over the bread broken in small pieces, and allow to soak for about half an hour. Then beat up with a fork, adding the sugar, yolks of eggs and the flavouring. Lastly, mix in the whites of eggs beaten to a stiff froth. Pour the mixture into a greased pie-dish and bake in a moderate oven for about 30 minutes, or until set and nicely browned.

N.B. Cocoa may be used instead of chocolate, in which case more sugar will be necessary.

554 Breadfruit Pudding

half a small-sized breadfruit
1 tablespoonful flour
2 yolks of eggs
2 tablespoonfuls sugar
a grate of nutmeg
1 dessertspoon brandy
salt
a little milk, if necessary

Cut the breadfruit in pieces, remove the skin and wash well in cold water. Put the pieces into a saucepan, cover with cold water, add a little salt and boil until it is cooked. Drain off the water and mash the breadfruit. Add to it the flour, mix well and stir in the yolks of eggs well beaten and the rest of the ingredients. Mix all together and add a little milk, if necessary. Pour the mixture into a buttered pie-dish and bake in a moderate oven.

555 Brown Betty Pudding

1 lb. hard, green skinned apples
½ lb. coarse browned crumbs (crushed rusks are very good)
3 oz. demerara sugar
2 oz. butter
mixed spice and freshly ground cinnamon to taste
a good pinch of grated nutmeg
custard sauce, or cream

Peel and slice the apples thinly, then chop small. Butter a pie-dish, and mix the spices with the sugar. Soak apples in water. Put alternate layers of crumbs, apples, sugar, and small bits of butter in the dish until all have been used up. Bake in a hot oven for the first 15 minutes, then reduce the heat and allow to cook slowly until the apples are tender.

The water which clings to the apples is usually sufficient but a little more may be added, if liked moist. Serve hot with custard.

556 Chocolate Custard Pudding

Make in the same way as Baked Custard Pudding (Recipe 544) adding 2 teaspoonfuls of cocoa or grated chocolate to it.

557 Coconut Bread Pudding

¼ lb. stale bread
2 oz. grated coconut
¼ lb. sugar
1 breakfastcup milk
3 eggs
vanilla flavouring

Break the bread in small pieces and put it into a basin. Boil the milk and pour it over the bread and allow to soak for half an hour. Then beat it up with a fork, add the coconut, and the yolks of eggs, sugar, and flavouring beaten together. Lastly, stir in the whites of eggs beaten to a stiff froth. Pour into a greased pie-dish and bake in a moderate oven for about 40 minutes or until nicely browned. Turn out of the dish, sprinkle over with sugar and serve.

558 Coconut Custard Pudding

1½ teacupfuls finely grated coconut
2 teacups milk
2 tablespoonfuls sugar
3 eggs
vanilla flavouring
a pinch of salt

Soak the coconut in the milk for half an hour, then mix in the sugar, flavouring, salt and the eggs well beaten. Pour into a greased pie-dish and bake in a moderate oven until firm to the touch and lightly browned. The pudding should be stirred up once or twice towards the beginning of the baking to prevent the coconut settling at the bottom of the dish.

N.B. If liked, the pie-dish may be lined with pastry before putting in the pudding mixture.

559 Coffee Meringue Pudding

1 rounded dessertspoonful cornflour
2 gills milk
1 gill strong black coffee
2 eggs
1½ oz. sugar
1 oz. butter
a little rum for flavouring
1 small apricot jam sponge sandwich
2 level tablespoonfuls castor sugar

Mix the cornflour with a little of the cold milk and heat the rest. Beat the yolks of eggs with the sugar, and stir in the hot milk. Return to the saucepan, stir in the cornflour and coffee, and cook over gentle heat, stirring all the time, until smooth and thickened. Stir in the rum and butter.

Pour a little in the bottom of a glass baking dish, put the cake in the centre, and pour the rest of the custard over. Allow to cool.

Whisk the whites of the eggs to a very stiff froth, stir in the castor sugar, and whisk again until thick and glossy. Spread over the top with the blade of a knife, and pipe the rest of the mixture round the edge. Bake in a moderate oven until the meringue is very lightly browned and set. Serve hot or cold.

560 Cup Pudding

2 oz. butter
2 oz. flour
¼ teaspoon baking powder
2 oz. soft sugar
3 eggs
flavouring
apricot jam

Beat the butter to a cream, add the sugar and then the flour and eggs by degrees, and keep beating the mixture until light and frothy. Flavour to taste with chopped lime-rind. Butter some small cups or tins, half fill them with the mixture and bake in a moderate oven until nicely browned and firm to the touch. Turn out and serve with a little Apricot Jam on the top of each, and custard sauce.

561 Currant Tart

short crust
currants
castor sugar
mixed spice
some finely powdered cardamoms and cinnamon
grated nutmeg
(all fresh spices sieved together)

Line an aluminium plate with the short crust rolled out rather thin. Wash and pick the currants and sprinkle them all over the paste in a thick layer right up to the edge. Colour the sugar with the mixed spice and add the fresh spices to give a more pronounced flavour, and sprinkle over the currants. The currants should be left moist and a few drops of water may be sprinkled over the sugar to give added moisture. Cover with another layer of paste, rolled out very thin and press the edges together. Crimp all round the edge with a fork, and snip the paste with scissors in neat lines all over the rest of the covering. Bake in a quick oven until the pastry is cooked. The top may be glazed with beaten egg to improve the appearance of the tart. Serve hot or cold.

562 Devonshire Pudding

4 apples
2 tablespoonfuls butter
castor sugar to sweeten
grated rind of half a lime
3 tablespoonfuls halved stoned raisins
4 oz. breadcrumbs
2 eggs
cream or custard

Bake the apples until very soft, remove all the pulp and beat this in a basin until smooth. Add the butter, and enough castor sugar to sweeten the finished pudding—about 4 level tablespoonfuls, but this depends on the sweetness of the apples.

Beat the eggs well, add the breadcrumbs and the prepared fruit, then the rind of lime and raisins. Beat all well together with a wooden spoon, turn into a buttered pie-dish, and bake in a hot oven for 15 minutes. Serve hot, with cream or custard.

563 Fig Pudding

stewed figs
2 oz. butter
2 oz. flour
2 oz. soft sugar
3 eggs
a pinch of salt
¼ teaspoon baking powder

Beat the butter and sugar to a cream, add the eggs, and lastly the flour with baking powder mixed in it. Butter a shallow pie-dish and put some stewed figs at the bottom. Pour the batter on the top and bake in a moderate oven for about half an hour or until nicely browned and well risen. Sprinkle with sugar and serve hot.

564 Lemon Delight

2 tablespoons butter
1 cup sugar
3 eggs
2 heaped tablespoons flour
1 level tea spoon baking powder
1 cup milk
juice and grated rind of a lemon or 2 ripe limes

Cream the butter and sugar till soft and light, and add the unbeaten egg yolks one by one, beating for five minutes after each addition. Sift the flour and baking powder together twice or thrice, then add in spoonfuls to the creamed mixture. Gradually add the milk, stirring well all the time to prevent lumps forming. Now add the juice and grated rind of the lemon or limes, mix well, and, last of all, stir in very lightly the stiffly beaten whites of the eggs. Pile the mixture into a well buttered baking dish and place this in a tin of cold water.

Bake in a moderate oven for 40 minutes or till the top is delicately browned.

565 Macaroni and Cheese Pudding

2 oz. macaroni
1 oz. grated cheese
2 tablespoonfuls sugar
1 teacup milk
a little butter

Make in the same way as Macaroni Pudding, adding the grated cheese to it. Pour the mixture into a greased pie-dish, sprinkle over with some grated cheese, put some small pieces of butter here and there on the top, and bake in a moderate oven until delicately browned.

566 Macaroni Pudding

3 oz. macaroni
1 pint milk
2 tablespoonfuls sugar
2 eggs
a grate of nutmeg
a pinch of salt

Break the macaroni in short lengths and throw it into a saucepan of boiling water. Allow it to cook until quite tender, then drain off the water. Add the milk to the macaroni and boil until the milk is almost absorbed, strring all the time. Remove the saucepan from the fire, add the sugar, salt, and nutmeg, and lastly the eggs well beaten. Pour the mixture into a greased pie-dish and bake in a moderate oven until nicely browned.

567 Meringue Tartlets

short crust (Recipe 1353)
pineapple jam
the white of one large egg
level dessertspoonful castor sugar
a few drops of lime juice
the yolk of the egg beaten with a few drops cold water

Make the pastry, and cut out into 12 rounds not more than 2½ inches in diameter and ¼ inch thick. From six of these cut out an inner round leaving a ring about ¼ inch wide all round, or a trifle less. Place the rounds on a floured tin, and brush all round the outer edge with beaten egg, then press the rings on lightly keeping them neatly in position. Brush over the tops with beaten egg and bake in a quick oven.

Have ready a meringue mixture, made by whisking the white of egg to a very stiff froth, adding the castor sugar and whisking again until very smooth and glossy. Mix a few drops of lime juice with the jam, put a spoonful into each pastry case, and cover with the meringue, pressing it down into the cavity with the back of a teaspoon. Pipe a small rose of the same mixture in the centre, and return to the hot oven just long enough to set and colour the meringue—placing the tin just under the browning shelf for this purpose.

568 Pineapple Custard

stewed pineapple flavoured with cloves and cinnamon (about 3 thick slices, cut into quarters, will be sufficient)
3 eggs
½ pint milk
1 level tablespoonful castor sugar
a few drops of vanilla essence and an extra dessertspoonful of the sugar for the decoration

Place the pineapple in the bottom of a glass baking dish arranging it neatly, and reserving one section for garnishing.

Beat the yolks of the eggs in a basin with the sugar, heat the milk and pour over it stirring well to mix. Return to the saucepan used for the milk and stir over gentle heat until just warmed through again, then pour over the pineapple and bake in a very slow oven until set. Allow to chill thoroughly. Meanwhile, whisk the whites of the eggs until stiff, add the sugar and whisk again until very thick and glossy. Pile up the mixture in rough, uneven cones on top of the custard and place thin slices of the fruit at intervals round the dish. Chill until required.

If a hot pudding is preferred, proceed as directed above, placing the meringue mixture on the custard as soon as it is cooked. Return to the oven until lightly browned on top and serve at once. The heat of the oven must be increased before the decorated pudding is put in or the meringue will be tough instead of light and frothy.

569 Pineapple Meringue Pie

1 oz. short crust pastry
2 tablespoons jam
1 pineapple, sliced
3 eggs
4 oz. sugar

Line a pie dish with the pastry, and flute the edge. Spread the jam over the pastry. Remove all traces of skin, "eyes", and centre stalk from the slices of pineapple and arrange a layer of them over the jam . Sprinkle with sugar. Arrange another layer of pineapple slices, and sprinkle with more sugar. Bake in a hot oven till the pastry is light brown in colour, then top the pie with a meringue made from the whites of the eggs and 2 oz. sugar. Bake till the top is delicately browned. Serve hot with a custard made from the yolks of the eggs.

570 Pineapple Pudding

1 medium-sized ripe pineapple	**2 oz. sultanas**
sugar	**2 oz. powdered rusks**
	whites of 2 eggs

Peel and cut the pineapple lengthwise in about 14 pieces. Arrange a layer of them in a pie-dish, dust over with sugar, lay on a few sultanas and sprinkle some of the powdered rusk over them. Then put in another layer of pineapple with sugar, sultanas and powdered rusk. Use up all the fruit arranging in layers. Whip up the whites of eggs to a stiff froth, add a tablespoonful of sugar and pile this meringue on the top of the pudding. Bake in rather a cool oven until lightly browned and firm to the touch.

571 Potato Pudding

½ lb. potatoes	**½ teaspoon baking powder**
3 oz. soft sugar	**¼ teaspoon chopped lime-rind**
2 oz. butter	**a pinch of salt**
½ teacup milk	**2 tablespoonfuls jam or marmalade**
3 eggs	

Boil or steam the potatoes and mash them perfectly smooth. Mix in the butter, sugar, salt, baking powder, lime-rind, the eggs well beaten and the milk. Put the jam or marmalade into a greased pie-dish, pour the potato mixture on the top of it and bake in a moderate oven for about half an hour.

572 Queen of Puddings

¼ lb. grated bread	**3 eggs**
2 oz. sugar	**a grate of nutmeg**
1 oz. butter	**a few drops of lime juice**
1 pint milk	**jam**

Mix the bread, butter and half the sugar together and add the nutmeg or any other flavouring which may be preferred. Bring the milk nearly to the boil and pour it over the bread mixture and allow to soak for a few minutes. Then stir in the yolks of the eggs, put the mixture into a buttered pie-dish and bake in a moderate oven for about 30 minutes. Let it cool, then spread a thick layer of jam on the top. Beat the whites of the eggs to a stiff froth, add the remainder of the sugar and a few drops of lime juice and pile on top of the pudding. Return to the oven until crisp and lightly browned.

573 Rice Pudding

1 teacup boiled table rice	**2 eggs**
1 breakfastcup milk	**a grate of nutmeg**
1½ tablespoons sugar	**a pinch of salt**

Mix the rice with the milk, add the sugar, salt, nutmeg, and the yolks of eggs well beaten. Lastly, stir in the whites of eggs beaten to a stiff froth. Pour the mixture into a well-greased pie-dish and bake for about half an hour in a moderate oven.

574 Sponge Cake Pudding

pastry
6 small sponge cakes
2 tablespoonfuls jam
2 tablespoons wine or brandy
1½ tablespoons sugar
1 breakfastcup milk
2 eggs
almond flavouring

Line a pie-dish with pastry. Cover the bottom of the paste with a layer of jam, over which place the sponge cakes cut in slices Pour over them the wine or brandy and allow to soak. Meanwhile, make a custard with the milk, eggs, sugar and flavouring and pour it over the sponge cakes. Bake in a moderate oven for about 40 minutes.

575 Tapioca Pudding

Make in the same way as Sago Pudding (Recipe 548).

Boiled and Steamed Puddings

Some Preliminaries

Preparations of Moulds and Basins—See that the mould or basin in which the pudding is to be cooked is perfectly dry before being greased. Then grease it with fresh butter or dripping. The mould is sometimes decorated with raisins, almonds or preserved fruits. Have the mould ready before beginning to mix the pudding.

To Chop Suet—Either beef or mutton suet may be used for puddings, but beef suet is generally preferred. Remove all skin and fibre from it, place it on a chopping board and shred it finely with a knife. Sprinkle it liberally with flour (taken from the quantity given in the recipe), and then chop it very finely with a knife.

How to Boil a Pudding— A pudding mixture can either be boiled in a mould covered with a cloth, or in a floured and scalded cloth only. When a basin is used it must be well greased, and the mixture should fill it, or the water will get into it and the pudding be spoiled. If a larger basin has to be used than can be filled with the mixture, it should be filled up with a round of bread, which is afterwards removed. Tie over it securely a cloth that has been wrung out of boiling water and sprinkled with flour. If no basin is used and the pudding is cooked in a floured and scalded cloth, a small saucer or plate should be put under the pudding to keep it from sticking to the pan. Plunge the pudding into a saucepan of fast-boiling water—there must be sufficient water to completely cover it—and boil steadily until the pudding is cooked; as the water boils away more boiling water must be added. Light puddings should be gently boiled and solid puddings boiled fast.

How to Steam a Pudding—Put the pudding mixture into a mould (it should not fill more than three-quarters) and cover the top of the mould with a piece of greased paper, then set it in a saucepan of boiling water reaching half-way up the mould, cover the saucepan and keep the water at simmering point until the pudding is cooked. If the water boils away more boiling water must be added.

How to Turn out a Pudding—Puddings should stand a few minutes in the mould or basin in which they were cooked before being turned out, in order that some of the steam may escape. If turned out too quickly they are liable to crack. Remove the cloth or paper from the top, beat the sides of the mould with the palms of the hands and shake it gently. It should then come out easily. If there is any difficulty in turning the pudding out, it may be dipped into a pan of cold water for an instant before the cloth or paper is removed.

591 Amber Pudding

6 oz. grated bread
2 oz. flour
3 oz. suet
¼ lb. sugar
2 tablespoons golden syrup
1 teaspoonful baking powder
1 dessertspoonful chopped candied peel
a grate of nutmeg
a pinch of salt
4 eggs
a little milk, if necessary

Mix all the dry ingredients together in a basin, add the eggs well beaten and mix together adding a little milk, if necessary. Pour the mixture into a well-greased mould and steam slowly for 1½ hours. Turn out and serve at once with Syrup Sauce (Recipe 723)

592 Boiled Apple Pudding

For the CRUST :
3 oz. finely shredded suet
6 oz. flour
1 level teaspoonful baking powder
1 saltspoonful salt
water

1 lb. firm, green-skinned apples
3 tablespoonfuls brown sugar
the juice of half a lime
mixed spice to taste
water
butter

Peel and slice the apples, and cover with cold water. Sieve the flour and baking powder together twice, add the salt and suet, and mix well, then add enough cold water to mix to a fairly stiff paste. Roll out on a lightly-floured board to about ¼ inch thickness, and use for lining a small, well-buttered pudding basin. Save the scraps of paste for the top. These must be gathered up, lightly kneaded together, and rolled out to a round to fit to the edge of the basin.

Put a layer of apple at the bottom of the prepared basin, cover with sugar and a dusting of spice, repeat until all the apples are used up, but do not put sugar or spice on top of the last layer. Pour in enough water to come a little less than half way up the basin, moisten the top edges of the paste, and press the cover of paste on top so that it joins on well to the lining, and comes to the edge of the basin. Cover with a large piece of buttered grease-proof paper, tied round the top of the basin but fitting very loosely over the top to allow plenty of space for the crust to rise to its full height. Steam for about 2 hours, keeping a kettle of boiling water handy to replenish the water at the bottom of the pan as it boils away.

593 Boiled Batter Pudding

3 oz. flour
2 oz. sugar
1 oz. butter
1 pint milk
3 eggs
½ teaspoon baking powder
a pinch of salt

Beat the butter and sugar to a cream, mix the baking powder with the flour, add them gradually, and the eggs without beating them. Then add the milk by degrees, and the salt, and beat well until the batter is full of air bubbles. Pour into a buttered basin, tie a floured and scalded cloth over the top and plunge the pudding into a saucepan of fast-boiling. water. Move the basin about for a few minutes to prevent the flour settling in any part. When done, turn it out of the basin and serve with wine or any sweet sauce. It must boil for 1¼ hours.

N.B. This pudding may be steamed instead of boiled.

594 Cabinet Pudding

a few slices of bread and butter
sugar
½ pint milk
2 eggs
2 oz. sultanas
almond or vanilla flavouring

Butter a pudding mould and decorate the inside with sultanas. Cut the crusts off the bread, then cut it in small squares. Arrange a layer of bread in the prepared mould, sprinkle with sultanas and sugar, then a layer of bread again with sultanas and sugar until the mould is half full. Beat up the eggs, add the milk and flavouring and a little sugar, mix all well together, pour it over the bread and let it stand for half an hour, so as to soak the bread thoroughly. Cover the pudding with a piece of buttered paper and steam very slowly for one hour. Turn it out of the mould and serve with Custard or Jam Sauce.

N.B. If a richer pudding is wanted, sponge cake can be used instead of bread and butter, and preserved fruits, almonds etc. added to it. The custard can also be made richer by adding more eggs, and a little wine or liqueur may be used for flavouring.

595 Canary Pudding

the weight of two large eggs in butter, castor sugar and flour
1 heaped teaspoonful baking powder
grated rind of 1 small orange and a teaspoonful of the juice
glace cherries and butter for the moulds
raspberry jam sauce
greased paper to fit steamer

Beat the butter and eggs together in a bowl until thick and creamy, and of a pale colour. Sieve the flour twice, and crush any lumps there may be in the baking powder. Beat the eggs well. Have the small moulds ready, well buttered, and with a glace cherry stuck into the centre bottom of each mould. See that the steamer is ready with boiling water, as the puddings must not stand after mixing.

Add the beaten eggs, a little at a time, to the creamed mixture, and beat well between each addition until all are used up. Now add the flour, a spoonful at a time, and beat in thoroughly until the mixture has a light, bubbly appearance. Stir in the baking powder, and three-quarter fill each mould. Place in the steamer, cover with the paper, and cook until well risen and spongy to the touch. Turn out on to a hot dish, and pour the warm sauce over each. Serve at once.

596 Caramel Pudding

CARAMEL:

3 tablespoonfuls sugar
3 tablespoons cold water

CUSTARD:

4 or 5 eggs
¾ pint milk
1 teaspoonful sugar
vanilla flavouring
a pinch of salt

Put the sugar and water into a saucepan and boil quickly, without stirring, until it assumes a pale coffee colour, then stir it well. Warm a plain mould, pour in the caramel and keep turning it round and round until the interior is completely coated with the caramel which will become hard almost immediately. Now make the custard. Beat the eggs and to them add the sugar, flavouring and salt. Heat the milk and pour it slowly over the egg mixture, stirring all the time. Then pour the custard very carefully into the prepared mould, cover with buttered paper and steam very gently for an hour, when it should set. Let it stand a few minutes before turning it out. The caramel will form a sauce round and over the pudding. It can be served hot or cold.

597 Chocolate Caramel Pudding

Make in the same way as Caramel Pudding (Recipe 596), adding 1 oz. chocolate or cocoa to the custard.

598 Chocolate Pudding I

1 oz. cocoa
3 tablespoonfuls sugar
1 pint milk
6 eggs
vanilla flavouring
2 tablespoons boiling water

Mix the cocoa smoothy with the water, add the milk which must be boiling, the flavouring, the sugar and the eggs well beaten. Mix thoroughly, pour the mixture into a well-greased mould, cover with greased paper and steam slowly for half an hour.

599 Chocolate Pudding II

¼ lb. chocolate
¼ lb. sugar
¼ lb. flour
¼ lb. butter
3 eggs
1 teacup milk
½ teaspoon baking powder
vanilla flavouring

Grate the chocolate and put it into a saucepan with the milk. It must be stirred until perfectly smooth and then allowed to cool. Beat the butter and sugar to a cream and mix in the dissolved chocolate. Then add one egg and a little flour and beat the mixture well, then a second egg and some more flour, then the third egg and the remainder of the flour mixed with the baking powder. Beat the mixture well, add the flavouring and pour into a well-greased mould. Cover with greased paper and steam for 2 hours. Turn out and serve with Chocolate or Custard Sauce flavoured with vanilla.

600 Christmas Pudding

½ lb. flour
½ lb. stale bread
½ lb. suet
1 lb. sugar
½ lb. currants
½ lb. raisins
½ lb. sultanas
¼ lb. ginger preserve
¼ lb. mixed candied peel
¼ lb. shelled almonds
6 eggs
a wineglass each of brandy, sherry and rose-water
½ nutmeg (grated)
½ teaspoon each of powdered cardamoms and cinnamon
¼ teaspoon powdered cloves
1 teaspoon salt

Wash, pick and dry the currants, stone and cut the raisins in halves, wash and steam the sultanas, cut the ginger preserve in small pieces, shred the candied peel finely, grate the bread into fine crumbs, blanch and chop the almonds, chop the suet finely and sieve the flour. Mix all these ingredients together, adding the spices. Then beat the eggs and add them and also the brandy, rose-water and sherry. If a very dark pudding is liked, colour with a little Burnt Sugar (Recipe 1612). Put the mixture into a well-greased mould, cover the top with a good layer of flour and tie over it a scalded and floured cloth. The pudding, instead of being put into a mould, may be boiled in a cloth.

Plunge the pudding into a large saucepan of boiling water—there must be sufficient water to completely cover it—and boil from 8 to 10 hours. Make the pudding a few days before Christmas. When wanted, reboil for a couple of hours, turn it on to a dish, and at the moment of serving, pour a wine-glass of brandy round it, light the brandy and send the pudding to table encircled with flames.

N.B. A ring, a thimble, a button and a small coin are sometimes put into the pudding. The person who gets the ring will, it is supposed, be the first of the company present who will marry; the recipient of the thimble will be an old maid; the one who gets the button will remain a bachelor; and the person to whom the coin comes will become wealthy.

601 Coconut Caramel Pudding

2 oz. finely grated coconut
2 oz. semolina
2 oz. sugar
1 pint milk
3 eggs
rose or vanilla flavouring

CARAMEL:
3 tablespoonfuls sugar
3 tablespoons water

Put the milk and semolina into a saucepan and stir over the fire until the semolina is quite cooked and the mixture thick. A little butter may be added, if liked. Take the saucepan off the fire, let the contents cool a little, then add the coconut, sugar, flavouring and the eggs well beaten. Make the caramel and line a plain mould with it as in Recipe 596. When cool, fill up with the coconut mixture, cover with greased paper and steam slowly for about 40 minutes or until firm to the touch. Stand a few minutes before turning out and serve either hot or cold.

602 Cornflour Pudding

3 level tablespoonfuls cornflour
5 eggs
lemon flavouring
2 tablespoonfuls sugar
1 pint milk
a pinch of salt
sultanas or raisins

Mix the cornflour to a smooth paste with a little of the milk. Put the remainder of the milk into a saucepan and bring to boiling point. Remove the saucepan from the fire and pour the mixed cornflour into it, stirring all the time. Return to the fire and boil for 10 minutes longer, stirring constantly. Let the mixture cool a little, then stir in the sugar, salt, flavouring and the eggs well beaten. Grease a mould, decorate it with sultanas or raisins, pour the mixture into it and steam for 1½ hours.

603 Date Pudding

½ lb. dates
¼ lb. sugar
¼ lb. suet
2 oz. stale bread
2 oz. flour
2 eggs
½ teaspoon mixed spice
½ teaspoon baking powder
1 teacup milk
a pinch of salt

Stone the dates and cut them in small pieces. Sieve the flour into a basin, add the suet finely chopped, the sugar, the bread grated, baked powder, and salt, and mix all well together. Then add the eggs well beaten and the milk and stir well together. Pour the mixture into a well-greased mould, cover with greased paper, and steam steadily from 2 to 3 hours. Turn out and serve with any suitable sauce.

604 Ginger Preserve Pudding

¼ lb. flour	**2 tablespoons ginger syrup**
¼ lb. soft sugar	**¼ teaspoon baking powder**
¼ lb. preserved ginger	**3 eggs**
2 oz. butter	

Beat the butter and sugar to a cream. Then add one egg and a little flour and beat well, then a second egg and some more flour, beat again, then the third egg and the remainder of the flour and beat well for a few minutes. Cut the ginger into small pieces, put it into the mixture, add the ginger syrup and mix well; lastly, mix in the baking powder. Put into a well-buttered basin, cover with buttered paper and steam for 1½ hours. Turn it out and serve with custard sauce.

605 Golden Pudding I

¼ lb. flour	**3 eggs**
¼ lb. stale bread	**2 tablespoons of golden syrup**
¼ lb. suet	**½ teaspoon baking powder**
2 oz. sugar	**a pinch of salt**

Grate the bread and mix together with the flour, suet, sugar, baking powder and salt. Beat the eggs, add the golden syrup to it and mix with the dry ingredients. Pour the mixture into a well-greased mould, cover with greased paper and steam from 2½ to 3 hours. Serve with Golden Syrup.

606 Golden Pudding II

4 oz. each of fine white bread-crumbs, finely-chopped suet, and marmalade	**2 eggs**
	enough milk to moisten
	butter
2 oz. castor sugar	**custard or marmalade sauce**

Mix the suet and sugar with the crumbs. Beat the eggs with a tablespoonful milk, and add the marmalade. Stir in the dry ingredients, adding milk as needed to bring to a consistency that will drop from the spoon. Turn into a buttered pudding basin, cover with buttered grease-proof paper and steam for 2 hours.

Serve very hot, with hot custard or a marmalade sauce, made by melting down two or three tablespoonfuls marmalade with a little water to bring to pouring consistency.

607 Roly-Poly Pudding

¼ lb. flour	**a pinch of salt**
½ lb. chopped suet	**cold water**
¼ teaspoon baking powder	**jam**

Mix the suet into the flour, add the baking powder and the salt and mix into a stiff paste with a little cold water. Roll out into an oblong shape about a quarter of an inch thick, spread a layer of jam over the surface of the paste, leaving a margin of about an inch all round the edge. Wet round the edges of the paste with cold water and roll up lightly in the form of a bolster, sealing the edges firmly. Dip a pudding cloth in boiling water, flour it well and roll up the pudding in it, securing the edges with string. Plunge the pudding into a saucepan of boiling water with a plate at the bottom of it and boil from 1½ to 2 hours. Take off the cloth carefully and serve very hot.

608 Semolina Pudding

2 oz. semolina	**2 eggs**
1 oz. sugar	**lemon flavouring**
1 pint milk	**a pinch of salt**

Put the milk into a saucepan and heat it over the fire. Then sprinkle in the semolina and simmer slowly until the semolina is cooked and the mixture thick. Take the saucepan off the fire, let the contents cool a little, then add the sugar, flavouring and the eggs well beaten. Put the mixture into a greased mould, cover with greased paper and steam for half an hour.

609 Souffle Pudding

2 oz. flour	**6 yolks of eggs**
1½ oz. soft sugar	**4 whites of eggs**
1½ oz. butter	**vanilla or almond flavouring**
2 teacups milk	**a pinch of salt**

Melt the butter in a saucepan, add the flour and sugar, mix well together and add the milk. Stir over the fire until it boils and is thick. Remove the saucepan from the fire and when the contents have cooled a little add the yolks of the eggs beaten together with the flavouring. Mix well together. Add the salt to the whites of eggs, beat to a very stiff froth and mix it by degrees with the other mixture, stirring it in as lightly as possible. Pour immediately into a greased mould and steam very gently for about three quarters of an hour or until it is firm to the touch and will turn out. Serve with any nice sauce.

610 Sponge Pudding

3 oz. flour	**½ teaspoon baking powder**
1 oz. butter	**vanilla flavouring**
2 tablespoonfuls sugar	**a pinch of salt**
2 eggs	**2 tablespoonfuls jam**
½ teacup milk	

Beat the butter and sugar to a cream, add the eggs, beating them well in, then gradually mix in the flour. Beat well, add the milk and beat again. The mixture should be of the consistency of a thick batter that will just drop from the spoon. Lastly, mix in the flavouring, salt, and the baking powder. Butter a pudding basin, put the jam at the bottom, and pour the batter gently over it; cover with a piece of buttered paper and steam for 1 hour. Then turn out carefully and serve at once.

611 Steamed Bread Pudding

½ lb. stale bread
1 pint milk
¼ lb. sugar
2 oz. sultanas
3 eggs
a grate of nutmeg
a little chopped lime rind

Break the bread in small pieces, put them into a basin, heat the milk to boiling point and pour it over the bread. Cover the basin and let the bread soak for half an hour. Beat the eggs and sugar together, add the nutmeg and lime-rind and mix together with the bread, adding also the sultanas. Put the mixture into a greased mould, cover with greased paper and steam for 2 hours.

N.B. This pudding may be baked instead of steamed. Currants or dates may be used instead of sultanas.

612 Steamed Jam Pudding

¼ lb. stale bread
2 oz. sugar
1 oz. butter
3 eggs
1 teacup milk
vanilla flavouring
2 tablespoonfuls jam

Break the bread in small pieces and put it into a basin, pour the milk boiling hot over it and let it soak for a few minutes. Beat the butter and sugar together, then add the eggs and flavouring, beat well and mix together with the bread. Grease a pudding mould, put the jam at the bottom, pour the mixture over it and steam for about 1 hour. Turn out and serve hot.

613 Variegated Pudding

2 oz. butter
2 oz. flour
2 oz. sugar
3 eggs
¼ teaspoon baking powder
vanilla
rose and lemon flavouring
1 dessertspoon grated chocolate
carmine and yellow colouring

Beat the butter to a cream, add the sugar, and then the flour and eggs by degrees, and keep beating the mixture until light and frothy. Then divide into three equal parts. Melt the chocolate in a tablespoon of water and add to one part, flavouring it with vanilla. Colour the second part a pretty pink with a few drops of carmine and flavour it with rose. To the third part add a few drops of yellow colouring and flavour with lemon. Have a well-greased mould ready and put in the mixtures with a spoon intermixing the colours. Fill it rather irregularly and then shake the mixture down. The mould must not be more than three-quarters full. Cover with a greased paper and steam for about 1½ hours or until cooked. Turn out and serve with Custard or Wine Sauce.

614 Vattalappam—Vla (pron. Flah)

MALAY PUDDING

10 eggs
1 lb. jaggery
2½ teacups thick coconut milk
a grate of nutmeg
a pinch of powdered cinnamon
½ teaspoon powdered cardamoms
a pinch of salt

Beat the eggs, yolks and whites separately. Then beat well together; mix in the jaggery finely scraped, the coconut milk, spices and salt. Pour into a greased mould, cover with greased paper and steam for about 1¼ hours or until firm to the touch. Serve in the mould.

Cold Sweets

General Remarks

Cold desserts besides being popular have the great advantage that they can be prepared beforehand. A jelly or any other cold mixture should not be made too firm. It should be just stiff enough to retain its form when turned out of the mould. One of the chief things in making jelly is to get the jelly clear. Special attention should be paid to the clearing and straining process. All utensils used must be perfectly clean. The jelly should not be poured into the mould until it has cooled a bit.

Preparation of Moulds—Either china or tin moulds can be used. For most jellies and cold puddings, the moulds are used wet. If tin moulds are used see that they are perfectly clean. They should be well washed with hot water and then rinsed out in cold water.

How to Use Gelatine—Gelatine is used for stiffening purposes and is obtainable in sheets, strips and powder. Sheet or leaf gelatine is perhaps the best kind to use. It is always best to soak the gelatine in cold water for a couple of hours. The usual proportion to allow is 1 oz. gelatine to 1 pint liquid, but as gelatine varies in strength it is not possible to give exact quantities. Then again, in hot weather more gelatine should be used than in cold, and the jelly for a large mould should be made stiffer than for a small one. Experience will be found the best guide and a trial or two of the gelatine will soon teach the proper quantity necessary.

Straining Jelly—Any kind of cloth will do for straining jellies. The cloth should be well scalded with boiling water before it is used in order to heat it and so get the jelly quickly through. The cloth must never be squeezed or the jelly will not be clear. Should the jelly not be clear on a first straining, strain it 2 or 3 times until it runs through perfectly clear.

To Unmould Jellies and Other Cold Sweets—Have ready a basin of very hot water, dip the mould in it for a few seconds if the mould is made of tin, or a couple of minutes if made of china, take it out and wipe the moisture off the mould with a cloth. Beat the sides of the mould with the palm of the hand until the jelly seems quite loose in the mould, place the dish in which it is to be served over it and then gently turn it over. Give another slight shake and lift the mould carefully.

621 Apple Supreme

1 pint port wine jelly
6 medium-sized apples
6 oz. soft white sugar
1 leaf gelatine
1 tablespoonful water
a few thin strips of rind of lime
2 cloves
1 inch cinnamon
cream

Peel and core the apples, put into a stew-pan and fill the cavities with some of the sugar. Dissolve the rest of the sugar in about $\frac{1}{2}$ pint or a little more of water, add to the apples in the pan, with the spices and lime . Cover, and simmer very gently, turning the apples over once and basting frequently with the syrup until the fruit is soft without having lost its shape.

Lift out very carefully and when cool place in the refrigerator to chill thoroughly, allowing the syrup to drain off well.

Meanwhile, pour half of the jelly into the bottom of a shallow glass dish, and allow to set. Dissolve the gelatine in the tablespoonful of water, and add to the rest of the jelly while it is still warm. Stir well to mix, cool, and put to set in a shallow plain mould. It must set quite firm.

When the jelly in the dish is set but not quite hard arrange the chilled apples on it and continue chilling.

Leave the cream to chill very well and when the stiff jelly is ready scoop out small pieces of it with a salt spoon, mix with a little of the cream, and fill up the apple cavities with it neatly. Decorate the top of the jelly in the dish with the rest of the stiff jelly scooped out as before, and serve. Hand the rest of the cream separately. If liked, this may be slightly sweetened with castor sugar.

622 Apricot Blancmange

1 pint milk
2 tablespoonfuls cornflour
2 tablespoonfuls sugar
almond flavouring
tinned apricots

Mix the cornflour to a smooth paste with a little cold milk, bring the rest of the milk to boiling point, add this to the cornflour, stirring all the time and return all to the saucepan. Add the sugar and stir until thickened and cooked. Flavour to taste, pour into a border mould and allow to cool. Turn out on a glass dish and pile the apricots in the middle.

623 Apricot Chiffon Pie

For the PASTRY:

4 oz. butter
8 oz. flour
½ teaspoon salt
1 teaspoon baking powder
iced water

For the FILLING:

1 tablespoon unflavoured gelatine, softened in ¼ cup cold water
3 eggs
1½ cups apricot puree from tinned apricots
1 cup brown sugar
1 tablespoon lime juice
2 oz. white sugar
1 tin evaporated milk

Sift flour and baking powder and add salt.

Rub butter into flour with the fingertips, and aerate till light and all the pieces are the size of fine breadcrumbs. Mix to a dough with iced water, roll out, and line a shallow baking dish with it. Weigh down with raw rice and bake in a moderately hot oven till done.

Prepare the filling by beating the yolks of the eggs, the brown sugar and the salt together. When well mixed, add the apricot pulp and lime juice and cook over gentle heat till thick, stirring all the while. Take it off the fire and leave aside for a little time. Dissolve the gelatine in half a cup of boiling water, and when entirely dissolved add it to the apricot mixture. Chill the mixture in a bowl till it is firm. Boil the tin of evaporated milk in a pan of water for half an hour. Measure out quarter pint and whip it till it is frothy, also whip the whites of the eggs with a pinch of salt till very stiff. Add the 2 ozs. of white sugar to the egg whites, and beat again. When the apricot mixture is firm, whip it up with a rotary beater or a heavy wire whisk, and fold in the beaten evaporated milk and the egg whites. Pile it into the pie-shell, and chill till firm.

624 Basket Pudding

1 day-old sponge cake, baked in a round tin approximately 6 inches in diameter and 3 inches deep
a good assortment of tinned or fresh stewed fruit or tinned fruit salad
1 strip of angelica 9 inches long and about ½ inch wide
8 glace cherries
about 14 small "leaves" cut from a strip of angelica

For MOISTENING:

mix 3 tablespoonfuls rum or sherry with 2 tablespoonfuls of the syrup from the fruit, and sugar to taste.

For COVERING:

beat together 5 oz. sieved icing sugar
1 oz. sieved cocoa powder
3 oz. fresh butter
when thick and creamy, stir in rum or sherry to give a good flavour—about 1 tablespoonful

The cream should be just stiff enough to spread nicely, and, if too soft, a little more sieved sugar and cocoa may be added

With a very sharp knife cut out the centre of the cake leaving an inch depth at the bottom and about $\frac{3}{4}$ inch all round the sides. Place on a round serving-dish or fancy plate, with a lace paper d'oyley underneath. Very carefully coat the entire outside surface of the cake and the narrow rim at the top with the chocolate cream covering, and with a fruit fork mark wavy lines on the cream to represent the weave of the basket. Place in the refrigerator to chill until the cream is quite firm, then moisten the whole of the inner surface of the cake with the moistening mixture, and return to chill.

If tinned fruit salad is used $1\frac{1}{2}$ large tins will be required; but if an assortment of tinned fruit is preferred (and this is certainly more satisfactory) 1 tin each of greengages, pears, peaches, apricots, and cherries is a suitable selection. The small "picnic" size will be ample. Turn out into separate bowls, and select two of each of the best shaped fruit for the top of the basket, with about 6 of the cherries. Drain these on a clean cloth.

Fill up the basket to the rim with the rest of the fruit, cutting the pears into three pieces, and the peaches into four. The stones may be removed from the greengages and cherries, if liked. Care must be taken to keep the basket a good shape when filling up with the fruit, and as soon as possible it must be returned to the refrigerator. Do not allow too much of the syrup to cling to the fruit, or it will soften the cake than necessary.

While the basket is hardening again coat the strip of angelica on both sides with the chocolate cream, marking as before. If the angelica is washed in warm water and well dried this removes the sugar crystals and makes it pliable so that it can be bent into a nice curve to form the handle. The leaves are also improved by having the crystals removed in the same manner. Leave about $\frac{3}{4}$ inch of the plain angelica at each end of the strip as this will be pressed into the sides of the cake and will be easier to handle when fixing in position. Trim the top of the basket with the drained fruit, curved side uppermost, placing the glace cherries here and there to add a bright note of colour, and arranging the angelica leaves wherever they look best. Make a small incision with a skewer at opposite sides of the basket towards the inside rather than the outside edge (as this helps to keep it firmly in position) and press in the handle carefully. Look over the basket for any patches of cream which may need forking again to improve the appearance. Place in the refrigerator to chill until required.

Hand cream, or the balance of the fruit syrup, if liked, when serving.

625 Charlotte Russe

1 pint clear orange jelly
glace cherries and angelica for decoration
3 tablespoonfuls sherry mixed with 1 tablespoonful water and 1 heaped dessertspoonful castor sugar
½ pint milk
a thin ring of sponge cake to fit loosely into the plain round mould or tin used
½ pint cream
1 tablespoonful sherry
1 level tablespoonful castor sugar
1 oz. leaf gelatine
½ gill water

Choose a plain mould, measuring about 6 inches in diameter and 3 inches deep. Place a thin layer of the jelly at the bottom, and allow to set quite firm. Dip the cherries and small "leaves" cut from the angelica in some of the liquid jelly, and arrange them attractively on the jelly foundation. Chill thoroughly to set very firmly in position, then pour on a little more jelly and set again. Finally pour in just enough liquid jelly to cover the decoration, and leave to set. The mould must now be turned on its side, and the liquid jelly poured on, a small spoonful at a time, so that the entire surface is evenly coated with the jelly. Each spoonful of the jelly must set before the mould is turned slightly to allow the next spoonful to be poured in, and care must be taken to see that each successive addition of liquid jelly joins up with the previous one. The operation will be hastened, and simplified, if the mould is placed on a bed of crushed ice for this part of the decorative work. As soon as the jelly completely covers the inside of the mould it may be stood upright again, provided it is kept in the refrigerator to prevent the jelly from liquefying again. Meanwhile, warm the milk and allow the sugar to dissolve in it, add the gelatine dissolved in the water, and stir until thoroughly mixed. Pour into a bowl, and when cold stir in the cream and the sherry. As soon as the mould is ready, slip the ring of sponge cake into it, taking care not to damage the thin jelly covering. The cake should be at least a day old, or it will crumb untidily when the ring shape is being cut from it. The sides of the ring should not be more than ¾ inch thick, and a very sharp knife must be used for cutting out the centre. Moisten the cake quickly with the sherry mixture, all over the inside, by tilting the mould and turning it round and round gently while pouring on the liquid a spoonful at a time. Stir the cream mixture, and pour it into the cake case gently until it is completely filled but not overflowing. Allow to set firmly, then pour over the balance of the orange jelly, and leave to set until very firm.

To unmould, dip into just warm water, wipe the outside quickly, and invert on to an ice-cold dish with a paper d'oyley underneath, and serve immediately.

Charlotte Russe made in this way, although somewhat coplicated and requiring time and patience for perfect results, is a delicious and very attractive sweet, and is actually not as difficult as the more usual variety made with sponge fingers—as these have to be very perfectly arranged in the mould, and very carefully baked, to ensure a neat, even appearance.

626 Chocolate Biscuit Pudding

1 pint cream
whites of 2 eggs
2 level tablespoonfuls castor sugar
a few drops vanilla essence
½ lb. chocolate biscuits
glace cherries or grated chocolate for decorating

Whip the cream in a basin and whisk the whites of the eggs until very stiff, then gradually fold the eggs into the cream, adding the sugar a little at a time, until thoroughly blended. Flavour with vanilla. Crush the biscuits with a pastry roller until broken up into fairly small pieces. To avoid powdering them place between two pieces of white kitchen paper.

Put a layer of the cream mixture in a glass dish, cover with a thin layer of the biscuits and continue in this order until all are used up, the cream being the last layer. Stand in the refrigerator until thoroughly chilled. Just before serving decorate the top of the cream with halved glace cherries, or chocolate grated on a suet grater, which produces very light, curled flakes.

Another method is to crush the biscuits in smaller pieces, and place in layers (or stir into the mixture, as liked) in one of the ice trays. Freeze until firm, dip the tray into hot water to loosen the cream at the sides, and turn out quickly. Cut into slices, and serve on fancy glass plates, with the grated chocolate sprinkled over.

627 Chocolate Chiffon Pie

one heaped tablespoon unflavoured gelatine softened in ¼ cup cold water
4 eggs
1 cup sugar
one pie shell
2 level tablespoons cocoa or two heaped tablespoons chocolate powder
vanilla
whipped cream

Dissolve the softened gelatine in a little more than half a cup of boiling water and make sure that it is entirely dissolved before adding the cocoa or chocolate. Stir well till smooth. Add the beaten egg yolks, half a cup of sugar, a pinch of salt and vanilla to taste. Chill.

Beat the whites of eggs with a pinch of salt till very stiff and frothy and add the remaining sugar. When the gelatine mixture starts to thicken, beat it well with a fork. Gradually fold in the beaten whites of eggs, and mix well but do not beat.

Pour the mixture into the pie shell and chill till firm. Serve with whipped cream.

628 Chocolate Mould

2 oz. chocolate
2 oz. sugar
1 pint milk
½ oz. sheet gelatine

Break the chocloate in small pieces and put it into a saucepan with a teacup of milk. Dissolve slowly, over the fire, until perfectly smooth. Then remove the saucepan from the fire and add the remainder of the milk, the gelatine cut in pieces, the sugar and the flavouring. Stir again over the fire until the gelatine is dissolved. Let the mixture cool a little, then pour into a wet mould. When cold and set, turn out and serve plain or with Custard Sauce.

629 Chocolate Mousse

4 oz. grated chocolate
1 gill milk
2 small eggs and the yolks of four more
2 tablespoonfuls castor sugar
2 teaspoonfuls rum
¼ pint thick fresh cream, or a medium-size tin of cream

Melt the chocolate with the milk over a low flame, stirring gently all the time, then increase the flame slightly and, still stirring, allow it to boil well until it becomes like a thick batter. Chocolate burns very easily, so care must be taken to avoid this by lifting the pan off the flame every now and then while boiling. Allow to cool, while beating all the eggs and the sugar together in a fairly large basin, with the rum. When well beaten add the chocolate, then stand the basin over a saucepan containing hot water, and whisk over moderate heat until the mixture is warm and thick enough to hang on the end of the whisk. At no time should the basin rest actually on the water beneath, or it will begin to cook before it is properly beaten and the mousse will be ruined. Whisking should be done in one direction only. As soon as it is thick enough, lift off the basin, wipe the bottom to remove the steam, and continue whisking until quite cold. Whip the chilled cream until thick and light, stir very lightly into the chocolate mixture, and turn into a freezing tray and freeze for about 3 hours. Turn out on to an ice-cold dish, on which a lace-edged paper d'oyley has been placed. Where no refrigerator is available the mousse may be turned into a "bombe" mould with a well-fitting lid, packed in ice and salt, and allowed to freeze for at least four hours.

630 Clear Jelly

1 oz. leaf gelatine
¾ pint cold water
¼ pint lime juice
3 oz. sugar
1 inch piece cinnamon
2 cloves
rind of 1 lime
whites and shells of 2 eggs

Put into a saucepan the water, gelatine, sugar, lime juice and rind, the cinnamon, cloves, the egg shells which should be washed and crushed, and whites of the eggs lightly beaten. The pan should not be more than half full or the jelly will boil over. Whisk over the fire until it just begins to boil and not longer. Then let it boil up as high as it will without boiling over. Lessen the fire and let it simmer for 10 minutes. Remove from the fire, allow it to stand for 10 minutes, then strain through a scalded jelly bag or cloth. The jelly will not be clear the first time, so strain it 2 or 3 times until it runs through perfectly clear. Then mould and use as required.

631 Coffee Cream Mould

¼ pint cream
¾ pint milk
1 oz. leaf gelatine
2 tablespoonfuls castor sugar
1 tablespoonful coffee essence
1 tablespoonful water

Cut up the gelatine into fairly small pieces, and rinse in cold water to soften, then add 1 tablespoonful water and dissolve over gentle heat.

Stir milk and sugar together over a low flame until the sugar is dissolved; but do not allow the milk to become too hot or it will curdle when the gelatine is added. Pour in the liquid gelatine, stirring all the time until it has mixed well with the warm milk, and turn into a bowl. When cold, stir in the cream and the essence. Chill until just on the point of setting, then turn into a mould rinsed out with iced water.

When quite set the cream will be firm to the touch and have a shiny appearance on top. Dip the mould into warm water to loosen the cream slightly, wipe off quickly, and invert on to a cold dish. A light tap will cause the cream to come away from the mould easily.

632 Coffee Jelly

1 teacup strong coffee
½ oz. sheet gelatine
2 oz. sugar
vanilla flavouring

Soak the gelatine in the water and put it into a saucepan. Add the coffee and the sugar and dissolve slowly over the fire. Strain through a cloth and add the flavouring. Pour in to a wetted mould and chill until set. Turn out on a glass dish and just before serving pile whipped cream over the top.

633 Cornflour Blancmange

2 oz. cornflour
1 pint milk
1½ oz. sugar
1 oz. butter
lemon flavouring

Mix the cornflour to a smooth paste with a little of the milk. Put the remainder of the milk into a saucepan, add the sugar, and bring to boiling point. Remove the saucepan from the fire and pour the mixed cornflour into it, stirring all the time. Add the butter and flavouring and stir again over the fire 10 minutes longer. Pour into a wet mould and set it aside until cold. Turn out when wanted and serve jam or stewed fruit with it.

N.B. The butter may be omitted, if a plainer mould is wanted.

634 Custard Jelly

2 eggs
1 breakfastcup milk
10 oz. sugar
¼ oz. prepared moss (sold in strands or flakes)
a pinch of salt
3 pints water
vanilla flavouring

Make a thin custard with the eggs, 2 oz. sugar, and milk. Wash the moss, put it into a saucepan, add the water and boil until the moss is quite dissolved. Then add the remainder of the sugar and when dissolved, strain and add it to the custard with a pinch of salt and the flavouring. Mix together and pour into a wet mould. Turn out when wanted.

635 Fruit Jelly

1 pint orange jelly
sections cut from 1 large or 2 small mandarin oranges
1 Jaffna mango peeled and cut into ¼ inch thick slices
16 glace cherries
a few "leaves" cut from a strip of angelica

Make the jelly, and allow to chill. Pour a layer into the bottom of a plain round mould, rinsed with iced water. Put in the ice-compartment of the refrigerator to set quickly. Meanwhile prepare the fruit by cutting rounds from the mango with a very sharp fluted pastry cutter about 1¼ inches in diameter. From these cut out an inner round with a smaller cutter. Keep on a damp cloth until required. Cut the cherries in halves, and remove the sections of fruit from the mandarins by splitting the curved side of the inner skin which covers each section. Take out the seeds, and place on the cloth. Wash the sugar from the angelica leaves, and dry well.

As soon as the first layer of jelly has set firm, place five mango rings round the edge of the mould and one in the centre, with half a cherry in the centre of each, rounded side downwards. Each piece of fruit must be dipped in the liquid jelly before being placed in position. Return to the refrigerator to set the fruit in position, then pour in a spoonful of liquid jelly at a time—taking care not to cause air bubbles while doing so—until the jelly is level with the top of the fruit. Set again, and pour in as much liquid jelly as was used for the first layer in the mould. Set firmly, then decorate the next layer with sections of mandarins.

When these have been set to the level of the fruit with jelly, put the small rounds of mango all round the edge of the tin, with an angelica leaf between each. If the mould is turned on its side for this part of the decoration, and the fruit has taken up a fair amount of liquid jelly, the pieces will set firmly to the edge in a very short time, and by turning it round and round as each set of leaves and mango are firmly fixed, a very neat arrangement can be achieved. When the mould has been completely circled, stand upright again, and pour in liquid jelly to a depth of ¼ inch. Set firmly, then pour in more to come above the side decoration, and set.

The next layer consists of halved cherries and angelica leaves, set as before, and last of all another layer of orange, with about ½ inch depth of jelly to finish off the mould.

Allow to remain in the ice-compartment until wanted. Wipe off the moisture from the outside of the mould, wrap round with a cloth wrung out of very hot water for a minute or so, and invert on to an ice-cold dish. It is not advisable to dip the mould in hot water for turning out this jelly, as the side decoration may slip out of place owing to the fact that there is only a thin layer of jelly between it and the mould.

Orange jelly made from fresh fruit is, of course, the best to use; but when this jelly is wanted in a hurry a good brand of prepared jelly may take its place.

636 Fruit Shortcake

6 oz. flour
6 oz. butter
2 level tablespoonfuls castor sugar
1 very small egg
½ teaspoonful baking powder
stewed or tinned fruit
cream
castor sugar for dusting

Cream the butter and sugar together for 5 minutes. Beat in the egg, and cream together for a minute longer. Sieve the flour and baking powder together twice, and mix with the butter and sugar. Bake in two very shallow sandwich tins, spreading it evenly over the surface, first buttering the tins and dusting them with flour. When lightly browned on top, and slightly shrunk away from the sides of the tins, the cakes are ready. Ease round the edge with a knife, and leave for a couple of minutes to cool, then very carefully turn out and finish cooling on a wire cake rack. These cakes are extremely brittle, especially before they are quite cold, and the greatest care must be observed in turning them out of the tins. Place one cake on the serving dish, and cover with a layer of fruit from which the syrup has been drained.

Press down lightly with a fork and dredge with sugar. Cover with the other cake, top with fruit arranged attractively, and dredge with a little more sugar. Serve the cream, and the syrup from the fruit, separately.

Almost any fruit may be used. Remove stones, if any, very neatly. Perhaps the best kind of tinned fruit is strawberries, but apricots are very nice.

637 Fruit Sponge

1 day-old sponge cake, baked in a tin about 6 inches in diameter and 3 inches deep
red-currant or guava jelly
roasted cadjunuts or walnuts chopped coarsely
any mixed stewed fruit or tinned fruit salad
3 tablespoonfuls syrup from the fruit
2 tablespoonfuls rum or 3 of sherry
1 white of egg
1 tablespoonful sifted icing sugar
cream or creamy custard sauce

Cut out the centre of the cake with a very sharp knife, leaving a shell all round about ¾ inch thick, and the same depth of cake at the bottom. Pack the centre with softly-crushed tissue paper, so that the cake holds its shape nicely. Place on the serving-dish with a fancy paper d'oyley beneath. Carefully spread the jelly all round the edge with a knife, then press the nuts into it until completely covered. Decorate the top edge of the cake in the same manner. Brush away any fallen nuts from the dish, and fasten a band of grease-proof paper round. Chill thoroughly to set nuts firmly.

Mix the fruit, removing any stones, and mix syrup with the rum or sherry. All must be well chilled. Remove tissue paper carefully, and pour the syrup mixture all over the inside to moisten the cake well. Arrange the fruit in the cavity and chill again.

Beat the white of the egg to a very stiff froth, mix in the sugar and beat again until very light and glossy. Put into a paper cornucopia with a small fancy icing-tube at the end and, removing the paper band, pipe a well-spaced decoration round the top of the cake, leaving the nut-covered top showing through between. Pipe the rest of the meringue round the bottom edge, and serve at once.

638 Ginger Creams

½ pint milk
2 level tablespoonfuls castor sugar
yolks of four eggs
1 oz. leaf gelatine
2 tablespoonfuls water
2 tablespoonfuls ginger syrup
3—4 knobs of preserved ginger
1 gill of cream

Make a custard with the milk, eggs, and sugar. When cool add the gelatine dissolved in the water, and mixed with the syrup. Stir very well, and gently, until thoroughly mixed. When quite cold whisk the cream with a fork until slightly thickened, stir into the prepared cream, and chill. As soon as the cream is on the point of setting turn in the finely-chopped ginger, and put into small fancy moulds rinsed with iced water. Set until quite firm.

Serve on individual plates which have been previously chilled and covered with a small fancy paper d'oyley.

639 Honeycomb Mould

1 pint milk
¾ oz. leaf gelatine
3 eggs
2 oz. castor sugar
a few drops of vanilla essence
2 scant tablespoonfuls water

Beat the yolks of the eggs in a basin with the sugar, stir in the warmed milk, and pour into a saucepan. Cook the custard very slowly over a low flame, stirring constantly. Do not allow to boil or it will curdle.

Dissolve the gelatine in the water and add to the warm custard, stirring until well mixed. Allow to become quite cold, then add the vanilla to taste and fold in the stiffly-whisked whites of the eggs. This must be done lightly but thoroughly. Turn into a fancy mould rinsed with iced water, and leave in the refrigerator to set. When turned out there should be a topping of clear jelly with the fluffy cream below.

640 Ice Pudding

1 pint thick custard
½ pint cream
½ lb. mixed crystallized fruit
1 tablespoonful brandy

Stir the cream into the cold custard, add the fruit chopped into small pieces, and the brandy. Freeze until very hard.

Pack an ice-cold "bombe" mould with the mixture, fasten the lid securely with a strip of adhesive tape, and stand in a pail of broken ice mixed with salt for at least an hour. Turn out on to a very cold dish, and serve at once.

641 Jellied Oranges

medium-sized oranges of a good shape
¾ to 1 gill orange jelly for each, according to size of fruit
a little marashino to flavour
marshmallow cream and glace cherries to decorate

Wash and dry the oranges, and cut off a slice from the stem end of each—large enough to allow of scooping out the pulpy juice sacs without damaging the cases. Wipe out the insides of each with a damp rough cloth to remove any loose pith, and then chill the cases very thoroughly.

Remove the unbroken sacs from the rest of the pulp, and mix in with the liquid jelly. Flavour to taste with maraschino, and leave in the refrigerator until just beginning to set. Stir well to mix in the fruit evenly and fill up the orange cases with the jelly. Chill until set firm.

Put a little mound of marshmallow cream on top of each, with a glace cherry in the centre. Serve at once.

642 Jellied Sponge

plain sponge cake, baked in a sandwich-tin about 8 inches diameter and 1 inch deep
1 tablespoonful water mixed with 1 tablespoonful castor sugar and 3 tablespoonfuls sherry
4 tablespoonfuls sieved apricot jam
1½ tablespoonfuls sherry
¾—1 cupful chopped walnuts
¼ pint chilled cream

When the cake is quite cold turn it upside down on a thick fold of cloth and moisten well with the sweetened water and sherry mixed until the sugar is dissolved.

Invert on to a flat serving dish. Heat the jam in a small saucepan, stir in the sherry, and stir over a very low flame until clear. Keep hot by standing in a bowl of hot water.

With the back of a small spoon spread the warm jelly in a circle about 2½ inches in diameter in the centre of the cake and cover with the chopped nuts. Mark off an outer ring round the edge of the cake about 1—1½ inches wide, and spread the jelly over this and down round the outer side of the cake, using a knife for the side as it is easier to spread. Cover with the rest of the nuts. Lift the pan containing the jelly out of the hot water, wipe off the moisture, and pour the jelly when slightly cooled all over the rest of the top of the cake which is exposed, spreading it evenly with the back of a small spoon. Put into the refrigerator to chill, and serve with the cream handed separately.

643 Jelly with Fruit

Clear Jelly or Moss can be used for this and any fresh fruit such as grapes, strawberries, oranges, plantains, etc. The grapes and strawberries may be used whole, the plantains must be sliced and the oranges divided in sections. Small pieces of tinned fruit may also be used but they must first be well drained from the syrup.

Rinse a jelly mould with cold water and place it in a basin of broken ice. Pour some liquid jelly into the mould, sufficient to cover the bottom of it, and let it set. Then arrange some of the prepared fruit on the top and put in another layer of jelly. When this is set, a little more fruit and more jelly. Repeat until the mould is quite full. Do not put too much fruit into the mould. Let it set and turn out when wanted.

644 Lemon Chiffon Pie

1 pie shell
1 tablespoon unflavoured gelatine softened in ¼ cup cold water
1 cup sugar
juice of one large lemon or two limes
4 eggs

Beat the yolks of the eggs with half the quantity of sugar, add the lemon juice, and cook over a pan of boiling water till thick and smooth, stirring all the time. Dissolve the gelatine in half a cup of boiling water and add it to the mixture. If liked, add the grated rind of half a lemon as well. Chill till the mixture thickens. Beat the whites of eggs with a pinch of salt till stiff, add the remaining sugar and beat again. Fold into the lemon mixture, pour into the pie-shell, and chill till firm.

645 Meringues

4 whites of eggs
a pinch of salt
5 or 6 oz. sugar
any filling liked

Put the whites into a basin, add a pinch of salt and whip them as stiffly as possible. Powder and sieve the sugar and mix it in very lightly, and with a tablespoon set portions of the mixture on sheets of buttered paper, each piece should be about the size and shape of a duck egg. Leave a space of an inch between each meringue. Sprinkle some sugar over them, place the sheets on a flat baking tin and set them in a very gentle oven. As soon as they are crisp and have acquired a pale yellow tint, remove them from the oven. Turn the paper on which the meringues have been baked upside down upon the table, wet the paper on the back with a brush or cloth dipped in cold water, and the meringues can be easily detached from it. Turn the meringues over and scoop out the soft part from the centre. Place them back on the tin and put again into the oven for a few minutes to dry.

The meringues may be finished off in many different ways:—A whipped cream nicely flavoured, some jelly or jam or any other filling. Fill the meringues with any of the above, put two meringues together, and pile them on a glass or silver dish.

646 Moss Jelly I

¼ oz. prepared moss (sold in strands or flakes)
½ lb. sugar
a pinch of salt
3 pints water
juice of half an orange

Wash the moss well, put it into a saucepan with the water and let it boil until the moss has quite dissolved. Take it off the fire, stir in the sugar, add the salt and orange juice and strain through a jelly cloth. Pour into a wetted mould and set aside until cold.

N.B. Wine may be added, if liked, and a little jam placed at the bottom of the mould before the jelly is poured in.

647 Moss Jelly II

2 oz. fibre moss
½ lb. sugar
rose or any flavouring liked
6 pints water
whites and shells of 2 eggs
a pinch of salt

Wash the moss thoroughly, pick it over carefully and soak it overnight in cold water. Then lift it out of the water, put it into a saucepan with the water and simmer slowly for about 1 hour or until the moss is boiled. If necessary, add more boiling water. Strain and add the sugar, salt, the egg shells which should be washed and crushed and the whites of the eggs lightly beaten. Then follow directions given for Clear Jelly (Recipe 630). Add the flavouring after the jelly has been strained. Pour into a wet mould and set it in a cool place till wanted. Turn out and serve plain or with Custard Sauce.

648 Nut Cream

yolks of 4 eggs
6 oz. castor sugar
½ pint milk
½ pint cream
1 oz. gelatine
a little cold water
4 oz. cadjunuts or almonds
vanilla essence to flavour

Lightly roast the nuts and grind them, then put into a basin and pour the boiling milk over. Cover and allow to become cool. Beat the yolks of eggs in a basin with the sugar until thick and creamy, and of a pale golden colour. Mix this with the milk and nuts, turn into a saucepan, and stir over the gentle heat until just on the point of boiling (to cook the eggs). Cool and then chill, and stir in the chilled cream. Dissolve the gelatine in about 2 tablespoonfuls water and stir this into the rest, adding vanilla essence to flavour. Pour into a mould rinsed with iced water and leave in the refrigerator to set.

649 Orange Jelly

1 breakfastcupful each of strained orange juice and hot water
3 oz. castor sugar
1 oz. leaf gelatine
1 brimming tablespoonful strained lime juice
very thinly cut rind of 2 oranges

Dissolve the gelatine in the hot water, add the sugar and rind, and as soon as the sugar has dissolved allow to boil up. Reduce the flame to a glimmer, and leave the saucepan over this gentle heat for about five minutes.

Put the orange and lime juice in a basin, and pour the other mixture into it through a very fine strainer or a piece of muslin. Allow to cool, then chill slightly and pour into a mould rinsed with iced water. Set until firm.

If a sweeter jelly is preferred, a little more sugar may be added, especially if the lime juice is very strong or the oranges not sweet.

650 Orange Sponge

¾ pint orange juice
2 oz. sugar
2 whites of eggs
½ oz. gelatine
½ pint water
1 tablespoon sherry

Put the sugar, gelatine and water into a saucepan and dissolve slowly over the fire. Take it off the fire and strain into a basin. When nearly cold, strain in the orange juice, add the whites of eggs and sherry and whisk all together until very stiff. Pour the mixture into a wet mould and set aside until firm. Turn out on a glass dish when wanted.

651 Peach Trifle

1 large sponge cake
1 tin peaches
a glass of wine
a little sugar
1 pint custard

Take a round sponge cake about the size of a dessert plate and 4 inches in thickness. The cake should be at least one day old. Scoop out the centre so as to leave a case of sponge cake and place it on a glass dish. Pour the wine over and let it soak. Turn half the contents of the tin of peaches into a stewpan and let the fruit stew for a short time in its syrup, adding a little sugar. Let the peaches cool and then fill up the hollow of the cake with them. Make a thick custard and, when cool, pour it over the filled cake. Arrange the rest of the peaches round the cake.

652 Pineapple Royale

slices from a ripe, juicy kew pine
1 teacupful of the juice
half a cupful of small cubes of pineapple
1 dessertspoonful strained lime juice
sugar to sweeten to taste
½ pint thick cream
2 level dessertspoonfuls castor sugar
some glace cherries cut in quarter
chopped walnuts

Mix the juice of pineapple and lime together with sugar to sweeten. Stir until dissolved, then add the cubes of pineapple and put in an icy-tray to partially freeze. Meanwhile, whisk the cream and castor sugar together, add the cherries, and chill thoroughly. Chill the slices of pineapple, and cut into small sections. Stir the cream mixture into the pineapple juice in the tray, and let it freeze, stirring once or twice during the process. When nicely firm, serve piled up on the sections of pine arranged at the bottom of each ice-cream plate, and sprinkle with the nuts.

653 Port Wine Jelly

½ pint port wine
½ pint water
4—5 leaves gelatine (a little more than 1 oz.)
the rind and juice of ½ lime
4 oz. castor sugar
½ inch piece cinnamon
1 or 2 tablespoonfuls brandy
cochineal or red colouring

Dissolve the gelatine in the water over a moderate flame. Add the sugar, rind, and juice of lime, and the cinnamon, and whisk with a wire beater over gentle heat until it boils. Reduce the flame and simmer for a few minutes, then strain through a jelly bag. Add the wine and brandy and improve the colour by adding cochineal or other red colouring. When cool, pour into a fancy mould rinsed with iced water, and set until firm.

654 Ribbon Jelly

clear jelly or moss jelly **carmine or cochineal**
flavouring

Divide the jelly in two equal parts. Flavour one part with essence of rose and colour it pink with few drops of carmine or cochineal. Flavour the other part with essence of lemon. Rinse a jelly mould with cold water and place it in a basin of broken ice. Pour a small quantity of red jelly into it, let this set, then pour in a small quantity of the pale jelly and repeat this until the mould is full. One colour must always be perfectly firm before pouring in the other or the effect would be spoilt by the two colours running into each other. Turn out when wanted.

655 Rice Flour Blancmange

2 oz. rice flour **1 teaspoon butter**
2 oz. sugar **a pinch of salt**
1 pint milk **flavouring**

Mix the flour to a smooth paste with a little of the milk. Heat the rest of the milk in a saucepan and pour it over the flour stirring all the time. Return all to the saucepan, add the sugar and stir over the fire until boiling. Then add the flavouring and the butter and boil, stirring all the time, until the flour is thoroughly cooked and the mixture very thick. Pour into a wet mould and let it stand until cold and set. Turn out and serve with jam or stewed fruit.

656 Rhubarb Trifle

stewed rhubarb **1½ oz. sugar**
2 oz. cornflour **1 oz. butter**
1 pint milk **½ pint custard**

Mix the cornflour to a smooth paste with a little of the milk. Put the remainder of the milk into a saucepan, add the sugar and bring to boiling point. Remove the saucepan from the fire and pour the mixed cornflour into it, stirring all the time. Add the butter and stir again over the fire for 10 minutes longer. Pour into a mould that has been rinsed out with cold water and set aside until cold. Turn out on a glass dish, arrange the stewed rhubarb round it and pour the custard over.

657 Rum Barada

The weight of 2 eggs in butter, castor sugar and sieved flour
1 heaped teaspoonful baking powder
a few drops vanilla essence

For MOISTENING:
1 heaped dessertspoonful castor sugar
2 scant tablespoonfuls water
2 tablespoonfuls rum

For COATING:
2 scant tablespoonfuls sieved apricot jam
1 tablespoonful rum

For THE FILLING:
2 oz. each butter, castor sugar, ground almonds or cadju-nuts flavoured with a few drops of almond essence
2 tablespoonfuls thick cream
the yolk of 1 egg
2 teaspoonfuls rum, if liked
1 large bulb of preserved ginger chopped very small may be added

For DECORATION:
glace cherries and angelica "leaves"

Make a cake of the first lot of ingredients, beating butter and sugar to a pale cream, adding the beaten eggs, the flour sieved 3 times with the baking powder, and the flavouring, in this order. Bake in a buttered and floured ring mould, in a moderate oven, until palely-golden brown on top and easing away from the sides of the mould slightly. Cool on a wire rack.

Prick the cake all over on the underside, and here and there on the top and sides, with a small-pronged fork taking care not to damage the "crust". Pour in the moistening mixture liberally on the underside with a teaspoon and moisten the rest at the fork pricks to ensure that the inside will not dry in any part.

Place on the serving dish, and brush over the whole of the outside crust and down into the cavity with the coating mixture. This must be first placed in a small saucepan, stirred to mix thoroughly, and placed over a very low flame until it is hot and clear in appearance. Sir very gently white heating. Use a clean dry pastry brush for coating, taking care not to disturb the crumbs of the cake crust. The cake should now have a clear jellied appearance. Chill very well. Prepare the filling by beating the butter until soft. Add the sugar and cream together for a few minutes, then add the rum by degrees. Beat all together until pale in colour and thick. Add the yolk of egg, mix in well and put in the ground nuts and cream and beat again for a few minutes. If chopped ginger is used it must now be added. Chill the mixture, then pile it up in the hollow centre of the cake, rounding it nicely. Put the rest of the mixture into a cornucopia made of double greaseproof paper with a plain meringue tube in the end. Pipe a neat decoration all round the centre filling of cream resting on the top edge of the cake, and decorate all round the base of the cake in the same manner. Put an alternate garnish of halved cherries and angelica leaves on this decoration (top and bottom), and arrange a cluster of cherries and leaves on top of the centre filling. Serve ice-cold. If made some time before it is to be used the barada should be covered over with a cone of greaseproof paper while it is chilling in the refrigerator.

658 Rum Cream

1 wineglassful rum	**½ oz. gelatine**
2 oz. castor sugar	**½ pint milk**
2 yolks of eggs	**1 tablespoonful water**

Beat the yolks and sugar together in a basin, and stir in the almost boiling milk. Return to the saucepan and stir over gentle heat until the custard thickens. Do not allow it to boil. Cut the gelatine into small pieces and rinse in cold water, then put in a small pan with a tablespoonful of water and stir over low heat until dissolved. Turn into the warm custard and stir until well mixed and no streaks of gelatine are visible. Allow to chill until it looks thick and is slightly set round the edge of the basin, then stir in the rum and turn into a mould rinsed in cold water. When set firm it is ready for use.

659 Sago Pudding or Mould

¼ lb. sago	**2 teacups water**
6 oz. jaggery	**2-inch piece cinnamon**
½ teacup coconut milk	**salt**

Wash the sago well and soak it in water for about 20 minutes. Turn it into a saucepan, add the water and cinnamon and cook until the sago is boiled and very thick. Then remove the piece of cinnamon, add the jaggery, coconut milk, and a pinch of salt and stir constantly until the mixture is very thick. Pour into a wet mould and set it aside until cold and firm. When wanted, turn out and serve with thick coconut milk to which a pinch of salt must be added.

660 Snow Eggs

4 eggs	**salt**
1 pint milk	**vanilla flavouring**
sugar	

Put the milk into a shallow saucepan and bring to the boil; sweeten to taste and flavour with vanilla. Add a pinch of salt to the whites of eggs and beat them to a very stiff froth. Drop tablespoonfuls of this egg froth into the boiling milk. A few seconds will cook each 'spoonful on one side, then turn it over and when cooked on the other side place in a glass dish. Having cooked all the egg froth, strain the milk free from any bits of egg that may have been left in it. Beat the yolks of eggs, add sugar and flavouring to taste and pour the milk slowly on to this mixture, stirring all the time. Return to the saucepan and stir carefully over the fire until the custard thickens. *Let it cool, then pour* round the snow eggs in the dish.

661 Surprise Pudding

½ lb. plain sponge cake baked in a round tin
1 large tin strawberries (or other fruit)
½ lb. tin thick cream
4 tablespoonfuls sherry or 3 of rum
4 tablespoonfuls fruit syrup
castor sugar for dredging
the whites of 3 large or 4 small eggs
2 heaped tablespoonfuls castor sugar

The cake is all the better for being a couple of days old. Cut it across into 3 slices. Place the bottom slice in the dish in which the pudding is to be served, which must be either of fire-proof glass or plated, and round in shape. Mix the syrup and sherry together, and moisten the cake slightly with some of it, then cover with a layer of the fruit. Dredge with castor sugar and coat with the cream (previously turned into a basin, whipped for a few minutes, and thoroughly chilled). Over this place the middle layer of cake, moisten, cover with fruit, sugar and cream as before. Put the last layer over and moisten with the balance of the syrup and sherry. Allow to chill for several hours on the lowest shelf of the refrigerator.

About 15 minutes before the pudding is required whisk the whites of the eggs to a very stiff froth, stir in the castor sugar, and whisk again until stiff. Entirely cover the prepared cake with this meringue mixture spread smoothly with a knife and pipe a decoration round the top and bottom edges with the balance. Stand the dish on an old bread board or in a baking tin with several layers of paper below it, and put into a very quick oven to lightly brown and set the meringue. Serve immediately.

662 Tipsy Cake

1 large sponge cake
1 or 2 glasses of sherry or brandy
1 pint custard
almonds
raspberry or apricot jam

Cut the cake in 3 or 4 slices, spread each piece with jam and put the cake together again. Place it in a glass dish, pour the wine over it and let soak for about an hour, basting it occasionally with the wine until it is all absorbed. Make the custard as directed in Recipe 716 and when cool pour it over the cake. Blanch the almonds, cut them in strips and stick them all over the cake.

663 Trifle

6 small sponge cakes
milk
sugar
¼ pint custard
jam
almonds

Split the sponge cakes, spread them with any nice jam, press the two halves together and arrange them in a glass dish. Pour a little sweetened cold milk over the cakes and let them soak for half an hour. Make a good thick custard and when cold pour it over the sponge cakes. Blanch and halve some sweet almonds and sprinkle over the trifle.

664 Vanilla Cream Trifle

3 eggs
½ pint milk
1 heaped dessertspoonful castor sugar
a few drops of vanilla essence
1 small day-old sponge cake
apricot jam
½ pint cream or ½lb. tin of cream
sugar to taste

For MOISTENING THE CAKE:
1 tablespoonful cold water
3 tablespoonfuls sherry
1 level tablespoonful castor sugar

For DECORATION:
the whites of 2 of the eggs (above) and 1 level tablespoonful castor sugar

Make a custard with the yolks and one white of the eggs, the milk and the first lot of sugar, flavouring it with vanilla essence to taste. Put a thin layer of this, while hot, in the bottom of the dish, and place the lower half of the cake on top. Sprinkle the cake with some of the moistening mixture, mixed together, and spread it with a thick layer of apricot jam. It is advisable to pass the jam through a coarse sieve to remove skin and the kernels from the fruit stones. Put the other half of the cake on top, and sprinkle with the rest of the moistening mixture. Pour the balance of the custard over, and when cold put in the refrigerator or on ice to set the custard.

Whip the cream for five minutes, standing the bowl containing it in a larger bowl with crushed ice round. Add the sugar to taste, and whip again for five minutes. Spread on top of the custard, and chill very thoroughly. Some brands of tinned cream whip up fairly stiff—quite stiff enough for this purpose—and unless pure fresh cream is used a good brand of tinned cream is to be preferred.

Whisk the whites of the eggs to a stiff froth with a rotary beater, add the sugar, and whisk again until smooth and glossy. Put into a large paper cornucopia with a fancy tube in the end, and pipe any attractive decoration desired in lines or circles over the top of the cream. leaving a small space between for the cream to show through. Leave in the refrigerator until required.

Fritters

FRITTERS are usually composed of some sweet mixture, or fruit coated with a light batter, or the sweet ingredients or fruit is mixed with the batter.

The batter used should be light and smooth and just sufficiently thick to coat completely the article to be fried. The batter is better for being made a couple of hours before it is required.

Special attention should be given to the frying of fritters, for if not properly done they will turn out heavy. Use ghee or dripping for frying; and a deep pan, for the ghee must well cover the article to be fried. The ghee must be boiling before being used. Do not put too many fritters into the pan at one time or they will cool the ghee too much and it will soak into them; allow the ghee to become quite hot again before putting in the second lot. Fry them a nice brown, turning them when required. When done, lift them out with a perforated spoon, letting the oil drip well from them, and drain on paper.

Serve the fritters very hot, sprinkled with sugar, or serve a nicely flavoured sugar syrup separately.

671 Batter for Frying I

¼ lb. flour
1 teacup milk
1 egg
a pinch of slat

Put the flour and salt into a basin and mix to a smooth batter with half of the milk. Beat in the egg and the remainder of the milk. Beat well until perfectly smooth and full of air-bubbles. Let it stand for some time before using.

672 Batter for Frying II

¼ lb. roasted rice flour
1 teacup coconut milk
1 egg
a pinch of salt

Make the batter according to directions given in the previous recipe.

673 Bread Fritters I

2 or 3 slices stale bread
1 teacup milk
2 eggs
1 teaspoon butter
a pinch of nutmeg
salt and carbonate of soda
soft sugar

Break the bread in small pieces and put it into a basin with the butter. Heat the milk and pour it over the bread. Allow this to soak for about 15 minutes, then stir in the yolks of eggs and add the salt and nutmeg; mix well together. Whisk the whites of eggs to a stiff froth and stir them in very lightly at the last along with the carbonate of soda. Drop spoonfuls of the mixture into boiling ghee and fry them to a golden brown colour. Drain and dust over with soft sugar.

674 Bread Fritters II

5 or 6 slices stale bread
1 breakfastcup milk
2 eggs
a grate of nutmeg
sugar syrup (Recipe 1081)

Cut the bread in slices about half an inch thick, remove the crusts and cut each slice in two. Beat the eggs, add the milk and nutmeg to them and pour over the bread. Let this soak a short time without allowing the bread to become too moist. Fry in boiling ghee or dripping until of a golden brown colour on both sides. Drain well, arrange the fritters on a dish, pour some sugar syrup over them and serve hot.

675 Bread and Butter Fritters

slices of bread and butter
jam
frying batter I or II (671, 672)
sugar

Spread half the slices of bread and butter with any nice jam, cover with the other slices, press them together and cut in small squares or long pieces. Dip them in the batter and fry to a golden brown colour. Drain well, sprinkle with sugar and serve.

676 Breadfruit Fritters

breadfruit
salt
ground saffron
oil

For the SUGAR COATING:
1 lb. sugar
1 teacup water
½ wineglass rose water

Cut the breadfruit in quarters, remove the core and peel it. Cut in thin slices, then into strips, and put them into cold water. Wash well, drain, and mix with a little ground saffron and salt. Then drain off all the water. Have ready a pan of boiling oil, put in the slices of breadfruit, a little at a time, and fry to a golden colour, shaking them so as to cook them equally. When ready lift them out with a perforated spoon and drain on paper. Then coat with sugar.

Sugar Coating—Put the sugar and water into a saucepan and boil them together until they form a thick syrup. Then add the rose water and stir until the syrup is very thick. Reduce the fire and put the fried breadfruit into the syrup, stirring carefully so that the breadfruit is all nicely coated. Take the pan off the fire and continue stirring until the sugar crystallizes. Keep in an air-tight tin.

677 Fried Stringhoppers

stringhoppers **oil for frying** **syrup**

Dry the stringhoppers in the sun for a couple of days until they are crisp. Then fry in boiling oil until of a light brown colour. Drain well, pour some thickened kitul or coconut syrup over them and serve hot.

678 Pancakes

½ lb. flour
a pinch of salt
1 pint milk
3 yolks of eggs
2 whites of eggs
ghee or dripping for frying
refined or soft sugar

Put the flour into a basin, add the salt and about half the milk and beat to a perfectly smooth batter; then beat in the yolks of eggs and by degrees the remainder of the milk, and beat it thoroughly. Let the batter stand for about half an hour before using it. Whisk the whites of the eggs to a stiff froth and stir them in very lightly at the last. Put a little ghee or dripping into a frying pan—the pan must be a perfectly clean one—and make it very hot. Then quickly pour in the batter, a little more than a tablespoonful to a pan 5½ inches in diameter. Let it fry for about 2 minutes until set and lightly browned on the underside, then toss it over or turn over with the blade of a knife. Brown on the other side and slip the pancake on to a plate. Each pancake will require a little fresh ghee added to the pan. When done sprinkle each pancake with sugar and roll up. Serve them hot.

N.B. A little lime juice may be added to the sugar, if liked, or the pancakes may be varied by spreading them with any nice jam before rolling them up. Coconut milk may be used for mixing the batter.

679 Pineapple Fritters

slices of pineapple
soft sugar
a little wine
frying batter I

Soak the slices of pineapple in a little wine and sugar for about an hour. Then dip them in the batter and fry in boiling ghee. Sprinkle with sugar and serve hot.

680 Plantain Fritters I

frying batter
sugar or jaggery syrup
1 or 2 sour plantains

Peel and cut the plantains in two lengthwise, dip them in the batter and fry to a golden brown colour. Pile on a dish and serve hot with jaggery or sugar syrup.

N.B. A little scraped jaggery may be mixed with the batter.

681 Plantain Fritters II

3 sour plantains
¼ lb. roasted and sifted rice flour
2 tablespoons coconut milk
1 egg
a pinch of salt
powdered sugar or syrup

Peel the plantains, which should be quite ripe, and mash them into a pulp. Add to them the flour and salt, beat in the egg and then the milk by degrees. Mix well together and drop spoonfuls of the mixture into boiling ghee, and fry a golden brown colour. Dust over with powdered sugar, or sugar or jaggery syrup may be served separately.

682 Plantain Fritters without Batter

sour plantains
soft sugar

Peel and split the plantains in two lengthwise and fry them in boiling ghee or dripping, turning them so that they may brown on both sides. Drain well and sprinkle liberally with sugar.

683 Sponge Cake Fritters

slices of sponge cake
jam
2 or 3 tablespoons of soft sugar
milk or wine
frying batter I

Spread each slice of cake with jam, sandwich them together and cut them in small squares or long pieces. Pour a little cold milk or wine over them and let them soak for a few minutes. Then dip them in the batter and fry to a golden brown colour. Sprinkle with sugar and serve.

Souffles and Sweet Omelettes

A SOUFFLE is a light pudding which must be served very hot. Eggs form the principal ingredient and they must be fresh. The success of souffles depends largely upon the whites of the eggs being beaten to a very stiff froth: if the eggs are not fresh, this will not be possible.

Moulds or tins in which souffles are to be steamed should be greased very thickly with butter and have a double band of buttered paper, wide enough to stand 3 or 4 inches above the top of the tin, tied round its rim to support the souffle when it rises above the level of the tin. Also have ready a round of buttered paper to cover the top.

In baked souffles it is not necessary to have the band of paper round the tin. The mixture should not more than half fill the mould as it rises very much when cooking.

Before beginning to make the souffle have everything in readiness. The mould or tin in which it is to be steamed or baked, a saucepan of boiling water if the souffle is to be steamed, or the oven ready to receive it if it is to be baked.

To steam a souffle, place the mould containing it in a saucepan of boiling water to reach half-way up the sides. Steam slowly and steadily until well risen and firm to the touch. If cooked too quickly, it will rise rapidly without becoming firm, and will sink again when it is turned out. Steamed souffles are usually turned out of the moulds, but baked souffles, are sent to table in the dish or dishes in which they are cooked. A baked souffle must be cooked in a moderate and steady oven until it is well risen and firm to the touch.

The success of a souffle depends to a great extent upon the whites of the eggs being thoroughly beaten, steady cooking and quick serving.

691 Chocolate Souffle

3 oz. chocolate
1 oz. flour
2 oz. soft sugar
1 gill milk
4 yolks of eggs
5 whites of eggs
vanilla flavouring

Break the chocolate in small pieces and put it into a saucepan with half the milk. Cook over a slow fire, stirring all the time, until the chocolate is melted. Remove the saucepan from the fire and allow the chocolate to cool a little. Then mix in gradually the flour, sugar, flavouring, yolks of eggs and the remainder of the milk. Stir over the fire again till boiling. Then remove from the fire, and when nearly cold, add the whites of the eggs beaten to a stiff froth. Pour the mixture into a buttered dish and bake in a moderate oven until well risen and firm to the touch. Sprinkle with sugar and serve immediately. It will take from 15 to 20 minutes to bake.

692 Omelette Souffle

4 eggs
1½ oz. sugar
1 tablespoonful jam
vanilla flavouring
1 dessertspoonful flour

Separate the yolks from the whites of the eggs, add the sugar to the yolks and beat together until creamy, then stir in the flour and flavouring. Beat the whites of eggs to a stiff froth and mix them lightly with the batter. Pour the mixture into a well-buttered omelette pan and bake in a brisk oven from 10 to 15 minutes. When firm to the touch, turn the omelette on to a sugared paper, put the jam in the centre, fold over and serve at once.

693 Pineapple Souffle

2 tablespoonfuls pineapple preserve (Recipe 1118)
2 oz. butter
2 oz. flour
2 oz. sugar
4 eggs
1 gill milk
rose flavouring

Heat the butter in a saucepan, stir in the flour and mix well together with a wooden spoon. Then add the milk and stir over the fire until the mixture thickens and draws away from the sides of the saucepan. Remove the saucepan from the fire, let the contents cool slightly, then beat in the yolks of eggs, the sugar, flavouring and pineapple preserve. Beat the whites of eggs to a stiff froth and stir them in lightly at the last. Pour the mixture into a prepared souffle mould and steam very gently from 40 to 50 minutes. Turn out and serve at once with pineapple (or any other suitable) sauce poured round it.

694 Plantain Souffle

4 sour plantains
3 eggs
1 wineglass orange juice
sugar

Peel the plantains and mash into a pulp with a spoon. Add the sugar, orange juice and yolks of eggs and mix well together. Have the whites of eggs beaten to a stiff froth and stir them in at the last. Pour the mixture into a well-buttered souffle dish, and bake until well risen and firm to the touch. It will take about 20 minutes to cook. Sprinkle with sugar and serve at once.

695 Rice Flour Souffle

2 oz. roasted rice flour
4 oz. soft sugar
2 oz. butter
4 eggs
vanilla flavouring
a pinch of salt
1 pint milk

Mix the flour to a smooth paste with a little of the milk, and put the remainder into a saucepan to heat. When hot add the flour and stir over the fire until boiling. Then add the sugar, salt, and the butter and cook for 10 minutes longer. Remove the saucepan from the fire and when the mixture is off the boil stir in the yolks of eggs and the flavouring. Beat the whites of eggs to a stiff froth and stir them in lightly at the last. Pour the mixture into a buttered dish and bake in a moderate oven for about 30 minutes or until well risen and nicely browned. Sprinkle with sugar and serve as quickly as possible.

696 Sago Souffle

Make in the same way as Tapioca Souffle (Recipe 698).

697 Semolina Souffle

2 oz. semolina	**4 eggs**
2 oz. soft sugar	**a pinch of salt**
1 pint milk	**rose or vanilla flavouring**

Rinse out a small saucepan with cold water, and put into it the semolina and the milk. Stir over the fire with a wooden spoon until it boils and the mixture thickens. Take the pan off the fire and add the sugar, salt and flavouring. Then add the yolks of the eggs, one at a time, beating the mixture well together between each. Lastly, stir in the whites of eggs beaten to a very stiff froth. Pour the mixture into a well-buttered mould and steam gently for about 40 minutes or until the souffle is well risen and firm to the touch. Turn out carefully and serve at once, with jam or Custard Sauce poured round it.

698 Tapioca Souffle

2 tablespoonfuls tapioca	**½ pint milk**
2 oz. soft sugar	**lemon flavouring**
2 oz. butter	**a pinch of salt**
4 eggs	

Wash the tapioca and put it into a saucepan with the milk and butter and cook over the fire stirring occasionally until the tapioca turns quite clear. Then remove the saucepan from the fire, and when the contents have cooled a little, stir in the sugar, salt, yolks of eggs and flavouring. Lastly, add the whites of eggs beaten to a stiff froth. Pour the mixture into a prepared souffle mould and steam very slowly from 30 to 40 minutes or until the souffle is well risen and firm to the touch. Serve with any nice sauce.

699 Vanilla Souffle

1 oz. flour	**3 yolks of eggs**
1 oz. butter	**4 whites of eggs**
1 oz. soft sugar	**vanilla flavouring**
1 gill milk	**a pinch of salt**

Melt the butter in a saucepan, add the flour and mix well together with a wooden spoon. Then add the milk and stir over the fire until the mixture thickens and draws away from the sides of the saucepan. Remove the saucepan from the fire and add the sugar, salt and flavouring. Then add the yolks of eggs, one at a time, and beat well together. Beat the whites of eggs to a stiff froth and stir them in lightly at the last. Pour the mixture into a well-buttered souffle mould and steam very gently from 30 to 40 minutes or until well risen and firm to the touch. Turn out and serve with jam or Custard Sauce.

700 Chocolate Omelette

1½ oz. chocolate
2 tablespoons milk
1 oz. sugar
1 oz. butter
3 yolks of eggs
5 whites of eggs
vanilla flavouring

Break the chocolate into small pieces and put it into a saucepan with the milk. Stir over the fire until the chocolate is melted and free from lumps. Remove the pan from the fire and allow the chocolate to cool a little. Put the sugar, yolks of eggs and flavouring into a basin, beat well together, then mix in the chocolate. Lastly, stir in the whites of eggs beaten to a stiff froth. Melt the butter in an omelette pan and when hot pour in the mixture. Allow the omelette to set over a moderate fire, and when cooked on the underside fold over, dredge with sugar and serve very hot.

701 Jam Omelette

4 eggs
1 oz. butter
1 dessertspoonful soft sugar
a tablespoonful jam
vanilla flavouring
a pinch of salt

Make in the same way as Sweet Omelette (Recipe 704). Warm the jam and put it in the centre of the omelette before folding it over. When ready, slip the omelette on to a dish, sprinkle it over with sugar and serve quickly.

702 Plantain Omelette

2 sour plantains
1 dessertspoonful sugar
1 oz. butter
4 eggs
a pinch of salt

Peel the plantains and cut them in slices about ⅛ inch in thickness. Then make an omelette with the eggs and sugar (Recipe 704), and put the plantain in the centre of the omelette before folding it over. Turn on to a dish, sprinkle with sugar and serve at once.

703 Rum Omelette

to every 3 eggs allow 1 heaped tablespoonful castor sugar
1 teaspoonful rum for mixing
2 tablespoonfuls rum pouring over and castor sugar for dredging

Beat the yolks of the eggs and the sugar together with a whisk until thick, and pale in colour, and then stir in the rum. Whisk the whites until very stiff and shiny in appearance. Have ready a hot omelette pan, well greased, and a sheet of white kitchen paper thickly dusted with castor sugar. Fold the whites into the other mixture very lightly, and pour into the prepared pan. Cook until nicely browned and set over a moderate flame, cutting the bottom of the omelette with the blade of a knife while cooking to allow the centre to cook through nicely. This must be done very lightly or the omelette will be heavy. When set, slip the omelette on to the prepared paper, and fold over in half. Slide on to a very hot dish, pour the warmed rum over and set alight. Serve at once.

For a very sweet omelette two tablespoonfuls of raspberry jam, warmed sufficiently to make it spread quickly may be poured over the centre of the omelette just before folding.

704 Sweet Omelette

4 eggs
1 oz. butter
1 dessertspoonful sugar
vanilla or lemon flavouring
a pinch of salt

Separate the yolks from the whites of the eggs. Put the yolks into a basin with the sugar and flavouring and heat to a cream. Add a pinch of salt to the whites of eggs and whip to a very stiff froth, then stir lightly into the yolks. Melt the butter in an omelette pan. When hot, pour in the mixture and while the omelette is setting underneath, loosen it at the sides with a knife. When it is nicely browned on the underside, slip a knife under it and double over first from one side and then from the other towards the centre. Then turn it on to a dish, dredge with sugar and serve quickly.

Sweet Sauces

711 Butter Sauce

2 oz. fresh butter
3 oz. icing sugar
1 dessertspoon brandy
flavouring

Beat the butter to a cream, add the sugar and beat until it is quite foamy. Flavour with the brandy and almond or vanilla essence. This sauce should not be made until shortly before it is to be served.

712 Caramel Sauce

2 tablespoons sugar
2 tablespoons water
1 breakfastcup custard sauce flavoured with vanilla

Put the sugar and water into a saucepan and let it cook without stirring until it assumes a nice golden brown colour. Mix it well until quite smooth and then mix together with the custard.

713 Chocolate Sauce

2 oz. chocolate
½ pint water
1½ oz. soft sugar
1 dessertspoon cornflour
1 dessertspoon brandy
vanilla essence

Grate the chocolate and put it into a saucepan with the sugar and half the water and stir over the fire until quite dissolved. Mix the cornflour smoothly with the remainder of the water and add to the contents of the saucepan; stir over the fire a few minutes longer and add the brandy and vanilla.

714 Coconut Sauce

2 tablespoonfuls finely grated coconut
¼ lb. soft sugar
2 oz. fresh butter
2 whites of eggs
rose flavouring
1 dessertspoon brandy

Beat the butter to a cream, add the sugar and beat again until frothy. Then mix in the coconut, add the brandy and flavour with essence of rose: Beat the whites of eggs to a stiff froth and mix in lightly.

715 Cornflour Sauce

1 teaspoon cornflour
1 teacup milk
1 tablespoon sugar
2 eggs
lemon flavouring

Mix the cornflour smoothly with a little cold water. Put the milk into a saucepan and bring to the boil, mix in the cornflour and let it cook from 5 to 10 minutes, stirring all the time. Then remove the saucepan from the fire and allow the contents to cool slightly. Beat the yolks of eggs and sugar together, add the flavouring and mix with the sauce. Return the saucepan to the fire and re-heat the contents but do not boil again. Pour the custard into a basin and when somewhat cooled, stir in very lightly the whites of eggs beaten to a stiff froth.

716 Custard Sauce

1 pint milk
3 eggs
2 tablespoons sugar
flavouring

Beat the eggs, yolks and whites, lightly together, mix in the sugar and flavour to taste with nutmeg, chopped lime rind or any essence. Boil the milk in a saucepan, take it off the fire and pour in quickly the egg mixture, stirring all the time. Return the saucepan to the fire and stir very carefully until the sauce thickens but do not allow it to boil or it will curdle. Continue stirring for a couple of minutes after it has been taken off the fire.

717 Jam Sauce

1 tablespoonful raspberry, strawberry or any other jam
1 tablespoonful sugar
¼ pint water
a squeeze of lime juice
2 or 3 drops carmine

Put the jam, sugar and water into a small saucepan, bring them to the boil and add the lime juice and colouring.

718 Lime Sauce

3 tablespoons sugar
juice of 2 limes
the finely chopped rind of 1 lime
1 wineglass brandy
2 or 3 drops carmine or cochineal
1 breakfastcup water

Put the water and lime rind into a saucepan and boil for 5 minutes, then add the sugar and simmer until a fine syrup is produced; strain into it the lime juice, add the colouring and lastly the brandy.

719 Marshmallow Sauce

4 oz. marshmallows
1 gill water
about 6 oz. sieved icing sugar
the whites of 2 eggs

Cut the marshmallows into small pieces, and put into a double-saucepan, the inner one being of china. If this is not available a pudding basin may be placed over a saucepan of boiling water, the basin wide enough to rest firmly on the edge with the bottom resting in the water.

Allow to melt, then add the icing sugar and stir until smooth. Remove the inner pan and beat thoroughly until quite smooth and cool. Fold in the stiffly-whisked whites of eggs, and whisk all together until thick. The quantity of sugar will depend on the size of the eggs. If the sauce appears to be too liquid more sieved sugar may be added. Any flavouring may be used, and this may be decided in accordance with the flavouring of the dish with which the sauce is served. A small quantity of rum gives a very good flavour.

720 Pineapple Sauce

2 tablespoons pineapple preserve
1 tablespoon sugar
1 teacup water
½ glass of wine
a squeeze of lime juice

Make a syrup with the sugar and water and when it thickens stir in the pineapple preserve, wine and lime juice.

721 Raspberry Jam Sauce

6 tablespoonfuls raspberry jam
the strained juice of half a very small lime
3 tablespoonfuls water
1 leaf gelatine
1 teaspoonful sherry
a little castor sugar

Put the jam and 1 tablespoonful water in a small saucepan, stir over a low flame, and heat thoroughly. Strain to remove seeds. Cut the gelatine into small pieces, and dissolve in the rest of the water, strain into the warm jam syrup, and add sugar, if a very sweet sauce is wanted. Stir over a low flame until hot but not boiling, then remove from the fire and add the sherry and lime to taste. Use as required for sweet puddings.

722 Raspberry Sauce

2 tablespoons raspberry jam
2 tablespoons soft sugar
1 teaspoon lime juice
3 whites of eggs
vanilla flavouring
2 or 3 drops carmine or cochineal

Beat the whites of eggs to a very stiff froth, gradually adding the sugar. Then mix in the jam, lime juice, vanilla and colouring.

723 Syrup Sauce

2 tablespoons golden syrup
1 dessertspoon lime juice
1 teacup water

Put all the ingredients into a saucepan, bring to the boil and boil for 10 minutes longer.

724 Vanilla Sauce

2 eggs
1 breakfastcup milk
1 oz. sugar
vanilla flavouring

Make according to directions given for Custard Sauce (Recipe 716).

725 Wine Sauce

¼ glass sherry
¼ pint water
1 tablespoon jam
1 tablespoon sugar
a squeeze of lime juice

Put the sugar and water into a saucepan and boil for about 10 minutes. Then add the sherry, jam and lime juice and bring to the boil.

Fruit Salads and Dessert Fruit Dishes

FRUIT, cooked or uncooked, is recognized as a wholesome food and one that should, whenever possible, be served at every meal. When fresh fruit is not obtainable, **stewed fruits** are always acceptable and they may be served with a milk pudding or blancmange, if a more substantial sweet course is wanted.

Fruit Salads are very popular and are easily prepared. All kinds of fruit in season may be used in the making of a salad, such as mangoes, papaws, apples, pineapples, plantains, oranges, grapes, etc. When fresh fruit is scare, tinned peaches, apricots or any other tinned fruit could be used together with fresh fruit. Some candied fruit or chopped almonds is sometimes mixed with the fruit or sprinkled on the top of the salad.

The fresh fruit must be sound and perfectly ripe. The mangoes, papaws, apples, and pineapple should be peeled and cut in dice or small slices; the plantains peeled and sliced; oranges should be peeled, the white skin and the pips removed, and divided into sections; grapes may be used whole or cut in two and the seeds removed.

The dressing of a fruit salad is usually a syrup made of sugar and water and flavoured with wine or fruit juice, or a sprinkling of sugar with wine or fruit juice.

The perfecting touch to a fruit salad is to chill well before serving.

731 Apples Baked

firm green-skinned apples
fine brown or castor sugar, as preferred
mixed spice to taste
1 glace cherry for each apple
some thick cream

Wash and core the apples, place in a pie-dish with water to come up to about ½ inch round them. Fill up the centres with the sugar mixed with a little spice. Bake in a moderate oven, and when the water is quite hot stir in another dessertspoonful sugar for each apple used and baste the fruit with the syrup several times during cooking. When the apples are soft inside, and the skin wrinkled, remove from the oven and cool. Arrange on a glass dish, and chill thoroughly, then put a cherry on top of each, pour over a little of the syrup, and serve with chilled cream.

732 Apple Salad

4 apples **a glass of port wine** **sugar**

Peel, core and slice the apples very thinly. Place them in a glass dish, sprinkle over with sugar and pour the wine over them. Stand in a cold place for an hour before serving.

733 Apples Stewed

1 lb. apples | **¾ pint water**
4 to 6 oz. sugar | **a few drops cochineal or carmine**

Peel the apples, cut them in quarters and remove the cores. Put them into a saucepan with the water and let them cook slowly until the apples are quite tender. Then add the sugar and stir for about 10 minutes or until the sugar is quite dissolved. Lift the quarters of apple carefully on to a glass dish, boil the syrup for a few minutes longer, colour it pink with a few drops of colouring, let it cool slightly and pour it over the fruit. Serve with cream or custard.

734 Avocado or Alligator Pear Salad

Cut the fruit in two, remove the stone and scoop out the pulp with a spoon. Add sugar or scraped jaggery to taste and mix well. Fill the avocado skins with the sweetened pulp and serve.

735 Apricots Stewed

1 lb. dried apricots | **water** | **6 to 8 oz sugar**

Wash the apricots well, put them into a basin with enough cold water to cover them and let them soak overnight. Then put the apricots and the water in which they were soaked into a saucepan and let them stew gently until the fruit is quite tender. Add the sugar and stir until it is dissolved.

N.B. If liked, a little wine may be added, and cream or custard may be served separately.

736 Bananas Spiced

ripe bananas
strained lime juice
castor sugar
mixed spice
butter
2 tablespoonfuls water to every banana used

Peel the fruit, and place them on a dish, the bottom of which has been covered with lime juice. Prick the fruit well with a fork, so that the lime flavour can penetrate, and pour the juice over every now and then. Butter a glass baking dish liberally, roll the bananas in the sugar until completely coated, and place them side by side in the dish. Sprinkle each with the spice, pour in the water, and bake in a moderate oven until soft. Baste with the syrup frequently, and turn over once during cooking.

They may be eaten either hot or cold. If the latter, they must be thoroughly chilled.

Serve with cream.

737 Dates with Custard

½ lb. dates — **a glass of wine**
2 oz. sugar — **custard**

Stone the dates and put them into a dish, sprinkle over with sugar, pour in the wine and bake for 10 minutes. Pour the custard over it and serve either hot or cold.

738 Dates Stewed

1 lb. dates — **1 glass of wine**
¼ lb. sugar — **¼ pint water**

Remove the stones from the dates, put them into a saucepan, add the sugar and the water and stew slowly for about half an hour. Add the wine just before taking it off the fire.

739 Figs Stewed

1 lb. dried figs — **water** — **6 to 8 oz sugar**

Stew in the same way as Apricots (Recipe 735).

740 Granadilla Salad

Take a nice ripe granadilla, cut it in two lengthwise and scoop out all the juice and seeds into a bowl. Then pull out the tough skin in the fruit next to the seeds and scrape out the pulp from the fruit with a spoon. Mix the pulp with the juice and seeds, add sugar to taste and a wineglass of brandy or any nice wine. Place in a cool place until wanted.

741 Grapefruit

Cut the fruit in halves, crosswise. Take out the membrane in the centre and loosen the sections round the edge with a sharp knife. Sprinkle well with castor sugar and put aside in a cool place for a few hours before serving. Then serve with a spoon.

742 Jak Stewed

½ lb. ripe jak — **1 breakfastcup water** — **¼ lb. sugar**

The jak—the hard variety—must be quite ripe. Remove the seeds and weigh the fruit. Then put it into a saucepan, add the water and simmer gently until the fruit is tender. Add the sugar and stir until it is dissolved. Serve with or without custard.

743 Mangoes Stewed

1 lb. mangoes — **8 to 10 oz. sugar**

Bombay mangoes are nice for stewing. The fruit should be sound and just ripe. Peel the mangoes, cut them in small slices and weigh the fruit. Put the fruit into a stewpan along with the sugar and stir over the fire until the fruit is cooked, and looks transparent. Then lift the slices of mangoes on to a glass dish, boil the syrup a few minutes longer, let it cool slightly and pour over the fruit.

N.B. A little wine may be added, if liked.

744 Mixed Fruit Salad I

2 oranges
2 mangoes
3 plantains
a small pineapple
a small papaw
½ lb. sugar
¼ pint water
1 glass wine
1 tablespoon brandy

Prepare the fruit (see beginning of chapter) and mix it lightly in a deep glass dish or salad bowl. Boil the sugar and water until they form a syrup, then allow to cool, add the wine and brandy and pour over the fruit. Chill for about one hour before serving.

745 Mixed Fruit Salad II

¼ lb. grapes
2 apples
2 oranges
2 plantains
2 slices pineapple
½ tin peaches
a few candied cherries
a tablespoon chopped almonds
½ lb. sugar
1 gill fruit syrup
a glass of liqueur
a glass of sherry

Prepare the fruit and mix it in a deep glass dish or salad bowl. Make a syrup with the sugar and tinned fruit juice and allow to cool. Then add the liqueur and sherry and pour over the fruit. Garnish with the cherries and chopped almonds and chill for at least an hour

N.B. Tinned cream mixed with sugar and vanilla or a vanilla flavoured custard and wafer biscuits may be served separately.

746 Mixed Fruit Salad from Dried Fruit

The most delicious fruit salads can be made from dried fruits such as apricots, figs, prunes, apples, etc., when fresh fruit is not obtainable. Wash the fruit thoroughly, put them into a basin with sufficient cold water to cover them and let them soak overnight. Then put the fruit and the water in which they were soaked into a saucepan and stew slowly until the fruit is tender. Add sugar according to taste and some fruit juice. There are some very nice fruit juices sold in bottles. A little wine may be added if wished, also some chopped nuts.

747 Orange Salad

6 oranges **a wineglass of brandy or wine** **sugar**

Peel the oranges carefully, removing all the white pith. Cut them in thin slices and take out the seeds. Arrange the slices on a glass dish, sprinkle over with powdered sugar sufficient to sweeten, and pour over it the brandy or wine. Chill well. This salad should be made at least half an hour before it is wanted.

748 Orange and Plantain Salad

4 oranges **6 oz. sugar**
6 plantains **½ teacup water**

Peel the oranges and remove all the white pith. Then cut them in very thin slices or divide the oranges in sections and take out the seeds. Peel the plantains and cut them also in slices using a silver knife to prevent discoloration. Arrange the fruit in a deep glass dish; boil the sugar and water together until they form a syrup, let it cool slightly, then pour over the fruit. Place on ice or in a cool place until wanted.

749 Papaw Stewed

1 lb. papaw **4 to 6 oz. sugar** **½ pint water**

Choose half-ripe fruit. Peel the papaw, cut it in convenient-sized pieces and remove the seeds. Then weigh the fruit and put it into a saucepan along with the water and simmer slowly until the fruit is cooked. Add the sugar and stir until it is dissolved. Then lift the pieces of fruit on to a glass dish and let the syrup boil a few minutes longer. Let it cool slightly and pour over the fruit.

N.B. A little wine may be added, if liked.

750 Peaches Stewed

1 lb. peaches **4 to 6 oz. sugar** **½ pint water**

Pare, halve and stone the peaches. Make a syrup with the sugar and water, put in the peaches and stew gently until they are quite soft without being broken. Then take them out carefully and place on a glass dish. Allow the syrup to cool slightly and pour it over.

751 Pears Stewed

1 lb. pears **a few drops of cochineal or carmine**
6 to 8 oz. sugar **1 pint water**
1 inch piece cinnamon
2 or 3 cloves

Peel the pears, cut them in halves or quarters according to size, remove the cores, and put them into a saucepan along with the water, cinnamon and cloves. Let them simmer gently until tender, from 1 to 1½ hours. Then add the sugar and the colouring and stir carefully until the sugar is dissolved. Lift the fruit carefully on to a glass dish, boil the syrup for a few minutes longer, let it cool slightly, and then pour it over.

N.B. A little port wine may be added if wished.

752 Pineapple and Custard

pineapple **sugar** **custard (Recipe 716)**

Pare the pineapple and cut it in two lengthwise, then cut each half into 6 or 8 pieces also lengthwise. Weigh the fruit and allow ¾ lb. sugar to each pound of fruit. Prick the pieces of pineapple over with a fork and put them into a saucepan with the sugar. Boil together, stirring constantly, until the syrup is thick and the fruit transparent. When cold, put it into a glass dish and pour the custard over it.

753 Pineapple Salad I

1 medium-sized pineapple **2 tablespoons orange juice** **sugar**

Pare the pineapple and cut it in small cubes. Put the fruit into a deep glass dish, add the orange juice and sprinkle over with sugar. Mix lightly together. This should be done at least a couple of hours before the salad is wanted as the sugar must be quite dissolved.

754 Pineapple Salad II

slices of ripe, sweet pineapple
1 dessertspoonful of chopped crystallized fruit for each slice
thick tinned cream sweetened to taste with castor sugar

Cut the pineapple slices about ½ inch thick, and cut out the core from each. Cut each slice into sections of a convenient size for eating, and arrange these on ice-cream plates, keeping the round shape of each slice with the well defined cavity in the centre. This must be filled with the crystallized fruit, piled up high, after each slice has been neatly coated with the sweetened cream. This is quite easy to do, if the cream is whipped in a basin with the sugar until rather frothy, then allowed to chill until smooth and thick enough to spread. Take up a teaspoonful of the cream at a time, pour it gradually over the pineapple, and smooth with the back of the spoon.

It is impossible to give accurate quantities as the size of the pines varies considerably. For slices 3½ inches in diameter after the outer skin has been pared away, from 4—5 teaspoonfuls cream will be needed.

755 Pineapple Stewed

1 lb. pineapple
6 oz. sugar
½ pint water
12 peppercorns
1 inch piece cinnamon
2 or 3 cloves
a few drops cochineal or carmine
1 dessertspoon flour

Pare the pineapple and cut it in slices. Weigh it and put the fruit into a saucepan with water, peppercorns, cinnamon and cloves and simmer gently until the fruit is cooked. Then add the sugar and a few drops of colouring and stir until the sugar is dissolved.

Lastly add the flour dissolved in half a teacup of cold water and stir for a few minutes longer until the flour is cooked and the gravy thick.

N.B. If liked, jaggery may be used instead of sugar.

756 Plantain and Custard

plantains **jam** **custard**

Peel the required number of plantains and split them in two lengthwise. Spread each piece with any nice jam and place the halves together again. Arrange in a glass dish and pour over it a custard made as given in Recipe 716.

757 Plantain Stewed

1 lb. sour plantains
6 oz. sugar
½ pint water
12 peppercorns
1 inch piece cinnamon
2 or 3 cloves
a few drops cochineal or carmine
1 dessertspoon flour

Choose nice ripe plantains, peel and then weigh them and cook in the same way as Stewed Pineapple. If liked, a custard may be served separately.

758 Prunes Stewed

½ lb. prunes **3 oz. sugar** **water**

Wash the prunes well and put them into a basin with sufficient cold water to cover them. Let them soak overnight or at least for 6 hours. Then turn the prunes and the water in which they have been soaked into a saucepan and let them simmer gently until the fruit is perfectly tender. Add the sugar and stir until the sugar is dissolved.

N.B. A piece of lime rind or a little wine may be added, if liked.

759 Raisins Stewed

½ lb. muscatel raisins **2 oz. sugar** **water**

Wash and pick the raisins free from stalks and stew in the same way as prunes.

760 Rhubarb Stewed

1 lb. rhubarb **6 to 8 oz. sugar** **water**

Wash the rhubarb, peel it, if coarse, and cut it in short lengths. Put it into a saucepan with a little water and heat over a slow fire until the sugar is melted. Then allow the fruit to simmer until it is tender but unbroken. Stewed rhubarb is nice served with blancmange.

761 Rice Border for Stewed Fruit

¼ lb. rice
1 cupful water
1 cupful milk
2 oz. castor sugar
1 dessertspoonful butter
a few drops of vanilla essence
stewed fruit

Wash the rice and drop into the cupful of freshly-boiling water, with a pinch of salt added. Cook until most of the water has been absorbed, then drain and put into a double boiler with the milk, previously heated with the sugar. Cover, and cook slowly until the milk is absorbed and the grains puffed out and soft. Put the butter in with it and allow to melt, then stir well and turn into a ring mould rinsed with water. Press down to take the shape of the mould well, and chill until wanted.

Turn out on to a round dish, and fill up the centre with any fresh, stewed or tinned fruit, handing the syrup separately.

762 Strawberries and Cream

strawberries sugar cream

Pick and wash the strawberries carefully. Put them into a glass dish, sprinkle some sugar over them and toss the two lightly together. Then whip the cream, sweeten to taste and pile this on top of the strawberries.

763 Tomatoes Stewed

1 lb. tree tomatoes 6 to 8 oz sugar ¼ pint water

Remove the stalks from the tomatoes and put them into a basin of boiling water, let them stand for a couple of minutes, then lift them out, peel them and cut them in halves. Make a syrup with the sugar and water, put in the tomatoes and stew them gently until they are tender without being broken.

764 Water Melon Salad

water melon sugar wine

Cut the melon in quarters and remove all the seeds. Then take the fleshy part, break it in pieces and put it into a glass dish. Sprinkle well with sugar and pour over it a glass of some good wine.

Rice—Curries—Sambols

In Ceylon the preparation of rice and curry is an important branch of cookery, though unfortunately much neglected, as a result of which many of the old tasty curries are forgotten, or are totally unknown to most of the present generation.

This chapter includes as comprehensive a selection of recipes for different preparations of rice, curries, and sambols as possible.

For other recipes, see chapters entitled Kandyan-Sinhalese and Tamil Recipes.

Chutneys and Pickles are in the next chapter.

For Milk Rice (Kiribath), Hoppers (Appa), Stringhoppers (Iddi Appung), Pittu, Roti, and other preparations from rice-flour, see chapter entitled Rasa Kavili.

General Hints

Boiling Rice—It is not possible to give the exact quantity of water required for boiling rice. The amount of water varies with the different kinds of rice, and it is useful to remember that newly-hulled rice requires less water than rice which has been kept for some time. Normally 2 quarts of water to a measure of rice (or 2 cups water to one cupful rice) would suit.

To prepare rice for boiling, first winnow it to remove broken grains and chaff. Then carefully remove any stones it may have mixed with it. Wash the rice well, and remove any pieces of dirt or any grains that float on top.

Boil the rice in a saucepan or pot. When nearly all the water is absorbed, press a few grains between the fingers; if the rice is hard, add a little hot water. Reduce the heat. When all the water is absorbed, add salt to taste and stir the rice well with the handle of a wooden spoon to ensure even moisture throughout and to prevent the rice forming into lumps. A 2-inch piece of rampa may be boiled with the rice for flavour.

Types of rice which get sticky should be first cleaned and washed, then plunged into boiling water to which a little salt has been added, and kept on a quick fire till the grains are cooked through. The water should then be drained off, and the pot left on hot coals to dry the excess moisture.

Curries and Sambols—In making curries and sambols, some skill is needed to judge the exact quantities required of the different flavouring agents used. Though the quantities of ingredients are given in the following recipes, no hard and fast rules can be laid down. The knowledge can be easily acquired with a little practice. Individual tastes must be taken into consideration, and the dishes made pleasing to the palate.

It is a well known fact that curries and sambols cooked in ordinary chatties taste much better than when cooked in saucepans.

Coconut Milk—*To Extract the Milk*—To each coconut (scraped) add a teacupful of water and squeeze the coconut well, then strain through a coconut-milk strainer. This milk is known as the thick milk or first extract. The coconut can be squeezed twice or even three times more, adding water each time.

In cold climates it is advisable to use hot water for squeezing coconut instead of cold.

Quantities—In this chapter the quantities of ingredents will be found to be given in perhaps the most practicable method in ordinary use. Instead of by weight the quantities are given, for the most part, in spoonfuls.

Rice

771 Buriani

1 measure buriani-rice
2 lb. lean mutton
¼ lb. ghee
¼ lb. red onions (sliced)
2- inch piece cinnamon
6 cardamoms (powdered)
6 cloves
2-inch piece rampa
½ stem lemon-grass
salt
a little diluted Spanish saffron

Cut the mutton in about 2-inch squares and put them into a saucepan. . Pour in a sufficient quantity of boiling water to cover the meat and let it simmer until the mutton is cooked but not too tender. Melt the ghee in a saucepan and when very hot put in the rampa and lemon-grass and one-third of the onions and stir until the onions are fried. Then turn in the rice well washed and stir for a few minutes. Add the mutton and the stock (add boiling water, if the stock is not sufficient for boiling the rice) and the rest of the ingredients, except the cardamoms and saffron, and boil until the rice is cooked. Mix in the cardamoms when the rice is half-cooked. When the rice is ready, take a small portion of it separately and mix with it the saffron which both colours and flavours. Then mix the coloured rice together with the other and dish it out neatly.

N.B. Spanish saffron is obtainable at the Bombay sweet shops in Colombo.

An Onion Sambol usually accompanies Buriani. Most of the curries served with Ghee Rice (see 773) go well with Buriani.

772 Egg Rice

1 measure table-rice
6 or 8 eggs
2 oz. ghee or dripping
2 oz. red onions
20 peppercorns
6 cloves
2-inch piece cinnamon
salt

Wash and boil the rice, adding the cinnamon, cloves, peppercorns and salt. Keep the rice warm while you prepare the egg. Beat the eggs, first the whites separately, then add the yolks and beat together. Heat the ghee in a saucepan or chatty, put in the onions and let them boil—they must not brown—then turn in the beaten egg, stir briskly for a minute or two, put in the boiled rice and mix well together. Before adding the rice to the egg remove the piece of cinnamon.

The usual curries served with Egg Rice are the same as for Ghee Rice.

773 Ghee Rice

1½ measures table-rice
6 oz. ghee
6 oz. red onions (sliced)
25 peppercorns
8 cloves
salt
4-inch piece rampa
½ stem lemon-grass
3-inch piece cinnamon
15 cardamoms (powdered)
a sufficient quantity of meat stock to boil the rice

Heat the ghee in a saucepan or chatty, and when very hot, put in one-third of the onions, and a small piece each of the rampa and lemon-grass, and stir until the onions are fried. Then turn in the rice which must be well washed, and stir for a few minutes, add the stock and the rest of the ingredients, except the cardamoms and boil until the rice is cooked. Mix in the cardamoms when the rice is half-cooked.

Curries etc. to be served with Ghee Rice: Fowl Malay Badun (Recipe 813), Liver and Brinjal Curry (821), Sathey Malay Curry (834), Plantain Curry (847), Brinjal Pahi (864), Chilli Sambol (866).

774 Italian Risotto

½ lb. table-rice
1½ cupfuls chicken stock very well flavoured with vegetables, (**celery, carrot, onion, peppercorns, etc.**)
1 Bombay onion
2 oz. butter
1 cupful thick tomato puree
pepper and salt to taste
2 oz. grated cheese
the white meat from the chicken

Boil the chicken with seasonings as usual. Strain the stock from it, and measure.

Wash the rice very well. Chop the Bombay onion very finely, and fry in the butter without browning. Turn the rice into the pan, and stir well until it takes up all the butter, then pour in the stock and cook until all of it has been absorbed and the rice grains are soft without being mushy. Put in the pieces of chicken cut into fairly small pieces, the tomato puree, and season to taste. Last of all stir in the cheese, mix all well together, and serve on a hot dish.

A good accompaniment to this dish is a very dry chicken curry, the chicken being cut up into quite small pieces.

775 "Lampries" (Dutch Lomprijst)

The rice is prepared like Ghee Rice (Recipe 773). Partially boil the fowl, mutton, and beef (of which the lampries curry is made), and use the stock for boiling the rice. When the rice, curries, etc., are cooked, have ready pieces of plantain leaf, 14×12 inches. Put about 3 tablespoonfuls of rice on each leaf, pour a dessertspoonful of thick coconut milk over the rice, and arrange a little of the curry, a couple of frikkadels, and a little of each of the sambols on the rice, fold up the leaves, making them into neat oblong parcels, and fasten the two ends with pieces of ekel. Then bake the lampries in a moderately hot oven for about 20 minutes. 1½ measures of rice will be sufficient for about 24 lampries.

N.B. Before using the plantain eaves, they must be washed, wiped dry, and warmed over the fire.

Curries etc. to be enclosed in the Lampries: Lampries Curry (Recipe 818), Frikkadels (814), Brinjal Pahi (864), Chilli Sambol (866), Cucumber Sambol (868, 869), Prawn Blachang (874).

776 Pilau

1 measure table-rice	**2 oz. shelled almonds**
1 fowl	**2 inch piece rampa**
8 slices of bacon (fried)	**2-inch piece cinnamon**
4 eggs	**12 cardamoms (powdered)**
¼ lb. ghee	**pepper and salt**
¼ lb. red onions	**a pinch of ground saffron**
¼ lb. sultana raisins	**ghee for frying the fowl and eggs**

Pluck and draw the fowl, wash it and put into a stewpan with sufficient water to cover it, and boil slowly until the fowl is partially cooked. Then remove the fowl from the stock (the stock is used for boiling the rice), cut it into neat joints, rub over with pepper and salt, and fry a nice brown in hot ghee. Heat ¼ lb. ghee in a saucepan or chatty and fry half the onions together with the rampa; when the onions are browned, put in the rice well washed, the remainder of the onions, the cinnamon, and a sufficient quantity of fowl stock to boil the rice. Add the raisins and cardamoms when the rice is half-cooked, and mix in the almonds as soon as the rice is taken off the fire. When ready, dish the rice neatly, with the pieces of fowl embedded in the rice, and arrange the bacon (fried) and eggs (cut in halves) on the top. The eggs must be boiled hard, then shelled, rubbed over with salt and saffron and fried a golden brown in ghee.

777 Stringhopper Pilau

25 stringhoppers (Recipe 1036)
1 chicken
4 slices ham
3 eggs
2 oz. ghee
2 oz. red onions
2 oz. sultana raisins
1 oz. shelled almonds
2-inch piece rampa
½ stem lemon-grass
8 cardamoms (powdered)
pepper
salt
a pinch of ground saffron
ghee for frying the chicken and eggs

Pluck and draw the chicken, wash it and put into a stewpan, add a little water and boil slowly until the chicken is partially cooked. Then cut it into neat joints, rub over with pepper and salt and fry a nice brown in hot ghee. Break up the string-hoppers. Heat 2 oz. ghee in a saucepan and fry the onions (sliced) together with the rampa and lemon-grass. When the onions are browned, put in the stringhoppers and stir well for 10 minutes adding the cardamoms. Mix in the almonds and sultanas as soon as it is taken off the fire.

When ready, dish the stringhopper pilau neatly with the pieces of chicken embedded in it, the ham fried and cut in pieces and the eggs cut in quarters on the top. The eggs must be boiled hard, shelled, rubbed over with salt and saffron and fried a golden brown in ghee.

778 Savoury Rice

2 breakfastcupfuls boiled rice
4 large eggs
2 dessertspoonfuls shredded red onions
1 dessertspoonful chopped green chillies (seeds removed)
2 leeks (chopped)
4 scant tablespoonfuls melted ghee
salt and pepper to taste

Fry the leeks in the ghee for about 5 minutes, then add the chillies and onions and fry all together until cooked but not brown. Beat the eggs in a basin with salt and pepper, turn into the same pan and fry all together, "scrambling" the eggs into rather coarse pieces, by mixing round and round with a wooden spoon. Now add the cooked rice, a big spoonful at a time, and mix well with each addition. Pile up on a hot dish and serve.

This is a very tasty way of serving rice. With meat or chicken curry it takes the place of the heavier ghee or yellow rice, although it is quite good by itself.

779 Savoury Rice Mould

savoury rice (Recipe 778)
a little butter
filling mixture

Prepare the rice as directed, and pack it firmly into a lightly buttered ring mould, pressing down with the back of a spoon until it is level with the top of the mould. Smooth off with the blade of a knife. Put into a very hot oven for about 5 minutes.

Invert on to a hot dish, and give a sharp tap to loosen the mixture from the sides. The mould should then lift off easily, leaving an attractive border, the cavity of which should be filled with any suitable accompaniment—creamed fish or chicken, curried mince, a chicken badun curry, or rather dry fish curry.

780 Yellow Rice

1½ measures table-rice or good muttusamba rice
3 oz. ghee or dripping
6 oz. red onions (sliced)
2 oz. pounded Maldive fish
8 cloves
25 peppercorns
15 cardamoms (powdered)
a few sprigs of fennel
salt
4-inch piece rampa
½ stem lemon-grass
a small sprig of curry-leaves
a sufficient quantity of ground saffron to colour the rice
a sufficient quantity of coconut milk to boil the rice (the extract of 2 coconuts)

Heat the ghee in a chatty or saucepan, and when very hot, fry one-third of the onions, together with a small piece each of the rampa and lemon-grass, and a few curry-leaves. Keep stirring until the onions are browned then turn in the rice well washed, stir for about 3 minutes, and add the coconut milk with which must be mixed the rest of the ingredients, except the cardamoms, which mix in when the rice is half-cooked.

N.B. Meat boilings may be used for boiling the rice instead of coconut milk.

Curries etc. to be served with Yellow Rice: Fried Egg Curry (Recipe 806), Fowl Badun (812), Liver Curry (820), Pork Badun (824), Sathey Curry (833), Brinjal Curry (842), Chilli Sambol (866), Coconut Sambol (867), Cucumber Sambol (868, 869).

Curries — Fish, Meat &c.

(For other curries, see Kandyan-Sinhalese and Tamil Recipes)

791 Beef Badun

Wash the meat, cut it in slices about half an inch thick, and chop them lightly. Then prepare in the same way as Beef Smoore (Recipe 795) omitting the lime-pickle, and boiling the meat in coconut milk (second extract) instead of water.

792 Beef Curry

2 lb. beef
15 dry chillies (ground)
a pinch of ground saffron
1 dessertspoonful sliced red onions
3 cloves of garlic (chopped)
2 slices green ginger (chopped)
¼ teaspoon fenugreek
2-inch piece rampa
½ stem lemon-grass
a small sprig of curry-leaves
2-inch piece cinnamon
juice of half a lime
1 dessertspoonful ghee or dripping
salt
1 teacup thick coconut milk
3 teacups second extract of coconut milk

Wash and cut the meat into small pieces and put into a chatty with the second extract of milk, the chilli, saffron, garlic, ginger and salt, and half each of the onions, rampa, lemon-grass, curry-leaves, cinnamon and fenugreek, and boil until the meat is tender. Then add the thick milk and the lime juice, and let it boil 10 minutes, Heat the ghee in a chatty and fry the remainder of the ingredients, then turn in the meat mixture and let it simmer for 10 minutes longer.

793 Beef Malay Curry

2 lb. beef
20 dry chillies (pounded)
1 dessertspoonful white cummin seed (ground)
a pinch of ground saffron
1 dessertspoonful sliced red onions
3 cloves of garlic (chopped)
3 slices green ginger (chopped)
2-inch piece rampa
½ stem lemon grass
a small sprig of curry-leaves
¼ teaspoon fenugreek
2-inch piece cinnamon
6 cardamoms (powdered)
4 cloves (powdered)
2 pieces aromatic ginger (powdered)
1 dessertspoonful ghee or dripping
salt
juice of one lime
1 teacup thick coconut milk

Wash and cut the meat into 1½-inch squares. Put it into a chatty, with 6 teacups of water, the chilli, saffron, garlic. ginger, rampa, lemon-grass, curry-leaves, cinnamon, salt, and half the onions, and boil gently until the meat is very tender and the gravy reduced to about a cupful. Heat the ghee and fry the remainder of the onions together with the fenugreek, then turn in the meat preparation to which must be added the coconut milk mixed with the cummin, cardamoms, aromatic ginger, cloves and lime juice, and let it simmer for about 15 minutes longer.

794 Beef Mustard Curry

Prepare in the same way as Beef Curry (Recipe 792), adding a dessertspoonful of mustard seed (ground) to the other ingredients.

795 Beef Smoore

3 lb. beef
1 tablespoonful sliced red onions
6 cloves of garlic (chopped)
6 slices green ginger (chopped)
2-inch piece cinnamon
4-inch piece rampa
½ stem lemon-grass
a small sprig of curry-leaves
1½ tablespoons coriander seed
1½ teaspoons white cummin seed
1 teaspoonful sweet cummin seed (roasted and grounded together)
½ teaspoon fenugreek
1½ wineglasses vinegar
half a pickled lime
2 tablespoonfuls ghee
1 teacup thick coconut milk
salt
a pinch of ground saffron
20 dry chillies (roasted and ground)

Wash the meat, prick it over with a steel skewer or fork and put it into a chatty with 3 teacups of water and all the ingredients, except the coconut milk and ghee, and boil gently until the meat is tender. Then add the coconut milk and boil for 15 minutes longer. Remove the gravy, put in the ghee and fry the meat. Pour back the gravy and stir for a couple of minutes.

796 Brain Badun

The brain must not be cut into slices but cooked whole. Prepare in the same way as Beef Badun (Recipe 791).

797 Brain Pudichchi

Prepare in the same way as Fish Pudichchi (Recipe 810).

798 Curried Chicken

Prepare in the same way as Curried Hare (Recipe 816).

799 Chicken White Curry

1 chicken
1 dessertspoonful sliced red onions
a few sprigs of fennel
2 cloves of garlic and 2 slices green ginger (chopped)
a pinch of ground saffron
10 dry chillies (ground)
a dessertspoonful of coriander seed
1 teaspoonful of white cummin seed and ½ teaspoon sweet cummin seed (ground together)
¼ teaspoon fenugreek
1 dessertspoonful ghee
1-inch piece cinnamon
2-inch piece rampa
¼ stem lemon-grass
a small sprig of curry-leaves
juice of half a lime
1 teacup thick coconut milk
1½ teacups second extract of coconut milk

Cut the chicken in joints and put them into a chatty with the second extract of coconut milk, the fennel, garlic, ginger, saffron, ground chillies, fenugreek, cinnamon and salt and half each of the onions, rampa, lemon-grass and curry-leaves. Cook until the chicken is half done, then add the thick milk mixed with the coriander and cummins, add also the lime juice and cook until the chicken is tender. Heat the ghee in a chatty and fry the remainder of the ingredients, turn in the chicken preparation and allow to simmer a few minutes longer.

800 Crab Curry

4 medium-sized crabs
30 dry chillies (ground)
a pinch of ground saffron
1 dessertspoonful sliced red onions
4 cloves of garlic (chopped)
2 slices green ginger (chopped)
¼ teaspoon fenugreek
2 tablespoonfuls scraped coconut and
1 teaspoonful raw-rice (ground together)
2-inch piece cinnamon
2 handfuls of "drum-stick" leaves
salt
juice of 1½ limes
3 teacups thick coconut milk
½ teacup second extract of coconut milk

Break the crabs into pieces and put them into a chatty with the rest of the ingredients, except the thick milk, the ground coconut and rice, and the lime juice, and let it boil until the gravy is all absorbed. Then add the thick milk mixed with the ground coconut and rice, and the lime juice. Let it simmer slowly for about 10 minutes longer.

801 Cuttle-Fish Badun

Clean and cut the fish in rings and boil in water until tender. Then prepare in the same way as Fowl Badun (Recipe 812). Cuttle fish is also nice made into black curry. First boil the fish and then make according to directions given in Recipe 823, omitting the cardamoms.

802 Dry Fish Curry

½ lb. dry fish
2 oz. tamarin
2 teaspoons white cummin seed and 1 teaspoon sweet cummin seed (lightly roasted and ground together)
20 dry chillies (lightly roasted and ground)
a pinch of ground saffron
2½ wineglasses vinegar
1 tablespoonful coriander seed
2-inch piece rampa
¼ stem lemon-grass
a small sprig of curry-leaves
2-inch piece cinnamon
1 dessertspoonful sugar
½ teacup thick coconut milk
coconut oil

Wash and cut the dry fish into convenient sized pieces. Squeeze the tamarind in the vinegar and mix with the ground coriander, cummins, chillies and saffron, and add the rampa, lemon-grass, curry-leaves and cinnamon. Mix all together and put the dry fish into this mixture. Let it remain for about an hour or so. Then take the dry fish out of the gravy and fry it in oil. Mix the coconut milk with the gravy and pour it over the fried dry fish and stir over the fire until the ingredients are cooked. Just before taking it off the fire, mix in the sugar.

803 Dry Fish and Brinjal Curry

½ lb. dry seer
1 lb. brinjal
12 large curry chillies
10 or 12 cloves of garlic
½ lb. red onions
15 dry chillies
3 tablespoons coriander
2 teaspoons small cummin
½ teaspoon large cummin
small piece cinnamon
pinch of saffron
2 oz. tamarind squeezed in a sufficient quantity of vinegar
first and second milk of one coconut

Cut the brinjals in four lengthwise and rub the pieces with saffron and salt. Wash the chillies and slit them down one side. Remove the seeds and soak them in salt water. Wash the dry fish and cut it into 2-inch pieces. Fry all the ingredients in coconut oil—first the dry fish, then the chillies, garlic, brinjals, and red onions, taking one lot of ingredients out before adding the next. Mix all the curry stuffs with the coconut milk, add salt and tamarind to taste, and put on to boil. When boiling, add the fried ingredients and allow to simmer till the gravy is thick. If desired, add a tablespoon of sugar and mix well just before serving.

804 Duck Padre Curry

2 ducks
¾ oz. dry chillies
½ oz. coriander seed
¼ oz. white cummin seed
3-inch piece of cinnamon
2-inch piece of rampa
½ stem lemon-grass
a small sprig of curry-leaves
1 tablespoonful sugar
3 tablespoonfuls vinegar
½ oz. sweet cummin seed
1 tablespoonful sliced red onions
6 cloves of garlic
6 slices of green ginger
a wineglass of arrack or whisky
1 tablespoonful dripping
pepper
salt
coconut milk (the extract of one coconut)

Roast, pound, and sieve the chillies, coriander and cummins, each ingredient separately. Cut the ducks into neat joints and put them into a saucepan or chatty with sufficient coconut milk to cover, mix in the powdered ingredients, add the onions, garlic, ginger, cinnamon, pepper, salt, rampa, lemon-grass, curry-leaves and vinegar, and boil for half an hour. Then add the sugar and arrack and let it simmer gently until the duck is tender. Heat the dripping in a saucepan or chatty and fry the pieces of duck, then add the gravy and stir for a couple of minutes. Serve the curry neatly in a dish, and cover the top with Fried Potatoes (Recipe 426).

805 Egg Curry

4 hard-boiled eggs (cut in halves lengthwise)
1 teaspoonful Maldive fish
1 dessertspoonful sliced red onions
1 ripe or green chilli (cut lengthwise)
a few sprigs of fennel
a pinch of ground saffron
a slice of green ginger (chopped)
1 clove of garlic (chopped)
a few curry-leaves
¼ teaspoon fenugreek
a small piece of cinnamon
juice of half a lime
salt
½ teacup thick coconut milk
1½ teacups second extract of coconut milk

Put all the ingredients, except the thick milk and the lime juice, into a chatty and boil until the ingredients are cooked. Then add the thick milk and the lime juice and stir well or it will curdle. Add the eggs, stir for a few minutes, take it off the fire and continue stirring for a couple of minutes longer.

N.B. The gravy by itself is known as coconut soup or anang.

806 Fried Egg Curry

8 eggs
1 dessertspoonful sliced red onions
2 cloves of garlic (chopped)
2 slices green ginger (chopped)
2-inch piece rampa
¼ stem lemon-grass
a small sprig of curry-leaves
2 inch piece cinnamon
a few sprigs of fennel
1 dessertspoonful coriander seed
1 teaspoonful white cummin seed
½ teaspoon sweet cummin seed (roasted and ground together)
¼ teaspoon fenugreek
juice of half a lime
ghee or dripping
1½ teacupfuls coconut milk (extract of half a coconut)
1 dessertspoonful pounded Maldive fish
salt
a pinch of ground saffron
10 dry chillies (ground

Boil the eggs hard, shell them, rub over with salt and saffron, and fry a nice golden brown colour in hot ghee. The eggs must be picked over with a stout pin before frying so as to prevent them from bursting. Then make the gravy. Heat a dessertspoonful of ghee and fry half the onions, a small piece each of the rampa and lemon-grass, and a few curry-leaves, then add the coconut milk and the rest of the ingredients, except the lime juice, and boil until the gravy is thick, stirring now and again. Put in the eggs, add the lime juice, and let it simmer for a few minutes longer.

807 Poached Egg Curry

Make the gravy as for Fried Egg Curry (Recipe 806). When the gravy boils, break the eggs one at a time into a cup and carefully slip them into the gravy, and cook until the whites seem set.

808 Fish Ambul-Thiyal

2 slices seer fish
25 dry chillies (ground)
1 teaspoonful white cummin seed (ground)
½ teaspoon ground pepper
a pinch of ground saffron
¼ teaspoon fenugreek
2-inch piece cinnamon
salt
1 dessertspoonful sliced red onions
2 cloves of garlic (chopped)
2 slices green ginger (chopped)
2 inch piece rampa
¼ stem lemon-grass
a small sprig of curry-leaves
3 pieces dried gamboge (finely ground)

Wash the fish and put the slices into a chatty. Add a teacup of water and all the ingredients and let it simmer until the gravy is thick.

809 Fish Pindun Curry

2 slices seer fish
1 dessertspoonful sliced red onions
3 cloves of garlic (chopped)
2 slices green ginger (chopped)
2-inch piece cinnamon
2-inch piece rampa
¼ stem lemon-grass
a small sprig of curry-leaves
1 dessertspoon vinegar
1 dessertspoonful coraínder seed
1 teaspoonful white cummin seed & ½ teaspoon sweet cummin seed (roasted and ground together)
½ oz. tamarind (squeezed in vinegar)
2 teacups coconut milk
coconut oil
pepper
salt
¼ teaspoon fenugreek
a pinch of ground saffron
12 dry chillies (roasted and ground)

Wash the fish and rub it over with pepper, salt, and saffron, and fry to a light brown in hot oil. Then make the gravy. Put the coconut milk into a chatty, add the rest of the ingredients, and boil until the ingredients are cooked. Then put in the fish and keep on a slow fire for a few minutes longer.

810 Fish Pudichchi

2 slices seer fish
15 dry chillies (ground)
a pinch of ground saffron
3 dessertspoonfuls sliced red onions
2 cloves of garlic (chopped)
2 slices green ginger (chopped)
2-inch piece cinnamon
2-inch piece rampa
¼ stem lemon-grass
a small sprig of curry leaves
¼ teaspoon fenugreek
juice of half a lime
1½ teacups coconut milk
salt

Wash the fish, cut each slice in four and put into a chatty. Add all the ingredients except the lime juice, and boil until the fish is cooked, adding the lime juice when the curry is half-cooked.

811 Fish Smoore

2 lb. seer or para fish
pepper
salt
a pinch of ground saffron
1 tablespoonful ghee
1 tablespoonful sliced red onions
4 cloves of garlic and 4 slices green ginger (chopped)
2-inch piece cinnamon
3-inch piece rampa
¼ stem lemon-grass
a small sprig of curry-leaves
1 tablespoonful coriander
1 teaspoonful white cummin seed and half teaspoon sweet cummin seed (roasted and ground together)
15 dry chillies (roasted and ground)
¼ teaspoon fenugreek
1 wineglass vinegar
1½ teacups coconut milk

Wash the fish and rub it over with pepper, salt and saffron, and fry to a light brown in ghee. Then add all the ingredients and allow to simmer until the ingredients are cooked.

812 Fowl Badun

1 fowl
1 tablespoonful sliced red onions
4 cloves of garlic (chopped)
2 slices green ginger (chopped)
a pinch of ground saffron
20 dry chillies (roasted and ground)
¼ teaspoon fenugreek, 1 tablespoonful coriander seed, 1 teaspoonful white cummin seed, ½ teaspoon sweet cummin seed (roasted and ground together)
1 tablespoonful ghee
salt
2-inch piece cinnamon
2-inch piece rampa
¼ stem lemon-grass
a small sprig of curry-leaves
1 wineglass vinegar
3 teacups coconut milk (extract of one coconut)

Cut the fowl into neat joints, and put it into a chatty with the coconut milk and the rest of the ingredients, excepting the ghee, and boil until the fowl is tender and the gravy reduced to very little. Then remove the fowl from the gravy and fry it in ghee, pour back the gravy and keep on a slow fire for a couple of minutes longer.

813 Fowl Malay Badun

1 fowl
20 dry chillies (ground)
1 dessertspoonful white cummin seed (ground)
1½ teaspoons sweet cummin seed (slightly roasted and pounded)
a pinch of ground saffron
¼ teaspoon fenugreek
1 dessertspoonful sliced red onions
3 cloves of garlic (chopped)
2 slices green ginger (chopped)
2-inch piece rampa
½ stem lemon-grass
a small sprig of curry-leaves
2-inch piece cinnamon
lime juice to taste
1 tablespoonful ghee or dripping
3 teacups coconut milk (the extract of one coconut)

Have the fowl drawn and trussed as for roasting. Put it into a chatty, add the coconut milk and the rest of the ingredients, except the sweet cummin and lime juice, and boil until the fowl is tender and the gravy reduced to about a cupful. (The sweet cummin and the lime juice must be added when the curry is half-cooked). Then remove the gravy, put in the ghee, and fry the fowl a nice brown. Pour back the gravy, and let it remain a few minutes longer on a slow fire.

814 Frikkadels (Dutch: Forced-meat Balls)

1 lb. beef
a thick slice of bread (grated)
1 tablespoonful of chopped red onions
2 cloves of garlic (chopped)
2 slices green ginger (chopped)
1 teaspoonful chopped fennel
powdered cinnamon
cloves and pepper
salt
1 egg
juice of half a lime
egg and breadcrumbs
ghee or dripping

Mince the meat finely or pass it through a mincing machine. Season the meat with pepper, salt, cloves, and cinnamon, add the onions and grated bread, and moisten with the lime juice and the egg slightly beaten. Mix well together and make into small balls, about the size of a marble; dip in beaten egg, roll in breadcrumbs and fry in hot ghee.

815 Frikkadel Curry

Make the frikkadels as directed in Recipe 814, and the gravy as for Fried Egg Curry (Recipe 806). When the gravy is ready, put in the frikkadels and keep on a slow fire for 10 minutes.

816 Curried Hare

1 medium-sized hare
1 oz. dry chillies
½ oz. coriander seed
¼ oz. white cummin seed
⅛ oz. sweet cummin seed
½ teaspoon fenugreek
1 tablespoonful sliced red onions
a pinch of ground saffron
4 cloves
garlic (chopped)
2 slices green ginger (chopped)
2- inch piece cinnamon
2- inch piece rampa
½ stem lemon-grass
a small sprig of curry-leaves
1 wineglass vinegar
1 tablespoonful ghee or dripping
salt
coconut milk (the extract of one coconut)

Roast and grind the chillies, coriander and cummins. Skin and paunch the hare and cut it into small neat joints. Put them into a saucepan or chatty with a sufficient quantity of coconut milk to cover the pieces. Add the rest of the ingredients and let it simmer gently until the hare is tender and the gravy has reduced. Heat the ghee in a saucepan or chatty and fry the pieces of hare, then add the gravy and stir for a couple of minutes. Serve with Fried Potatoes (Recipe 426).

817 Kuruma Iraichchi

1 lb. beef
1 tablespoonful coriander seed (ground)
1 dessertspoonful white cummin seed (ground)
3 cloves of garlic (chopped)
3 slices green ginger (chopped)
2-inch piece rampa
$\frac{1}{4}$ stem lemon-grass
a small sprig of curry-leaves
1 teaspoonful sweet cummin seed (pounded)
a pinch of ground saffron
1 teaspoonful powdered pepper
4 cloves
salt
2-inch piece cinnamon
1 dessertspoonful sliced red onions
a few sprigs of fennel
2 ripe chillies (sliced)
1 tablespoonful ghee or dripping
1 wineglass vinegar
1 teacup thick coconut milk

Wash the meat and cut it in slices about half an inch thick and chop them lightly. Put the meat into a chatty with 2 teacups of water and all the ingredients except the coconut milk, cummins, and ghee, and boil until the meat is tender. Then remove the gravy, put in the ghee, and fry the meat. Mix the cummins with the coconut milk, add it to the gravy, pour the whole over the meat and let it simmer over a slow fire until the gravy is thick.

[For Kuruma Iraichchi (White Curry), see Recipe 988]

818 Lampries Curry (Lampries: Recipe 775)

1 fowl
$\frac{1}{2}$ lb. mutton
$\frac{1}{2}$ lb. beef
$\frac{1}{2}$ lb. pork
1 dessertspoonful sliced red onions
4 cloves of garlic (chopped)
3 slices green ginger (chopped)
2-inch piece cinnamon
10 cardamoms (powdered)
$\frac{1}{4}$ teaspoonful fenugreek
3-inch piece rampa
1 teaspoonful coriander seed, 1 teaspoonful white cummin seed, $\frac{1}{2}$ teaspoon sweet cummin seed (roasted dark and ground together)
$\frac{1}{2}$ stem lemon-grass
a small sprig of curry leaves
1 dessertspoonful ghee or dripping
juice of one lime
3 teacups of coconut milk (the extract of one coconut)
a pinch of ground saffron
$\frac{1}{4}$ lb. dried prawns (roasted and pounded)
25 dry chillies (roasted dark and ground)

Partially boil the fowl, mutton, and beef, and use the stock for boiling the rice. Cut the different boiled meats and the pork into very small pieces, and put into a chatty with the coconut milk, the ground ingredients, the garlic, ginger, cinnamon, fenugreek, and salt, and half each of the onions, rampa, lemon-grass, and curry leaves, and boil until the meat is tender, adding the prawns, cardamoms, and lime juice when the curry is half-cooked. Heat the ghee in a chatty and fry the remainder of the ingredients, then turn in the meat preparation and allow to simmer a few minutes longer.

819 Liver Badun

Prepare in the same way as Beef Badun (Recipe 791).

820 Liver Curry

1 lb. liver
10 dry chillies (roasted and ground)
1 dessertspoonful white cummin seed (ground)
2 slices green ginger (chopped)
2-inch piece rampa
$\frac{1}{4}$ stem lemon-grass
a small sprig of curry-leaves
2 pieces aromatic ginger (powdered)
a pinch of ground saffron
1 dessertspoonful sliced red onions
salt
3 cloves of garlic (chopped)
10 cardamoms (powdered)
$\frac{1}{4}$ teaspoon fenugreek
$\frac{1}{2}$ wineglass vinegar
1 dessertspoonful ghee or dripping
1 teacup thick coconut milk

Wash and boil the liver, and cut it into thin slices and then into fine strips about half an inch long. Put the liver into a chatty, add the coconut milk and all the ingredients and boil until the ingredients are cooked. Then remove the gravy, put in the ghee, and fry the liver; pour back the gravy and stir for a couple of minutes.

821 Liver and Brinjal Curry

$\frac{1}{2}$ lb. liver
3 medium-sized brinjals
10 dry chillies (powdered)
a pinch of ground saffron
1 dessertspoonful sliced red onions
2 cloves of garlic (chopped)
2 slices green ginger (chopped)
2-inch piece rampa
$\frac{1}{4}$ stem lemon-grass
a small sprig of curry-leaves
2-inch piece cinnamon
1 dessertspoonful coriander seed, and 1 teaspoonful sweet cummin seed (slightly roasted and ground together)
4 cardamoms (powdered)
2 pieces aromatic ginger (powdered)
1 teaspoonful ghee or dripping
salt
coconut oil
$\frac{1}{2}$ oz. tamarind (squeezed in coconut milk)
$1\frac{1}{2}$ teacups coconut milk
$1\frac{1}{2}$ teaspoons white cummin seed (ground)

Cut the brinjals into small square pieces, mix with salt and saffron and fry in oil. Wash and boil the liver and cut it into small pieces. Mix the coconut milk, the ground ingredients, the chilli, garlic, ginger, cinnamon, cardamoms, aromatic ginger, tamarind and salt, and half each of the onions, rampa, lemon-grass, and curry-leaves together, and add the liver and brinjal. Heat the ghee and fry the remainder of the ingredients, then turn in the whole mixture and let it simmer until the ingredients are cooked.

822 Liver Finkel Curry

1 lb. liver
4 dry chillies (ground)
a pinch of ground saffron
4 cloves of garlic (chopped)
3 slices green ginger (chopped)
a few sprigs of fennel
2-inch piece rampa
¼ stem lemon-grass
powdered cinnamon
cloves and pepper
1 dessertspoonful sliced red onions
a small sprig of curry-leaves
1 dessertspoonful ghee or dripping
salt
2 tablespoons vinegar
2 teacups coconut milk

Wash and boil the liver. Then cut it in tiny dice and season with pepper, salt, cloves and cinnamon. Heat the ghee in a chatty and fry half the onions, a small piece each of the rampa and lemon-grass, and a few curry-leaves; when the onions are fried, put in the liver and the rest of the ingredients, and let it simmer until the gravy is thick.

823 Mutton Black Curry

1 lb. mutton
½ lb. sheep's liver
1 sheep's heart
1 tablespoonful sliced red onions
a small sprig of curry-leaves
2-inch piece cinnamon
1 tablespoonful coriander seed, 1 teaspoonful white commin seed and ½ teaspoon sweet cummin seed (roasted and ground together)
2 cloves of garlic
2 slices green ginger
1-inch piece cinnamon
3 cloves of garlic (chopped)
2 slices green ginger (chopped)
2-inch piece rampa
¼ stem lemon-grass
a few curry-leaves
15 cardamoms (powdered)
½ teaspoon fenugreek
1 dessertspoonful ghee or dripping
salt
4 teacups coconut milk (extract of one coconut)
juice of 1½ limes
a pinch of ground saffron
25 dry chillies (roasted dark and ground)

Wash and cut the mutton, liver, and heart into small pieces, a little smaller than for an ordinary beef curry. The roasted ingredients must be browned very dark as the curry should be dark in appearance. Put the meat into a chatty with the coconut milk, the ground ingredients, the ginger, garlic, cinnamon, salt, three-fourths of the onions, and half each of the rampa, lemon-grass, curry-leaves, and fenugreek, and boil gently until the meat is tender, adding the lime juice when the curry is half-cooked. Heat the ghee in a chatty and fry the remainder of the ingredients, then turn in the meat mixture, and keep on a slow fire for a few minutes longer.

824 Pork Badun

2 lb. pork
1 dessertspoonful sliced red onions
4 cloves of garlic (chopped)
2 slices green ginger (chopped)
2-inch piece rampa
¼ stem lemon-grass
a small sprig of curry-leaves
1 tablespoonful coriander seed
1 teaspoonful white cummin seed, ½ teaspoon sweet cummin seed (roasted and ground together)
2-inch piece cinnamon
¼ teaspoon fenugreek
1 wineglass vinegar
½ teacup thick coconut milk
salt
30 dry chillies (roasted and ground)

Wash and cut the pork into squares of about 2 inches, and put into a chatty with 1½ teacups of water and all the ingredients, except the coconut milk, and boil until the pork is tender. Then add the coconut milk and let it simmer for 10 minutes longer. Remove the gravy and allow the pork to fry a nice brown. No ghee need be added as there should be sufficient fat in the pork for frying. Pour back the gravy and stir for a couple of minutes.

825 Pork Padre Curry

3 lb. pork
¾ oz. dry chillies
½ oz. coriander seed
¼ oz. white cummin seed
⅛ oz. sweet cummin seed
1 tablespoonful sliced red onions
6 slices green ginger and 4 cloves of garlic (chopped)
2-inch piece rampa
½ stem lemon-grass
a small sprig of curry-leaves
3-inch piece cinnamon
3 tablespoons vinegar
a wineglass of whisky
1 tablespoonful sugar
pepper
salt
coconut milk (the extract of 1 coconut)

Roast, pound and sieve the chillies, coriander and cummins, each ingredient separately. Wash and cut the pork into squares of about two inches and put them into a saucepan with sufficient coconut milk to cover. Mix in the powdered ingredients, add the onions, garlic, ginger, cinnamon, pepper, salt, rampa, lemon-grass, curry-leaves and vinegar and boil for half an hour. Then add the sugar and whisky and let it simmer gently until the pork is tender. Remove the gravy and allow the pork to fry a nice brown. No dripping need be added as there should be sufficient fat in the pork for frying. Then pour back the gravy and stir for a couple of minutes. Serve the curry neatly in a dish and cover the top with Fried Potatoes (Recipe 426).

826 Pork Red Curry

2 lb. pork
30 dry chillies (ground)
a pinch of ground saffron
1 dessertspoonful sliced red onions
4 cloves of garlic (chopped)
3 slices green ginger (chopped)
2-inch piece cinnamon
2-inch piece rampa
¼ stem lemon-grass
a small sprig of curry-leaves
¼ teaspoon fenugreek
4 pieces dried gamboge
1 dessertspoonful ghee or dripping
salt
½ teacup thick coconut milk
juice of ½ lime

Wash the pork and cut it into small pieces. Put into a chatty with 1½ teacups of water, the chilli, saffron, garlic, ginger, cinnamon, gamboge and salt, and half-each of the onions, fenugreek, rampa, lemon-grass and curry-leaves, and boil gently until the meat is tender. Then add the milk and lime juice, and let it boil for 10 minutes. Heat the ghee in a chatty and fry the remainder of the ingredients, then turn in the meat mixture and keep on a slow fire for a few minutes longer.

827 Pork Smoore

Prepare in the same way as Beef Smoore (Recipe 795).

828 Pork Thiyal

2 lb. pork
30 dry chillies (ground)
4 cloves of garlic (chopped)
3 slices green ginger (chopped)
2-inch piece cinnamon
2-inch piece rampa
a pinch of ground saffron
1 dessertspoonful sliced red onions
¼ stem lemon-grass
a small sprig of curry-leaves
¼ teaspoon fenugreek
6 pieces dried gamboge
salt (finely ground)

Wash the pork and cut it into small pieces. Put the pork into a chatty with about 1½ teacups of water, and all the ingredients and allow to boil until the pork is tender and the gravy thick.

829 Prawn Badun

Choose large prawns for badun. Prepare in the same way as Beef Badun (Recipe 791).

830 Prawn Curry

50 small prawns
20 dry chillies (ground)
a pinch of ground saffron
1 dessertspoonful sliced red onions
3 cloves of garlic (chopped)
2 slices green ginger (chopped)
2-inch piece cinnamon
¼ teaspoon fenugreek
1 dessertspoonful ghee
½ teacup thick coconut milk
2 tablespoonfuls scraped coconut and 1 teaspoonful raw-rice (ground together)
2-inch piece rampa
¼ stem lemon-grass
a small sprig of curry-leaves
juice of one lime
salt
1 teacup second extract of coconut milk

Wash and shell the prawns and put them into a chatty with the second extract of milk, the chilli, saffron, garlic, ginger, cinnamon and salt, and half each of the onions, fenugreek, rampa, lemon-grass and curry-leaves, and boil until the prawns are nearly cooked. Then add the thick milk mixed with the ground coconut and rice, and the lime juice, and stir for a couple of minutes. Heat the ghee in a chatty and fry the remainder of the ingredients, then turn in the prawn mixture, and let it simmer on a very slow fire for about 15 minutes.

831 Prawn and Tomato Curry

¼ lb. dried prawns (roasted and lightly pounded)
9 medium-sized half-ripe tomatoes
30 dry chillies (roasted and pounded)
1 tablespoonful pounded Maldive fish
1 dessertspoonful sliced red onions
a pinch of ground saffron
3 cloves of garlic (chopped)
2 slices green ginger (chopped)
2-inch piece rampa
¼ stem lemon-grass
a small sprig of curry-leaves
1 oz. tamarind (squeezed in coconut milk)
3 teacups coconut milk
salt
1 tablespoon coconut oil

Heat the oil in a chatty and fry half the onions together with a small piece each of the rampa and lemon-grass, and a few curry-leaves. Mix the rest of the ingredients together, and when the onions are browned turn in the whole mixture and let it boil; when nearly cooked, lessen the fire and allow to simmer very gently until the gravy dries up.

832 Salmon Curry

1 tin salmon
1 dessertspoonful sliced red onions
15 dry chillies (ground)
2 cloves of garlic and 2 slices green ginger (chopped)
2-inch piece cinnamon
2-inch piece rampa
¼ stem lemon-grass
3 small sprigs of curry-leaves
a few sprigs of fennel
¼ teaspoon fenugreek
juice of half a lime
1 dessertspoonful dripping
1 teacup coconut milk
salt

Heat the dripping in a chatty and fry half the onions, a small piece each of the rampa and lemon-grass and a few curry-leaves. Then add the gravy from the tinned fish, the coconut milk and the rest of the ingredients. When the gravy boils up add the salmon and keep on a slow fire for a few minutes longer.

833 Sathey Curry

1½ lb. beef
1 dessertspoonful sliced red onions
1 oz. tamarind (squeezed in coconut milk)
1 tablespoonful ghee
4 cloves of garlic (chopped)
3 slices green ginger (chopped)
2-inch piece rampa
¼ stem lemon-grass
a small sprig of curry-leaves
¼ teaspoon fenugreek
2 pieces aromatic ginger (powdered)
8 cardamoms (powdered)
1 teaspoonful powdered pepper
1 dessertspoonful coriander seed, and 1 teaspoonful white cummin seed (roasted and ground together)
3 teacups coconut milk (extract of half a coconut)
salt
a pinch of ground saffron
25 dry chillies (roasted and ground)
½ teaspoon sweet cummin seed (roasted and powdered)

Wash and cut the meat into half-inch squares, mix with the saffron and pepper, add just a little salt water, and boil until the meat is tender, and the water all absorbed. Then put in 1½ dessertspoons of ghee and fry the meat. Next, skewer the meat on pieces of ekel, 3 inches long—4 pieces of meat on each. Then make the gravy. Heat the remainder of the ghee, and fry half of the onions until lightly browned; add the coconut milk mixed with the rest of the ingredients, except the sweet cummin, cardamoms and aromatic ginger, and let it simmer until the gravy is thick. Then put in the meat, add the remainder of the ingredients, and keep on a slow fire for about 10 minutes longer.

834 Sathey Malay Curry

2 lb. beef
30 dry chillies
1 tablespoonful coriander seed
1 teaspoonful white cummin seed
1 teaspoonful sweet cummin seed
1 dessertspoonful sliced red onions
salt
4 cloves of garlic
3 slices green ginger
4-inch piece rampa
½ stem lemon-grass
a small sprig of curry-leaves
2-inch piece cinnamon
6 cardamoms
2 pieces aromatic ginger
1½oz. tamarind (squeezed in salt water)

Wash the meat and cut it into one-inch squares. Slightly roast and pound together the coriander and cummins; also slightly roast and pound the chillies. The following ingredients *viz.*: The onions, garlic, ginger, rampa, lemon-grass, curry-leaves, cinnamon, cardamoms, and aromatic ginger must also be pounded. Mix all the pounded ingredients together, add the tamarind and salt, and rub the mixture well into the meat. Let it remain for an hour. Then fix the meat on skewers, 4 pieces of meat on each, and grill over a clear fire, turning the satheys frequently until they are cooked. When ready, arrange the satheys on a dish and pour the gravy over them.

N.B. Buffalo meat is considered better than ordinary beef for the sathey.

For the Gravy

1 dessertspoonful coriander seed
1 teaspoonful white cummin seed
1 teaspoonful sweet cummin seed
¼ teaspoon fenugreek
a pinch of ground saffron
1 dessertspoonful sliced red onions
3 cloves of garlic (chopped)
2 slices green ginger (chopped)
2-inch piece rampa
¼ stem lemon-grass
a small sprig of curry-leaves
2-inch piece cinnamon
6 cardamoms (powdered)
2 pieces aromatic ginger (powdered)
juice of half a lime
1 dessertspoonful ghee or dripping
2 teacups thick coconut milk (the extract of one coconut)
salt

Pound the coriander and white cummin together, and slightly roast and pound the sweet cummin. Mix the coriander and the cummins with the coconut milk and strain through a coconut milk strainer. Then add to it the saffron, garlic, ginger, cinnamon, cardamoms, aromatic ginger and salt. Heat the ghee in a chatty and fry the onions together with the rampa, lemon-grass, curry-leaves, and fenugreek, then turn in the mixture and let it simmer slowly, stirring all the time, until it thickens. Add the lime juice when the gravy is half-cooked.

835 Sathey with White Gravy

Cook the meat and skewer on ekels as directed in Recipe 833. Then arrange the satheys on a dish and pour the gravy over them.

For the Gravy

2 teacups thick coconut milk
1 teaspoonful sweet cummin seed (slightly roasted and pounded)
a pinch of ground saffron
1 dessertspoonful sliced red onions
2 cloves of garlic (chopped)
1 slice green ginger (chopped)
10 cardamoms (powdered)
2 pieces aromatic ginger (powdered)
2-inch piece rampa
¼ stem lemon-grass
a small sprig of curry-leaves
1 teaspoonful ghee
1 teaspoonful flour
juice of half a lime
salt

Heat the ghee in a chatty and fry half the onions together with a small piece each of the rampa and lemon-grass, and a few curry-leaves, then add the coconut milk and the rest of the ingredients, except the cummin, aromatic ginger, cardamoms, flour and lime juice. Let it boil until the ingredients are cooked, then add the flour mixed smoothy with a little coconut milk, and the lime juice, stir for a few minutes until the flour is boiled: sprinkle in the cummin, cardamoms, and aromatic ginger, and when the gravy is very thick, pour it over the meat.

836 Tripe Curry

2 lb. tripe
20 dry chillies (pounded)
1 dessertspoon white cummin seed (ground)
a pinch of ground saffron
1 dessertspoonful sliced red onions
3 cloves of garlic and 3 slices green ginger (chopped)
2-inch piece rampa
½ stem lemon-grass
3 small sprig of curry-leaves
½ teaspoon fenugreek
2-inch piece cinnamon
6 cardamoms
4 cloves and 2 pieces aromatic ginger (powdered)
salt
1 dessertspoonful ghee or dripping
juice of 1 lime
1½ teacups thick coconut milk

Use the honeycomb tripe. Wash the tripe well in warm water, put it into a saucepan, cover with cold water and let it simmer for some time. Then take it off the fire and scrape the tripe quite clean. Cut it in 1½-inch squares, return to the saucepan with fresh cold water and let it boil from 3 to 4 hours or until very tender. Then drain off the water, put the tripe into a chatty, add the coconut milk, the chilli, cummin, saffron, garlic, ginger, cinnamon, cloves, cardamoms, aromatic ginger, salt, and half each of the onions, rampa, lemon-grass and curry-leaves. Allow to simmer slowly until the ingredients are cooked. Heat the ghee in a chatty and fry the remainder of the onions, rampa, lemon-grass and curry-leaves and the fenugreek, turn in the tripe preparation, add the lime juice and let it simmer for about 10 minutes longer.

837 Udder Badun

Wash and boil the udder until tender. Then cut it into slices half an inch thick, and prepare in the same way as Beef Badun (Recipe 791).

Curries—Fruit, Vegetables &c.

(For other curries, see Kandyan-Sinhalese and Tamil Recipes)

841 Ambarella Curry

4 well-seasoned ambarellas
1 dessertspoonful sliced red onions
1 dessertspoonful pounded Maldive fish
6 dry chillies (ground)
a pinch of ground saffron
2-inch piece rampa
¼ stem lemon-grass
a small sprig of curry-leaves
2-inch piece cinnamon
salt
1 teacup coconut milk
a dessertspoon of dripping

Peel and cut the ambarellas in four lengthwise. Heat the dripping in a chatty and fry half the onions together with a small piece each of the rampa and lemon-grass and a few curry-leaves. Mix the rest of the ingredients together, and when the onions are browned, turn in the whole mixture and let it boil, stirring occasionally until the ingredients are cooked.

842 Brinjal Curry

4 medium-sized brinjals
1 dessertspoonful mustard seed (ground)
8 dry chillies (roasted and ground)
1 dessertspoonful pounded Maldive fish
1 dessertspoonful sliced red onions
salt
3 cloves of garlic (chopped)
2 slices green ginger (chopped)
2-inch piece rampa
¼ stem lemon-grass
2-inch piece cinnamon
¼ teaspoon fenugreek
½ wineglass vinegar
coconut oil
1½ teacups coconut milk

Cut the brinjals in slices lengthwise, rub over with salt and saffron, and fry in oil. Then prepare the gravy. Put the coconut milk into a chatty, add the rest of the ingredients, and boil until the gravy is very thick. Then add the fried brinjal and let it simmer for a few minutes longer.

843 Chilli Curry

25 large green chillies
¼ lb. Maldive fish (pounded)
2-inch piece rampa
juice of half a lime
¼ stem lemon grass
2 oz. red onions (sliced)
a pinch of ground saffron
a small sprig of curry-leaves
2 teacups coconut milk
salt
coconut oil

Cut a small slit in the chilli, lengthwise, and remove the seeds. Then make the stuffing. Mix together three-fourths of the Maldive fish and three-fourths of the onions, add salt to taste and moisten with a little lime juice. Fill the chillies with this mixture, tie them round with pieces of thread and fry them in oil. Next prepare the gravy. Put the coconut milk into a chatty with the remainder of the Maldive fish and onions, the saffron, rampa, lemon-grass, curry-leaves and salt, and boil until the gravy is thick. Then put in the stuffed chillies, add the lime juice and keep on a slow fire for a few minutes longer.

844 Dhall Curry

⅛ measure dhall
1 dessertspoonful sliced red onions
1 dessertspoonful pounded Maldive fish
a pinch of ground saffron
1 green chilli sliced
1-inch piece cinnamon
1-inch piece rampa
¼ stem lemon-grass
a small sprig of curry-leaves
salt
½ teacup thick coconut milk
1½ teacups second extract of coconut milk
1 teaspoonful ghee

Wash the dhall well in several changes of water removing any discoloured ones which float on top of the water. Put the dhall into a chatty with the second extract of milk, the Maldive fish, saffron, chilli, cinnamon and half each of the onions, rampa, lemon-grass and curry-leaves. Simmer slowly until the dhall is cooked, then add the thick milk and the salt and stir for a couple of minutes. Heat the ghee in another chatty and fry the remainder of the onions, the rampa, lemon-grass and curry-leaves, turn in the curry and keep on a slow fire for a few minutes longer.

845 Mango Curry

2 well-seasoned mangoes
1 dessertspoonful sliced red onions
1 dessertspoonful pounded Maldive fish
6 dry chillies (ground)
a pinch of ground saffron
2-inch piece rampa
¼ stem lemon-grass
a small sprig of curry-leaves
2-inch piece cinnamon
salt
1 teacup coconut milk
a dessertspoon of dripping

Peel and cut the mango in small slices. Heat the dripping in a chatty and fry half the onions together with a small piece each of the rampa and lemon-grass and a few curry-leves. Mix the rest of the ingredients together and when the onions are browned turn in the whole mixture and let it boil stirring occasionally until the ingredients are cooked.

846 Pineapple Curry

1 medium-sized well-seasoned pineapple
1 dessertspoonful sliced red onions
1 dessertspoonful pounded Maldive fish
6 dry chillies (ground)
1 teaspoonful mustard seed (ground)
½ teaspoon sweet cummin seed (lightly roasted and powdered)
a pinch of ground saffron
2-inch piece rampa
¼ stem lemon-grass
a small sprig of curry-leaves
2-inch piece cinnamon
salt
1 teacup coconut milk
a dessertspoonful dripping

Pare the pineapple and cut it in small dice. Heat the dripping in a chatty and fry half the onions together with a small piece each of the rampa, lemon-grass and a few curry-leaves, then add the coconut milk and the rest of the ingredients except the cummin. Let it simmer until the ingredients are cooked, then sprinkle in the cummin and let it simmer for 10 minutes longer.

847 Plantain Curry

4 ash plantains
1 dessertspoonful sliced red onions
2 green chillies (sliced)
1 dessertspoonful pounded Maldive fish
¼ teaspoon fenugreek
a pinch of ground saffron
2-inch piece cinnamon
2-inch piece rampa
a small sprig of curry- leaves
a few springs of fennel
salt
coconut oil
2½ teacups coconut milk (the extract of half a coconut)

Skin the plantains, cut them in two across and slice them lengthwise; rub over with salt and saffron and fry them in oil. Then make the gravy. Put the coconut milk into a chatty with the rest of the ingredients, and boil until the ingredients are cooked, then put in the plantain and let it simmer until the gravy is thick.

848 Shoeflowers Curried

about a dozen shoeflowers
1 dessertspoonful sliced red onions
1 dessertspoonful pounded Maldive fish
2 green chillies (sliced)
a pinch of ground saffron
1 teaspoonful mustard seed (ground)
1-inch piece cinnamon
salt
1 dessertspoon vinegar
½ teacup thick coconut milk
2 teacups second extract of coconut milk

For the BATTER:

¼ lb. flour
1 teacup milk
1 egg
salt

Take the ordinary single red shoeflower (hibiscus), wash it, remove the calyx and break off the stamen. Drain off the water, make a smooth batter with the flower, milk and egg and add salt to taste. Dip the flowers in the batter and fry in oil. Then make the gravy. Put the second extract of coconut milk into a chatty, add the onions, Maldive fish, green chillies, saffron and salt and allow to boil up. Then add the fried shoeflowers and allow to simmer for about 5 minutes. Mix the ground mustard with the thick coconut milk, add the vinegar and stir this into the curry. Cook for about 5 minutes longer, stirring all the time.

849 Snakegourd Curry

1 snakegourd
¼ lb. beef (prepared as for patties)
2 hard-boiled eggs
¼ teaspoon fenugreek
a pinch of ground saffron
2-inch piece rampa
¼ stem lemon-grass
1 dessertspoonful pounded Maldive fish
1 dessertspoonful sliced red onions
a small sprig of curry-leaves
juice of half a lime
2 teacups coconut milk
coconut oil
salt

Cut the snakegourd across in 2½-inch length pieces, take out the seeds, rub the pieces over with salt and saffron and fry in oil. Fill up the pieces with the curry, putting a piece of boiled egg into each. Now make the gravy. Put the coconut milk into a chatty, add the rest of the ingredients, except the lime juice into each. Now make the gravy. Put the coconut milk into a chatty, add the rest of the ingredients, except the lime juice and boil until the ingredients are cooked. Then put in the pieces of stuffed snakegourd, add the lime juice, and allow to simmer slowly until the gravy is thick.

850 Sweet Pumpkin Flowers Curried

Prepare in the same way as Shoeflowers Curried (Recipe 848).

851 Vegetable Curries

Nearly all vegetables are curried in the same way. Prepare the vegetables and put into a chatty with a sufficient quantity of the second extract of coconut milk, a few sliced red onions, some pounded Maldive fish, a ripe chilli, a pinch of ground saffron, a clove of garlic, a slice or two of green ginger, a small piece of cinnamon, and salt to taste. Boil until the vegetable is cooked, then add a little thick milk and allow to simmer for about 10 minutes longer. The quantities of the ingredients must be regulated by the amount of the vegetable.

Sambols

861 Billing Sambol

50 small billings
12 dry chillies (pounded)
1 tablespoonful pounded Maldive fish
1 dessertspoonful sliced red onions
a pinch of ground saffron
3 cloves of garlic (chopped)
2 slices green ginger (chopped)
2-inch piece cinnamon
2-inch piece rampa
¼ stem lemon-grass
a small sprig of curry leaves
4 tablespoons coconut oil
salt

Cut the billings into fine strips, lengthwise, put into salt water and let it remain for about half an hour. Then squeeze out all the water, and mix the billings and the rest of the ingredients together. Heat the oil in a chatty, turn in the mixture and fry for a few minutes.

862 Bittergourd Sambol

4 bittergourds
1½ teaspoons pounded Maldive fish
1 dessertspoonful sliced red onions
1 green chilli (sliced)
a pinch of ground saffron
juice of half a lime
2 tablespoons coconut milk
salt

Cut the gourds across in slices, remove the seeds, rub over with a little salt and saffron and fry in oil. Put the fried gourd into a dish, mix the rest of the ingredients with the coconut milk and pour over the gourd.

863 Blachang

6 salted "hurullas" (jardy)
30 dry chillies (roasted and ground)
2 oz. Maldive fish (pounded)
2 oz. red onions (sliced)
2 tablespoonfuls scraped coconut (ground)
3 cloves of garlic (chopped)
2 slices green ginger (chopped)
2-inch piece rampa
¼ stem lemon-grass
a small sprig of curry-leaves
2-inch piece cinnamon
1 teaspoonful sugar
2 tablespoons coconut oil
salt
2 oz. tamarind (squeezed in coconut milk)
1½ teacups thick coconut milk

There is a particular kind of jardy that dissolves in cooking and blachang is best made of this sort of fish. Wash the fish, put it into a chatty with a teacupful of water and boil it. When well boiled, strain. Heat the oil and fry a couple of sliced onions, a small piece each of the rampa and lemon-grass, and a few curry-leaves, and when the onions are browned, add the strained fish liquor and the rest of the ingredients, except the ground coconut and sugar. When about half cooked, add the coconut and sugar and let it simmer on a slow fire until cooked.

864 Brinjal Pahi

4 medium-sized brinjals
1 tablespoonful mustard seed (ground)
¼ stem lemon-grass
a small sprig of curry-leaves
1 teaspoonful sugar
1 tablespoonful pounded Maldive fish
1 tablespoonful sliced red onions
4 cloves of garlic (chopped)
3 slices green ginger (chopped)
3 ripe chillies (sliced)
2-inch piece cinnamon
2-inch piece rampa
1 tablespoonful coriander seed
1½ teaspoons white cummin seed
½ teaspoon sweet cummin seed (ground together)
1 wineglass vinegar
1½ oz. tamarind (squeezed in salt water)
coconut oil
salt
½ teacup thick coconut milk
a pinch of ground saffron
20 dry chillies (ground)

Slice the brinjals lengthwise, rub over with salt and saffron and fry in oil. Mix the ground ingredients with the vinegar and tamarind, and then mix in the rest of the ingredients, except the coconut milk and sugar, Heat 2 tablespoons of oil in a chatty, and when very hot turn in the brinjal mixture, and the coconut milk, and let it simmer on a slow fire for about 15 minutes stirring all the time. Mix in the sugar just before taking it off the fire.

865 Brinjal Sambol

Prepare in the same way as Bittergourd Sambol (Recipe 862).

866 Chilli Sambol

2 oz. dry chillies (roasted and pounded)
2 oz. dried prawns (roasted and pounded)
¼ lb. Maldive fish (pounded)
¼ lb. red onions (sliced)
3 cloves of garlic (chopped)
4 slices green ginger (chopped)
2 ripe chillies (sliced)
2-inch piece cinnamon
3-inch piece rampa
¼ stem lemon-grass
a small sprig of curry-leaves
2 oz. tamarind (squeezed in coconut milk)
juice of half a lime
1½ teaspoons sugar
4 tablespoons coconut oil
4 teacups coconut milk (the extract of one coconut)
salt

Heat half the oil in a chatty and fry a tablespoonful of the onions, and a small piece each of the rampa and lemon-grass, and a few curry-leaves; when the onions are browned, add the remainder of the oil, let it get hot, then put in the rest of the ingredients, except the coconut milk, tamarind, lime juice, and sugar, and let the whole fry for a few minutes, stirring all the time. Then add the coconut milk, tamarind and lime juice, and let it simmer, first over a brisk fire, then keep on warm coals until the gravy dries up. Mix in the sugar before lessening the fire. This sambol needs frequent strring or it will adhere to the chatty.

867 Coconut Sambol (Goda Sambol)

½ a coconut (scraped)
10 dry chillies
1 dessertspoonful Maldive fish
1 tablespoonful sliced red onions
juice of one lime
salt

Pound together the chillies, Maldive fish, onions, and salt, then add the coconut and pound lightly. Moisten with the lime juice and mix well together.

N.B. Instead of being pounded, the ingredients may be lightly ground.

868 Cucumber Sambol I

1 cucumber
1 dessertspoonful pounded Maldive fish
1 dessertspoonful sliced red onions
2 ripe chillies (finely sliced)
2 tablespoons thick coconut milk
juice of half a lime
salt

Peel the cucumber and cut the fruit across in two. Then pare it thinly, lengthwise, cutting round and round the fruit until you reach the seed part of it. Then roll up the pieces together, and cut across in very fine strips. Put it into salt water, let it remain for a few minutes, then squeeze out all the water and put the cucumber into a dish; add the ingredients and mix well together.

869 Cucumber Sambol II

1 cucumber
20 dry chillies (roasted and powdered)
1 tablespoonful powdered Maldive fish
1 tablespoonful sliced red onions
2 cloves of garlic and 2 slices green ginger (chopped)
a few grains of fenugreek
2-inch piece cinnamon
2-inch piece rampa
¼ stem lemon-grass
a small sprig of curry-leaves
1 oz. tamarind (squeezed in water)
salt
2 tablespoons thick coconut milk
1 tablespoon coconut oil

Peel the cucumber, cut it in two lengthwise and remove the seeds. Then cut it in pieces and put it into a chatty along with the chillies, Maldive fish, garlic, ginger, fenugreek, cinnamon, tamarind, salt, three-fourths of the onions and half each of the rampa, lemon-grass and curry-leaves. Let it simmer until the ingredients are cooked. Heat the oil in another chatty and fry the remainder of the onions, rampa, lemon-grass and curry-leaves, then turn in the cucumber preparation and stir for a couple of minutes. Add the coconut milk and cook for 5 minutes longer.

870 Dry Fish Sambol

Roast the dry fish over coals and break it into small pieces. Then add to it sliced red onions and green chillies, lime juice or vinegar, and salt, if necessary; mix all well together.

871 Ground Chilli Sambol

25 ripe chillies (sliced)
¼ lb. red onions (sliced
2 oz. Maldive fish (lightly pounded)
lime juice
sugar
salt
coconut oil

Fry the chillies, onions, and Maldive fish in oil and grind them finely, using lime juice to moisten; add sugar and salt to taste.

872 Onion Sambol I

¼ lb. Bombay onions
1 dessertspoonful sliced red onions
2 or 3 green chillies
juice of half a lime
salt

Slice the Bombay onions finely and mix together with the red onions and green chillies (sliced). Moisten with the lime juice and add salt to taste.

873 Fried Onion Sambol

¼ lb. Bombay onions (cut in slices)
10 dry chillies (broken in small pieces)
juice of half a lime
1 tablespoonful pounded Maldive fish
salt
4 tablespoons coconut oil

Heat the oil in a chatty and fry all the ingredients together.

874 Prawn Blachang

½ lb. dried prawns (roasted and pounded)
12 dry chillies (roasted)
1 dessertspoonful sliced red onions
2 cloves of garlic
2 slices green ginger
juice of 2 limes
salt

Grind the prawns very finely together with the chillies, onions, garlic, ginger, and salt; moisten with the lime juice and mix well together.

875 Prawn Sambol

¼ lb. dried prawns (roasted and lightly pounded)
¼ lb. red onions (sliced)
15 ripe and green chillies (sliced)
juice of half a lime
4 tablespoons coconut oil
salt

Heat the oil in a chatty and fry the onions and chillies, then add the prawns and let the whole fry a couple of minutes; take it off the fire and add salt and lime juice to taste.

876 Seeni (Sugar) Sambol

Prepare in the same way as Chilli Sambol (Recipe (866)

877 Shoeflower Sambol

2 doz. shoeflowers (single red)
1 tablespoon thick coconut milk
1 dessertspoonful sliced red onions
1 dessertspoonful pounded Maldive fish
1 green chilli (sliced)
salt
a squeeze of lime juice
1 teaspoonful ghee or butter

Wash the shoeflowers, pick off the petals and put them into a chatty. Add the coconut milk, onions, Maldive fish, chilli and salt and let it simmer slowly until the gravy is almost absorbed. Then add the lime juice and ghee and allow to simmer for 5 minutes longer, stirring all the time.

878 Stringhopper Sambol

½ coconut (finely scraped)
1 tablespoonful pounded Maldive fish
1 dessertspoonful sliced red onions
salt
6 dry chillies (ground)
a pinch of ground saffron
3 green chillies (cut lengthwise)
a few curry-leaves
1-inch piece rampa
1-inch piece cinnamon
juice of half a lime

Put all the ingredients except the coconut into a chatty, add half a teacup of water and boil until the ingredients are cooked. Then add the coconut, stir well and boil a couple of minutes longer.

879 Tomato Sambol

Bake the tomatoes under hot ashes, then wash them well and break into pieces. Add a little thick coconut milk, some pounded Maldive fish, a few sliced red onions, a sliced green chilli, a squeeze of lime, and a little salt, and mix well together.

Chutneys and Pickles

THESE form a necessary accompaniment to rice and curry. The vinegar used for chutneys and pickles should be of the best quality. The jars or bottles into which chutneys and pickles are put must be perfectly clean and dry. Cork them tightly so as to exclude air or seal the bottles, if to be kept long. Successful chutneys and pickles can be turned out by carefully following the direction given for making them.

Chutneys

891 Dried Apricot Chutney

½ lb. dried apricots
½ lb. sugar
½ oz. dry chillies
¼ oz. garlic
¼ oz. green ginger
¼ bottle vinegar
salt

Wash the apricots well and put them into a basin with sufficient cold water to cover them, and let them soak overnight. Then remove the seeds and put the apricots and the water in which they were soaked into a saucepan and simmer slowly until the fruit is tender, mashing the fruit with a spoon. Grind the chillies, garlic and ginger with vinegar. Put the remainder of the vinegar into a saucepan, add the sugar, ground ingredients and salt and stir over the fire until the ingredients are cooked. Then add the stewed apricots and let the whole boil till of a good consistency for chutney.

892 Date Chutney

1 lb. dates
¼ lb. sugar
1 oz. dry chillics
½ oz. garlie
½ oz. green ginger
½ bottle vinegar
salt

Stone the dates and grind them; also grind the chillies, garlic and ginger with vinegar. Make a syrup of the sugar and the remainder of the vinegar, add the ground ingredients and salt, and boil until the syrup is thick. Let it cool, then mix in the dates.

893 Ginger Preserve Chutney

½ lb. jar ginger preserve
½ oz. garlic
6 oz. sugar
¾ oz. dry chillies
½ oz. green ginger
¼ bottle vinegar
salt

Grind the chillies, garlic and green ginger with vinegar, Cut the preserved ginger into very small pieces. The preserve should be fresh and syrupy. Make a syrup of the sugar and the remainder of the vinegar, add the ground ingredients and salt and boil until the ingredients are cooked. Then mix in the syrup from the preserved ginger and the cut ginger and let the whole boil till of a good consistency for chutney.

N.B. Chow-chow preserve can be prepared in the same way.

894 Lime Pickle Chutney

1½ lb. pickled limes	**1 oz. mustard seed**
1½ lb. sugar	**1 oz. garlic**
½ lb. sultanas	**1 oz. green ginger**
1½ oz. dry chillies	**¾ bottle vinegar**

Cut the limes into fine strips. Remove the stalks from the sultanas. Grind the chillies, mustard, garlic and ginger with vinegar. Dissolve the sugar in the remainder of the vinegar add the ground ingredients and boil until the syrup is thick. Allow to cool, then add the lime pickle and the sultanas and mix well together.

895 Lovi-Lovi Chutney

1 lb. lovi-lovi pulp	**½ oz. garlic**
1¼ lb. sugar	**½ oz. green ginger**
¼ lb. sultanas	**¼ bottle vinegar**
1 oz. dry chillies	**salt**
1 oz. mustard seed	

Pick the stalks from the lovi-lovis which must be quite ripe, and wash the fruit. Put them into a saucepan with sufficient water to cover and simmer gently until the fruit is quite tender. Then drain off the water (this juice can be used for making jelly) and rub the fruit through a sieve fine enough to keep back the seeds. Wash the sultanas and remove the stalks. Grind the chillies, mustard, garlic and ginger with vinegar. Make a syrup with the sugar and the remainder of the vinegar, add the ground ingredients and salt and bring to the boil. The add the sieved fruit pulp and boil till of a good consistency for chutney. Let it cool and then mix in the sultanas.

896 Mango Chutney

1 lb. green mangoes	**1 oz. garlic**
1 lb. sugar	**1 oz. green ginger**
¼ lb. sultanas	**½ bottle vinegar**
1½ oz. dry chillies	**salt**
1 oz. mustard seed	

Peel and slice the mangoes, sprinkle them with salt and dry for a day in the sun. Then bruise the slices. Wash the sultanas and remove the stalks. Grind the chillies, mustard, garlic and ginger with vinegar. Dissolve the sugar in the remainder of the vinegar, add the salt and the ground ingredients and boil until the syrup is very thick. Then add the mango and boil for 10 minutes longer. Allow the chutney to cool and then mix in the sultanas.

897 Sweet Mango Chutney

1 lb. ripe Bombay mangoes
1¼ lb. sugar
¼ lb. sultanas
1 oz. dry chillies
½ oz. mustard seed
½ oz. garlic
½ oz. green ginger
1 teaspoon salt
½ bottle vinegar

Choose sound fruit not too ripe. Peel the mangoes, cut them in small slices and weigh the fruit. Wash the sultanas and remove the stalks. Grind the chillies, mustard, garlic and ginger with vinegar. Put the mango and sugar into a saucepan and stir over the fire until the fruit is cooked, mashing the fruit with the spoon while stirring. Then add the ground ingredients and salt mixed smoothly with the remainder of the vinegar and boil till of a good consistency for chutney, stirring all the time. Let it cool, then mix in the sultanas.

898 Pineapple Chutney

1 medium-sized ripe pineapple
6 oz. sugar
½ oz. dry chillies
¼ oz. garlic
¼ oz. green ginger
¼ bottle vinegar
salt

Pare the pineapple and cut it into very small dice. Grind the chillies, mustard, garlic, and ginger with vinegar. Add all the ingredients to the pineapple and boil until it is well cooked and the chutney is of a good consistency.

899 Sweet Pumpkin Chutney

1 lb. sweet pumpkin
1 lb. sugar
¼ lb. sultanas
1 oz. dry chillies
½ oz. garlic
½ oz. green ginger
½ bottle vinegar
salt

Peel the pumpkin, cut it in pieces and remove the seeds and the stringy part from the centre and weigh the fruit. Wash it well and boil in slightly salted water. When tender, drain well and mash the fruit to a pulp. Wash the sultanas and remove the stalks. Grind the chillies, garlic and ginger with vinegar. Put the remainder of the vinegar into a saucepan, add the sugar and the ground ingredients and salt and stir over the fire until the ingredients are cooked. Then add the pumpkin and let the whole boil until of a good consistency for chutney. It must be stirred constantly. When cool, mix in the sultanas.

900 Tamarind Chutney

1 lb. tamarind
1½ lb. sugar
½ lb. sultanas
1½ oz. dry chillies
1 oz. mustard seed
1 oz. garlic
1 oz. green ginger
1 bottle vinegar
salt

Squeeze the tamarind well in vinegar and strain it through a coarse net. Wash the sultanas and remove the stalks. Grind the chillies, mustard, garlic and ginger with vinegar. Make a syrup of the sugar and the remainder of the vinegar, add the ground ingredients and salt and bring to the boil. Add the tamarind and boil till of a good consistency for chutney. Let it cool and mix in the sultanas.

901 Tomato Chutney

1 lb. ripe tomatoes	**½ oz. green ginger**
1 lb. sugar	**¼ bottle vinegar**
1 oz. dry chillies	**salt**
½ oz. garlic	

Grind the chillies, garlic and ginger with vinegar. Scald the tomatoes and remove their skins. Cut them into slices, add the remainder of the vinegar and boil until the fruit is soft. Add the sugar, the ground ingredients and salt, and boil the whole gently till of a good consistency for chutney.

902 Green Tomato Chutney

1 lb. green tomatoes	**½ oz. garlic**
1 lb. sugar	**½ oz. ginger**
1 oz. dry chillies	**½ bottle vinegar**
1 oz. mustard seed	**salt**

Slice the tomatoes, sprinkle them with salt and leave until the next day. Grind the chillies, mustard, garlic and ginger with vinegar. Boil the prepared tomatoes in the remainder of the vinegar until the fruit is soft. Add the sugar, the ground ingredients and salt, and boil the whole gently until of a good consistency for chutney.

903 Woodapple Chutney

1 lb. woodapple	**1 oz. garlic**
1 lb. sugar	**1 oz. green ginger**
¼ lb. sultanas	**1 bottle vinegar**
1½ oz. dry chillies	**salt**

Break the shell and scoop out the inside of the fruit with a spoon and weigh it. Squeeze the fruit well in vinegar, using about half the vinegar, and strain it through coarse net. Wash the sultanas and remove the stalks. Grind the chillies, garlic and ginger with vinegar. Make a syrup of the sugar and the remainder of the vinegar, add the ground ingredients and salt and bring to the boil. Then add the woodapple and boil till of a good consistency, for chutney. Let it cool and mix in the sultanas.

Pickles

911 Ambarella Pickle

Choose well-seasoned fruit. Cut the ambarellas in four lengthwise and peel off the skin. Then boil them in vinegar until tender and put them into mustard prepared as follows:

To half a bottle of vinegar allow 1½ oz. mustard seed, ¾ oz. dry chillies, ½ oz. each of garlic and green ginger, and salt to taste. Grind the mustard, chillies, garlic and ginger in vinegar and mix all the ingredients smoothly with the remainder of the vinegar.

912 Beetroot Pickle

beetroots	**cinnamon**
peppercorns	**salt**
cloves	**vinegar**

Wash the beets well and be careful not to break or pick the outside skin as this will cause bleeding and both colour and flavour would be lost. Put the beets into a saucepan of boiling water and allow to simmer until tender. When cool, peel them, slice, and place in jars or pickle bottles. Take as much vinegar as will cover the sliced beetroot when in the jar, and boil it, adding seasoning in the proportion of 1 teaspoonful of peppercorns, 10 cloves, a 2-inch piece of cinnamon and a teaspoon of salt to each bottle. Allow to cool, then pour this spiced vinegar over the beets, and cover the jars tightly.

913 Billing Temperado

Prepare in the same way as Mango Temperado (Recipe 924), using salted and dried billing.

914 Bittergourd Pickle

Cut the bittergourds across in two, and slice them lengthwise, then run two cuts down each slice, but do not separate them. Boil the bittergourd in vinegar and put into prepared mustard. To prepare the mustard, see Recipe 920.

915 Brinjal Pickle

Cut the brinjals into rather thick slices lengthwise, and run two or three cuts down each slice, but do not separate them. Boil in vinegar and prepare in the same way as in the following recipe.

916 Brinjal and Chilli Pickle

4 medium-sized brinjals	**⅛ oz. green ginger**
25 green chillies	**2-inch piece rampa**
½ oz. dry chillies	**½ stem lemon-grass**
¾ oz. mustard seed	**a small sprig of curry-leave**
½ oz. coriander seed	**2-inch piece cinnamon**
¼ oz. white cummin seed	**salt**
⅛ oz. sweet cummin seed	**¾ bottle vinegar**
¼ oz. garlic	**coconut oil**

Cut the brinjals in slices lengthwise, rub over with salt and saffron and fry in oil; also fry the green chillies. Grind the coriander, white cummin and sweet cummin together—the garlic and ginger together, and the dry chillies and mustard together. These ingredients must all be ground with vinegar. Mix the ground ingredients smoothly with the rest of the vinegar, add the fried brinjal and chilli, the rampa and lemon-grass slightly bruised, the curry-leaves, cinnamon and salt, and mix well together.

917 Chilli Pickle

green chillies
vinegar
peppercorns
cloves
cinnamon
salt

Wash the chillies, wipe them dry and put them into a bottle with vinegar and spices in the proportion of ½ teaspoon peppercorns, 10 cloves, 2-inch piece cinnamon and ½ teaspoon salt to each pint of vinegar. The vinegar must cover the chillies in the bottle. Cover the bottle tightly and keep it in the sun every day for a week, when the pickle will be ready for use.

918 Stuffed Chilli Pickle

capsicum chillies
green papaw
mustard seed
dry chillies
saffron
garlic
green ginger
salt
vinegar

Make small slits in the chillies lengthwise, remove the seeds, and boil them in vinegar until partially done. Grind the mustard, dry chillies, garlic and ginger with vinegar. Grate the papaw finely, add a little vinegar and salt and boil it. Take it off the fire and mix with the ground ingredients in the proportion of ½ oz. each of chilli and mustard and ¼ oz. each of garlic and ginger to ½ lb. grated papaw. Fill the chillies with this mixture and put them into mustard prepared as follows:—

To ½ a bottle of vinegar allow 1½ oz. mustard seed, ¾ oz. dry chillies, ½ oz. each of garlic and ginger, a pinch of ground saffron and salt to taste. Grind the mustard, chillies, garlic and ginger with vinegar, and mix all the ingredients smoothly with the remainder of the vinegar.

919 Coconut-Cabbage Pickle

Cut the coconut-cabbage into pieces, and steep in salt water for about 8 hours. Then drain and put into prepared mustard. To prepare the mustard, see Recipe 920.

920 Cucumber Pickle

1 medium-sized cucumber
¾ oz. mustard seed
½ oz. dry chillies
¼ oz. green ginger
¼ oz. garlic
¼ bottle vinegar
a pinch of ground saffron
salt

Choose a rather tender cucumber, wash it and cut it across in two. Cut it in pieces lengthwise and remove the seed portion.

Sprinkle the cucumber with salt and let it remain for about 6 hours. Drain well and put into prepared mustard.

To Prepare the Mustard—Grind the mustard seed, chilli, garlic and ginger with vinegar. Then mix it all with the remainder of the vinegar, adding a little more vinegar, if the mixture is too thick.

921 Pickled Dates

dates
vinegar
peppercorns
cloves
cinnamon
salt

Choose fresh firm dates. Remove the stones by making an incision lengthwise in each date and press the fruit together again. Put the dates into a jar or pickle bottle and cover with spiced vinegar made as follows.—Take as much vinegar as will cover the dates in the jar and boil it adding seasoning in the proportion of 1 teaspoon of peppercorns, 8 cloves, 2-inch piece cinnamon and a teaspoon of salt to each bottle of vinegar. Pour the vinegar hot over the dates and leave the jar uncovered until the vinegar is cool. Then cork securely. The pickle will be ready for use in a week's time.

922 Pickled Fish

6 slices salted seer fish
4 oz. tamarind
1 oz. dry chillies
1 oz. coriander seed
½ oz. white cummin seed
¼ oz. sweet cummin seed
½ oz. garlic
¼ oz. green ginger
4-inch piece rampa
1 stem lemon-grass
a small sprig of curry-leaves
3-inch piece of cinnamon
10 ripe chillies
1 bottle vinegar

Use fish that has been salted 3 or 4 days. Wash it and dry in the sun for 2 days. Grind the coriander and cummins together, the garlic and ginger together, and the dry chillies by themselves, all with vinegar. Then mix these ground ingredients smoothly with a little vinegar. Squeeze the tamarind in the remainder of the vinegar, and add it to the mxed ingredients, also the rampa and lemon-grass slightly bruised, the curry-leaves, cinnamon, and the ripe chillies cut lengthwise. Mix all together and put the fish into this gravy. This preparation of fish could be kept for about a week. When required, take a slice or two of the fish with a little of the gravy, heat some ghee or oil in a pan and fry the fish. Then heat the gravy in the same pan, and pour over the fish.

923 Lime Pickle Temperado

1½ lb. pickled limes
12 ripe and green chillies
1½ oz. dry chillies
¾ oz. mustard
¼ oz. white cummin seed
⅛ oz. sweet cummin seed
⅛ oz. black cummin seed
⅛ oz. fenugreek
4-inch piece cinnamon
1 stem lemon-grass
4 tender lime leaves
3 tender mango leaves
1 wineglass gingelly oil
3 wineglasses vinegar
a small piece of asafoetida about the size of a peppercorn
½ oz. garlic
½ oz. green ginger

Slightly roast the mustard, cummin, fenugreek, cinnamon and the green and ripe chillies from which the seeds should be removed. Roast each ingredient separately. Then roast together the rampa, lemon-grass, and the lime and mango leaves; also slightly roast and pound the dry chillies. Cut the ginger into half inch pieces, and sightly bruise them, also the garlic which should not be peeled. Heat the oil in a chatty, put in the asafoetida and when fried throw the piece away. Then fry the garlic and ginger, and add the limes which must be each cut in four, and the rest of the ingredients and let it simmer for a few minutes, stirring, all the time.

924 Mango Temperado

4 dried mangoes
¾ oz. dry chillies
½ oz. mustard seed
½ oz. coriander seed
¼ oz. white cummin seed
⅛ oz. sweet cummin seed
¼ oz. garlic
⅛ oz. green ginger
a pinch of ground saffron
2-inch piece cinnamon
1 tablespoonful sliced red onions
1 dessertspoonful pounded Maldive fish
2-inch piece rampa
½ stem lemon-grass
a small sprig of curry-leaves
4 ripe chillies
1 dessertspoonful sugar
1 teacup thick coconut milk
¼ bottle vinegar
coconut oil

Wash the mangoes well and drain off the water. Grind the coriander and cummin together, the ginger and garlic together and the dry chillies and mustard together. These must all be ground with vinegar and then mixed smoothly with the rest of the vinegar. Add the mangoes, the Maldive fish, coconut milk and the ripe chillies cut lengthwise, and mix well together. Heat some good coconut oil in a chatty and fry the onions, rampa, lemon-grass, curry-leaves and cinnamon. When the onions are browned turn in the mango preparation, and keep on a slow fire for about 20 minutes, stirring occasionally.

925 Mixed Pickle I

red onions
green chillies
green papaw
French beans
lovi-lovi
olive
mustard seed
dry chillies
saffron
green ginger
garlic
salt
sugar
vinegar

Take equal quantities of red onions, green chillies and papaw, and half these quantities each of tender French beans, green olives and ripe lovi-lovis. Peel the onions, cut the chillies in two lengthwise, half-way up; peel and cut the papaw into convenient sized pieces, removing the seeds, and cut the beans in two lengthwise. Boil the chillies, onions, papaw, French beans and olives in vinegar, each ingredient separately. Cut the lovi-lovis in halves, put them into salt water and let them remain for a couple of hours, then drain. Prepare the mustard as given below, put the boiled ingredients and the lovi-lovis into it and mix well together.

To Prepare the Mustard—To each bottle of vinegar allow 3 oz. mustard seed, 2 oz. dry chillies, 1 oz. each of garlic and ginger (all ground with vinegar), a good pinch of saffron, a tablespoonful of sugar, and salt to taste. Mix the ground ingredients smoothly with the vinegar.

926 Mixed Pickle II

red onions	**garlic**
green chillies	**green ginger**
green papaw	**English mustard**
French beans	**ground saffron**
caulifowers	**sugar**
vinegar	**salt**
dry chillies	

Take equal quantities of each kind of vegetable. Peel the onions, make a slit in the chillies and remove the seeds, peel and cut the papaw in convenient sized pieces removing the seeds, string and cut the French beans as for boiling, break the cauliflower into sprays using only the flower part. Put the prepared vegetables into boiling brine of moderate strength and cook for about 10 minutes, then drain. Allow sufficient vinegar to completely cover the vegetables and to each bottle of vinegar, allow ½ oz. dry chillies, ¼ oz. each of garlic and green ginger, 1 oz. mustard, a good pinch of saffron and ½ teaspoon of sugar. Grind the chillies, garlic and ginger with vinegar and mix the mustard smoothly with a little vinegar, Boil the ground ingredients in the remainder of the vinegar, then take the pan off the fire and mix in the mustard and sugar. Put in the vegetables, mix well together and put into jars or bottles and cork tightly.

927 Bombay Onion Pickle

½ lb. Bombay onions	**2-inch piece cinnamon**
½ teaspoon peppercorns	**salt**
6 cloves	**¼ bottle vinegar**

Cut the roots and tops off the onions, peel them and cut each into four. Put all the ingredients into a saucepan and boil until the onions are tender.

N.B. Cabbage can be pickled in the same way.

928 Onion and Chilli Pickle

½ lb. red onions	**2-inch piece cinnamon**
25 green chillies	**salt**
½ teaspoon peppercorns	**½ bottle vinegar**
6 cloves	

Prepare in the same way as Bombay Pickle.

929 Pineapple Pickle

1 medium-sized half-ripe pineapple
¾ oz. mustard seed
½ oz. dry chillies
¼ oz. garlic
¼ oz. green ginger
a pinch of ground saffron
¼ bottle vinegar
salt

Pare the pineapple and cut it into small dice. Grind the mustard, chillies, garlic and ginger with vinegar. Mix these ingredients smoothly with the remainder of the vinegar, add the pineapple and mix well together, adding salt to taste.

930 Polos Pahi (Tender Jak Pickle)

a very tender small jak
½ oz. dry chillies
½ oz. mustard seed
¼ oz. garlic
⅛ oz. green ginger
¼ bottle vinegar
1 dessertspoonful sugar
salt

Cut the jak into pieces and boil it. Then pare off the skin, remove the core and grind the jak finely; also grind the dry chillies, mustard, garlic and ginger with vinegar. Then grind all these ingredients together adding salt to taste. Heat the vinegar in a chatty and when very hot put in the jak preparation and stir over the fire for a couple of minutes. Mix in the sugar when it cools.

931 Pickled Pork

1 pig's head
2 oz. mustard seed
½ oz. dry chillies
1 oz. green ginger
12 small cloves of garlic
12 ripe chillies
a pinch of ground saffron
salt
½ bottle vinegar

The head of the pig is usually used for pickling. Split it in two, wash it and boil it, Remove the meat from the bones and cut into rather large pieces. The above ingredients will be sufficient for about 2 lbs. of boiled pork. Wash and dry the mustard in the sun, then bruise and remove the husk. Grind the dry chillies with vinegar. Scrape the ginger and slice it; peel the garlic. Skewer 2 cloves of garlic, 2 slices green ginger, and 2 ripe chillies in turn in pieces of ekel. Mix the ground chlli and saffron smoothly with the remainder of the vinegar, add salt, and put in the pieces of boiled pork and the skewered ingredients. Keep in a well covered jar. The pickle will be ready for use in 24 hours. It may be served as it is, but is nicer fried.

To Fry—Take a few pieces of the pork and a little of the gravy. First fry the pork in a little dripping, then warm the gravv in the same pan and pour it over the fried pork.

N.B. If liked, the mustard, instead of being dried and husked, may be ground in the usual way with vinegar.

Kandyan-Sinhalese Recipes

941 Alakola Ambul Curry

2 tablespoonfuls ground dried chillies (or preferably half a handful of green or dried heen miris)
10 red onions, sliced
1 tablespoonful powdered Maldive fish
10 pieces goraka
curry-leaves
2 or 3 slices green ginger
4 or 5 cloves of garlic
half a handful coconut cut in tiny pieces
a pinch of uluhāl and turmeric
2 or 3 small pieces cinnamon
2 cupfuls cold water
also 25 tender (unopened) leaves of Alakola (Alocasia) and mustard and coconut oil for "tempering"

Place all the ingredients except the Alakola, mustard and coconut oil, together in a chatty with the water, and cook. Meanwhile, cut the leaves into 2 or 3-inch pieces and wash thoroughly. When the ingredients have boiled sufficiently, put in the Alakola leaves and continue cooking all together until the gravy is almost entirely absorbed. Temper with the coconut oil and mustard.

942 Angunakola Mallung

angunakola leaves
½ a scraped coconut
1 dessertspoonful of powdered Maldive fish
a pinch of saffron
1 dessertspoonful salt water
a little lime juice
4 red onions, sliced finely
4 green chillies, sliced finely
peeled red onions and fried dry chillies to garnish

Break the angunakola leaves free of stems, wash well and cut very finely—almost like threads. Mix in the same bulk of scraped coconut, and add the rest of the ingredients, mixing them all together thoroughly with the hand. Heat the salt water in a chatty and throw in the prepared leaves, etc. Keep turning over a moderate fire for about 5—7 minutes, and before taking off the fire sprinkle in a little lime juice.

Arrange the mallung on a dish, and garnish with the fresh onions and fried chillies.

N.B. **Gotukola** can be cooked in the same manner. Both kinds of leaves should look fresh and green when cooked, and should not be kept too long on the fire.

943 Ash-Pumpkin Curry

1 medium-size, well-matured ash pumpkin
⅛ lb. dried chillies (slightly roasted and ground)
8—10 red onions, sliced
1 tablespoonful broken but not powdered Maldive fish
4—5 cloves of garlic
rampa
sera
curry-leaves
8 pieces dry goraka
3 cloves
3—4 sliced green chillies
¼ oz. ground turmeric
a small quantity uluhāl
salt
the milk of 1½ coconuts

Scrape the ash off the pumpkin and thoroughly fork the fruit, then cut into square or rectangular pieces, leaving the hard and forked skin intact. Wash well. Place in a vessel and add the ingredients and also tiny pieces of coconut. Bring to the boil over a good flame, and boil until the gravy is thick, then add about 2 tablespoonfuls of coconut oil, a small quantity of sooduru (cummin) some mustard and sliced red onions, and, if necessary, lime and salt, and allow the vessel to be on a glowing fire for a few minutes.

944 Breadfruit Ambul Curry

3 matured breadfruit, and the same ingredients as for Jak Curry (Recipe 950).

Remove the skin of the fruit, cut into sections of 1½—2 inches, and put into cold water to which the juice of half a lime has been added. Wash well, then cook as described for Jak Curry.

945 Breadfruit Mallung

See Recipe 959.

946 Butsarana Dalu Badun

The tender leaves of Butsarana (Mussaenda)
Batter as in Recipe 953

Proceed as directed in the recipe quoted using the tender leaves instead of the Katufumurunga flowers. This makes a delicious Badun.

947 Dried Sprat Bola Curry (Halmessan Bola Ambul)

½ lb. sprats
1 tablespoonful rice-flour
15 green chillies
1 tablespoonful ground chillies
a few cloves of garlic
⅛ lb. red onions
¼ oz. ground turmeric
½ oz. ground salt
curry-leaves
2 small pieces cinnamon
about 25 pieces of coconut (cut very small, not grated)
lime or tamarind
oil for frying
4 cupfuls coconut milk

Clean and soak the sprats for 3 hours, wash well, and grind thoroughly into a paste. Mix in the rice-flour, and shape into balls the size of a small marble. Fry these in oil until nicely browned and drain. Split the chillies and fry lightly in the same oil.

Cook the other ingredients in the coconut milk until three-quarters done, then put in the fried chillies and sprat balls, adding lime or tamarind and salt to taste. Cook until the gravy is further reduced.

N.B. Instead of the sprats in above recipe take ½ lb. Maldive fish. Powder it and grind to a paste, adding rice-flour as above.

Form into balls, and cook in the same manner. This is known as **Maldive Fish Bola Curry** (Umbalakade Bola Ambul).

948 Gotukola Mallung

See Recipe 942

949 Green-Cadju Curry

green cadjus
1st and 2nd milk of one coconut
1 dessertspoonful ground or powdered dry chilli
a sprig of curry-leaves
a piece of rampa and lemon grass
coconut oil
3 sliced red onions
1 dessertspoonful coriander powder
4 green chillies
4 red onions
3 slices green ginger
3 cloves garlic
salt to taste
3 sliced green chillies
sprig of curry-leaves
1 teaspoonful mustard seed

Cut and clean the cadjus, put into a chatty with sufficient of the two milks of the coconut to cover, and add the rest of the first lot of ingredients. Allow to cook slowly. Meanwhile, heat the oil and fry the other ingredients in it, then stir the cadjunut mixture well and turn it into the second chatty. Cook on a moderate fire until the cadjus are tender, stirring with the handle of a wooden spoon to prevent breaking up the fruit. Continue cooking until the gravy dries up. If preferred, the dry chillies can be omitted and more of the green chillies used instead.

950 Jak Curry (Kos Ambul)

36 kos madul (pericarps) with the seeds
milk of 1 whole coconut
6 red onions
pinch of ground saffron
1 tablespoonful ground chillies (or according to taste)
3 cloves of garlic
1 tablespoonful powdered Maldive fish
curry-leaves
2 pieces cinnamon
3 or 4 green chillies chopped
2 tablespoonfuls coconut oil
a little mustard
salt
lime
oil, mustard, and red onions for "tempering"

Cut the pericarps at the end to remove the seeds, from which remove the skins. Wash, and boil the seeds lightly in a mixture of saffron, salt, and water, then re-introduce them into the pericarps. Put the ingredients into a vessel and cook until the gravy is thick. Temper before serving.

951 Tender-Jak Curry (Polos Ambul)

1 young jak fruit
¼ oz. each turmeric and powdered coriander
1 oz. dried chillies
¼ oz. powdered cummin
10 small red onions
¼ lb. well-broken Maldive fish
a small piece of cinnamon
a few curry-leaves
20 very tiny pieces of cut coconut
half a handful dried goraka
salt
coconut milk
coconut oil, mustard seed, maha-duru, red onions for "tempering"

The jak used for this curry must be of the age of one month to six weeks, not more.

Remove the green skin, cut lengthwise into eight sections and divide these. Do not remove the core, but round it off, or cut vertically to round pieces ¼ inch in thickness. Wash well in water to which the juice of a lime has been added. Drain, and put into a pan adding and thoroughly mixing with a paste made by grinding together the turmeric, dried chillies, powdered coriander, and powdered cummin. Now put in the red onions, Maldive fish, cinnamon, curry-leaves, coconut, goraka, and salt. Add enough coconut milk to cover, and cook over a quick fire until half cooked, then reduce the heat and allow to cook until the oil has formed from the milk. At this stage prepare the "tempering" and add it to the curry, shaking the pan slightly, then finish cooking, on a slow fire for about five minutes longer.

N.B. Tender jak can also be cooked whole, after skinning.

952 Jak Seed Curry

about 40 jack seeds
1 dessertspoonful coconut
2 cupfuls thick milk
1 dessertspoonful Maldive fish
1 teaspoonful rice
8 dry chillies
1 teaspoonful white cummin
1½ teaspoonfuls coriander
salt to taste

Wash the seeds well in water. They will burst when boiled well. Wash them slightly and put into another chatty with the milk, ½ quantity of red onions, and other ingredients. When the curry is cooked, temper in the pot and add the remaining quantity of onions.

953 Katurumurunga Flower Badun

12 opened katurumurunga flowers
oil and one egg
¼ lb. flour
coconut milk
salt and pepper
butter (optional)

Make a batter of the flower, egg, and coconut milk, adding pepper and salt to taste. Remove the green ovary from the flowers and, holding them by the stalk, dip each in the batter so that it is well coated. Fry in boiling oil. The addition of a little butter is an improvement. Drain, and serve hot.

954 Katurumurunga Flower Omelette

Make a batter as in the foregoing recipe, but thicker by reducing the quantity of coconut milk. Shred the flowers, wash well and squeeze well until almost dry. Mix the shredded flower with the batter, and fry in butter.

The addition of a little finely-chopped bacon or ham is a great improvement.

955 Kung-Koong Curry

kung-koong leaves
ground or powdered dry chilli
sliced red onion
sliced green chillies
Maldive fish
lime juice, or vinegar
salt to taste
coconut oil

Wash and clean the leaves well, and according to the quantity used add 1 teaspoonful or 1 dessertspoonful of powdered chilli, 3 or 4 sliced red onions, the same of green chillies sliced, a dessertspoonful Maldive fish, lime juice or vinegar, and salt to taste. Mix all the ingredients together, and fry in hot oil.

N.B. **Onion leaves** may be cooked in the same manner.

956 Maldive Fish Bola Curry

See Recipe 947.

957 Madukoku Ambula

25 tender madukoku
2 dessertspoonfuls roasted and ground chillies
1 dessertspoonful powdered Maldive fish
8 red onions sliced
curry-leaves
rampa
2 cloves garlic
a pinch of saffron
milk of ½ coconut
juice of 1 lime
salt
oil to temper

Boil the madukoku in water, and peel them. Cut the stalks into pieces about 2 inches in length, and put into a chatty with the ingredients. When the curry is cooked temper it with coconut oil.

958 Mugunuwenna Mallung

a handful of mugunuwenna leaves
½ coconut scraped
a piece of saffron ground
1 dessertspoonful Maldive fish ground
4 sliced red onions
salt

Wash the leaves well and shred as finely as possible. Put into a chatty and sprinkle with a little salt. Add the Maldive fish and cook until the leaves are tender and the mallung dry. Grind the coconut with the saffron and onions, and mix in well with the mallung. Cook for only 3 minutes.

959 Moongpialie Mallung

1 cupful clean moongpialie
3 cupfuls water
½ scraped coconut
a pinch of saffron
1 teaspoonful Maldive fish
2 cloves of garlic
2 slices green ginger
½ teaspoonful mustard seed
salt to taste

The moongpialie must be well cleaned and then washed thoroughly. Boil it in the water, mashing well with a wooden spoon during the process. After scraping the coconut grind it well with all the rest of the ingredients, and then add this mixture to the moongpialie, and cook on a slow fire until dry.

N.B. Half-matured **breadfruit** and **green papaw** sliced finely may be made in the same manner, but with both of these the fruit should only be boiled and not mashed.

960 Onion Leaves Curry

See Recipe 955.

961 Green Papaw Mallung

See Recipe 959

962 Potato Badun

potatoes, about ½ lb.
thick coconut milk
a pinch of saffron
a dessertspoonful ground or powdered dry chilli
a sprig of curry-leaves
a piece of rampa and lemon grass
a dessertspoonful Maldive fish
salt to taste
2 slices green ginger
3 cloves of garlic
coconut oil, and 3 or 4 sliced onions

Boil and peel the potatoes, put into a chatty with sufficient thick coconut milk to cover, and add the rest of the ingredients. Allow to cook over a moderate fire. Meanwhile, fry the onions in the oil in another chatty, and when browned nicely turn the contents of the first chatty into this. Cook over a moderate fire until the gravy dries up.

963 Titta Tibbatu Mallung

½ measure of the fruit
a pinch of ground chillies
10 green chillies, sliced
10 small red onions, sliced
1 dessertspoonful powdered Maldive fish
curry-leaves
salt to taste
½ coconut scraped
oil and mustard seed for tempering

Put the fruit into a "koraha" and crush, then wash about four times in fresh water. Put into the pan with all the ingredients (except the coconut and the tempering) and cook for about 5 minutes, then add the coconut and cook for a further 3—4 minutes until the curry is dry. Temper with the oil and mustard seed.

964 Tomato Curry

1 lb. fully ripe tomatoes
1 dessertspoonful powdered chillies (or according to taste)
salt
1 tablespoonful powdered Maldive fish
4 cloves of garlic
8 red onions
curry-leaves
rampa
1 tablespoonful tiny pieces of coconut

Steep the tomatoes in boiling water and remove the skins. Add all the ingredients and cook to the consistency of a pulp.

N.B. Avoid using coconut milk or oil; but if liked a little ghee may be used to improve the flavour, or tempering may be done with ghee after cooking is completed.

Tamil Recipes

981 Ash-Plantain Pachchadi

2 ash-plantains
scraped coconut
12 red onions
3 green chillies
1 dessertspoonful thick coconut milk
lime juice and salt

Boil the ash-plantains, and while hot mash them up. Grind enough scraped coconut very finely to make a ball the size of a large lime. Slice the onions and chillies very fine, and mix all together with the coconut milk, adding lime juice and salt to taste.

N.B. If liked, the ash-plantains may be roasted instead of boiled.

982 Chicken Curry (Badun)

1 good-sized chicken cut into joints
12 dried chillies ground
1 teaspoonful sweet fennel
½ teaspoonful cummin
10 peppercorns (all these to be roasted and ground)
4 cloves of garlic
¼-inch ginger
1-inch cinnamon
2-inch piece of rampa
2-inch piece sera
curry-leaves
a pinch of saffron
1 breakfastcupful 2nd milk of the coconut
½ cupful 1st milk
6 red onions, sliced
2 tablespoonfuls ghee
salt and lime juice to taste

Wash the chicken well, put into a saucepan with all the ground ingredients, the garlic and ginger sliced fine, the cinnamon, rampa, sera, curry-leaves, saffron, and the second milk. Add salt and lime juice to taste, and cook until the chicken is tender. Then add the first milk and allow to simmer for 10 minutes longer. Remove meat and gravy from the pan, and pour into it the ghee. Fry the onions, in this, and when they are lightly browned put back the chicken, and cook for 10 minutes over a slow fire, then pour in the gravy and simmer until this is quite thick.

983 Curd Pachchadi

1 cupful curd
1 teaspoonful finely-chopped ginger
6 large green chillies ground
ground coconut to the size of a large lime
a small piece of asafoetida fried and powdered
a few curry-leaves cut finely
some mustard seeds

Mash the curd and add the ground coconut, ginger, chillies and asafoetida. Mix well. Fry the mustard and curry-leaves, add to the pachchadi, and mix well. If the curd is not too sour, a little lime juice may be added to taste.

984 Curd Vadai

1 chundu broken black-gram (ulunthu)
½ lb. red onions cut coarsely
5 green chillies
½ teaspoonful finely-chopped ginger
ground coconut the size of a large lime
salt to taste
ghee for frying

For the CURD:

2 cupfuls curd
½ cupful water
curry-leaves
1 teaspoonful mustard seeds
a small piece asafoetida fried in a little ghee and powdered
salt to taste
1 teaspoonful ghee

To make the vadai, soak the gram for 4 hours. Wash it well until the black skin comes away, then grind to a smooth paste. Add the onions. chillies, ginger, ground coconut, and salt. Mix well, and fry, then set aside to cool.

Meanwhile, mash the curd, add the water gradually, and mix well. Now add asafoetida and salt to taste. Fry the mustard and curry-leaves in the teaspoonful ghee, and put into the curd and mix well.

When the vadai is cold pick it lightly with a fork, pour over just enough hot water to be absorbed. Arrange in the dish in which it is to be served, and pour the curd mixture over.

985 Curry Powder for Vegetables

1 lb. dried chillies
6 oz. coriander seed
2-inch piece of saffron
1 oz. pepper
1 oz. cummin

Roast all the ingredients except the saffron. Cut this up and pound with the rest. Sift well, and store in a dry, well-corked bottle. Use a perfectly dry spoon for removing the required quantity of the powder when wanted.

This curry-powder is added to vegetable curries according to taste. When carefully made it will keep for several months.

986 Flavouring for Vegetable Curries

1 tablespoonful ghee
6 red onions sliced
2 dried chillies broken in small pieces
a pinch of cummin
a pinch of fenugreek
a good pinch of mustard seeds
a few curry-leaves

Heat the ghee thoroughly in a pan, then put in the onions and dried chillies. While these are frying add the cummin, fenugreek, and mustard. As soon as the mustard begins to crackle throw in the leaves, turn in the prepared vegetable curry, and cover the pan immediately. (By doing this the full flavour of all the ingredients is retained). Remove the pan from the fire, and stir to mix well before serving.

987 Garlic Curry

the cloves of 4 rather large garlics
¾ lb. red onions
8 green chillies
1 teaspoonful fenugreek
1 breakfastcupful 1st and 2nd coconut milk in equal quantities
1 teaspoonful ground chillies
a pinch of saffron
tamarind juice and salt to taste
coconut milk

Fry the whole cloves of garlic, the peeled red onions also whole, and the green chillies in a little coconut oil, without letting them get brown. Strain, and keep aside. Remove the pan from the fire and put the fenugreek into the hot oil for 2 minutes, then strain this also and set aside.

Mix the ground chillies and saffron with the coconut milk, adding salt and tamarind to taste, then put in the fried ingredients and allow to boil once, then reduce heat and simmer for a few minutes until the gravy thickens.

988 Kuruma Iraichchi (White Curry)

1 lb. mutton
1 large Bombay onion
2 inches each of rampa and sera
a pinch of saffron
curry-leaves
¾ cupful thick coconut milk
fennel leaves
12 red onions
½ teaspoonful powdered pepper
vinegar and salt to taste
1 tablespoonful ghee
2 cupfuls of water

Cut the mutton into 2-inch pieces, and score it across a little with a sharp knife, then put it into a pan with the sliced Bombay onion, the rampa, sera, saffron, curry-leaves, and pepper. Add vinegar and salt to taste, and boil until the meat is tender. Now add the coconut milk and let it boil again for a little while, then put in the fennel cut into two or three pieces, and cover for 5 minutes.

Slice the red onions fairly fine and fry them lightly in the ghee, then add to the contents of the pan. Simmer slowly over a gentle heat until it thickens.

For Kuruma Iraichchi, see Recipe 817.

989 Kool

2 tablespoonfuls palmyrah-root flour
50 prawns
½ lb. seer boiled (bones and skin removed)
⅛th measure rice
1 heaped teaspoonful ground dried chillies, or according to taste
15 long beans
tamarind juice and salt
3 bottles water
⅛th part of a medium sized jak and some of the seeds

Soak the flour in water and strain. Do this two or three times.

Put the three bottles of water into a pan and bring to the boil, then put in the well-washed rice, the beans broken into small pieces, the jak seeds split into two, and allow to cook. When well-boiled add the prepared jak cut into small pieces. Allow this to boil until cooked, then add the soaked flour, ground chillies, and tamarind juce and salt to taste. Last of all put in the boiled and shelled prawns, the seer broken into small pieces, and simmer all together. Remove from the fire before the liquid becomes too thick.

990 Masala Vadai

¼ measure dhall
1½ teaspoons very finely powdered Maldive fish
2 tablespoons finely sliced red onions
1 dessertspoonful powdered dry chillies
a good pinch of ground saffron
1 dozen curry-leaves
salt

Wash the dhall well in several changes of water removing any discoloured ones which float on top of the water. Put the dhall into a bowl with cold water to cover and let it soak for a couple of hours. Then drain and grind the dhall finely and add to it the Maldive fish, onions, dry chillies, saffron, curry-leaves broken in pieces and salt to taste. Mix well together and shape into small flat rounds about one-third of an inch thick, and fry in hot oil to a golden brown colour. This quantity will make about 2 dozen little fritters.

N.B. If liked, a prawn can be placed on the top of each fritter before they are fried. Wash and trim the prawns but do not remove the heads and tails. Add a little salt, boil them slightly and place one on the top of each fritter pressing the prawn in a bit.

991 Mulligatawny (White)

For the STOCK:
2 medium-sized fowls or 2 lb. breast of mutton
2-inch piece each of rampa and sera
18 curry onions, sliced
8 cloves of garlic, sliced
¼ teaspoonful sweet fennel
½ inch piece of ginger sliced finely
2 inch piece cinnamon
a few curry-leaves
3 bottles water
a few tomatoes
salt to taste

For SEASONING and THICKENING:
8 dried chillies
1 tablespoonful coriander
1 teaspoonful sweet fennel
¼ teaspoonful cummin
¼ teaspoonful peppercorns
gram (kondai-kadala)
1½ breakfastcupfuls thick coconut milk
a pinch of saffron
lime juice and salt to taste

For FLAVOURING:
sliced red onions
curry-leaves
a good-pinch of sweet fennel
ghee

Joint the fowls, or cut the mutton in medium-sized pieces, and put into a saucepan with the water and all the rest of the first lot of ingredients. Boil until the meat is tender.,

Roast and grind the dried chillies, then lightly roast the coriander, sweet fennel, cummin, and peppercorns, and grind these well.

Roast the gram and grind well. (The quantity when ground should be the size of a small orange).

Mix all these ground ingredients with the coconut milk, add the saffron, and pour into the mulligatawny, adding lime juice and salt to taste.

Fry the last lot of ingredients in ghee, first slicing the onions, and add to the rest of the mixture. Stir well, and remove from the fire.

This mulligatawny is best served with stringhoppers.

992 Murunga ("Drumstick") Curry

6 murungas
12 red onions
6 long chillies
2 breakfastcupfuls 1st and 2nd coconut milk in equal quantities
1 or 2 dessertspoonfuls curry powder
salt and thick tamarind juice to taste
ghee for frying

Cut the murungas into pieces 2½ inches long, and fry. Fry the red onions and the chillies whole. Put all into a vessel with salt and tamarind to taste, the coconut milk, and curry powder. Bring to the boil once, then allow to simmer gently until cooked. Remove from the fire.

N.B. The following **vegetables** may all be cooked in the same manner: ash-plantains, brinjals, long beans, bittergourd, snakegourd, and potatoes with Bombay onions in equal quantities.

993 Mutton Curry (White)

1 lb. mutton
15 red onions
4 fairly large green chillies
2 inches each of rampa and sera curry-leaves
4 cloves garlic
½ inch green ginger
lime juice and salt to taste
1 heaped teaspoonful uncooked rice
½ teaspoonful sweet fennel seed
½ cupful thick coconut milk
a pinch of saffron
1½ cupfuls 2nd milk of coconut

Cut the mutton into fairly large pieces, score across each piece a few times with a sharp knife, and put into a pan with the sliced red onions, the chillies cut into four lengthwise, garlic and ginger sliced finely, rampa and sera, a pinch of saffron, salt and lime juice to taste, and the 2nd milk. Boil all together until the meat is tender. Meanwhile, roast the rice until brown, then pound it. Roast the sweet fennel lightly and pound this. Sift each separately. When the meat is ready, and there is just a little gravy left with it, pour in the thick milk. Boil up once, then add the prepared rice and the fennel, cover the pan, and cook over a very low flame until the gravy thickens. Remove from the fire.

994 Pepper Water (Rasam)

2 dessertspoonfuls coriander
½ dessertspoonful cummin
1 teaspoonful peppercorns
1 small garlic
1 bottle water
tamarind juice and salt to taste
a pinch of mustard seed
1 dessertspoonful coconut oil or ghee
4 sliced red onions
a few curry-leaves
2 dried chillies broken in small pieces

Crush the coriander and put it into a pan with the water, cummin, peppercorns, and garlic (do not remove the skin of this) and bring to the boil twice. Add the tamarind juice and salt to taste.

Heat the oil or ghee, and in it fry the rest of the ingredients, then turn the contents of the other pan into the pan with the ghee, etc., and bring to the boil once. Remove from fire.

995 Potato Curry (Dry)

1 lb. potatoes
1 level dessertspoonful chilli powder
2 medium-sized Bombay onions
3 tablespoonfuls ghee
curry-leaves
salt to taste

Boil the potatoes in their skins, then peel and cut them up into fairly small "chunks". Add the chilli powder and salt, and set aside, mixing well. Heat the ghee until it boils, then add the onions sliced and let them "boil" in it until nearly cooked. Add a few curry-leaves, and the potatoes, and cook over a low flame for about 10 minutes. Stir well to mix thoroughly, then finish cooking over a very low flame until the curry has a "fried" appearance and is quite dry.

996 Prawn Vadai

1 chundu ulunthu
6 oz. red onions (chopped)
2 oz. green chillies (chopped)
50 prawns cut up small
⅛ teaspoon cummin & ⅛ teaspoon peppercorns (ground together)
a few curry-leaves
coconut oil for frying
salt to taste

Soak the ulunthu overnight. Wash it well until the black skin comes away and grind to a paste not too smooth. Add the onions, chillies, curry-leaves, all chopped fine, and the prawns. Mix well and fry.

997 Rasam

See Recipes 994 and 999.

998 Thosai

1 chundu ulunthu (broken black gram)
2 chundus uncooked rice
¼ teaspoon fenugreek & ⅛ teaspoon cummin (ground together)
½ teaspoon peppercorns
1 tablespoon good coconut oil or ghee
12 to 15 red onions sliced
3 dried chillies broken in small pieces
a few curry-leaves
salt to taste
a little gingelly oil

Soak rice and fenugreek together and the ulunthu separately for about 8 to 10 hours. Then wash the ulunthu well until the black skin comes away, and also wash the rice which has been soaked with the fenugreek. Then grind all to a very smooth paste. Mix all together, put into a pan, cover and leave overnight. In the morning it should be well risen. Add water and mix to a thick batter. Heat the ghee thoroughly in a pan, then put in the onions and dried chillies. While these are frying add curry leaves. When it is golden brown, remove the pan from the fire and add the fried ingredients to the rice and ulunthu batter. Mix in the ground pepper and cummin. Heat an iron girdle and rub it over with a cloth dipped in gingelly oil. Then add a coconut spoon full of the batter and smoothen it out with the back of the spoon to the size of a dessert plate. When baked on one side, turn over and cook for a few minutes longer.

999 Tomato Rasam

½ lb. ripe tomatoes
2 Bombay onions
4 cloves
a small piece of cinnamon
12 red onions
curry-leaves
¼ measure husked dhall
6 peppercorns
a pinch of saffron
1 tablespoonful and 1 teaspoonful ghee
lime juice and salt to taste
2 bottles water

Put the water into a pan, and when it boils add the saffron, teaspoonful ghee, and well-washed dhall. Boil together until the dhall is quite soft, then mash it well and strain.

Turn into a clean pan and add the finely-sliced Bombay onions, cloves, cinnamon, peppercorns, and tomatoes cut in pieces. Boil, mash the tomatoes up, and boil again, then strain and add lime juice and salt to taste.

Put the tablespoonful ghee into a pan, and when boiling add the sliced red onions. Fry to a golden colour, then add a few curry-leaves, and pour the strained rasam into it. Cover, and remove from the fire.

1000 Uppu Ma

1 cupful semolina
1½ cupfuls butter-milk
15 to 20 cadjunuts chopped coarsely
8 dried chillies cut into small pieces
curry-leaves
mustard
salt to taste
a small piece of asafoetida soaked in a teaspoonful water after frying and pounding
ghee for frying

First fry the chopped nuts in the ghee, then lift out and set aside. Then fry the chillies, and when these are brown add the mustard and curry-leaves and fry for a little while. Now turn in the semolina, and allow to fry over a moderate flame until golden brown in colour. Add the butter-milk, salt, and prepared asafoetida, and stir over a low flame until all the liquid has been absorbed. Stir in the nuts.

1001 Vegetable Curries

See Recipe 992.

Puddings

1006 Kesari-Bath

1 breakfastcupful each of semolina and milk
sugar to taste
3 or 4 powdered cardamoms
1 teaspoonful rose-water
20 cadjunuts
30 sultanas
2 teaspoonfuls ghee
2 teaspoonfuls powdered sugar-candy

Cut the nuts into large pieces, fry in the ghee until a pale golden colour, and drain. Next fry the sultanas in the ghee, and when they are nicely puffed out drain these also. Now turn the semolina into the ghee, and allow it to "roast" over a moderate flame until it is a nice golden brown colour. Pour in the boiling milk, and cook until it is all absorbed, then add the sugar to taste and stir well. Remove from the fire, and add the sultanas, nuts, sugar-candy, cardamoms, and rose-water. Mix all well together.

1007 Payasam

3 tablespoonfuls semolina
1 bottle milk
2 cups water
20 cadjunuts chopped in large pieces
1 tablespoonful sultanas
sugar to taste (about 3 tablespoonfuls)
4 cardamoms pounded
a few drops essence of rose
2 tablespoonfuls ghee

Fry the nuts and sultanas separately in the ghee, and drain. Then fry the semolina in the ghee until it is golden brown in colour. Use a low flame to prevent colouring too quickly. Boil the water and pour into the semolina, and stir over a low flame for about 5 minutes, then add the boiling milk and the sugar, and allow to boil up two or three times, stirring all the time. Just before serving add the fried nuts and sultanas, the rose essence, and cardamoms, stir well.

Payasam should be liquid rather than stiff, and may be served warm or well-chilled, according to fancy.

Rasa Kavili (Sweetmeats)

(SINHALESE AND OTHER CEYLON SWEETS)

THE Sinhala title of this chapter is familiar to most Ceylonese. It is a comprehensive term and embraces the recipes here both individually and generally. Some of these preparations are in everyday use in nearly every Ceylonese home.

Milk Rice (Kiribath), Hoppers (Āppa), Stringhoppers (Iddi-Āppung), Pittu, and Roti are included here.

In these recipes care has been taken to give the quantities in such a way that even a novice can attempt them with a fair amount of success. Every one of these is a tried recipe, and if the directions are followed carefully there should be no failure.

1021 Aggala

½ measure muttusamba rice
¼ measure coconut syrup
powdered pepper
salt

Roast and pound the rice and sieve it. Put the syrup into a pan, add a pinch of salt, and stir over the fire until it thickens. Then take the pan off the fire. Reserve one-fourth of the powdered rice for coating the aggalas when they are ready. Mix a good pinch of pepper with the rest of the powdered rice and add it to the syrup as soon as it is taken off the fire. Mix well until it forms into a stiff paste, and before it cools form into balls about the size of a small lime. Coat them well with the powdered rice which had been reserved.

1022 Alu-Eluvang

½ measure rice-flour
2 eggs
3 teacups coconut milk
salt
pani-pol (Recipe 1049)

The flour must be finely sieved. Put it into a basin and mix to a smooth paste with half of the milk, adding salt to taste. Beat in the eggs and add the rest of the milk gradually. Melt a little dripping in a frying pan and when quite hot pour in enough batter to cover the bottom of the pan thinly. When cooked underneath, —do not cook both sides—turn on to a plate, place a spoonful of pani-pol in the centre and roll up as you would a pan-cake. It must be rolled at once before it cools or it will crack in the rolling.

1023 Aluvā I

½ measure well-roasted and sieved rice-flour
¼ measure coconut syrup
25 cadjunuts or 2 tablespoonfuls moong-ata
a pinch of roasted and powdered sweet cummin
½ teaspoon ghee or butter
salt

Put the syrup into a pan and stir over the fire until it thickens. Then add the flour, reserving about one-fourth of it for coating the aluva, and stir well and briskly. Mix in the cadjunuts cut in pieces or the moong-ata slightly roasted and husked, the cummin, salt and ghee. Mix all together and turn it quickly on to a floured board. Knead with the hand and flatten out, coating the top with flour. Cut into diamond shaped pieces.

N.B. The flour should not be allowed to boil too long in the syrup as that makes the aluva sticky.

1024 Aluva II

½ measure well-roasted and sieved rice-flour
1 lb. sugar
¾ teacup water
25 cadjunuts
rose-water
salt

Put the sugar and water into a pan and stir over the fire until it thickens. Flavour with rose-water and then proceed to make the aluvā as directed in the previous recipe.

1025 Āppa (Hoppers)

½ measure slightly roasted rice-flour
¾ teacup coconut water
1 teacup thick coconut milk
1 teacup second extract of coconut milk (extract of one coconut)
salt
1 tablespoon of toddy or a good pinch of corbonate of soda

Mix the flour with the coconut water and toddy overnight, kneading it well. About 2 or 3 hours before baking the hoppers add the coconut milk very gradually, first the thick milk and then the second extract, and stir the mixture well, mixing in the soda if it is used. Cover and let it stand.

Place a little iron pan over a light fire, grease it, pour a spoonful of the batter, cover with a chatty containing burning coals and bake till done. Before covering the pan, take it up with both hands and give it a circular twist till about half an inch more of the pan is thickly coated with the batter which, when the hopper is baked, forms the crisp brown border.

N.B.—As hoppers are usually baked early in the morning it is advisable to use hot water for squeezing the coconut instead of cold.

The inside of a hopper pan should not be washed but greased with butter or gingelly oil and wiped.

The hoppers often stick to the pan and give trouble. This could be prevented by frying the yolk of an egg in the pan and rubbing the pan over with it. Hoppers can also be baked on a gas stove using a tight fitting lid to cover the pan instead of a chatty with coals.

1026 Bittara Āppa I (Egg Hoppers)

Prepare the batter in the same way as in the previous recipe. Pour a spoonful of the batter into the pan, and when the hopper is half baked make a slight depression in the centre with the ladle and break an egg carefully into it. Cover the pan and bake till the egg is cooked. The time will depend on how the egg is liked, soft or hard.

1027 Bittara Appa II (Egg Hoppers)

½ measure slightly roasted rice-flour
¾ teacup coconut water
1½ teacups coconut milk
3 or 4 eggs
2 tablespoonfuls sugar
a grate of nutmeg
a good pinch of carbonate of soda
a few sultanas
salt

Mix and prepare the batter as directed in Recipe 1025. Beat the eggs and sugar together, add the nutmeg and stir it into the batter after adding the coconut milk. Pour a spoonful of the batter into a hopper pan and when half baked sprinkle in a few sultanas. Cover the pan again and bake till done.

1028 Hakuru Āppa (Jaggery Hoppers)

Prepare the batter and bake the hoppers as directed in Recipe 1025, mixing in ½ lb. jaggery (scraped) into the batter when adding the coconut milk.

1029 Asmi

1 measure rice-flour
1 teacup thick coconut milk
a handful of "dhoul kurundu" leaves squeezed in a cup of second extract of coconut milk
salt
oil for frying

For the SYRUP
½ lb. sugar
¼ teacup water
essence of rose
cochineal

The flour must be very finely sieved through voile and the coconut milk carefully strained through a kitchen towel. Put the flour into a basin, add the milk very gradually and knead well with the hand. Then add salt to taste and 3 tablespoons of the leaf juice (strained), which is added to make the batter slimy. The batter should be of a thick, slimy consistency. Have ready a deep round-bottom pan about three-fourths full of boiling oil. Take a spoonful of the batter and pour it through an āsmi spoon (a large coconut shell spoon with a perforated bottom and an upright handle) into the boiling oil moving the spoon round and in all directions until a complete network is formed. Release the edges with an oil spoon, fold over to form a semi-circle and press the edges together. Turn over and fry the other side. Drain on paper. The āsmis should be put away for a day or two and then fried again when they will swell out. Then decorate the top of the āsmis with thickened syrup pouring it in a zigzag design.

To Prepare the Syrup—Put the sugar and water in a saucepan and thicken it over the fire. Flavour with rose and colour it pink with a few drops of cochineal. Pour it over the āsmis before it hardens.

1030 Atiraha I

1 measure rice-flour
$\frac{1}{8}$ measure kappi
$\frac{1}{2}$ measure coconut syrup
salt
oil for frying

Put the syrup into a saucepan and stir over the fire until it thickens, then add the kappi slightly roasted. Stir well and add the flour very gradually and stir with a straight wooden ladle until it is boiled and is of a thick consistency, adding salt to taste. Take it off the fire and turn on to a pastry board to cool. Pour 2 teacups of water into the pan in which the mixture was cooked and stir over the fire for a few minutes until it thickens into a congee. Allow it to cool. Then knead the paste well with the hand adding enough of the congee to soften the paste sufficiently to be able to form into balls which are flattened on oiled plantain leaves into rounds. Fry a few at a time in boiling coconut oil in a deep pan.

N.B. Kappi is the remainder of the flour left over in the sieve after the rice has been pounded and sieved. This must be winnowed and the little grains like sago separated and used.

1031 Atiraha II

1 measure rice-flour
1 lb. and 2 oz. sugar
rose water
salt
ghee for frying

Make the sugar into a syrup by adding a teacup of water to the sugar and boiling it. Flavour the syrup with rose-water and then proceed to make the atirahas as in previous recipe. Fry them in ghee.

1032 Bibikkan

$\frac{1}{2}$ measure rice-flour
1 lb. finely scraped coconut
$\frac{3}{4}$ lb. jaggery (scraped)
2 oz. moong-ata
salt
a good pinch of carbonate of soda

Mix the flour, coconut and jaggery in a basin, adding salt to taste. Then add the moong-ata slightly roasted and husked, and the soda, and mix well together. Place a "kenda" leaf or a round of plantain leaf in the middle of a hopper pan, pour a spoonful of the batter into it and bake in the same way as directed in Recipe 1025.

N.B. The coconut should not be too dry.

1033 Galkisse Bibikkan

½ measure slightly roasted and sieved rice-flour
¾ measure coconut syrup
2 lb. scraped coconut
2 oz. sultanas
25 cadjunuts
½ teaspoon roasted and finely powdered sweet cummin
salt

Put the syrup into a saucepan and stir over the fire until it boils, then add the coconut, which must be pounded after being scraped, and stir for a few minutes. Take it off the fire and allow to cool. When cold, mix in the flour and cummin and add salt to taste. Pour the mixture into prepared pans and sprinkle the top with a few sultanas and cadjunuts split in halves. These bibikkans are usually baked between 2 chatties with coals at the bottom and in the upper chatty. They can also be baked in a moderate oven.

N.B. To Prepare the Pans—Take round fluted pans about 6½ inches in diameter and 1½ inches high. Grease the pans well with butter or ghee and dust them with American flour, shaking out all the flour that does not adhere.

1034 Halapa

½ measure slightly roasted rice-flour
¾ lb. jaggery (scraped)
1 lb. scraped coconut
salt

Put all the ingredients into a basin and mix well together with the hand. Place a dessertspoonful of the mixture on a "kenda" leaf, flatten it out and fold the leaf in two. Then steam the halapas.

The Method of Steaming—Tie a pudding cloth over the mouth of a fairly open chatty pot three-quarters full of water. Cover it with a chatty large enough to cover the rim of the pot and bring the water to the boil. Then place the halapas a few at a time on the improvised steamer and steam from 15 to 20 minutes or until sufficiently boiled. As the water in the steaming pot boils down more boiling water must be added.

1035 Kurakkan Halapa

¼ measure kurakkan-flour
¼ measure rice-flour
¾ lb. jaggery (scraped)
1 lb. scraped coconut
salt

Mix the two kinds of flour together and prepare the halapas in the same way as in the previous recipe.

N.B. If liked, a little pani-pol (Recipe 1049) could be placed in the centre of the halapa before folding it over.

1036 Idi-Āppung (Stringhoppers)

½ measure rice-flour **1 teacup boiling water** **salt**

Sieve the flour finely and put it into a cone shaped basket (gotuwa) and steam over a chatty pot of boiling water. When ready, turn it on to a sieving (aswatty) and sieve it while hot, rubbing it gently through with the palm of the hand.

Instead of steaming, if liked, the flour could be roasted and very finely sieved. Put the prepared flour into a chatty, add salt to taste and mix well using the handle of a kitchen ladle. When well mixed put some of the paste into an idi-āppung mould and press it through on to the idi-āppung mats (watties) which should be previously greased. Place about 3 or 4 of these mats at a time over a chatty pot of boiling water—the mats are arranged with a cane ring between each. Cover with an idi-āppung steaming pot cover and steam until the idi-āppungs are boiled.

N.B. The gotuwa, aswatty, idi-āppung watties as well as the mould and steaming pot cover are all procurable in the market.

Stringhoppers are usually served with: Mulligatawny (see Recipe 991), Fowl Badun (812), Frikkadels (814), Liver Curry (820), Chilli Sambol (866), Stringhopper Sambol (878).

1037 Idi-Āppung (Stringhopper) Dodol

8 to 10 idi-āppungs
½ lb. jaggery
1 teacup coconut milk
1-inch piece cinnamon
a pinch of slightly roasted and powdered sweet cummin

Pour a little of the coconut milk over the idi-āppungs and break them up. Put the jaggery, coconut milk and cinnamon into a pan and stir over the fire until it forms a thick syrup. Then add the idi-āppungs, sprinkle in the cummin and stir until the mixture thickens. Turn it on to a flat buttered dish, smooth the top with a greased piece of plantain leaf, and cut into diamond shaped or square pieces when cold.

1038 Kalu Dodol

½ lb. rice-flour
2½ lb. jaggery
½ teaspoon powdered cardamoms
6 pints coconut milk (the extract of 3 large coconuts)

To get the milk from the coconut add a sufficient quantity of water to the grated coconut and extract the thick milk, then add more water and extract the second quantity of milk. Then pound the refuse of the coconut in a flour pounder and add water to get a further quantity of milk. The three extracts of milk must make 6 pints. Put the milk into a large brass pan and add the flour and the jaggery which must be scraped or broken up. Keep on the fire and stir all the time. As the mixture thickens a brass or iron spoon must be used for stirring. As it proceeds to thicken and oil forms which must be removed from time to time with a spoon. Add the cardamoms about 15 minutes before taking the dodol off the fire. Much depends on the stirring, as the mixture is liable to burn. When very thick turn it on to a flat dish. A few cadjunuts may be chopped and added to the mixture at the same time as the cardamoms. Good kitul jaggery must be used, preferably dark cakes.

The above quantity will take about 2½ hours to make.

1039 Konda Kavum I

1 measure rice-flour
½ measure coconut syrup
salt
oil for frying

The flour must be very finely sieved. Put it into a basin, add the syrup and mix well together, adding a little salt and a little hot water, if the batter is too thick. If not sure of the consistency it is best to fry a kavum and see whether it is right before adding the water. Have ready a deep round-bottom pan of boiling coconut oil. Pour in a spoonful of the batter and as it begins to fry and the centre rises, pour in a little more batter into the centre and insert an ekel in the middle of the fritter; not allowing it to go through. Keep twisting the ekel round and round and at the same time splashing the boiling oil on the fritter using an oil spoon for the purpose. This is to produce the konde. Press round the base of the konde with the spoon to get it into the proper shape. The kavums must have a nice brown colour when fried. Drain well.

It needs considerable practice to produce a well-shaped kavum.

1040 Konda Kavum II

1 measure rice-flour
¾ lb. sugar
ghee for frying
rose-water
salt

Make the sugar into a syrup by adding ½ teacup of water and boiling it and then flavour with rose-water. Make and fry the kavums as in the previous recipe.

1041 Moong-ata Kavum (Green Gram Kavum)

½ measure moong-ata flour
½ measure rice-flour
½ measure coconut syrup
1 dessertspoon ghee
salt

For the BATTER:

¼ measure rice-flour
½ tea-cup or a little less of coconut milk
1 egg
a pinch of salt
ground saffron

Put the syrup into a pan and stir over the fire until it boils. Then add the two kinds of flour gradually and keep on stirring until the flour is cooked and the mixture thickens. Just before taking it off the fire add the ghee and stir well. Turn the paste on to a pastry board to cool.

Pour 2 teacups of water into the pan in which the mixture was cooked and stir over the fire for a few minutes until it thickens into a congee, and allow it to cool.

Then knead the paste with the hand, adding a sufficient quantity of the congee, a little at a time, to soften the paste. It must be well kneaded or the paste will be lumpy. Flatten out on the board, smooth the top with a greased piece of plantain leaf and cut into diamond shaped pieces. Dip in batter and fry in boiling oil.

Prepare the batter as in the previous recipe.

1042 Pana Kavum

¼ measure well roasted and finely sieved rice-flour
½ teaspoon soft sugar
salt
yolk of 1 egg
coconut milk
oil for frying

SUGAR COATING:

¼ lb. sugar **2 tablespoons water** **1 dessertspoon rose-water**

Put the flour, sugar and salt into a basin, add the yolk of egg and enough milk to form a nice stiffish paste, and knead with the hand until quite smooth. Form the paste into different little fancy shapes with the hand or press the paste through a pana-kavum mould into a pan of boiling oil and fry to a nice brown colour. Then drain and coat with sugar.

To Prepare the Sugar Coating—Put the sugar and water into a pan and boil until they form a thick syrup. Then add the rose-water and stir until the syrup is very thick. Take the pan off the fire, toss in the little shapes and stir carefully until they get coated with the sugar.

1943 Kiribath (Milk Rice)

½ measure country-rice or raw-rice
2 teacups thick coconut milk
salt

Boil the rice as usual, and when the water is all absorbed but before the rice becomes grainy, add the coconut milk and salt and stir well with the handle of a kitchen ladle. Cover the pot and allow to boil on a slow fire until the milk is absorbed, when the rice will be ready.

For **Coppa Kiribath** (Cup Milk Rice), rinse out a seenakku cup with coconut milk and fill it with the milk rice, pressing it in somewhat, and make a depression in the centre with a finger. Fill it with pani-pol (Recipe 1049) and cover up neatly with the rice. Turn out of the cups.

For Seenakku cups, see illustration "Ceylonese Cooking Utensils".

1044 Kiri Dodol

½ measure rice-flour
¾ lb. jaggery
5 teacups coconut milk
25 cadjunuts
2-inch piece cinnamon
salt

Put the flour into a pan, add the milk gradually and stir until free from lumps. Then add the jaggery which may be scraped or broken up, the cinnamon and salt, and stir over the fire until the mixture thickens. Mix in the cadjunuts cut in small pieces a few minutes before taking the dodol off the fire. Turn it on to a flat buttered dish, flatten out with a piece of greased plantain leaf, and cut into diamond-shaped pieces when cold.

1045 Laddu

¼ measure muttusamba rice
½ lb. jaggery
½ lb. scraped coconut
salt

Roast, pound and sieve the rice. Pound the jaggery in a rice pounder, add the coconut, powdered rice and salt to taste and pound all together until well mixed. Then with the hand form the paste into oblong-shaped rolls.

1046 Lavariya

flour prepared as for idi-āppung (Recipe 1036)
pani-pol (Recipe 1049)

After the flour has been mixed, take portions of it, form into balls about the size of a lime and then flatten out on greased plantain leaves. Place a spoonful of pani-pol in the centre and fold over like a patty. Place 3 or 4 of these on a greased idi-āppung watty and steam as directed in Recipe 1047.

1057 Idi-Āppung (Stringhopper) Lavariya

Prepare the flour as for idi-āppung and pour it through an idi-āppung mould on to a "kenda" leaf which should be lightly greased. Place a little pani-pol (Recipe 1049) in the centre and fold over like a patty. Take it out of the leaf and place 3 or 4 of these on a greased idi-āppung watty. Then steam until cooked, placing only one watty at a time on the steaming pot and covering with an idi-āppung steaming pot cover.

1048 Moong-ata Guli (Green Gram Balls)

½ measure moong-ata flour
¼ measure well roasted and sieved rice-flour
¼ measure coconut syrup
¼ lb. sugar candy
salt

For the BATTER:

¼ measure rice-flour
½ teacup or a little less of coconut milk
1 egg
a pinch of salt
a pinch of ground saffron

Put the syrup into a pan, add a pinch of salt and stir over the fire until it thickens somewhat. Then take the pan off the fire and mix in the two kinds of flour and the sugar candy coarsely powdered. Mix well, first with the spoon and, when sufficiently cooled, work with the hands and form the mixture into balls about the size of a large marble. This must be done quickly or the mixture will crumble into powder. Dip the balls in batter and fry 3 or 4 of them together in hot oil. Drain on paper.

To Prepare the Batter—Put the flour into a basin and mix to a smooth batter with half of the milk, beat in the egg and the remainder of the milk, add salt to taste and enough saffron to make the batter a nice bright yellow.

N,B. The egg may be omitted, if wished.

1049 Pani-Pol (Jaggery & Coconut Filling)

½ lb. jaggery
½ lb. scraped coconut
½ teaspoon rice-flour
1-inch piece cinnamon
salt

Scrape the jaggery and put it into a saucepan with 3 tablespoons of water. Stir over the fire until the syrup thickens, then add the coconut, cinnamon and a pinch of salt. When the mixture thickens sprinkle in the flour and stir for a couple of minutes longer.

N.B. If the flavour is liked, a pinch of roasted and finely powdered sweet cummin could be added to it.

1050 Pasong

½ measure rice-flour
3 teacups coconut milk
10 oz. jaggery
salt

For the TOP DRESSING:

⅛ measure rice-flour 1 teacup thick coconut milk salt

The flour must be very finely sieved. Put it into a basin and add the coconut milk gradually, stirring it well. Mix in the jaggery (scraped) and a little salt. Have ready a chatty pot half full of boiling water with a steaming basket (gotuwa) on it. Place a few plantain leaf cones in it, fill them three parts with the batter, cover with a steaming pot cover and steam till the batter is half cooked. Then pour a spoonful of the dressing into each cone and steam again till the top is firm.

To Make the Dressing—Mix the flour and coconut milk together and add salt to taste.

N.B. To make the plantain leaf cones—take pieces of plantain leaf about 7 inches long and 4½ inches wide. Warm them until they become flexibie and twist into cones fastening with a piece of pointed ekel. Trim the tops with a pair of scissors.

1051 Pittu

½ measure rice-flour 1 lb. scraped coconut salt

Put the flour and coconut into a large deep chatty, add a little salt and mix with the hand in a circular movement forming the flour into little grains. If necessary, sprinkle in a little cold water while forming the grains. The coconut for pittu should not be too dry.

Half fill a chatty pot with water and bring to the boil. Then place the pittu bamboo on it making sure that no steam escapes between the pot and bamboo. Fill up the bamboo with the prepared flour, dropping it in very gently in handfuls. When the steam begins to escape through the top of the bamboo cover with a coconut shell and steam until the pittu is cooked. Take the bamboo off the pot and push the pittu on to a dish using a stout, round stick for the purpose. Serve with thick coconut milk.

1052 Coppa Pittu (Cup Pittu)

½ measure roasted and sieved rice-flour
½ lb. scraped coconut
salt
pani-pol (Recipe 1049)

Put the flour into a large deep chatty, add the coconut and salt and mix it using only the tips of the fingers (as you would rub fat into flour in making pastry). Sprinkle a few drops of cold water from time to time and mix it occasionally with a circular movement of the hand until the mixture becomes like fine breadcrumbs. Fill a seenakku cup* with the mixture pressing it in somewhat. Make a depressing in the centre with a finger, fill it with pani-pol and cover up neatly with the mixture. Turn out 4 or 5 of these on a lightly buttered idi-āppung watty and steam in the same way as idi-āppung (Recipe 1036), but using only one watty at a time It will take from 12 to 15 minutes to steam.

*See illustration, "Ceylonese Cooking Utensils."

1053 Kurakkan Pittu

¼ measure kurakkan-flour
¼ measure rice-flour
1 lb. scraped coconut
salt

Mix the two kinds of flour and the coconut together, add salt to taste and proceed to make the pittu as in the previous recipe.

Serve with coconut milk, scraped coconut and jaggery.

1054 Pol-Kotta

½ measure slightly roasted and sieved rice-flour
¾ lb. scraped coconut
2 oz. jaggery (scraped)
salt
kitul or coconut syrup

Put the flour, coconut and jaggery into a basin and mix well with the hand, adding salt to taste and a little boiling water, if necessary. It must be a stiffish paste. Make the paste into balls about the size of a lime, then take into the palm of the hand, shape into a roll and press it down with the tips of 3 fingers leaving a fairly deep impression. Then steam in the same way as halapa (Recipe 1034). When ready, pour some thickened syrup into the depressions and serve hot.

1055 Rōda-Kokis

½ measure rice-flour
2 teacups coconut milk
1 tablespoonful sugar
2 eggs
salt
oil for frying

Put the flour, sugar and salt into a basin, add about half of the coconut milk and mix to a smooth paste. Beat up the eggs and add them to the batter and also the rest of the milk gradually. Beat all well together until perfectly smooth. It should be thicker than a pancake batter. Have ready a deep, round-bottomed pan of boiling coconut oil. Take a kokis mould and dip it into the oil to make it hot. Then dip it into the batter taking care not to let the batter cover more than three parts of the mould. Plunge it into the hot oil and fry for a few minutes. Then slip the kokis out of the mould by shaking it a bit and let the kokis cook a minute or two longer to brown the inside. Drain on paper. The kokis will keep crisp in an air tight tin.

N.B. The sugar can be omitted or both sugar and eggs, in which case a little more coconut milk will be necessary.

1056 Roti

½ measure slightly roasted rice-flour
1 lb. scraped coconut
salt to taste
boiling water, if necessary

Put the flour and coconut into a basin, add salt to taste and mix well with the hand adding a little boiling water, if the paste is too dry. Form the paste into balls and flatten out on plantain leaves. Bake the rotties in an open rotty-chatty or pan over the fire. When one side is done turn over and bake the other side.

1057 Sago Dodol

¾ measure slightly roasted rice-flour
½ lb. jaggery
¾ teacup thick coconut milk
salt
1-inch piece cinnamon
a good pinch of roasted and powdered sweet cummin

Put the flour into a large deep chatty, add salt to taste, sprinkle in a little water and mix with the hand in a circular movement forming the flour into grains about the size of large sago. As the grains form, remove them into another vessel. Sprinkle in more water—very little at a time—and continue this process until all the flour has turned into grains. Have ready a steaming pot as directed in Recipe 1034 and steam the prepared flour. When ready spread it out to cool. Put the jaggery, coconut milk and cinnamon into a pan and stir over the fire until it is very thick, then add the steamed flour, sprinkle in the cummin and stir until it is quite stiff. Turn out on a buttered dish, flatten the top smoothly and cut into diamond shaped pieces.

1058 Seenakku I

½ measure rice-flour	½ lb. jaggery (scraped)
½ teacup coconut water	a good pinch of carbonate of soda
1 breakfastcup coconut milk	salt

The flour must be very finely sieved. Mix and prepare the batter as directed in Recipe 1061. When ready, pour the batter into seenakku cups* rinsed out with water, filling them three-parts. Have ready a wide-mouthed chatty pot half full of boiling water over which place the seenakku steamer (a round of tin fitting the mouth of the chatty and having round holes cut in it to fit the cups). Place the cups on the steamer, cover with a large chatty and steam till the batter is cooked. When ready the seenakku should be well risen and the centres split. As you take them off the fire, place the cups in a basin of cold water which will help the seenakkus to come out easily. Serve with scraped coconut.

N.B. When the water in the steaming pot boils down more boiling water must be added.

*See illustration, "Ceylonese Cooking Utensils."

1059 Seenakku II

½ measure rice-flour	10 oz. jaggery
3 teacups coconut milk	salt

The flour must be very finely sieved. Put it into a basin and add the coconut milk gradually, mixing it into a smooth batter. Then add the jaggery and a little salt and stir well. Pour the batter into seenakku cups* and steam as directed in the previous recipe. These seenakkus instead of rising will form a depression in the centre. Serve with scraped coconut.

*See illustration, "Ceylonese Cooking Utensils."

1060 Thala Guli (Gingelly Balls)

½ measure cleaned thala 1 lb. jaggery salt

First pound the thala, then add the jaggery and a little salt and pound well until an oily paste is formed. Mix well and make the paste into balls about the size of large marbles.

1061 Wandu Āppa (Steamed Hoppers or Wandu Hoppers)

½ measure rice-flour	½ lb. jaggery (scraped)
½ teacup coconut water	a good pinch of carbonate of soda
1 breakfast cup coconut milk	salt

Put the flour into a basin and mix with the coconut water, kneading it well. Cover and keep it for about 4 hours. Then add the coconut milk very gradually, mix well and add the jaggery, salt and soda. Stir all together, cover the basin with a cloth and let it stand for a couple of hours to allow the batter to rise. Have ready a small-mouthed chatty pot half full of boiling water and tie a pudding cloth over the mouth of it. The cloth should not be stretched but allowed to hang loosely. Place a "kenda" leaf in the middle of it and pour a spoonful of the batter into it. Cover with a string-hopper steaming pot cover and steam till it is cooked. The middle of a well done wandu āppa will be found to be well risen and split in the centre when ready. Serve with scraped coconut.

Dutch and Portuguese Sweets

A Ceylon cookery book would not be complete without some of these old recipes, reminiscent of eighteenth, seventeenth and sixteenth century Ceylon.

The recipes for Refined Sugar (1080) and Sugar Syrup (1081) are included here for convenience.

1071 Aardappelen Koek (Dutch)

POTATO CAKE

½ lb. potatoes
¼ lb. flour
2 eggs
1¼ pints coconut milk
a pinch of salt
soft sugar

Boil and mash the potatoes finely. Put the flour into a basin, add about half the milk and beat to a smooth paste. Then add the eggs well beaten and mix in the potatoes. Thin down with the remainder of the milk and add a good pinch of salt. Make small pancakes with the mixture as directed in Recipe 678 and serve them hot rolled up with sugar.

1072 Bolo de Coco (Portuguese)

COCONUT CAKE

1 teacup rice-flour
2 coconuts
1 lb. soft sugar
4 eggs
½ wineglass rose- water
25 cadjunuts
¼ teaspoon each powdered cardamoms and cinnamons
a pinch of powdered cloves

Scrape the coconut and grind it very finely. Put the yolks of eggs and sugar into a basin and beat well together. Then add the coconut and gradually mix in the flour. Add the rose-water and spices and lastly the whites of eggs beaten to a stiff froth. Pour the mixture into a flat tin that has been greased, sprinkle the top with the cadjunuts cut in fine strips, and bake in a moderate oven.

1073 Bolo Folhado "Bol Fiado" (Por uguese)

LAMINATED CAKE

PASTRY:

¾ lb. flour
2 oz. butter
1 teaspoon soft sugar
4 yolks of eggs
2 tablespoons toddy
about ½ teacup coconut milk
a pinch of salt

FILLING:

150 cadjunuts
1 lb. sugar
1 teacup water
½ wineglass rose-water

First prepare the filling—skin the cadjunuts and chop them *very* finely. Put the sugar and water into a preserving pan and stir over the fire until it forms a fairly thick syrup. Then add the cadjunuts and the rose-water, lessen the fire, and continue stirring until the mixture thickens, but it must not harden.

Make the pastry with the ingredients given above, and according to directions given in Recipe 1358. Roll out rather thinly and cut out four rounds, three to the size of a dessert plate and the fourth round an inch bigger. Flour a dessert plate and line it with the big round of paste allowing the edges to overlap. Divide the cadjunut mixture into three portions and spread one portion evenly on the paste lining the plate, cover with a round of paste, then a layer of cadjunut again and another round of paste, then the remaining portion of cadjunut and the last round of paste. Wet round the edge with white of egg and neatly fold up the edge of paste overlapping the plate. Then flute round the edges neatly with a knife. Roll out any trimmings of pastry, cut out some leaves, and decorate the top. Brush it over with beaten egg and bake in a moderately hot oven for about one hour or until nicely browned.

1074 **Boroa** (Portuguese)

SEMOLINA BISCUITS

1 lb. rulang or semolina
1 lb. soft sugar
1 lb. cadjunuts
yolks of 2 eggs
½ wineglass rose-water

Skin the cadjunuts and pound them to a paste, adding the rose-water, then put them into a basin with the rulang and sugar and mix together. Add the eggs well beaten and work up with the hand into a stiffish paste. Take small portions of the mixture and roll them into balls about the size of a large marble, then flatten them slightly and mark across in small checks with the back of a knife. Place them on a floured baking tin and bake in a moderate oven until nicely browned.

1075 **Broeder** (Dutch)

DOUGH CAKE

2 lb. dough
½ lb. soft sugar
¼ lb. fresh butter or ghee
½ lb. sultanas
20 yolks of eggs
½ teaspoon carbonate of soda
1 dessertspoon milk

First prepare the broeder pan, grease it well and decorate the bottom and sides of it with a few sultanas. Put the dough into a basin, add the yolks of eggs and beat well with the hand for about 20 minutes. Then add the butter, sugar, two-thirds of the sultanas and mix well together. Lastly, mix in the soda dissolved in the milk. Pour the batter into the prepared pan filling it three-quarters full, decorate the top with the remainder of the sultanas, and let it rise for about half an hour in the sun. Bake in a moderate oven from 1 to 1½ hours. When ready turn out of the pan and place the broeder upside down on a plate. Serve with fresh butter and refined sugar.

1076 Foguete (Portuguese)

"ROCKET"

PASTRY:

1 lb. flour
5 yolks of eggs
1 tablespoon butter
1 dessertspoon soft sugar
about a teacup of coconut milk
a pinch of salt

For FRYING:

ghee or coconut oil

PUMPKIN PRESERVE:

1 lb. pumpkin
2 lb. sugar
¼ lb. rulang
½ teaspoon powdered cardamoms
½ wineglass rose-water

SUGAR COATING:

1 lb. sugar **½ wineglass rose-water** **1 teacup water**

Make the pastry according to directions given in Recipe 1358 and the pumpkin preserve according to Recipe 1122. Roll the pastry out to the thickness of about ⅛ of an inch. Have ready little pieces of bamboo about 3 inches long and one inch in diameter. Butter them well and wrap a piece of paste over each, leaving the ends open and closing the paste along the sides, neatly wetting the join with white of egg. Mark or ornament according to taste. Have a pan of ghee or good coconut oil ready, smoking hot. Drop in the fuggetti and when slightly fried lift them off the oil and gently draw out the bamboos, return them to the oil and fry to a golden brown colour. Then fill the tubes with Pumpkin Preserve and coat with sugar.

Sugar Coating—Put the sugar and water into a preserving pan and boil until they form a thick syrup. Then add the rose-water and stir until the syrup is very thick. Reduce the fire and put the filled tubes into the syrup, stirring carefully so that the tubes all get a nice coating of sugar. Take the pan off the fire and continue stirring until the sugar gets crystallized.

1077 Ijzer Koekes (Dutch)

"IRON" (THIN) CAKES

½ lb. flour
½ lb. sugar
yolks of two eggs and white of one
1 breakfast cup of thick coconut milk
1 teaspoon very finely powdered cinnamon
a pinch of finely powered cloves
a saltspoon of salt

Mix the flour and sugar together, add the eggs well beaten and then the milk by degrees. The batter should be rather thicker than a pancake batter. Add the cinnamon, cloves and salt and mix well together. Heat the ijzer, rub it over with a little butter or ghee, pour a dessertspoon of the batter into it, close the ijzer and place it over a hot fire. When the koekje is browned on one side turn the ijzer over and cook the other side. Have ready a round stick about half an inch in diameter. As soon as each koekje is taken off the ijzer roll it round the stick and slip it on to a tin. Keep in an air-tight tin box.

1078 Pente Frito (Portuguese)

"FRIED COMB"

PASTRY:

½ lb. flour
1 teaspoon soft sugar
1 dessertspoon butter or dripping
yolks of 2 eggs
about a teacup of coconut milk
salt to taste

For FRYING:

ghee or coconut oil

SUGAR COATING:

¼ lb. sugar 1 dessertspoon rose-water 2 tablespoons water

Put the flour, sugar and salt into a basin, add the yolks of eggs and enough milk to form a stiffish paste and knead with the hand until quite smooth. Take small portions of the paste, roll them into balls and form into different fancy shapes. Fry in boiling ghee or oil till golden brown in colour; then drain them on paper and coat with sugar. To prepare the sugar coating see Recipe 1076.

1079 Poffertjes (Dutch)

FRITTERS

1 lb. dough
yolks of 8 eggs
2 oz. sultanas
1 breakfastcup coconut milk
a pinch of salt

Put the dough into a basin, add the salt and the yolks of eggs and beat well with the hand for about 20 minutes. Then add the milk by degrees, beating the batter well until it is perfectly smooth. Let it stand for about half an hour.

Place the poffertje pan over a fire and put a little butter or dripping into each receptacle. When very hot, put into each a spoonful or more of the batter—they must be nearly full—and sprinkle in a few sultanas. When cooked on one side turn over with a fork and keep on turning the poffertjes until of a golden brown colour. They must be perfectly round. Serve hot with sugar syrup.

1080 Refined Sugar

1 lb. sugar
whites and shells of 2 eggs
2½ teacups cold water
½ wineglass rose-water

Put the sugar into a preserving pan, add half a teacup of water, the whites of eggs and the shells well washed and crushed. Mix and beat with the hand for about 5 minutes; add the remainder of the water and stir over the fire until the sugar dissolves. Then allow the scum to boil well up to the top of the pan. Take it off the fire and when cool remove the scum and strain the syrup through a coarse cloth. Wash the pan, return the syrup to it, add the rose-water and stir over a gentle fire until it is very thick. Then take it off the fire and stir briskly until the sugar forms. Unless it is well stirred the sugar will be lumpy.

1081 Sugar Syrup

½ lb. sugar **a small teacup of water** **flavouring**

Put the sugar and water into a saucepan and boil them together until they form a syrup. Flavour with rose, vanilla or any flavouring preferred.

1082 Suikerbrood (Dutch)

LOAF SUGAR

1 lb. flour
¼ lb. roasted and sifted rice-flour
¾ lb. soft- sugar
yolks of 6 eggs
whites of 3 eggs
½ teaspoon chopped lime rind
a few drops of essence of lemon

Put the yolks of eggs and sugar into a basin and beat them together with a wooden spoon. Whip the whites of eggs to a stiff froth and mix them lightly with the yolks and sugar, along with the two kinds of flour. Then add the lime rind and essence and mix well together. Pour the mixture into a flat cake tin that has been greased, and bake in a moderate oven. When ready, turn out and allow to cool. When cold, cut into fingers 1 inch wide and 2½ inches long, and put them into the oven until lightly coloured and crisp.

1083 Wafel (Dutch)

WAFER-CAKE, WAFFLE

1 lb. dough
yolks of 8 eggs
a pinch of salt
1 breakfastcup coconut milk

Make the batter as given in Recipe 1079. Heat the wafel ijzer, rub it over with butter and put in about 2 tablespoons of the batter—the mould should not be too full—close it and place over a hot fire. When baked on one side, turn the opposite side of the ijzer over the fire. Serve hot with Sugar Syrup. (Recipe 1081).

Jams and Preserves

THE making of jams and jellies is a very interesting branch of cookery and one worth cultivating. Home-made jam is far superior to the bought variety and it is cheaper and more wholesome as well. Many cooks look upon jam and jelly-making as difficult, but by following the rules and hints given here the process will be found quite simple, and successful results may be looked for.

Hints on Jam-Making

THE fruit for jams should be just ripe, sound and freshly picked. It is a mistake to think that over-ripe fruit is good enough for jam. The fruit should be carefully looked over and all stalks removed. Good crepe sugar is the best to use for jams and jellies. From ¾ lb. to 1 lb. of sugar for each pound of fruit or fruit juice is the usual proportion, but the quantity of sugar will vary according to the nature of the fruit used. Individual taste can guide exact proportions. Brass and copper preserving pans are the best to use for making jams and jellies, and a wooden spoon for stirring. In stirring jams and jellies keep the spoon at the bottom of the pan and not lifted about. In straining jellies always let the juice drip—never squeeze the fruit or the jelly will not be clear. The time required for cooking of fruit will depend on the kind of fruit used and the rapidity with which it is boiled.

To ascertain whether the jam or jelly is ready, pour a little of the syrup into a cold plate; if it sets in a few minutes it is ready.

Remove the scum from the top of the jam or jelly before putting into jars or bottles. See that the jars or bottles are clean and dry and do not close up until the jam is quite cold. All jars and bottles should be well corked and air excluded by dripping the mouths of the bottles, after corking, into boiling resin.

1091 Ambarella Preserve

1 lb. ambarellas
1 lb. sugar
¼ pint water
½ wineglass rose-water
2-inch piece cinnamon

Choose well-seasoned fruit. Peel them, prick them well with a fork and put them into cold water at once. When all the fruit has been pricked, squeeze out the water and weigh it. Put the sugar and water into a preserving pan and bring to the boil, then add the ambarellas and the cinnamon and boil together stirring constantly, until the syrup is thick and the fruit transparent. Add the rose-water a few minutes before taking the preserve off the fire.

1092 Apple Jam

1 lb. apples (weighed after peeling and coring)
1 lb. sugar
a little water
a few drops of lemon flavouring

Peel, core and slice the apples very thinly. Put them into a preserving pan with a little water and stew them until reduced to a pulp. Then add the sugar and flavouring and boil until the jam will set.

1093 Apple Jelly

To each pint of apple juice, allow 1 lb. sugar and one dessertspoon of lime juice.

Wash the apples, neither peel nor core them, but cut them in 4 or 6 pieces according to size. Put them into a preserving pan with just sufficient water to cover them. Simmer gently until the fruit is reduced to a pulp, stirring occasionally with a wooden spoon. Then strain through a jelly cloth, measure the juice and put it into a preserving pan with the stated proportion of sugar and lime juice. Stir carefully until the sugar is dissolved and then boil until the jelly will set when tested on a plate.

1094 Apricot Jam (from Dried Fruit)

1 lb. dried apricots **1½ lb. sugar**

Wash the apricots, put them into a basin with sufficient cold water to cover them and 2 inches above the level of the fruit and let them soak for 12 hours. Then put the fruit and water into a preserving pan and simmer slowly until the fruit is tender. Add the sugar and boil gently until the jam will set.

1095 Billing Jam

1 lb. billings **1½ lb. sugar**

Pick off the stalks from the billings and wash the fruit. Then slice them and put them in water for a couple of hours. Squeeze out the water, weigh the fruit and put it into a preserving pan along with the above proportion of sugar and just a little water, if necessary. Boil together until of a thick consistency.

N.B. A small piece of cinnamon may be added, if the flavour is liked.

1096 Billing Preserve

1 lb. billings
1½ lb. sugar
¼ pint water
½ wineglass rose-water

Pick off the stalks and prick the fruit well with a fork, and put them into cold water. When all the fruit has been pricked, squeeze out the water, pressing the fruit well so as to get out some of the acid juice from it. Weigh the fruit; make a syrup of the sugar and water, bring to the boil, add the billings and boil until the syrup is thick and the fruit transparent. It must be stirred constantly. Add the rose-water a few minutes before taking the preserve off the fire.

1097 Carrot Jam

carrots	**lime juice**
sugar	**brandy**
warm water	**almonds**

Select young red carrots; wash, scrape them clean, and cut them in pieces. Put them into a preserving pan with sufficient warm water to cover them and let them simmer slowly until quite soft; then rub through a sieve. Weigh the pulp and to each pound allow 1 lb. sugar, 1 tablespoon each of lime juice and brandy and ½ oz. chopped almonds. Put the pulp into a preserving pan with the sugar, add the lime juice and boil, stirring all the time, until the jam will set. Then add the brandy and the almonds at the last.

1098 Damson Jam

1 lb. damsons **1 lb. sugar**

Pick off the stalks from the damsons, examine them carefully and wash them, if necessary. Then put them into a preserving pan and heat over a *slow* fire until the juice begins to flow. Now bring the fruit to the boil, add the sugar and boil again for 20 to 30 minutes or until the liquid will set. It must be stirred almost constantly.

1099 Damson Marmalade

damsons **sugar**

Pick off the stalks from the damsons and look over them carefully. Then wash and drain them well. Put them into a large earthenware jar with a lid, place in a pan half-full of boiling water, and steam until the fruit is tender. Then rub them through a coarse sieve. Measure the pulp and juice into a preserving pan and add ¾ lb. sugar to each pint. Boil together, stirring constantly, until the marmalade will set quickly when tested on a plate. When ready pour into glass jars and seal when cold. To flavour the marmalade a few of the kernels may be blanched and chopped and added, if liked.

1100 Date Jam

2 lb. dates	**a grate of nutmeg**
1 pint water	**1 teaspoon butter**
1 lb. sugar	**a few drops of lemon flavouring**

Stone the dates and put the fruit into a preserving pan, add the water and cook on a very slow fire until the fruit is hot, then add the sugar, butter and nutmeg and allow to cook, stirring well, until it begins to thicken. Add the flavouring and boil until the jam is quite thick.

1101 Fig Jam (from Dried Fruit)

1 lb. dried figs 1½ lb. sugar

Wash the figs well, put them into a basin with enough cold water to cover them and 2 inches above the level of the fruit, and let them soak overnight. Then break up the fruit and put it into a preserving pan along with the water in which it was soaked, and simmer gently, stirring frequently until the fruit is tender. Add the sugar and boil again until the jam will set.

1102 Guava Cheese

1 lb. sugar 1 tablespoon lime juice to 1½ lb. guava pulp

This can be made from the fruit pulp after the juice has been strained off for jelly. Rub the pulp through a sieve fine enough to keep back the seeds. Then weigh the sieved pulp and put it into a preserving pan with stated proportion of sugar and lime juice and boil, stirring constantly, until the mixture is quite thick and begins to draw away from the sides and bottom of the pan. It should cut quite solid in slices.

1103 Guava Jelly

To each pint of guava juice allow ¾ lb. of sugar and 1 tablespoon of lime juice.

Peel and slice the guavas and put them into a preserving pan with sufficient water to cover them. Simmer gently until the fruit is tender, stirring occasionally with a wooden spoon. Then strain through muslin, measure the juice and put it into a preserving pan with the stated proportion of sugar and lime juice. Stir carefully until the sugar is dissolved. Boil until the jelly will set, and remove any scum that rises.

1104 China-Guava Jelly

China guavas water sugar

Cut the tops and tails off the guavas and wash them thoroughly. Put them into a preserving pan, allowing 2 pints of water to each pound of fruit, and let them cook until the water is reduced by half and the fruit is quite soft but not too pulpy or the jelly will not be clear. Then strain through muslin, measure the juice and return it to a clean preserving pan along with 1 lb. sugar to each pint of juice. Boil until the jelly will set, and remove any scum that rises.

1105 Jambu Preserve

1 lb. jambus 1 lb. sugar ½ wineglass rose-water

The small pink jambus make nice preserve. They must be quite ripe. Make in the same way as Billing Preserve (Recipe 1096).

1106 Loquat Jam

¾ lb. sugar to 1 lb. stoned loquats

The fruit should be perfectly ripe. Wash the loquats, top and tail them and, splitting down, remove the stones and pitch-like cup in which they rest. Put the loquats into a preserving pan with sufficient water to cover them an inch above the level of the fruit, and simmer until the loquats are half-boiled. Then add the sugar and continue boiling slowly, stirring all the time, until the jam will set.

1107 Lovi-Lovi Jam

1¼ lb. sugar to 1 lb. lovi-lovi pulp

The fruit pulp that is left after the juice has been strained off for jelly (Recipe 1108) can be used for making the jam. Rub the fruit through a sieve fine enough to keep back the seeds. Then put the sieved pulp into a preserving pan with sugar in the stated proportion and boil together stirring constantly until of a thick consistency.

1108 Lovi-Lovi Jelly

To each pint of lovi-lovi juice allow 1 lb. sugar

Pick off the stalks from the lovi-lovis, which should be quite ripe, and wash the fruit. Then put them into a preserving pan allowing a pint of water to each lb. of fruit. Simmer gently until the fruit is quite tender and the water reduced by half. Then strain through muslin; measure the juice and return it to a clean saucepan with the stated proportion of sugar. Boil until the jelly will set when tested on a plate. Skim when necessary.

1109 Mango Jam

mangoes sugar

Bombay mangoes are the best for jam. Choose sound fruits not too ripe. Peel the mangoes and cut them in small slices, then weigh the fruit and allow 1 lb sugar to each pound of fruit. Put the fruit and sugar into a preserving pan and boil steadily until of a proper consistency and the fruit looks transparent. Mash the fruit with the spoon while stirring.

N.B. A small piece of cinnamon may be added, if the flavour is liked.

1110 Mango Preserve

1 lb. mangoes	**½ wineglass rose-water**
1 lb. sugar	**2-inch piece cinnamon**
¼ pint water	

Fibre mangoes are the best for preserve and the fruit must be well-seasoned and just ripening. Cut the mangoes lengthwise in halves or quarters according to size, peel off the skin and remove the kernel from the seed. Prick the fruit well with a fork and put into cold water at once. When all the fruit has been pricked squeeze out the water and weigh it. Put the sugar and ¼ pint of water into a preserving pan and bring to the boil, then add the mangoes and the cinnamon and boil together, stirring constantly, until the syrup is thick and the fruit transparent. Add the rose-water a few minutes before taking the preserve off the fire.

1111 Mulberry Jam

2 lb. mulberries — **½ pint water**
1½ lb. sugar — **1 tablespoon lime juice**

The mulberries should be just ripe and not too soft. Pick off the stalks, look over the fruit carefully, wash, and drain them. Put the mulberries into a preserving pan with the water and allow to simmer slowly until they are cooked. Then add the sugar and the lime juice and boil slowly, stirring all the time, until the jam will set.

1112 Nelli Preserve

Make in the same way as Billing Preserve (Recipe 1096).

1113 Nutmeg Jelly

To each pint of nutmeg juice allow 1 lb. sugar

The nutmeg fruit makes quite a nice jelly. Take ripe fruit, (as the fruit ripens it splits open and the stone or nutmeg usually drops off) peel them and put them into a basin with cold water and let them soak for 12 hours. Drain off the water, put the fruit into a preserving pan with just sufficient water to cover them and simmer slowly until the fruit is quite soft and pulpy. Then strain through muslin without pressing the pulp. Measure the juice and return it to a clean preserving pan with the stated proportion of sugar and boil gently until it jellies.

1114 Nutmeg Preserve

1 lb. nutmegs — **1 lb. sugar** — **½ pint water**

The nutmeg fruit makes quite a nice preserve. Take ripe fruit (as the fruit ripens it splits open and the stone or nutmeg usually drops off), cut them in quarters and prick well with a fork. Put the fruit at once into a basin with salted water and let it soak for 12 hours. Drain off the water and wash the fruit well in three or four changes of fresh water. Then squeeze out as much of the water as possible and weigh the fruit. Put it into a preserving pan with the sugar, add the water and boil gently, stirring constantly, until the syrup is thick and the fruit transparent.

1115 Orange Marmalade

1 lb. marmalade oranges — **2 lb. sugar** — **2 pints water**

Wipe the oranges with a damp cloth, cut each through lengthwise, then slice them crosswise as thinly as possible. Remove the pips as they come and drop them into a basin with about ½ a pint of cold water. Put the sliced oranges into another basin with the remaining 1½ pints of water and let them soak for 24 hours. Then put them into a preserving pan, add the water in which the pips have been steeped and boil slowly for about one hour or until the skins are tender. Add the sugar and boil half an hour longer or until the marmalade jellies, stirring frequently with a wooden spoon.

1116 Papaw Preserve

1 lb. papaw
2 lb. sugar
¼ lb. rulang
½ teaspoon powdered cardamoms
½ wineglass rose-water

Take a well-seasoned papaw and grate it; pour boiling water over it and let it remain for about half an hour. Then put it into a cloth and squeeze out the water from it. Weigh it and put it into a preserving pan with the sugar and stir over the fire for about 15 minutes. Add the rulang and the cardamoms and stir until of a thick consistency. Add the rose-water a few minutes before taking it off the fire.

1117 Passion Fruit Jam

1 lb. sugar to 1 lb. fruit pulp and juice

Wash the fruit, cut them in halves and scoop out all the juice and seeds into a bowl. Put the shells into another bowl and cover with cold water, adding just a little salt. Allow to soak for about 6 or-8 hours. Then boil in the same water for one hour and scoop out the inside of the shells with a spoon. Throw away the outside of the shells and the water in which they were boiled. Strain the juice and seeds through a jelly cloth or fine sieve leaving only the seeds. Add the strained juice to the scooped out fruit pulp, weigh it and put it into a preserving pan with the stated proportion of sugar. Boil, stirring constantly, for about 20 minutes or until the jam will set.

1118 Pineapple Preserve

1 lb. pineapple ¾ lb. sugar 2-inch piece cinnamon

Pare the pineapple and cut it into small dice. Then weigh the fruit and put it into a preserving pan with the sugar in the stated proportion and the cinnamon. Boil together until the syrup is thick and the fruit transparent. It must be stirred almost constantly. Remove the cinnamon before bottling the preserve.

1119 Plantain Jelly

sour plantains sugar water

The plantains must be quite ripe. Peel them and put them into a preserving pan allowing a pint of water to each pound of fruit. Simmer gently until the fruit is tender and the water reduced by half. Then strain through muslin, measure the juice and return it to a clean saucepan with ¾ lb. sugar to each pint of juice. Boil stirring all the time, until it jellies in falling from the spoon. Skim before putting into pots.

1120 Pommelo Marmalade

½ lb. pommelo rind | **1 lb. sugar**
2 oranges | **water**

Choose a ripe pommelo. Score the skin across with a sharp knife and pull off the peel in strips. Then weigh it and put the peel into a preserving pan with a sufficient quantity of cold water to cover it, and allow to boil for about 2 hours or until the peel is quite soft, changing the water about 6 times or so to take off a little of the bitter taste. Peel the oranges, divide them into sections and break the pulp into small pieces removing the pips and all refuse. Put the pips into a basin with about ¼ pint of cold water and let them stand until required. When the peel has been sufficiently boiled, take it up, squeeze out the water from it and cut it in strips. Put the sugar, the cut up peel, the orange pulp and the water in which the pips were steeped into a preserving pan and let all boil slowly together for about half an hour or until the white part of the strips of the peel is transparent.

1121 Pumpkin Preserve I

1 lb. pumpkin | **½ teaspoon powdered cardamoms**
2 lb. sugar | **½ wineglass rose-water**
¼ lb. rulang

Grate the pumpkin, put it into a cloth and squeeze out some of the water from it. Then weigh it and put it into a preserving pan along with the sugar and stir over the fire for about 15 minutes. Add the rulang and the cardamoms and stir until of a thick consistency. Add the rose-water a few minutes before taking it off the fire.

1122 Pumpkin Preserve II

1 lb. pumpkin | **½ wineglass rose-water**
1 lb. sugar | **¼ pint water**

Peel the pumpkin thinly and prick the fruit well with a fork. Then cut it across in two, divide each half into about 12 long-shaped pieces and remove the seeds and the pulpy part from the centre. Prick each piece well again and carefully squeeze out the water from it. The pieces of pumpkin should be kept whole, not allowed to break. Then weigh the fruit. Put the sugar and water into a preserving pan, bring to the boil and keep stirring until the syrup is quite thick. Then add the pumpkin and boil again, stirring constantly. When the syrup is very thick add the rose-water. As the syrup thickens reduce the fire and stir very carefully so that all the fruit will get a nice coating of sugar. Take the pan off the fire and continue stirring until the sugar crystallizes.

1123 Rhubarb Jam

1 lb. rhubarb 1 lb. sugar juice of half a lime

Get some red-stalked fresh rhubarb. Wash and wipe it but do not peel it unless the skin is very coarse. Cut it in small pieces and then weigh it. Put it into a basin in layers with the sugar and let them stand overnight. Then turn all into a preserving pan, add the lime juice, bring to the boil and boil steadily, stirring all the time for about 20 minutes or until the jam will set. Skim carefully before putting into pots.

1124 Roselle Jelly

To each pint of roselle juice allow ¾ lb. sugar

Wash the fruit well and cut it in small pieces. Put it into a preserving pan with sufficient cold water to cover it and let it cook until the fruit is quite soft and pulpy. Then strain through muslin, measure the juice and put it into a preserving pan with the stated proportion of sugar. Boil until the jelly will set when tested on a plate. When ready, pour into jars or bottles and cork in the usual way.

1125 Strawberry Jam

1 lb. strawberries ¾ lb. sugar

Remove the stalks from the strawberries and any discoloured ones. Put the berries into a preserving pan with just a little water and boil for about half an hour stirring constantly. Then add the sugar and boil for another half-hour or until the jam will set. It must be stirred all the time.

1126 Tomato Jam

1 lb. tomatoes 1 lb. sugar juice of half a lime

Choose red tomatoes. Put them into a basin, pour boiling water over them and let them remain for a few minutes. Then lift them out and remove the skins. Break up the fruit and put them into a preserving pan along with the sugar. Add the lime juice and boil until the jam will set, stirring almost constantly.

1127 Green Tomato Jam

1 lb. green tomatoes 1 lb. sugar juice of half a lime

Slice the tomatoes and put them into a preserving pan with the sugar and just a little water. Add the lime juice and cook until the tomatoes are quite tender and transparent. Pour into jars and cover when cold.

1128 Vegetable Marrow Jam

1 lb. marrow — **the grated rind and juice of half a lime**
1 lb. sugar

Peel the marrow, cut it in quarters, and remove the seeds and the soft part from the centre. Then cut into small pieces about an inch in size and weigh the fruit. Put it into a basin in layers with the sugar and sprinkle with the grated rind of the lime. Strain the lime juice over, cover the basin and let it stand overnight. Next day, boil all together for about one hour, or until the pieces of marrow look transparent and the jam will set. It must be stirred almost constantly.

1129 Woodapple Jelly

woodapples — **sugar** — **water**

Break the shell and scoop out the inside of the fruit with a spoon and weigh it. Allow $\frac{3}{4}$ lb. sugar and $1\frac{1}{2}$ pints water to each pound of fruit. Put the fruit into a preserving pan along with the water and let cook slowly for about half an hour, or until the water is reduced by about half. Then strain through muslin and return the juice to a clean saucepan, add the sugar and boil, stirring constantly, until it jellies in falling from the spoon. Skim before putting into pots.

Sweets

THE art of sweet making is one well worth acquiring. It is one of the most interesting branches of cookery. Home-made sweets are very acceptable for desserts, and they always sell well at bazaars. The making of sweets requires a certain amount of practice, and its success depends to a great extent upon boiling sugar to the right degree. Once this is mastered the making of sweets is easy work and many different varieties will suggest themselves to the worker. The hints and directions given in the following recipes should be carefully followed.

Unboiled Sweets follow Candies, Toffees, etc.

Candies, Toffees &c.

1141 Almond Rock

1 lb. sugar	**1 teaspoon lime juice**
½ lb. almonds	**½ teacup water**

Blanch the almonds and with a sharp knife cut them into strips, then dry them in a cool oven until they are a pale brown colour. Put the sugar and water into a saucepan and melt over the fire, stirring occasionally. Then add the lime juice and boil steadily, without stirring, until the mixture acquires a rich brown colour. Stir in the almonds, mix thoroughly, and pour the mixture into a shallow buttered dish. As it cools mark it off into pieces and when cold break them apart.

1142 Barley Sugar

1 lb. sugar	**1 teaspoon lime juice**
½ pint water	**lemon or vanilla flavouring**

Put the sugar and water into a saucepan and let them dissolve over the fire and then boil until it is brittle when tested in cold water. Add the lime juice and the flavouring and boil for a couple of minutes longer. Pour out on a shallow buttered dish and when slightly cooled cut it in narrow strips with a knife and twist the strips with the fingers into a spiral shape.

1143 Butter Scotch

1 lb. sugar	**1 teaspoonful glucose or a pinch of cream of tartar**
3 oz. butter	**lemon flavouring**
2 tablespoons water	

Put the sugar, butter, water and glucose or cream of tartar into a saucepan, set it over the fire and boil the mixture, stirring all the time, until the toffee is brittle when tested in cold water. Just before taking it off the fire add a few drops of essence of lemon and pour into a shallow buttered dish. When set mark off in lengths and when cold break them apart and wrap each length in paper.

1144 Chocolate Almonds

Blanch some Jordan almonds, toast them in the oven for a few minutes, then cover with a thin coating of fondant and leave them for a few minutes to harden. Prepare some covering chocolates as in Recipe 1146, coat the almonds with it, and place on buttered paper until set.

1145 Chocolate Caramels

½ lb. sugar
1 oz. grated chocolate or cocoa
1 oz. butter
1 pint milk
vanilla flavouring

Put the sugar, chocolate, butter and milk into a preserving pan, place it over the fire and stir constantly to prevent it burning; let it boil till quite thick. Remove the pan from the fire, add the flavouring and pour into a shallow dish which has been rinsed out with cold water. When slightly cool mark the caramel into squares. When cold, divide and wrap in pieces of paper.

1146 Chocolate Creams

Form the centres of fondant using either the cooked (Recipe 1151) or the uncooked (Recipe 1196). Flavour and colour the fondant variously, form into balls and flatten them at one end so that they will stand. Use a little icing sugar to prevent the fondant from sticking to the hands. Leave them for 24 hours to harden. Then coat them with a chocolate covering made as follows:—

Chocolate Covering—Take a cake of Cadbury's Mexican Chocolate or any other plain chocolate, break it in small pieces, put it into a cup and place the cup in a pan of boiling water. Stir over a gentle fire until the chocolate has melted, add syrup enough to bring it to the consistency of thick custard. Remove the saucepan from the fire, take up the creams with a hat pin, dip each one into the melted chocolate and slip them on the sheet of buttered paper. The chocolate should set at once and have a glossy appearance. Do not allow the chocolate to become too dry; re-heat it from time to time.

1147 Chocolate Marzipan

Flavour and colour some marzipan (Recipe 1198) as desired, roll it out on a pastry board, cut in small squares and leave to harden. Then cut with melted chocolate as directed in Recipe 1146.

1148 Coconut Ice

2 lb. sugar
½ lb. desiccated or finely grated coconut
1 breakfastcup water
flavouring
cochineal or carmine

Reserve 6 oz. sugar for the colouring, put the remainder of the sugar and the water into a preserving pan, and stir over the fire until the sugar has all melted. Bring to the boil and let it boil for 10 minutes stirring all the time. Then add the coconut and continue to stir until the mixture thickens. Flavour to taste and pour it on to a flat dish which has been rinsed out with cold water. Put the 6 oz. of sugar into the pan with a little water and stir over the fire until it thickens, then add a few drops of colouring to make it a pretty pink colour and pour it evenly over the white ice. Cut in squares or bars.

1149 Coconut Rock with Semolina

1 lb. semolina
1 lb. finely grated coconut
2 lb. sugar
½ wineglass rose-water
½ teaspoon powdered cardamoms
1 breakfastcup water

Put the sugar and water into a preserving pan and stir over the fire until they come to the boil. Then add the semolina and stir until it is well boiled. Next add the coconut, rose-water and cardamoms and keep stirring until the mixture begins to thicken. Remove from the fire and pour it out on a flat dish which has been rinsed out with cold water. Cut in squares or diamonds.

1150 Coconut Tablet

¼ lb. desiccated or finely grated coconut
½ lb. sugar
½ lb. jaggery
¾ teacup water

Put the sugar, jaggery and water into a preserving pan and stir over the fire until the sugar and jaggery have melted. Bring to the boil stirring all the time. Then add the coconut and continue to stir until the mixture thickens. Pour into a flat dish which has been rinsed out with cold water, and, when firm enough, mark it across in squares.

1151 Fondant

2 lb. sugar
1 dessertspoonful glucose or a pinch of cream of tartar
1 breakfastcup water
icing sugar

Put the ingredients into a saucepan and melt slowly over the fire, stirring all the time with a wooden spoon until the sugar is dissolved. Then bring to the boil quickly and boil without stirring until a little dropped into a cup of cold water will form a soft ball. Turn the fondant on to a dish that has been sprinkled with cold water, sprinkle the surface of the fondant also with a little cold water to prevent a crust forming and let it cool slightly. Then work it up with a wooden spoon keeping it well together. When cool enough, knead the mixture well with the hand until it becomes a stiff white mass, using a little icing sugar to prevent the mixture sticking. The fondant is now ready to be coloured and flavoured as desired.

1152 Fruit Candy

2 lb. sugar
¼ lb. butter
¼ lb. raisins
¼ lb. dates
¼ lb. figs
2 oz. candied peel
¼ lb. almonds
1 tablespoon vinegar

Stone and cut the raisins and dates, also cut the figs and candied peel; blanch and cut the almonds, all rather small. Put the sugar, butter and vinegar into a preserving pan and boil until it thickens, then add the rest of the ingredients and stir until thoroughly blended. Pour the mixture on to sheets of buttered paper and roll up like a roly-poly pudding. When wanted, remove the paper and cut in slices.

1153 Golden Caramels

1 lb. sugar
2 tablespoons water
2 oz. butter
2 tablespoons golden syrup
a teaspoon of lime juice

Melt the butter in a preserving pan and add the sugar, water and golden syrup. Stir until boiling, then add the lime juice and continue to boil, without stirring, until the toffee will harden when tested in cold water. Pour into a shallow buttered dish and when firm cut into squares.

1154 Marzipan Boiled

½ lb. sugar
1 white of egg
6 oz. ground almonds
1 teacup water
icing sugar

Put the sugar and water into a saucepan and bring them slowly to the boil. Skim well, put on the lid and let it boil for a couple of minutes. Then uncover it and boil rapidly until a little dropped into a cup of cold water will form into a soft ball. Take the saucepan off the fire, stir in the almonds and white of egg, return the pan to the fire and stir for a couple of minutes longer. Turn the mixture on to a pastry board well dusted with icing sugar and work, first with a wooden spoon and then with the hand, using icing sugar to prevent the mixture sticking. Flavour and colour as required.

1155 Halwa-de-Muscat

¾ lb. flour
3 lb. sugar
½ lb. ghee
½ bottle milk
1 wineglass rose-water
2 oz. shelled almonds

Put the flour into a coarse cloth, draw all the sides of the cloth together and tie with a string. Put it into an open vessel, add a little water and extract the starch from the flour. When the water becomes thick with starch keep it aside and use fresh water. This will have to be done 4 or 5 times using 2 bottes of water in all. The sticky substance left in the cloth is not used. Add the sugar to the starch water, put the mixture into a preserving pan and boil it, stirring all the time. When very thick add the milk, almonds split in halves, and the rose-water. The ghee must now be added a spoonful at a time. When very thick and transparent turn it on to a flat dish. A few almonds may be reserved and sprinkled on top of the muscat. As the mixture thickens a brass or iron spoon must be used for stirring.

1156 Papaw Muscat

1 lb. papaw
1½ lb. sugar
2 oz. rulang
1 tablespoonful ghee
½ wineglass rose-water
½ teaspoon powdered cardamoms

Choose a well-seasoned fruit. Scrape the papaw, put it into a bowl and pour boiling water over it. Let it remain for about 10 minutes, then put it into a cloth and squeeze out the water from it. Weigh the fruit and prepare in the same way as Pumpkin Muscat (Recipe 1159).

1157 Plantain Muscat

1 lb. sour plantains
2 lb. sugar
2 oz. ghee
2 oz. rulang
¼ teaspoon powdered cardamoms

The plantains must be quite ripe and should be weighed after being peeled. Mash the plantains well, put them into a preserving pan, and mix in the sugar. Stir over the fire until thick, then add the rulang which should be slightly roasted, and the cardamoms, and keep on stirring. When the mixture thickens and sticks to the sides of the pan add the ghee, a little at a time. Continue stirring until the sugar begins to harden on the sides of the pan. Then take it off the fire and spread the mixture on a flat buttered dish. Before it gets quite cold, cut into small diamonds or squares.

1158 Potato Muscat

½ lb. potatoes
1 lb. sugar
25 cadjunuts
¾ teacup water
1 dessertspoonful butter or ghee
rose flavouring
¼ teaspoon powdered cardamoms

Boil and mash the poatoes. Put the sugar and water into a preserving pan and boil until the sugar becomes a thick syrup, stirring all the time. Then remove the saucepan from the fire and mix in the mashed potatoes, stir well until quite smooth and add the cadjunuts cut in small pieces. Return to the fire and stir again until the mixture becomes very thick, then add the butter, flavouring, and cardamoms. When the sugar begins to harden on the sides of the pan, take it off the fire and turn it on to a buttered dish. Cut into diamonds or squares while still warm.

1159 Pumpkin Muscat I

1 lb. pumpkin
1½ lb. sugar
2 oz. rulang
1 tablespoonful ghee
½ wineglass rose-water
½ teaspoon powdered cardamoms

Scrape the pumpkin, put it into a cloth, squeeze out some of the water from it and then weigh it. Soak the rulang in cold water for about half an hour. Put the scraped pumpkin, rulang and sugar into a preserving pan and stir over the fire until the mixture thickens. Then add the rose-water, cardamoms and ghee and continue stirring until the sugar begins to harden on the sides of the pan. Take the pan off the fire, pour the mixture on to sheets of buttered paper and roll up like a roly-poly pudding. When wanted, remove the paper and cut the muscat in slices.

1160 Pumpkin Muscat II

1 lb. pumpkin
2½ lb. sugar
2 oz. rulang
½ lb. butter
1 pint milk
½ wineglass rose-water
½ teaspoon powdered cardamoms
50 cadjunuts

Prepare the muscat in the same way as in the previous recipe. The cadjunuts are ground and added.

1161 Sago Muscat

½ lb. sago
2 lb. sugar
¼ lb. ghee
½ wineglass rose-water
½ teaspoon powdered cardamoms
1 breakfastcup water

Soak the sago in water for about 12 hours, then drain off the water. Put the sugar and a breakfastcup of water into a preserving pan, bring to the boil, then add the sago and keep stirring all the while. When the mixture thickens and sticks to the sides of the pan, add the ghee, a dessertspoonful at a time until it is all mixed in. Stir the mixture well after each spoonful of ghee has been added. Next add the rose-water and cardamoms. Continue stirring until the sugar begins to harden on the sides of the pan, then take it off the fire and spread the muscat on a flat buttered dish. Before it gets cold, cut it into diamonds. As the mixture thickens a brass or iron spoon must be used for stirring it. Stir continuously as the mixture burns easily.

1162 Sweet Pumpkin Muscat

1 lb. sweet pumpkin
1 lb. sugar
2 oz. rulang
1 dessertspoonful ghee
½ wineglass rose-water
½ teaspoon powdered cardamoms

Grate the pumpkin, put it into a towel, squeeze out some of the water from it and weigh it. Soak the rulang in cold water for about half an hour. Put the scraped pumpkin, rulang and sugar into a preserving pan and stir over the fire until the mixture thickens. Then add the rose-water, cardamoms and ghee and continue stirring until the sugar begins to harden on the sides of the pan. Take it off the fire, spread the muscat on a flat buttered dish, and before it gets cold cut it into small squares or diamonds.

1163 Peppermint Tablet

1 lb. sugar
1 pint milk
1 oz. butter
essence of peppermint

Put the sugar, milk, and butter into a saucepan and stir over moderate heat till they come to the boil, then simmer from 10 to 15 minutes stirring all the time. When the mixture is sufficiently thick, remove the pan from the fire and add enough peppermint essence to impart a flavour. Stir well and pour into a shallow dish which has been rinsed out with cold water. Mark it into small squares and when it is cold, cut them apart.

1164 Rose Tablet

1 lb. sugar
1 teacup water
rose flavouring
cochineal

Put the sugar and water into a saucepan and stir over the fire until they come to the boil. Remove any scum and continue boiling until it gets very thick. Remove from the fire, add the flavouring and colouring and pour the mixture into a buttered dish. When set, mark it in squares. Cut in pieces when cold.

1165 Almond Toffee

1 lb. sugar
¼ lb. almonds
2 oz. butter
a pinch of cream of tartar
½ a teacup water

Blanch and split the almonds and dry them in the oven. Put the butter into a saucepan and melt it over the fire, add the sugar, water and cream of tartar and bring to the boil. Boil without stirring until the toffee breaks brittle when tested in cold water. Stir in the almonds, cook them a moment and pour the mixture into a shallow buttered dish. When set, mark in squares, and break in pieces when cold.

1166 Cadjunut Toffee I

100 cadjunuts
1 lb. sugar
½ wineglass rose-water
¾ tea-cup water

Skin the cadjunuts and chop them very finely. Put the sugar and water into a preserving pan and stir over the fire until the sugar is melted. Then add the cadjunuts and the rose-water and continue to stir until the mixture thickens. Remove from the fire and turn it on to a shallow dish which has been rinsed out with rose-water. Before it gets quite cold cut it into diamonds or squares.

1167 Cadjunut Toffee II

100 cadjunuts
1 lb. sugar
1 oz. butter
1 teacup milk
rose flavouring

Skin the cadjunuts and chop them very finely. Put the sugar, butter and milk into a preserving pan and stir over the fire until the sugar is melted. Then add the cadjunuts and continue to stir until the mixture thickens. Remove from the fire, flavour with a few drops of rose flavouring and turn it on to a shallow dish which has been rinsed out with cold water. When set, mark in diamond-shaped pieces and when nearly cold cut in pieces.

1168 Coconut Milk Toffee I

2 teacups thick coconut milk **1 lb. sugar**
½ teacup jaggery syrup **vanilla flavouring**

Put the coconut milk, syrup and sugar into a preserving pan and stir carefully over the fire until it thickens. Add the flavouring and pour it on to a flat dish which has been rinsed out with cold water. When set mark in squares and when nearly cold cut in pieces. Instead of putting it on to a buttered dish the mixture may be formed, with the hands, into balls or rolls and each wrapped in paper.

1169 Coconut Milk Toffee II

1 teacup thick coconut milk **flavouring**
1 lb. sugar **cochineal**

Put the milk and sugar into a preserving pan, place it over the fire and stir until it thickens. Remove from the fire, flavour to taste, and add a few drops of cochineal to colour pink. Pour out on a flat dish which has been rinsed out with cold water. When set mark it in small squares, and cut in pieces when cold.

1170 Coffee Toffee

1 tin condensed milk **1 teacup water**
1½ lb. sugar **very strong coffee to taste**

Put the sugar and water into a preserving pan and stir over the fire until the sugar is dissolved. Pour in the milk and stir constantly until the mixture thickens. Then add the coffee strained through muslin, and when the mixture is very thick pour it into a flat buttered dish. Mark it across in squares and when cold break it into pieces.

1171 Gingelly Toffee

½ lb. gingelly **¾ teacup water**
1 lb. sugar **rose flavouring**

Put the sugar and water into a preserving pan and stir over the fire until the syrup is quite thick. Then add the gingelly and the flavouring and continue to stir until the mixture thickens. Pour into a dish which has been rinsed out with rose-water, and when firm enough mark it across in small squares or diamond-shaped pieces.

1172 Golden Toffee

1 lb. soft sugar
2 tablespoons water
2 oz. butter
2 tablespoons golden syrup
1 tin condensed milk
vanilla flavouring

Melt the butter in a preserving pan, add the sugar and water and then the syrup. Boil for a few minutes and add the milk. Now stir constantly and boil for a quarter of an hour longer or until the mixture thickens and hardens when a little is tested in cold water. Then remove the pan from the fire, flavour with vanilla and when the mixture has ceased to boil pour it into a shallow buttered dish. When nearly set mark across with a knife into small squares or oblong-shaped pieces and cut in pieces when cold.

1173 Milk Toffee I

1 bottle milk **¾ lb. sugar** **flavouring**

Boil the milk until it is quite thick. Add the sugar and stir over the fire until the sugar has all melted. Then add the flavouring and continue to stir until the mixture thickens. Remove from the fire and pour out on a flat dish which has been rinsed out with cold water. When partly set mark across in small diamond-shaped pieces or squares, and cut in pieces when cold.

1174 Milk Toffee II

1 tin condensed milk
1½ lb. sugar
1 teacup water
almond or vanilla flavouring

Put the sugar and water into a preserving pan and stir over the fire until the sugar is dissolved. Lower the heat and add the milk, stirring it continuously as it burns easily. When very thick, remove from the fire, add the flavouring, and pour it on to a flat dish which has been rinsed out with cold water. When set mark in small squares, and when nearly cold cut into pieces.

1175 Nut & Fruit Toffee

2 lb. sugar
1 tin condensed milk
1 dessertspoonful butter
1 teacup water
1 dessertspoon vanilla essence
50 cadjunuts
½ lb. sultana raisins
2 dessertspoonfuls cocoa

Skin the cadjunuts, chop them somewhat roughly and toast them in the oven for a few minutes. Wash and pick the sultanas and dry them. Put the sugar and water into a preserving pan, and stir over the fire until the sugar is dissolved. Then add the butter, milk and cocoa which must be dissolved in a little boiling water. Stir constantly until the mixture thickens and hardens when a little is tested in cold water. Remove the pan from the fire, stir in the cadjunuts and sultanas and add the flavouring. Stir well together and pour into a buttered dish or tin. Mark it in squares and cut in pieces when cold.

1176 Walnut Toffee

1 lb. sugar
3 oz. shelled walnuts
2 oz. butter
a pinch of cream of tarter
½ teacup water

Toast the walnuts a few minutes in the oven and then spread them out on a buttered dish. Put the butter into a saucepan and melt it over the fire, add the sugar, water and cream of tartar and bring to the boil. Boil without stirring until the toffee breaks brittle when tested in cold water. Pour over the nuts and leave to set. Before it is quite cold cut it in strips.

1177 Turkish Delight

1 lb. sugar
1 oz. sheet gelatine
½ pint water
flavouring
colouring
icing sugar

Soak the gelatine in half the quantity of water for a few hours. Put the sugar with the remainder of the water into a saucepan and bring to the boil. Remove the saucepan from the fire, add the gelatine, return the saucepan to the fire and simmer the contents slowly for 20 minutes, stirrng all the time. Then strain and divide into two portions. Flavour one portion with rose and colour a pale pink with a few drops of cochineal. Flavour the remainder with lemon and colour yellow or leave it its natural colour. Pour the mixture, about an inch thick, into flat dishes, rinsed out with cold water. Leave it to get firm and cold. Then turn out and cut into squares and coat each piece thickly with icing sugar.

1178 Walnut & Coffee Candy

1 lb. sugar
¼ lb. shelled walnuts
1 gill strong coffee
½ gill milk
1 oz. butter

Put all the ingredients except the nuts into a preserving pan and stir over the fire until the mixture thickens. Add the nuts finely chopped. Mix well together and pour into a buttered dish. Mark it in squares and cut in pieces when cold.

Unboiled Sweets

1191 Coconut Bars

1 lb. icing sugar
6 oz. desiccated coconut
a pinch of cream of tartar
white of egg
flavouring
colouring

Sieve the sugar, add the cream of tartar and coconut and mix in sufficient whites of egg to form the mixture into a stiff paste. Knead well with the hand and flavour to taste. Cover the paste and let it remain for an hour. Turn it on to a sugared board and colour half the paste pink with a few drops of carmine. Roll out the white half and the pink half separately, to the thickness of half an inch, then press the pink paste upon the white and cut into small neat bars with a sharp knife. Leave to harden on sheets of white paper dusted over with sugar. A third strip of colour may be added by dividing the paste into three and colouring one portion green or yellow.

1192 Stuffed Dates

Choose small soft dates—those sold in boxes are the best, the larger kinds being too coarse and thick. Remove the stones from the dates without cutting the fruit in two. Then fill up the centres with an almond-shaped piece of fondant. If liked the fondant can be divided into several portions and coloured and flavoured differently.

1193 Easter Eggs

1 lb. icing sugar
½ lb. ground almonds
1 dessertspoon rose-water
white of egg
flavouring and colouring

Sieve the sugar, add to it the almonds and mix thoroughly. Add the rose-water, moisten with white of egg, and knead well. Then flavour and colour according to taste, see Recipe 1196. When perfectly smooth and uniform in colour allow the paste to rest a little while before shaping it, as the working out will have softened it somewhat. Divide the paste into pieces and form them, with the help of a spoon, to the shape and size of a small egg. Place them on sheets of white paper sprinkled with icing sugar and leave to harden in a warm dry place.

1194 Fondant Creams

Flavour and colour some fondant as desired, then take small portions of it and shape with the hands into balls, cones, or any fancy shapes liked, using a little icing sugar to prevent it sticking. Or the fondant may be rolled out on a pastry board and cut into small squares or fancy shapes with a vegetable cutter. Leave them to harden on sheets of white paper sprinkled with icing sugar.

1195 Fondant Slices

Take a small piece of pink fondant and roll it out with the hands into a thin roll like a lead pencil. Then roll out a piece of white fondant with a rolling pin into a long strip, and also roll out a piece of green fondant into a strip. Place the green strip on the white, lay the pink roll on it and roll up like a roly-poly pudding. Make the roll as smooth and even as possible. Cut it in slices and leave to harden.

1196 Fondant Uncooked

1 lb. icing sugar
1 white of egg
a pinch of cream of tartar
a little water

Sieve the sugar into a basin, add the cream of tartar and then mix in the white of egg and enough water to form a stiff firm paste. Knead with the hand until smooth, then cover the paste and let it remain for an hour. Turn the paste on to a pastry board that has been sprinkled with sugar, and work it with the hand for a few minutes. The fondant is now ready to be coloured and flavoured and used as required. This recipe is the foundation of a great number of uncooked sweets which can be flavoured and coloured to taste.

Colouring and Flavouring—Colour and flavour very cautiously. Light and delicate coloured sweets are much daintier than those of a brilliant hue, and over-flavouring should also be avoided. Divide the paste into four or as many portions as you like. Colour one portion pink and flavour with rose or strawberry, another green and flavour with almond or peppermint, a third yellow with lemon or orange flavouring; one portion may be left uncoloured and flavoured with vanilla. Chocolate colouring is got by mixing in a little grated chocolate and this flavours as well. Liqueurs too are used for flavouring. Knead well so that the colouring and flavouring are evenly distributed.

1197 Lemon Creams

1 lb. icing sugar
1 white of egg
1 tablespoon water
a few drops of lemon flavouring
candied peel

Mix the paste in the same way as in Recipe 1196 and let it rest for an hour. Then form the paste into small fancy shapes, using a little icing sugar to prevent sticking. Place a thin strip of candied peel upon each sweet and lay them on sheets of white paper sprinkled over with icing sugar, to dry.

1198 Marzipan

1 lb. icing sugar
½ lb. ground almonds
1 dessertspoon rose-water
white of egg

Sieve the sugar, add to it the ground almonds and mix thoroughly Add the rose-water, moisten with sufficient white of egg to form a stiff paste, and knead well. Flavour and colour as required. See Recipe 1196.

1199 Marzipan Fruits

Take some marzipan, divide into pieces the size of walnuts and shape them with the hands into balls to make apples. Use a narrow strip of angelica to form a stem, or the stalk of a raisin would do, and stick a clove at the other end of the apple. Now paint the apples with a small brush using vegetables colouring. Pears, cherries, peaches, etc., can be made in the same way. These dainty looking trifles are really not difficult to make. Lightness of touch and general daintiness is necessary in the making of these sweets, and with a little taste and ingenuity quite a variety of pretty sweets can be turned out.

1200 Marzipan Potatoes

Take some marzipan and form the paste into shapes resembling small potatoes of different sizes. Mark a few eyes in each with a skewer and roll them in finely powdered chocolate.

1201 Neapolitan Squares

This is made by preparing 4 different colours of fondant and using different flavouring (see Recipe 1196). Roll out each piece of paste separately to about ¼ inch in thickness. Place the layers one upon another and press them lightly together with a rolling pin. Set the block aside until dry and firm, then cut in squares.

1202 Peppermint Creams

1 lb. icing sugar — **essence of peppermint**
1 white of egg — **1 tablespoon water**

Sieve the sugar and add to it the white of egg and water and knead with the hand into a smooth soft paste. Flavour with a few drops of essence of peppermint and let it rest for an hour. Dust a pastry board with icing sugar and roll out the mixture to ⅛ inch in thickness. Cut into rounds with a small cutter and leave to dry on sheets of white paper sprinkled with icing sugar.

1203 Walnut Creams

Take a piece of fondant and place it between two shelled half walnuts and press them lightly together so that the cream comes out all round between the halves. Leave them to harden.

Cakes and Cake Icings

(For other cakes, see Bread & Biscuits
and Pastry & Pastry Cakes)

In all branches of cookery and especially in cake-making, the greatest care must be exercised to follow the instructions to the letter. The ingredients must be all weighed, and each ingredient added and mixed in the order and manner indicated. The success of the cake depends very much on the instructions being followed exactly; but, like in everything else, in cake-making too experience is necessary and can be gained by practice.

Preparation of Cake Tins

Cake tins should be prepared before beginning to mix the ingredients as most cakes will spoil, if, after having been mixed, they have to stand waiting till the tins are ready.

To Line a Round Cake Tin with Paper—The correct method in which to line a round cake tin is first to cut a double-band of paper about 2½ or 3½ inches deeper than the cake tin and somewhat longer than the circumference. Fold up an inch of this band and make a mark, then open out and make cuts at even distances along the marked-off inch. Cut two rounds of paper, the size of the bottom of the tin and place one round at the bottom of the tin. Then arrange the band of paper inside the cake tin with the notched part flat at the bottom and place the second round on the top of this. Two folds of paper will do for ordinary cakes but for very big cakes and rich fruit cakes use four or even more folds of paper for the bottom of the tin. Grease the paper well with butter.

To Line a Flat Tin with Paper—It will not be necessary to shape the paper. Just press the paper into the tin and fold in the corners. Butter the paper and dust it over with a mixture of flour and sugar.

To Prepare Small Cake Tins—Melt some butter and grease the inside of the tins. Then mix together one tablespoonful each of soft sugar and flour and sprinkle the buttered tins well with this mixture but shake out all that does not adhere. This preparation gives a nice dry coating to sponge cakes.

Preparation of Ingredients

The flour should be sifted and it must be perfectly dry, as damp flour will make any cake heavy. The Baking Powder should be mixed with the flour or added to the mixture just before it is put into the oven. Soft sugar is usually used for cakes but the ordinary crepe sugar pounded and sifted will do just as well. Eggs should each be broken separately into a cup before adding them to any mixture in case one should not be quite good. Fresh butter is usually used for cakes. Currants should be washed and dried in a cloth and they must be looked over well for stones.

Sultanas should be washed and the stalks removed and in raisins the stalks and also the stones removed. Sultanas and raisins are cut in small pieces. Remove the hard sugar from inside the candied peel and shred the peel finely. Ginger preserve and pumpkin preserve are cut into small pieces. All fruit should be mixed with a little dry flour (taken from the quantity given in the recipe) before being added to the cake mixture, so as to prevent them sinking to the bottom of the tin.

Almonds should be put into a basin of cold water and allowed to stand for a couple of hours. Then remove the skins and shred or chop them.

Cadjunuts should be dried in the sun or in a very moderate oven, being careful they do not take colour. Remove the skins while still warm and chop or pound them as required.

Hints on Baking

The most important as well as the most difficult point in cake-making is the baking, as the success of a cake depends to a great extent upon the proper management of the oven. The oven needs careful watching. To start with, the oven must be hot. If the cake is put into one not hot enough, it will turn out heavy. A simple test for getting the proper heat is to put a piece of white paper into the oven and if it turns yellow in 5 minutes the heat is moderate and suitable for most cakes. After a little experience the heat of the oven can be easily judged by thrusting the hand into the oven. Sponge and all light cakes require rather a quick oven; but a moderate oven is best for the thick fruit cakes. Cakes must be put into the oven directly they are ready and not kept standing once they have been mixed up. Before beginning to mix the cake see that the oven will be sufficiently hot to receive the cake as soon as it is ready. When the oven is too hot at first the cake rises in a cone in the centre or a crust forms on the top which prevents the cake from rising. A well-baked cake should rise evenly and be smooth on the top. If the cake rises at one side it means that the oven is hotter on that side, so the cake must be carefully turned so as to bake evenly. Should the oven be too hot at the bottom put a brick under the tin. If the top of the cake gets brown before it is ready cover with a double-fold of paper. The oven should not be opened until at least 5 minutes after the cake has been put in, and then too it must be carefully opened and closed as the slamming of the door creates a draught and causes the mixture to fall.

To ascertain whether the cake is sufficiently done, test by thrusting a skewer into the centre of the cake. If the skewer comes out clean the cake is cooked, but if it is at all sticky the cake needs further cooking. Cakes should be cooled on a wire tray or sieve.

Cakes

1211 Almond Cake

½ lb. flour
½ lb. soft sugar
¼ lb. butter
¼ lb. shelled almonds
6 eggs
essence of almonds
rose-water
½ teaspoon baking powder

Blanch the almonds and pound to a paste with a little rose-water, reserving a few split halves to put on the top of the cake. Beat the butter and sugar together. Then add the flour by degrees, and the eggs, and beat the mixture well for about 15 minutes. Add the almond paste and a few drops of essence of almonds and the baking powder at the last. Pour the mixture into a lined cake tin, cover the top with the half almonds, and bake in a moderate oven for about 1½ hours.

1212 Birthday Cake

½ lb. flour
½ lb. sugar
6 oz. butter
6 eggs
½ teaspoon baking powder
1 teaspoon essence of vanilla
candied cherries
water icing (Recipe 1273)

Cream the butter, add the sugar and then the eggs and flour by degrees, beating the mixture well after adding each egg. When it has been well beaten add the flavouring and then the baking powder at the last. Pour the mixture into a lined cake tin and bake in a moderate oven for about 1½ hours. When quite cold coat the cakes with Water Icing coloured green, and ornament with candied cherries.

1213 Butter Cake

1 lb. flour
1 lb. soft sugar
1 lb. butter
1 lb. eggs
1 teaspoonful baking powder
2 teaspoons essence of vanilla

Beat the butter and sugar to a cream, then add the yolks of eggs and the flavouring and beat all well together. Whip the whites of eggs to a stiff froth, and sieve the flour with the baking powder. Add alternately a little flour and a little white of egg to the mixture until all is lightly blended together. Pour the mixture into a papered cake tin and bake in a moderate oven for about 2½ hours or untill wel risen and cooked through.

1214 Cherry Cake

10 oz. flour
½ soft sugar
½ lb. butter
½ lb. candied cherries
7 eggs
1 teaspoonful baking powder
½ teaspoon essence of vanilla

Beat the butter to a cream, add the sugar and beat well again. Add one egg and a tablespoonful of flour and beat for a few minutes. Add the second egg and another spoonful of flour, and so on, repeating this process until all the eggs and flour have been beaten in. Then add the vanilla and the cherries cut into halves or quarters. Mix in the baking powder at the last. Pour the mixture into a lined cake tin and bake for about 2½ hours. The oven should be more than ordinarily hot at first as the cherries being heavy are apt to sink to the bottom of the cake, if slowly baked. When the cake has fairly risen reduce the heat.

1215 Chocolate Cake

½ lb. flour
¼ lb. butter
¼ lb. grated chocolate
¾ lb. soft sugar
6 eggs
½ teaspoonful baking powder
1 teaspoon essence of vanilla
a pinch of powdered cinnamon
a pinch of grated nutmeg
½ wine-glass rose-water
chocolate icing (Recipe 1264)

Beat the butter and sugar to a cream and mix in the chocolate, vanilla, spices and rose-water. Add one egg with a little of the flour, and beat for a few minutes, then another egg and more flour and so on until all the eggs and flour have been beaten in. Add the baking powder at the last. Pour the mixture into a lined cake tin that has been dusted out with flour and sugar, and bake for about 1½ hours or until it is quite firm. When cold, ice the cake with Chocolate Icing.

1216 Chocolate Layer Cake

¼ lb. flour
½ lb. soft sugar
¼ lb. grated chocolate
6 eggs
1 teaspoonful baking powder
2 teaspoons essence of vanilla
chocolate icing (Recipe 1264)

FILLING:
1 tablespoonful butter **3 tablespoons soft sugar** **cochineal**

Put the yolks of eggs and sugar into a basin and beat them together, then add the chocolate and the flavouring and beat for a few minutes. Whip up the whites of the eggs to a stiff froth and add a little of them alternately with a little of the flour until all is mixed in. Sprinkle in the baking powder at the last. Pour the mixture into a lined cake tin and bake in a moderate oven for about 1½ hours or until it feels dry when tested with a skewer. When ready turn out of the tin and allow the cake to cool. Then split the cake in three or four, according to its height, spread each piece with the filling and put the cake back into shape. Coat the cake with Chocolate Icing.

To Make the Filling—Beat the butter and sugar together, add the flavouring and colour it a pale pink.

1217 Chocolate Roll

2 eggs
2 oz. flour
4 oz. soft sugar
1 oz. finely grated chocolate
1 tablespoon water
vanilla flavouring
¼ teaspoon baking powder
butter icing (Recipe 1263)

Put the sugar and yolks of eggs into a basin and beat them well together until light and frothy. Then mix in the flour lightly and the whites of eggs beaten to a stiff froth. Melt the chocolate in the water and add it to the mixture. Flavour to taste and add the baking powder last. Have ready a flat tin of an oblong shape lined with buttered paper. Pour the mixture in to the depth of ¼ of an inch and bake in rather a quick oven from 10 to 12 minutes. When ready turn the cake on to a paper well sprinkled with sugar, and trim the edges neatly with a knife. Spread with Butter Icing flavoured with vanilla and coloured with cochineal, and roll up quickly while yet warm or else it will crack in so doing. When cold, cut in thick slices.

1218 Christmas Cake

1 lb. rulang
2 oz. flour
2 lb. soft sugar
a wineglassful each of brandy, rose-water and bees' honey
½ lb. ginger preserve
½ lb. chow-chow preserve
½ lb. mixed candied peel
25 yolks of eggs
8 or 10 whites of eggs
200 cadjunuts
1 lb. butter
1 lb. raisins
1 lb. sultanas
½ lb. currants
½ lb. pumpkin preserve
½ teaspoon each of powdered cardamoms and cinnamon
¼ teaspoon powdered cloves
½ a nutmeg (grated)
almond paste
royal icing (Recipe 1271)

First prepare the fruit. Stone and cut the raisins in three or four pieces, wash and stem the sultanas, wash, pick and dry the currants, cut the pumpkin preserve, ginger preserve, and chow-chow preserve in small pieces, shred the candied peel finely and skin and chop the cadjunuts. Mix the different kinds of fruit together with the flour. Put the butter and sugar into a large basin and beat well with a wooden spoon till very light and smooth. Then add the yolks of eggs, one at a time, beating well after each is added and mix in the rulang gradually, then add the fruit, cadjunuts, and spices, and lastly the brandy, rose-water and bees' honey, and the whites of eggs beaten to a stiff froth. Have ready a large round cake tin lined with two or three folds of white paper, well buttered. It is best to have about six folds of paper to the bottom of the tin. Pour in the mixture to the prepared tin and bake in a moderate and steady oven from 4 to 5 hours. When the cake begins to brown cover it with a double-fold of paper, to prevent it burning on the top. When ready, let it stand for a few minutes, then turn it out carefully and allow to cool. This cake improves with keeping, so it should be made at least a week before it is required, but the icing must be laid on only a day or two before. Cover the cake with a good coating of almond paste, then coat it with Royal Icing. Allow it to dry, then put some icing into a forcing bag and force it out on the top and sides of the cake in a pretty design.

1219 Coconut Cake

½ lb. roasted and sifted rice flour
1 lb. soft sugar
1 coconut
6 yolks of eggs
2 whites of eggs
100 cadjunuts
½ wineglass rose-water
¼ teaspoon powdered cardamoms

Scrape the coconut and grind it very finely. Pound 75 of the cadjunuts into a paste moistening with a little rose-water, if necessary, and cut the remainder of the cadjunuts into fine strips. Put the yolks of eggs and sugar into a basin and beat well together. Add the flour gradually and mix in the other ingredients. Lastly, add the whites of eggs beaten to a stiff froth. Pour the mixture into a flat cake tin that has been greased and dusted out with flour and sugar, sprinkle the top with the cut cadjunuts and bake in a moderate oven until the top is a nice brown colour. It will take about an hour to bake.

1220 Coffee Cakes

½ lb. flour
½ lb. soft sugar
¼ lb. butter
¼ lb. currants
4 eggs
2 tablespoons very strong coffee
1 teaspoonful baking powder
a little milk
coffee icing (Recipe 1266)

Beat the butter and sugar together. Then add the eggs one at a time along with the flour, and beat the mixture well after the adding of each egg. Then add the currants and the coffee, which must be strained, and enough milk to make the mixture just soft enough to drop from the spoon. Mix in the baking powder last of all. Have ready some fancy cake tins well greased with butter and dusted out with a mixture of flour and sugar. Three parts fill them with the mixture and bake in a moderate oven from 20 to 25 minutes. When ready turn out the cakes and while still warm coat them with Coffee Icing.

1221 Currant Cakes

½ lb. flour
½ lb. roasted and sifted rice flour
1 lb. soft sugar
¼ lb. currants
1 teaspoonful baking powder
10 or 12 eggs
essence of lemon
6 oz. butter

Beat the butter and sugar to a cream, then add the yolks of the eggs and beat a few minutes longer. Whip the whites of the eggs to a stiff froth, and sieve the flour with the baking powder. Add the whites of the eggs and the two kinds of flour by degrees. Mix very lightly and stir in the currants well cleaned, and the flavouring. Have ready some small tins well greased with butter and dusted out with flour and sugar. Three parts fill the tins with the mixture, put into rather a quick oven, and bake for 20 minutes or until cooked through.

1222 Dripping Cake

1 lb. flour	**¼ lb. candied peel**
6 oz. sugar	**4 eggs**
¼ lb. dripping	**1 teaspoonful baking powder**
½ lb. currants	**½ pint milk**

Mix the flour and baking powder together, rub in the dripping, add the fruit and sugar and mix well together. Then add the eggs well beaten and the milk, and beat the whole thoroughly. Pour the mixture into a greased tin and bake from 1½ to 2 hours.

1223 Experiment Cake

½ lb. flour	**2 oz. candied peel**
½ lb. soft sugar	**2 oz. almonds**
¼ lb. butter	**6 eggs**
¼ lb. sultanas	**1 teaspoonful baking powder**
¼ lb. currants	**a few drops of essence of almonds**

Beat the butter and sugar together with a wooden spoon until quite creamy and soft, then add the eggs alternately with a spoonful of the flour, beating well between each. Having previously cleaned and mixed with a spoonful of flour the currants and sultanas, add them and the candied peel chopped finely, then the almonds blanched and shredded. Mix all these thoroughly, then add the flavouring and last of all the baking powder; Pour into a tin lined with buttered paper and bake for about 1½ hours.

1224 Family Cake

1 lb. flour	**8 eggs**
½ lb. soft sugar	**1 teaspoonful baking powder**
½ lb. butter	**a few drops of essence of lemon**
½ lb. currants	**¼ teaspoon each of grated nutmeg and powdered cinnamon and cloves**
½ lb. sultanas	
¼ lb. candied peel	

Make in the same way as Experiment Cake.

1225 Fancy Assorted Cakes

Most of the small fancy cakes are made up from Sponge Cake, Rice-Flour Cake, Chocolate Cake, and other plain cake mixtures. They can be baked in small fancy tins, cut into two or three slices and sandwiched with jam, marmalade, butter icing, almond paste or any other filling; or baked in sandwich tins and cut into small triangles, diamonds, fingers, squares and rounds. Coat with icing and decorate with preserved fruit or chopped almonds, or a little piping in icing can be put on the top. By varying the colouring and the flavouring of the cake mixture, filling and icing, and also with a little practice, an endless variety of pretty fancy cakes can be turned out.

1226 French Cakes

½ lb. flour
1 lb. soft sugar
12 yolks of eggs
8 whites of eggs
½ teaspoon each of powdered cardamoms and grated nutmeg
¼ teaspoon each of powdered cinnamon and cloves

Put the sugar and yolks of eggs into a basin and work them together with a wooden spoon until light and full of air bubbles. Then add the spices and gradually work in the flour. Lastly, add the whites of eggs beaten to a stiff froth. Have ready some small sponge cake tins, well greased with butter and dusted out with a mixture of flour and sugar. Half fill them with the mixture and bake in a steady oven until brown and well risen. These cakes will take about 20 minutes to bake.

1227 Ginger Cake

½ lb. flour
2 teaspoonfuls of dry ginger
¼ lb. sugar
¼ lb. butter
¼ lb. preserved ginger
2 oz. golden syrup
4 eggs
¼ teaspoon carbonate of soda
2 tablespoonfuls milk

Cream the butter and sugar together and mix in the golden syrup. Beat up the eggs and add them gradually with the flour. When well beaten, add the powdered ginger and the preserved ginger cut in pieces about the size of sultana raisins, and lastly, the soda dissolved in milk. Pour the mixture into a lined cake tin and bake at once in a moderate oven for about 1½ hours.

N.B. If liked, the syrup from the preserved ginger can be used instead of the Golden Syrup.

1228 Holiday Cake

½ lb. flour
10 oz. soft sugar
½ lb. butter
2 oz. currants
25 cadjunuts
6 yolks of eggs
3 whites of eggs
½ teaspoon baking powder
½ wineglass rose-water

Cream the butter, add the sugar and the rose-water and mix well. Then add the yolks of eggs and beat a few minutes longer. Beat the whites of eggs to a stiff froth, and mix the flour and baking powder together. Add these two alternately to the other mixture mixing them in very lightly. Pour the mixture into a flat tin that has been lined with buttered paper, sprinkle the top with the cadjunuts which should be cut in strips, and the currants. Bake in a moderate oven until the top of the cake is a nice brown colour. It will take from 40 to 50 minutes to bake.

1229 Lemon Layer Cake

8 eggs
the weight of 8 eggs in sugar
the weight of 4 eggs in flour
¾ teaspoon baking powder
essence of lemon
water icing

FILLING:

1 tablespoonful butter
3 tablespoonfuls soft sugar
essence of lemon

Make the cake in the same way as Sponge Cake (Recipe 1242), and bake it in a round cake tin that has been lined with buttered paper. When the cake is well baked allow it to cool. Then cut the cake in three or four slices, according to its height, spread each piece with the filling and put the cake together again. Coat the cake with Water Icing (Recipe 1273).

To Make the Filling—Beat the butter and sugar together and add flavouring to taste.

1230 Love Cake I

½ lb. rulang
1 lb. soft sugar
¼ lb butter
100 cadjunuts
10 yolks of eggs
½ wineglass each of rose-water and bees' honey
¼ teaspoon each of grated nutmeg, lemon rind and powdered cinnamon

Put the yolks of the eggs into a basin, add the sugar and beat them together. Have the rulang and butter mixed together and add them next. Beat again till well mixed, then add the cadjunuts, finely chopped, rose-water, bees' honey, nutmeg, lemon rind, and cinnamon and mix well together. Pour the mixture into a flat cake tin lined with greased paper and bake in a moderate oven until the top is nicely browned and the cake cooked through.

1231 Love Cake II

1 lb. rulang
2 lb. soft sugar
200 cadjunuts
12 yolks of eggs
10 whites of eggs
½ wineglass each of rose-water and bees' honey
½ teaspoon chopped lime rind

Beat together in a basin the sugar and the yolks of eggs. Then add the rulang and mix well together, ıen the cadjunuts finely chopped, the rose-water, bees' honey and lime and rind, lastly, the whites of eggs beaten to a stiff froth. Pour the mixture in to a flat papered cake tin and bake in a moderate oven. When ready turn it out carefully and sprinkle the top thickly with sugar.

1232 Madeira Cake

½ lb. flour
6 oz. soft sugar
¼ lb. butter
6 eggs
½ teaspoon baking powder
½ teaspoon essence of vanilla
2 or 3 strips candied peel

Beat the butter to a cream, add the sugar and flavouring and mix well together. Beat the yolks of eggs in a separate basin and add them to the creamed butter and sugar and mix well for a few minutes. Have the whites of eggs beaten to a stiff froth and mix them in lightly. Next add the flour and baking powder and mix all lightly but thoroughly. Pour the mixture into a lined cake tin, place the strips of candied peel on the top of the cake and bake in a moderately hot oven for about 1½ hours.

1233 Marble Cake

½ lb. flour
½ lb. soft sugar
¼ lb butter
6 eggs
½ teaspoon baking powder
1 oz. grated chocolate
vanilla and lemon flavouring
carmine, yellow colouring

Beat the butter and sugar into a cream. Add one egg with a little of the flour and beat for a few minutes, then another egg and more flour and so on until all the eggs and flour have been beaten in. Then mix in the baking powder. Divide the mixture into four equal portions. Melt the grated chocolate in a tablespoon of water and add it to two of the portions in unequal quantities so that one may be dark and the other light. Flavour both portions with vanilla. Mix a little carmine and yellow colouring to make an orange colour and add it to the two remaining portions making one portion a pale and the other a deep orange. Flavour these two portions with lemon. Have ready a cake tin lined with buttered paper. Fill it with alternate spoonfuls of the different mixtures so that when baked the cake may cut out like variegated marble. Bake in a moderate oven for about 2½ hours or until cooked through.

1234 Mocha Cake

¼ lb. flour
6 oz. sugar
a few drops of essence of vanilla
6 eggs
½ teaspoon baking powder
mocha icing (Recipe 1268)

Put the yolks of the eggs and the sugar into a basin and beat them well together. Mix the flour with the baking powder and whip the whites of eggs to a stiff froth. Add alternately a little flour and a little white of egg to the mixture, mixing them in very lightly. Then add the vanilla. Pour the mixture into a round, rather shallow cake tin that has been greased and dusted out with flour and sugar, and bake in rather a hot oven from 20 to 30 minutes. When ready, turn out and allow the cake to cool. Then split the cake once or twice according to its height, spread each piece with a layer of the icing and put the cake together again. Coat the cake with icing, and put some icing into a forcing bag and force it out in a pretty design on the top of the cake.

1235 Orange Cake

6 oz. flour
½ lb. soft sugar
the grated rind of half an orange
¼ lb. butter
5 eggs
¼ teacup strained orange juice
½ teaspoon baking powder

ICING:
½ lb. icing sugar
juice of 1 orange

Cream the butter and sugar together, then add the beaten yolks of eggs and the orange rind. Beat in alternately the orange juice and the flour, then add the whites of eggs beaten to a stiff froth and lastly the baking powder. Pour the mixture into a cake tin lined with buttered paper and bake in a moderate oven for about 1 hour. When baked and quite cold, ice the cake with the following icing.

To Make the Icing—Sieve the icing sugar into a basin and add gradually enough strained orange juice to make a thick paste. Mix well until smooth and spread over the cake at once.

1236 Queen Cakes

½ lb. flour
½ lb. soft sugar
¼ lb. butter
2 oz. currants
6 eggs
¼ pint milk
½ teaspoon baking powder

Beat the butter and sugar to a cream and add the yolks of eggs, one by one, and beat well between. Then whip the whites of eggs to a stiff froth and stir them in alternately with a little flour until all is mixed in. Then add the milk and the currants and sprinkle in the baking powder at the last. Butter some small fancy tins, dust the insides with a mixture of flour and sugar, fill each tin rather more than half full, bake in a moderate oven from 20 to 25 minutes.

N.B. If liked, the mixture can be baked in paper cases instead of tins.

1237 Ribbon Cake

6 oz. flour
4 oz. butter
9 oz. soft sugar
6 eggs
a few drops of vanilla flavouring
1 oz. grated chocolate, carmine or cochineal
jam or butter icing (Recipe 1263)
royal icing (Recipe 1271)

Beat the butter and sugar to a cream. Then add the yolks of eggs and beat for about 10 minutes. Have the whites of eggs beaten to a stiff froth and stir them in alternately with a little of the flour, then add the flavouring. Mix lightly and divide the mixture into three equal parts. Melt the chocolate in a tablespoon of water and add it to one part, colour the second part with a few drops of cochineal or carmine, and leave the remaining part as it is. Pour the mixture into three shallow tins lined with buttered paper and bake in rather a quick oven for about 10 or 12 minutes. When the cakes are ready turn them out of the tins and allow to cool. Then place them one on top of the other with a thin layer of jam, or Butter Icing between. Ice the top of the cake with Royal Icing.

1238 Rice-flour Cakes

¼ lb. roasted and sifted rice-flour
½ lb. soft sugar
5 eggs
a few drops of essence of lemon

Put the sugar and yolks of eggs into a basin and beat them together until light and frothy. Have the whites of eggs beaten to a stiff froth and stir them in alternately with the flour, then add the flavouring. Pour the mixture in to a tin that has been greased and dusted out with flour and sugar, fill it only half full, and bake in rather a quick oven until well risen and firm to the touch. It will take from 30 to 40 minutes.

N.B. This mixture will make a good Jam Sandwich or Swiss Roll.

1239 Iced Sandwich Cake

8 eggs
the weight of 8 eggs in sugar
the weight of 4 eggs in flour
¾ teaspoon baking powder
essence of vanilla
water icing (Recipe 1273)

FILLING:
1 tablespoonful butter
2 tablespoonfuls soft sugar
2 tablespoonfuls raspberry or strawberry jam

Beat the ingredients up in the same way as Lemon Layer Cake (Recipe 1229). Pour the mixture into two shallow round tins that have been lined with buttered paper and bake in rather a quick oven for about 15 minutes, or until it is well risen and firm to the touch. When the cakes are ready, turn them out and allow to cool. Then spread the top of one cake with the filling and place the other cake on it. Cover the cake with a thin layer of the icing.

To Make the Filling—Beat the butter and sugar together, then mix in the jam.

1240 Jam Sandwich Cake

4 eggs
the weight of 4 eggs in flour butter and soft sugar
½ teaspoonful baking powder
a few drops of essence of vanilla
2 tablespoonfuls raspberry or any other jam

Put the butter and sugar into a basin and beat to a cream. Add one egg and a little flour and beat them lightly in; then a second egg and some more flour and beat again; then the third egg and more flour; then lastly the fourth egg and the remainder of the flour mixed with the baking powder. Add the flavouring and mix all together. Take two shallow round cake tins of the same size and line each with buttered paper, and dust out with a mixture of flour and sugar. Pour the cake mixture into the papered tins, divided as evenly as possible, and put into rather a quick oven at once and bake for about 15 minutes or until nicely browned and cooked through. Turn them out carefully on a sheet of sugared paper, and when cool, spread the top of one cake with jam and place the other cake on it, letting the brown side be on the top, and sprinkle sugar thickly over it.

N.B. If a plainer sandwich cake is wanted make as given in Recipe 1243.

1241 Seed Cake

½ lb. flour	**6 eggs**
¼ lb. soft sugar	**1 teaspoonful baking powder**
¼ lb. butter	**1 teaspoonful caraway seeds**

Beat the butter to a cream, then add the sugar and beat them together for a few minutes. Add one egg and a little of the flour and beat for a few minutes. Continue until all the eggs and the flour have been beaten in, then add the caraway seeds and sprinkle in the baking powder last of all. Pour the mixture into a lined cake tin and bake in a moderate oven for about 2 hours.

1242 Sponge Cake

10 eggs	**1 teaspoonful baking powder**
the weight of 10 eggs in sugar	**a few drops of essence of lemon**
the weight of 5 eggs in flour	**or a little chopped lime rind**

Put the yolks of the eggs and the sugar into a basin, and beat them together with a wooden spoon until light and full of air bubbles. Whip the whites of the eggs to a stiff froth and sieve the flour with the baking powder. Add alternately a little flour and a little white of egg to the mixture, mixing them in gradually and very lightly. Then add the lemon flavouring. Pour the mixture into a flat tin that has been greased and dusted out with flour and sugar, half fill the tin, and bake at once in a moderate oven from 30 to 40 minutes, or until brown and well risen.

N.B. This mixture may be baked in small tins and will make nice little cakes. 15 to 20 minutes will be sufficient to cook them.

1243 Swiss Roll

4 eggs	**½ teaspoon baking powder**
¼ lb. flour	**2 tablespoonfuls raspberry jam**
¼ lb. soft sugar	

Put the sugar and yolks of eggs into a basin and beat them well together until light and frothy. Then mix in the flour very lightly and the whites of eggs beaten to a stiff froth. Add the baking powder last. Have ready a flat tin of an oblong shape lined with buttered paper. Pour the mixture in to the depth of ¼ inch and bake in a quick oven from 10 to 12 minutes. The top of the cake must be nicely browned. When ready turn the cake on to a paper well sprinkled with sugar and trim the edges neatly with a knife. Spread the jam (slightly warmed) over the cake quickly and evenly and roll it up quickly while yet warm or else it will crack in so doing. When cold cut it into thick slices, and if liked cover each with some soft icing.

N.B. If the jam is thick mix it with a tablespoon of hot water. Any other kind of jam without stones could be used instead of raspberry. If liked, the cake mixture can be coloured pink by adding a few drops of carmine or cochineal.

1244 Tiffin Cake

½ lb. flour
½ lb. soft sugar
¼ lb. butter
¼ lb. sultanas
½ teaspoon baking powder
caraway seeds to taste
yolks of 4 eggs
½ teacup milk

Beat the yolks of eggs and the sugar together, add the butter and then the flour by degrees mixed with the baking powder. Mix in the milk, sultanas and caraway seeds, pour into a buttered tin and bake in a moderately hot oven.

1245 Wedding Cake

2 lb. rulang
¼ lb. flour
4 lb. soft sugar
2 lb. butter
2 lb. raisins
2 lb. sultanas
1 lb. currants
1 lb. mixed candied peel
1 lb. candied cherries
1 lb. ginger preserve
1 lb. chow-chow preserve
1 lb. pumpkin preserve
1 lb. shelled almonds
50 yolks of eggs
25 whites of eggs
2 wineglasses each of brandy, rose-water and bees honey
2 tablespoons each of essence of vanilla and essence of almonds
1 teaspoonful each of powdered cardamoms and cinnamon
½ teaspoon powdered cloves
1 nutmeg (grated)
almond icing (Recipe 1241)
royal icing (Recipe 1271)

Make in the same way as Christmas Cake (Recipe 1218). Pour the mixture into three lined cake tins of graduated sizes and bake in a moderate and steady oven. The largest cake will require from 6 to 7 hours to bake, and the smaller ones less according to size. The success of the cakes depends very much on the long, steady baking, and the oven needs careful watching. When the cakes begin to brown cover them with a double-fold of paper to prevent them burning on the top. When baked let them stand in the tins for about half an hour, then turn them out carefully and allow to cool. This cake should be made at least a week before it is required as it improves with keeping. The almond paste and icing should be laid on a couple of days before it is wanted. For icing and decorating of cakes see Recipe 1271.

Cake Icings

1261 Almond Paste or Icing

1 lb. shelled almonds
½ lb. icing sugar
½ lb. soft sugar
1 tablespoon brandy
1 tablespoon essence of vanilla
white of egg
rose-water

Blanch the almonds and pound a few at a time in a mortar to a paste, adding a little rose-water to prevent oiling. Sieve the icing sugar into a basin, add the soft sugar, ground almonds, vanilla and brandy and mix well together. Then add enough unbeaten white of egg to make a stiff paste. Knead well with the hand, adding the moisture very gradually as the paste becomes soft with working. Taste the mixture and if the flavour of the almonds is too faint, add a few drops of essence of almonds.

How to Use Almond Paste—The cake must be perfectly cold for icing. Trim the cake, make the top of it level, and spread the paste at least half an inch thick on the surface of the cake. Shape it first with the hands, then take a knife with a broad blade, wet it and make the sides and top of the cake as smooth as possible. Allow the almond paste to dry before putting on the sugar icing.

N.B. Cadjunut paste, flavoured with essence of almonds, makes a good substitute for almond paste, or make the paste with equal quantities of almonds and cadjunuts.

1262 American Frosting

½ lb. granulated sugar
2 egg whites
3 tablespoons water
¼ teaspoon cream of tartar
vanilla essence

Put the sugar, water and cream of tartar into a pan and boil without stirring till it reaches a temperature of 240 degrees F. or when a little dropped into cold water, forms a soft ball. Have ready the whites of eggs stiffly beaten but not dry and when the syrup is of the required temperature, pour it in a thin stream over the egg whites, beating all the time. Continue beating till the icing becomes thick and white and stiff enough to spread. Flavour with vanilla and spread at once before it gets too dry.

1263 Butter Icing

½ lb. icing sugar
¼ lb. fresh butter
colouring
flavouring

Sieve the sugar and beat it to a cream with the butter. Then add any flavouring and colouring desired and mix well together.

1264 Chocolate Icing

½ lb. icing sugar
2 oz. grated chocolate
rose-water
1 teaspoonful essence of vanilla
2 tablespoonfuls water

Dissolve the chocolate with just sufficient rose-water or warm water to form a smooth but thick paste. Put the sugar into a saucepan, add the water and stir over the fire with a wooden spoon until warm—do not allow to boil or the icing will not be glossy. Take the pan off the fire, stir in the chocolate paste, add the flavouring, and mix well together.

1265 Chocolate Butter Icing

Make the icing in the same way as Butter Icing (Recipe 1263), adding 2 oz. grated chocolate and flavour with essence of vanilla.

1266 Coffee Icing

½ lb. icing sugar
essence of vanilla
essence of coffee or very strong black coffee to taste

Sieve the sugar and put it into a saucepan. Add the coffee and stir over the fire with a wooden spoon until warm. Flavour with vanilla.

1267 Golden Icing

icing sugar
1 yolk of egg
1 dessertspoonful drained orange juice

Put the yolk of egg and a dessertspoonful of sugar into a basin and beat well together. Add the orange juice and beat again, then mix in gradually enough icing sugar to make the icing just soft enough to spread over the cake.

1268 Mocha Icing

Make in the same way as Butter Icing (Recipe 1263), adding one teaspoonful of coffee essence or very strong black coffee to taste.

1269 Raspberry Butter Icing

Add a few drops of essence of raspberry to Butter Icing (Recipe 1263), and colour pink with a few drops of carmine or cochineal.

1270 Rose Icing

¼ lb. icing sugar
essence of rose
white of egg
carmine

Sieve the sugar into a basin and add enough unbeaten white of egg to make it a stiff smooth paste. Flavour with a few drops of essence of rose and tint it a pale pink with a few drops of carmine.

1271 Royal Icing

1½ lb. icing sugar
6 whites of eggs
1 dessertspoon lime juice
blue colouring

Sieve the sugar into a basin, add the lime juice and the unbeaten whites of eggs by degrees and work together with a wooden spoon until it is light and very white. The exact quantity of white of egg depends on the size of the eggs. To make this icing very white

2 drops of stone washing blue may be stirred in. A little colouring may also be added to the icing when desired but it must be added very sparingly if a dainty effect is to be obtained.

To Ice a Cake with Royal Icing—Unless the cake has got a coat of almond paste the first thing to do will be to make the top of the cake level and then turn it upside down. Spread the icing on the top of the cake as smoothly as possible, using a broad flat knife. Dip the knife in cold water when it gets sticky. Then ice the sides of the cake, touch up the edges and allow the cake to dry. A wedding cake has usually two coats of icing, but the first coat must be quite dry before the second is put on, and that again perfectly dry before the ornamentation is put on.

To Ornament a Cake—It is best to make some fresh icing for the piping, paying particular attention to the beating process. The icing should be beaten up very lightly, using for the purpose a wooden spatula, which is a plain piece of wood, cut in the form of a miniature cricket bat. Beat the icing as quickly as possible until it is perfectly smooth and of the right consistency; it will require some hard beating to make it workable. The icing should be beaten until it shows no signs of sinking after the withdrawal of the wooden spoon. It is now ready for piping. For this ornamentation paper bags and fancy forcing pipes are usually used, but the forcing pipes are not absolutely necessary. To make the bags, use fine stiffish white paper, cut in triangular-shaped pieces and twisted into cone-shaped bags. Cut a small piece off the top of the bag, and if you are using a pipe slip it in. Half fill the bag with icing, and fold in the surplus paper at the top to prevent the icing escaping from that end. Now proceed to force out the icing in a pretty design on the top and sides of the cake. This piping will not be found very easy by a beginner but with patience and practice there is no reason why it should not be mastered. It is best to make a few experiments in ornamental icing before proceeding to ice a cake.

1272 Strawberry Butter Icing

Make in the same way as Butter Icing (Recipe 1263), adding a few drops of essence of strawberry, and colour with carmine or cochineal.

1273 Water Icing

½ lb. icing sugar	**flavouring**
2 tablespoons water	**colouring**

Sieve the sugar and put it into a saucepan. Add the water very gradually and stir over a slow fire, with a wooden spoon, until warm; but do not on any account allow it to boil or the icing will not be shiny and will crack while pouring over the cake. The icing should be thick enough to coat well the wooden spoon. Remove from the fire, flavour and colour as desired and pour over the cake.

Bread and Biscuits

BREAD-MAKING forms an important branch of cookery, but it is one which is apt to be neglected. Home-made bread is practically unknown in towns where there are bakeries. But the few recipes for bread-making given in this chapter will be found useful for those living on estates and out of reach of bakeries. The recipes for fancy breads, biscuits, etc., will be found worth trying.

Bread Scones and Buns

1281 Bath Buns

1 lb. flour
¼ lb. sugar
6 oz. soft sugar
2 oz. candied peel
1 oz. compressed yeast
4 eggs
1 gill milk
lemon flavouring
a little sugar candy

Sieve the flour into a basin and rub in the butter. Put the yeast into a small basin, add a teaspoon of sugar, mix well together and stir in the milk which should be warm. Make a well in the centre of the flour, strain in the yeast and milk, add the eggs, and knead to a light dough. Cover the basin with a cloth and let it stand in the sun for 1½ hours or until it is well risen. Then add the remainder of the sugar, the candied peel finely chopped and a few drops of lemon flavouring; mix well together. When well mixed make into small buns, lay them on a floured baking tin, brush over with beaten egg, and sprinkle them with a little coarsely powdered sugar candy or coarse sugar. Bake in rather a quick oven for 20 minutes or until they are quite done.

1282 Coconut Buns

½ lb. flour
2 oz. soft sugar
3 oz. desiccated coconut
a little grated lime rind
3 oz. butter
1 teaspoonful baking powder
1 egg
a teacup of milk

Rub the butter into the flour, add the dry ingredients and mix all well together. Then stir in the eggs and the milk and beat well again. Pour the mixture into well-greased patty pans and bake the buns in a moderate oven from 20 to 30 minutes.

1283 Hot Cross Buns

1 lb. dough
¼ lb. flour
1½ oz. butter
3 oz. soft sugar
4 oz. currants
4 yolks of eggs
1 teaspoon baking powder
½ teaspoon mixed spice

Make the dough according to Recipe 1289, or it may be bought from the baker. Put the dough into a basin, add the butter and the yolks of eggs well beaten and beat with the hand until smooth and light. Mix the baking powder with the flour and add it gradually to the dough, then mix in the sugar, the currants cleaned and picked, and the spice. Make up the dough into small round buns and lay them on a floured baking tin about 3 inches apart and set them in the sun to rise from 20 to 30 minutes. Form a cross with two strips of dough on the top of each bun, brush them over with milk and bake in a quick oven from 20 to 25 minutes.

1284 Raspberry Buns

6 oz. flour
6 oz. roasted rice-flour
¼ lb. soft sugar
1 teaspoon baking powder
2 eggs
a little milk
¼ lb. butter
raspberry jam

Sieve the flour into a basin, rub in the butter and add the sugar and baking powder. Make a well in the centre and add the eggs (2 yolks and one white beaten together) and enough milk to form a stiffish dough. Divide this into about 15 equal pieces and roll each piece into a ball. Make a hole on the top of each ball, put in a little jam and close up neatly. Then flatten them out a little, brush over with white of egg and sugar, place them on a floured baking tin and bake in a hot oven for about 15 or 20 minutes.

1285 Rice-flour Buns

3 oz. flour
3 oz. roasted rice-flour
3 oz. soft sugar
3 oz. butter
3 oz. currants
1 oz. candied peel
1 teaspoon baking powder
2 eggs

Sieve the two kinds of flour and the baking powder into a basin and rub in the butter lightly. Then mix in the sugar and the fruit. Next add the eggs, well beaten, and mix into a soft dough. Divide into small buns, place them on a floured baking tin, put into the oven immediately and bake for about 20 minutes. Just before removing the buns from the oven brush them over with sugar and milk.

1286 Sultana Buns

1 lb. flour
2 oz. butter
2 oz. sugar
¼ lb. sultanas
½ oz. compressed yeast
1 teacup milk
2 eggs
a pinch of salt

Sieve the flour into a basin, add the sugar and rub in the butter with the tips of the fingers until free from lumps. Put the yeast and salt into a basin, mix well and pour in the milk, which should be warm. Make a well in the centre of the flour, pour in the yeast mixture and work all together with the hand, adding a little more milk, if necessary. Then cover the basin and set it in a warm place for about 2 hours. When the dough is well risen, add the eggs well beaten and the sultanas and knead lightly until free from crack. Form into small buns and place them about 3 inches apart on a greased and floured baking tin. Set again to rise for about half an hour and bake in a moderate oven until brown and firm to the touch. A few minutes before removing them from the oven brush them over with sugar and milk to give them a gloss.

1287 Home-made Bread I

3½ lb. flour
1 oz. compressed yeast
2 teaspoons salt
1 teaspoon sugar
about 2 pints warm milk and water, or warm water

Sieve the flour into a basin, mix in the salt and make a well in the centre. Mix the yeast and the sugar well together until they become liquid, and add to it half of the milk and water. Mix well together and strain into the middle of the flour. Then mix in gradually from the sides as much flour as well be necessary to form a thick smooth batter. Sprinkle a little flour on the top, cover the basin with a thick cloth and set it in a warm place or in the sun for about half an hour, or until the batter is covered with air bubbles. Then work in the rest of the flour, adding enough warm milk and water to form a soft dough. Turn out on a floured board and work it and beat it well with the hands until it becomes smooth and no longer sticks to the fingers. Put the dough back into the basin, score it across with a knife and keep it to rise a second time. It will swell to about twice its original size in about an hour's time. Turn out on the board again and re-knead lightly. Make up quickly into loaves and place them on greased and floured baking tins. For a cottage loaf make one large ball with a smaller one on the top. Flatten the smaller ball and press a floured finger through the middle of both. Make a few slits at regular intervals round the sides. If the loaves are to be baked in tins, grease the tins and do not fill them more than half. Let them rise again in a warm place for 20 minutes, then bake in a hot oven. The time will depend on the size of the loaf. A 2-lb. loaf will take about one hour to bake. To find out whether the bread is sufficiently baked or not, tap the bottom of the loaf; if ready to be taken out of the oven it will give out a hollow sound. As soon as the bread is taken from the oven it should be placed on a wire sieve or turned on its side to allow the steam to escape.

1288 Home-made Bread II

1¾ lb. flour
½ oz. compressed yeast
1 teaspoon salt
½ teaspoon sugar
½ pint warm milk
½ pint warm water

Sieve the flour into a basin, mix in the salt and make a well in the centre. Put the yeast and the sugar into a bowl, mix it well together and stir in the warm milk. Strain this into the middle of the flour and mix lightly, adding the warm water by degrees until a soft dough is formed. Then sprinkle it lightly with flour and score it across with a knife. Cover the basin with a cloth and let it stand in a warm place for half an hour to rise. Then follow directions given in the preceding recipe.

1289 Dough for Bread

2 lb. flour
½ teacup toddy
½ teaspoon salt
½ teaspoon sugar
lukewarm water

Put the toddy into a bowl, mix in the sugar and half a teaspoon of flour and add to it half a teacup of warm water. Cover the bowl with a cloth and place it in the sun for about an hour. Sieve the flour into a basin, mix in the salt, make a well in the centre and pour the toddy mixture into it; mix lightly adding a little more warm water, if necessary. Now work it and beat it well, with the hands until it becomes smooth and elastic and does not stick to the fingers. Then cover the basin with a cloth and place it in the sun for about 1½ hours to rise. The dough is then ready to be used as required.

1290 Gingerbread

1 lb. flour
¼ lb. butter
6 oz. soft sugar
½ lb. golden syrup
2 oz. shredded candied peel
1 oz. powdered dry ginger
½ teaspoon carbonate of soda
½ teaspoon powdered cinnamon
a pinch of powdered cloves
3 eggs

Sieve the flour into a basin and mix in the dry ingredients. Heat the butter, sugar and golden syrup in a saucepan and stir them into the centre of the dry ingredients. Add the eggs well beaten, and beat all together for a few minutes adding a little milk, if necessary. Pour the mixture into a lined and buttered tin, rather a shallow one, and bake in a very moderate oven, for gingerbread burns very quickly. It will take from 1 to 1½ hours to bake.

1291 Jaggery Bread

2 lb. dough
1¼ lb. jaggery

Scrape the jaggery finely with a knife, add it to the dough, and beat well with the hand until the jaggery is well mixed into the dough. Then half fill a greased cake tin with the dough and keep it in the sun to rise for about half an hour. Bake in a good oven until thoroughly cooked.

N.B. A dessertspoon of butter and 2 well-beaten eggs added to this is an improvement.

1292 Raisin Bread

1 lb. dough
¼ lb. soft sugar
¼ lb. sultanas
4 yolks of eggs

Put the dough into a basin, add the yolks of eggs and beat well with the hand for about 10 minutes. Then add the sugar and the sultanas, washed and picked, and mix well together. Half fill a greased tin with the dough and keep it to rise in the sun for about half an hour. When well risen bake in a moderate oven until thoroughly cooked. When nearly ready glaze the top with a syrup of sugar and water.

1293 Plantain Cake

1 lb. sour plantains
¾ lb. jaggery
½ lb. flour
½ lb. dates
a grate of nutmeg
2 eggs
a pinch of salt
about a teacup of coconut milk

Peel the plantains, which should be quite ripe, weigh them and then squeeze them into the flour. Scrape the jaggery and mix it in. Add the eggs well beaten, the dates stoned and chopped fine, a grate of nutmeg and a pinch of salt. Mix well together and then add the coconut milk. Bake in a slow oven.

1294 Rock Cakes

½ lb. flour
1 teaspoonful baking powder
a pinch of salt
3 oz. soft sugar
3 oz. butter or dripping
2 oz. currants
1 oz. candied peel
a few drops of essence of lemon
2 eggs
a little milk

Mix the flour, baking powder, salt and sugar together. Rub in the butter or dripping lightly with the tips of the fingers, and add the currants well cleaned, the candied peel cut in fine strips, and the essence of lemon. Then make a well in the centre and add the eggs well beaten and enough milk to make a stiffish paste. Mix thoroughly and arrange in small rocky heaps on a floured baking tin, keeping them some distance from each other. Sprinkle with sugar and bake in a quick oven until brown and firm to the touch.

1295 Currant Loaf

1 lb. dough
2 oz. butter
2 oz. sugar
2 oz. currants
1 oz. candied peel
2 eggs
½ teaspoon mixed spice

Put the dough into a basin, add the butter, sugar, currants carefully cleaned, the candied peel finely shredded, the eggs well beaten and the spice. Knead all together until thoroughly mixed. Put the batter into a greased tin, cover with a cloth and let it rise for about half an hour in the sun. Then bake in a moderate oven. When nearly ready, glaze the top with a syrup of sugar and water.

1296 Date Loaf

½ lb. flour
2 oz. butter
4 oz. soft sugar
3 eggs
½ lb. dates
¼ lb. sultanas
¼ teaspoon carbonate of soda
½ teaspoon baking powder
½ teacup milk

Beat the butter and sugar together, add the eggs, then the carbonate of soda dissolved in the milk. Mix the baking powder with the flour and add it by degrees and lastly, stir in the dates, stoned and cut up small, and the sultanas. Pour the mixture into a greased loaf tin and bake in a moderate oven for about 1½ hours.

1297 Dough Nuts

½ lb. flour
1 teaspoonful baking powder
a pinch of salt
2 oz. butter
¼ lb. soft sugar
2 eggs
butter-milk
fat for frying
powdered sugar

Mix the flour, baking powder and sugar together, rub in the butter, and make a well in the centre. Add the eggs well beaten then gradually as much butter-milk as will make a stiff dough which will roll out like pastry. Roll out to about half an inch in thickness, and cut into rings. This could be done by having two cutters of different sizes. Cut a round with the largest, then another round out of the middle of that. Fry these, a few at a time, in boiling fat. Drain on paper. They will of course, swell out and be double the size when cooked. Sprinkle with powdered sugar.

1298 Tiffin Rolls

½ lb. flour
2 oz. butter
2 tablespoons soft sugar
1 egg
1½ teaspoons baking powder
½ teaspoon salt
milk

Sieve the flour and baking powder into a basin, add the sugar and salt and rub in the butter until free from lumps. Make a well in the centre, add the egg well beaten, and enough milk to make a light dough. Divide the dough into small rolls, make a slit the length of each roll on the tops, and brush over with a little milk. Place them on a floured baking tin and bake at once in a quick oven for about 20 minutes.

1299 Vienna Rolls

1 lb. dough
¼ lb. flour
1 oz. butter
1½ dessertspoons soft sugar
1 teaspoon baking powder
2 eggs

Any bread dough may be used for these. Work the butter and the yolks of eggs well beaten into the dough and mix in the sugar. Mix the baking powder with the flour, and add it to the dough.

Then turn it on to a floured board, re-knead it lightly, and role out to about a quarter of an inch or a little more in thickness. Cut out squares of about 5 inches, trim the edges evenly and cut each square into two triangular pieces. Then role up each triangle lightly, beginning at the broad end which will make the middle thicker than the sides. Draw the point over like a flap, paste it down with a little white of egg, and bend the roll to form a crescent letting the two ends nearly meet. Place the rolls on a floured tin and let them rise for 20 minutes in the sun. Bake in rather a quick oven for about 30 minutes or until they are cooked. Then brush over with beaten egg to make them shiny, and return to the oven for 5 minutes to dry.

1300 Currant Scones

½ lb. flour
1 oz. paisley flour
2 oz. butter
1 oz. soft sugar
¼ lb. currants
1 egg
a little milk

Sieve the flour into a basin, mix in the paisley flour, and rub in the butter. Add the sugar and the currants cleaned and picked. Make a well in the centre and add the egg well beaten, then gradually a little milk until a soft dough is formed. Knead well and roll out rather thick. Stamp out into rounds with a pastry cutter and brush over with milk. Place them on a floured baking tin and bake in a fairly hot oven for about 15 minutes. They must be served hot.

1301 Plain Scones

½ lb. flour
1 oz. paisley-flour
2 oz. butter
1 dessertspoon sugar
a pinch of salt
1 gill milk

Sieve the flour into a basin and mix in the dry ingredients. Then rub in the butter lightly, make a well in the centre and add enough milk to make a softish dough. Mix quickly and lightly and turn out on a floured board. Then roll out about half an inch in thickness and cut into rounds or triangles. Place them on a floured baking tin and bake in a hot oven for about 15 minutes.

1302 Potato Scones

½ lb. potatoes
1 lb. flour
¼ lb sugar
¼ lb. butter
½ oz. cream of tartar
¼ oz. carbonate of soda
1 pint milk

Boil the potatoes and mash them. Sieve the flour into a basin and mix in the sugar, cream of tartar and soda; then rub in the butter and add the mashed potatoes. Mix the whole into a nice dough with the milk. Form into a round about half an inch in thickness and cut across in eight pieces. Place on a floured baking tin, let them stand for 15 minutes, then bake in a hot oven, turning them over when they are half done.

1303 Tea Scones

½ lb. flour	**½ teaspoon cream of tartar**
2 oz. butter	**½ teaspoon carbonate of soda**
1 oz. soft sugar	**a pinch of salt**
2 eggs	**milk**

Sieve the flour into a basin and mix in the dry ingredients. Add the butter and rub together with the tips of the fingers until free from lumps.

Make a well in the centre, add the eggs well beaten and pour in enough milk to make a light dough. Turn out on a floured board and knead lightly until free from cracks. Form into a round shape rather more than half an inch in thickness, mark across in four with the back of a knife, place on a floured baking tin and bake in a good oven until well risen and firm to the touch. A few minutes before removing the scone from the oven break it through in four pieces by the marks and brush over with a little milk.

Biscuits

1311 Almond Biscuits

½ lb. flour	**essence of almonds**
¼ lb. soft sugar	**a few almonds**
¼ lb. butter	**1 teaspoon baking powder**
2 yolks of eggs	**milk, if necessary**

Cream the butter and sugar together and add a few drops of essence of almonds. Beat the eggs and add gradually with the flour. The baking powder must be mixed with the flour. Work up with the hand into a stiffish paste, using a little milk, if necessary. Roll out rather thinly, stamp it out into small rounds with a cutter, place them on a floured tin and bake in a moderate oven until a golden brown colour. Allow the biscuits to cool, brush them over with white of egg, and sugar mixed and sprinkle with the almonds which should be chopped and browned. Return to the oven for a few minutes to dry.

1312 Almond Rings

Make in the same way as Coconut Rings (Recipe 1321), substituting ground almonds for coconut and adding a few drops of essence of almonds.

1313 Bachelor's Buttons

5 oz. flour	**1 egg**
3 oz. soft sugar	**vanilla flavouring**
2 oz. butter	

Beat the butter and sugar together and add the flavouring, then work in the flour and the egg well beaten. Knead into a smooth paste, adding a little more flour, if necessary. Form into small balls the size of a large marble, using a little flour to prevent them sticking to the hands. Place the biscuits on a floured tin, sprinkle them with sugar and bake in a hot oven until a light brown colour.

1314 Butter Biscuits

10 oz. flour | **½ lb. soft sugar**
¼ lb. butter | **1 egg**
1 teaspoon baking powder | **a few almonds**

Beat the butter and sugar together then work in the flour and the egg well beaten. Do not add all the egg unless necessary. Knead well with the hand to a smooth paste and form into balls the size of a large marble. Put one or two split almonds on the top of each and flatten them slightly. Arrange them on a floured baking tin, leaving a little space between each biscuit, and bake in a moderate oven from 10 to 15 minutes.

1315 Caraway Biscuits

½ lb. flour | **2 eggs**
3 oz. soft sugar | **¼ oz. caraway seeds**
2 oz. butter | **1 teaspoon baking powder**

Put the eggs and sugar into a basin and beat them together. Then add the butter beaten to a cream and mix in the flour, baking powder and caraway seeds. Knead it well, roll out the paste rather thinly, and prick all over with a skewer. Cut it into rounds and bake in a moderate oven from 10 to 15 minutes.

1316 Cheese Biscuits

4 oz. sieved flour | **2 oz. grated cheese**
3 oz. butter | **salt and pepper to taste**

Sieve the flour, salt, and pepper together, and mix in the cheese. Cream the butter, stir in the dry ingredients, and work together into a smooth, stiff paste, which should form into a ball and leave the sides of the basin clean. Turn on to a floured slab or board, knead lightly, adding flour as required to prevent stickiness.

Roll the paste out to a little less than quarter-inch thick, and cut into rounds with a one-inch fluted pastry cutter. Place on a greased and floured tin, and bake in a fairly quick oven until tinged with colour and quite firm to the touch. Leave in the tin to cool for a few minutes, then lift carefully on to a wire rack. As soon as the biscuits are quite cold, pack in an air-tight tin. They will then keep fresh and crisp for at least ten days. They are, however, very brittle, especially when still warm, so they must be handled gently.

N.B. These biscuits may be eaten plain, but they make an excellent foundation for many savoury snacks. Perhaps the best "toppings" are those made with cheese mixtures, such as creamed cheese, fresh cream cheese, or a plain rarebit-mixture, with or without the addition of strips of green chillies, gherkins, halved olive, or small pickled onions. When the rarebit-mixture is used the biscuits should be placed under a red-hot grill for two or three minutes to brown the mixture lightly; but with the other toppings they should be served chilled.

1317 Chocolate Biscuits

¼ lb. icing sugar or powdered sugar
¼ lb. grated chocolate
1 dessertspoon flour
white of egg
vanilla essence

Sift the sugar and mix it with the chocolate and flour, then add the flavouring and enough beaten white of egg to form into a paste. Take small portions of the mixture, form into balls, and arrange on a floured baking tin, keeping them some little distance apart. Bake in a moderate oven for about 15 minutes.

1318 Cinnamon Sticks

½ lb. flour
¼ lb. soft sugar
2 oz. butter
3 yolks of eggs
1 teaspoonful very finely powdered and sifted cinnamon
a few drops of lemon flavouring
a little milk, if necessary

Rub the butter into the flour, add the other dry ingredients to it and mix all well together. Then add the yolks of eggs, flavouring, and a little milk, if necessary. Mix up to a nice stiff paste, divide into pieces and roll out in little long sticks. Place them on a floured baking tin and bake in a moderate oven from 15 to 20 minutes.

1319 Coconut Biscuits

2 oz. desiccated coconut
2 oz. soft sugar
1 teaspoon flour
white of 1 egg
essence of vanilla

Mix the coconut, sugar and flour together, add the flavouring and bind together with white of egg beaten to a stiff froth. Drop the mixture by teaspoonfuls on well-buttered paper, placing them 2 inches apart and bake in a slow oven until lightly coloured.

1320 Coconut Macaroons

½ lb. powdered sugar
¼ lb. desiccated coconut
3 whites of eggs
vanilla essence

Make in the same way as Macaroons (Recipe 1330).

1321 Coconut Rings

2 oz. desiccated coconut
¼ lb. butter
½ lb. flour
¼ lb. soft sugar
milk, if necessary

Beat the butter and sugar together, add the coconut and flour and mix to a paste adding a little milk, if necessary. Roll out to about a quarter of an inch in thickness and cut into rounds. Then take a smaller cutter and stamp out the middle of each biscuit to form rings. Bake in a moderate oven.

1322 Finger Biscuits

½ lb. dough
½ oz. butter
1 dessertspoon sugar
1 egg
a little flour, if necessary

Work the butter and the egg, well beaten into the dough and mix in the sugar. Knead the dough until it is elastic, adding a little flour, if the dough is too moist. Divide it into pieces about the size of an egg and roll them out into long sticks, a little thicker than a pencil. Place them on a floured baking tin and let them rise in a warm place for about 10 minutes. Brush over with a little milk and bake in a moderate oven until crisp and lightly browned.

1323 Garibaldi Biscuits

½ lb. flour
1 teaspoon baking powder
2 oz. soft sugar
2 oz. butter
2 oz. currants
a pinch of salt
a little milk

Mix the flour and baking powder together, add the salt and sugar and rub in the butter with the tips of the fingers. Then add the currants and enough milk to form a stiff paste. Knead well and roll out rather thinly on a floured board and prick all over with a skewer. Cut in squares, place them on a floured tin and bake for about 20 minutes.

1324 Ginger Biscuits

½ lb. flour
½ teaspoon baking powder
¼ lb. soft sugar
¼ lb. butter
1 oz. powdered dry ginger
1 egg
milk, if necessary

Mix the flour, baking powder, sugar and ginger together and rub in the butter until free from lumps. Then bind together with the egg, well beaten, and a little milk, if necessary. Knead well with the hand until free from cracks, then turn the paste on to a floured board and roll out thinly. Cut it into rounds or fancy shapes, place the biscuits on a floured tin and bake in a moderate oven for about 15 minutes.

1325 Ginger Nuts

½ lb. flour
¼ lb. soft sugar
3 oz. butter or dripping
1 tablespoon powdered ginger
3 tablespoons golden syrup
1 teaspoon baking powder

Put the butter and sugar into a basin and beat them together, then add the golden syrup, flour, ginger and baking powder and mix these ingredients well together. Work into a stiff paste, adding more flour, if necessary. Then form into balls the size of a large marble and flatten them slightly. Place on a buttered tin and bake in a moderate oven for about 20 minutes or until nicely browned.

1326 Ginger Snaps

½ lb. flour
3 oz. soft sugar
3 oz. dripping
about 3 tablespoonfuls golden syrup
1½ teaspoons powdered dry ginger
almonds

Sieve the flour and ginger into a basin, add the sugar, rub in the dripping and mix well together. Add enough golden syrup to make a very stiff paste and knead with the hands until smooth. Flour a rolling pin, roll out the paste and cut into rounds. Place them on a greased baking tin, put one or two split almonds on the top of each and bake in a moderate oven for about 20 minutes or until nicely browned.

1327 Jumbles

½ lb. flour
1 oz. paisley flour
3 oz. soft sugar
2 oz. butter
2 eggs
a little grated lime-rind
milk

Beat the butter and sugar together and add the lime rind, then add the eggs well beaten. Mix the paisley flour with the flour and stir them lightly into the other ingredients. Then add enogh milk to make a stiffish dough. Turn out on a floured board and divide it into small equal sized pieces. Roll each piece out with the hands to the length of a stick of lead pencil and twist them to form the letter "S" or figure "8". Place the jumbles on a greased tin and bake in a moderate oven from 15 to 20 minutes.

1328 Kisses

4 to 5 whites of eggs
1 lb. sugar
flavouring

Beat the whites of eggs as stiffly as possible—so stiff that they will not fall from an inverted bowl. Mix in the sugar gradually and continue to beat until very light and stiff. Flavour with a few drops of rose, vanilla, almond or lemon flavouring, and, if liked, they may be variously tinted. Drop the mixture by small spoonfuls on well buttered paper, leaving a space of about an inch between each. Lay the paper on a baking tin and place them in a very moderate oven until they are crisp. They will take from 40 to 50 minutes to cook.

1329 Lemon Rings

½ lb. flour
¼ lb. soft sugar
¼ lb. butter
2 eggs
1 teaspoon baking powder
½ teaspoon very finely chopped lemon rind
lemon flavouring

Beat the butter and sugar together and add the eggs well beaten. Then mix in the flour, baking powder, lemon rind and flavouring. Roll out the paste to about ¼ of an inch in thickness, cut into it rounds and then with a smaller cutter stamp out the middle of the rounds to form rings. Bake in a moderate oven for about 15 minutes.

1330 Macaroons

½ lb. powdered sugar
¼ lb. ground almonds
3 whites of eggs
a squeeze of lime juice

Sieve the sugar, put it into a basin and mix in the almonds. Add the lime juice and then the white of eggs very gradually; beat the mixture well. It must be just moist enough to drop from a spoon. Drop the mixture in small round heaps on white paper placed on a baking tin, leaving sufficient space between each to allow of a little spreading. Dust over with a little sugar and place a half blanched and split almond on the top of each macaroon. Bake in a very moderate oven from 20 to 30 minutes until crisp and lightly browned. When they are cold, damp the paper at the back of each macaroon and they can be easily detached from the paper. They can also be baked on wafer paper which is allowed to remain on them.

1331 Milk Biscuits

½ lb. flour
1 teaspoon baking powder
2 oz. butter
a pinch of salt
milk

Mix the flour, baking powder and salt together in a basin, rub in the butter and make a well in the centre. Then add enough milk to form a nice paste. Turn it out on floured board and knead well until free from cracks. Then roll out rather thinly and prick all over with a skewer. Cut it in rounds, place on a floured tin and bake in a moderate oven for about 15 minutes, or until the biscuits are light brown and crisp.

1332 Mixed Biscuits

1 lb. flour
½ lb. soft sugar
½ lb. butter
yolks of 6 eggs
1 teaspoon baking powder
flavouring

Put the butter and sugar into a basin and beat them together until of a creamy consistency. Beat the yolks of eggs and add it gradually with the flour until a stiffish paste is formed. Then mix in the baking powder. Turn the paste on to a floured board and knead well with the hand. Divide the paste into four, to one part add currants, to another chopped or ground almonds or cadjunuts, to another coconut, and flavour the remainder with vanilla or lemon. A great variety of biscuits can be turned out in this way. Roll each portion of paste out to ¼ of an inch in thickness, then cut in rounds or fancy shapes, place them on a floured tin, brush them over with milk and bake from 15 to 20 minutes in a moderate oven.

1333 Plain Biscuits

½ lb. flour
1 teaspoon baking powder
¼ lb. soft sugar
yolks of 2 eggs
milk

Mix the flour, baking powder and sugar together, add the yolks of the eggs well beaten and enough milk to form the whole into a paste. Knead well, roll out and cut into biscuits. Place them on a floured tin and bake in a moderate oven until brown and crisp.

1334 Ratafias

½ lb. ground almonds
1 oz. rice-flour
½ lb. soft sugar
2 to 3 whites of eggs
ratafia flavouring

Mix together the sugar, rice-flour, which must be slightly roasted, and the almonds, then add the whites of eggs very gradually, beating well with a few drops of essence of ratafia. The mixture must be just moist enough to drop from a spoon. Put the mixture into a forcing bag and force it out in pieces about the size of a cent on white paper placed on a baking tin, leaving a space between each biscuit. If liked, instead of using a forcing bag the mixture can be shaped with a teaspoon. Bake in a very moderate oven until a light brown colour. When done, damp the paper at the back of each biscuit to help in taking them off.

1335 Rice-Flour Biscuits

½ lb. rice-flour
1 egg
¼ lb. soft sugar
3 oz. butter
vanilla flavouring

Put the flour, which must be slightly roasted, and the sugar into a basin and rub in the butter until free from lumps. Moisten it with the egg well beaten and add a few drops of essence of vanilla. Knead into a smooth paste, form into balls, and flatten them slightly. Place the biscuits on a floured tin and bake in a moderate oven from 25 to 30 minutes.

1336 Shortbread

¼ lb. flour
¼ lb. rice-flour
¼ lb. butter
¼ lb. soft sugar
2 eggs

Mix the two kinds of flour together and rub in the butter. Add the sugar and then the eggs well beaten and work all into a smooth dough. Roll out to about ¼ of an inch in thickness, cut into oblong pieces, pinch them round the edges and prick the centre with a skewer. Place the biscuit on a floured tin and bake slowly in a moderate oven.

1337 Soda Biscuits

½ lb. flour
¼ lb. soft sugar
2 oz. butter
2 eggs
½ teaspoon carbonate of soda

Put the flour into a basin, rub in the butter until free from lumps, and mix in the sugar. Then add the eggs well beaten and mix the ingredients well together. Do not add all the egg unless necessary. Add the soda at the last and quickly roll out the paste to about ¼ of an inch in thickness. Stamp it out in small rounds with a cutter, place the biscuits on a floured tin and bake at once in rather a brisk oven from 15 to 20 minutes.

1338 Wine Wafers

½ lb. dough
½ oz. butter
1 teaspoonful soft sugar
salt

Work the butter into the dough, adding the sugar and salt and a little flour, if the dough is too moist. Roll out very thin, and cut into rounds. Place the biscuits on a floured tin and bake slowly in a moderate oven.

Pastry and Pastry Cakes

THE art of making pastry is one that should be mastered by every woman. It is a simple enough operation in itself, and practice will give the confidence and experience necessary for turning out good pastry. Light handling is the chief point: the lighter the handling, the better the pastry. Some people seem to have a natural gift for turning out light pastry, but with practice and patience and by carefully following the hints given below, others should be able to acquire the art.

Hints on Making Pastry

The flour should be of the best quality and absolutely dry. Pass the flour through a sieve before using it. When Baking Powder is used it should be sieved with the flour, and the pastry baked as quickly as possible, otherwise the effect of the baking powder will be lost. The butter or dripping should be rubbed into the flour with just the tips of the fingers and thumbs, not the palms of the hands. Fresh butter is better than salt. The water should be added gradually but quickly to prevent hard lumps being formed. See that the pastry board and rolling-pin are quite clean and dry. The hands must be very dry and cool and the pastry mixed in as cool a place as possible. Roll the pastry lightly, on the one side only, using even pressure and in one direction—always away from you. Lift the rolling-pin after each roll. Keep the pin and board from stickness by dredging them occasionally with flour, but use flour sparingly.

The Oven

Special attention should be paid to the oven—for the best prepared pastry, if not properly baked, will not turn out a success. A hot oven is required for pastry. The greatest heat should be underneath, so that the pastry may rise to its full height before it begins to brown and harden on the outside. The heat of the oven may be tested by placing a piece of white paper inside it, and if it turns a dark brown in about 3 minutes the heat is right.

To Glaze Pastry

Sweet pastry is usually glazed with slightly beaten white of egg and sugar, or with milk, or cold water and sugar. If a deeper colour is desired, brush the pastry over with beaten egg, using the yolk as well.

Kinds of Pastry

1351 Cornflour Pastry

2 oz. cornflour
1 teaspoonful baking powder
4 oz. flour
2 oz. butter
1 oz. soft sugar
a pinch of salt
1 yolk of egg
a little milk or water

Sieve the flour and baking powder into a basin and mix in the cornflour, sugar and salt. Rub in the butter and mix the whole into a stiff paste with the beaten yolk of egg and a little milk or water. Then roll out as wanted.

1352 Dripping Crust

1 lb. flour
3 oz. dripping
1 teaspoonful baking powder
1 teaspoonful soft sugar
a pinch of salt
3 yolks of eggs
1 white of egg
milk

Make in the same way as Short Crust (Recipe 1353).

1353 Short Crust

1 lb. flour
4 oz. butter
1 dessertspoonful soft sugar
a pinch of salt
2 teaspoons lime juice
cold water

Sieve the flour into a basin and mix in the sugar and salt. Add the lime juice, then rub in the butter and mix the whole into a stiff paste with a sufficient quantity of cold water. Turn out on a floured board and knead lightly with the hands until free from cracks. Then roll out as wanted.

1354 Suet Crust

1 lb. flour
6 oz. suet
1 teaspoonful baking powder
salt, cold water

Sieve the flour and baking powder and mix in the salt. Remove the skin and fibre from the suet and shred it finely with a knife. Dust it over with a little flour (taken from the quantity weighed for the paste), and chop it finely. The finer it is chopped the lighter the pastry will be. Then mix it well with the flour and work it all to a smooth paste adding a sufficient quantity of water. Knead it until free from cracks, and roll out as required.

1355 Flaky Pastry

1 lb. flour
½ lb. butter
a pinch of salt
2 teaspoons lime juice
cold water

Sieve the flour into a basin and add the lime juice and salt. Then rub in lightly with the tips of the fingers one-third of the butter, and add sufficient cold water to form the whole into a smooth paste. Mix with the hand as lightly as possible and turn out on to a floured board. Knead lightly until it is free from cracks and quite smooth. Flour the rolling-pin and roll the paste out into a long narrow strip about ¼ inch in thickness. Divide the remainder of the butter into four equal portions; put one portion on the pastry in small pieces and in even rows, dredge lightly with flour and fold the paste in three. Press the edges lightly with the rolling-pin and roll out the paste again into a long narrow strip. Repeat this process until the remaining portions of butter have thus been used. Then roll it out to the thickness required for use.

1356 Potato Pastry

¼ lb. potatoes | **1 yolk of egg**
¼ lb. flour | **salt**
2 oz. dripping | **milk**

Boil the potatoes and mash them. Sieve the flour and rub in the dripping, then mix with the potatoes and add the salt. Bind together with the yolk of egg and a little milk, if necessary. The paste should not be too moist. Roll out on a floured board and use as required.

1357 Puff Pastry

1 lb. flour | **2 tablespoons lime juice**
1 lb. butter | **cold water**
a pinch of salt

Let the butter lie in a basin of cold water for some time before using it. Then fold it in a clean cloth and squeeze out as much of the water as possible and pat it into a flat square cake. Sieve the flour into a basin, add the salt, make a hollow in the centre, strain the lime juice into it and add water gradually until a stiffish paste is formed. Turn this on to a floured board and knead it well with the hands until it is free from cracks and quite smooth. Then roll out the paste into a square or oblong shape about ¼ inch in thickness. Place the butter in the centre of the paste, fold one half over the butter, then the second half over that, enclosing the butter entirely, and press the edges together with the rolling-pin. Flour the board and rolling-pin, place the paste on the board with the side with no edge to your right hand, and remember to place the paste in this position every time it has to be moved. Then roll out the paste into a long narrow strip being careful that the butter does not break through. Fold it exactly in three, press the edges together, then roll it out again. Fold again and leave the paste as it is in a cool place for about 20 minutes. Repeat this until the paste has been rolled out seven times, put it away after every two rolls. The rolling should be done as evenly as possible, keeping the edges of the paste neat and even and the corners square. After it has made its last roll let it rest for 20 minutes, then roll out to the thickness required.

1358 Sweet Paste for Tarts

1 lb. flour
6 oz. butter
1 tablespoonful soft sugar
a pinch of salt
1 teaspoonful baking powder
4 yolks of eggs
2 whites of eggs
milk

Sieve the flour and baking powder into a basin and mix in the sugar and salt. Add one-third of the butter and rub together with the tips of the fingers and thumbs until as fine as breadcrumbs. Make a well in the centre, add the eggs well beaten and enough milk to make a softish dough. Turn on to a floured board and knead lightly until free from cracks. Then flour the board and roll the paste out into a long narrow strip. Divide the remainder of the butter into four equal portions, put one portion on the paste in small pieces, flour the surface lightly and fold it in three. Roll out the paste again and proceed as before until the three remaining portions of butter have been used. Then roll out the paste to the thickness required.

1359 Case for Vol-au-Vent

1 lb. very light puff pastry
1 beaten egg for glazing

Divide the paste into two equal pieces. Roll out the first to about $\frac{3}{4}$ inch thickness, keeping the top quite level.

With an oval vol-au-vent cutter, measuring about $6\frac{1}{2}$ by $4\frac{1}{2}$ inches, cut out a block of pastry, and place on a baking tin. With the next size smaller cutter (usually about $5\frac{1}{2}$ by $3\frac{3}{4}$ inches) mark off an inner oval very evenly, pressing the cutter down into the paste within a very short distance of the bottom, taking care not to cut right through by uneven pressing.

Roll out the other half of the paste and cut in the same manner, place on the baking tin, and with the smaller cutter cut right through the paste to the bottom of the tin.

Brush over the top of the second oval with beaten egg, and bake all in a hot oven, allowing the pastry to rise fully before it begins to brown.

When cooked, remove from the oven and place on a wire cake tray, then with a sharp, pointed knife slit right round the second piece where it is cut through, and separate the outer from the inner oval, lifting off the top layers of the latter to form the covering for the case. In the same manner lift off the inner section from the first piece, taking care not to damage the outer case. Scoop out the soft paste inside with a fork as quickly as possible, leaving a firm, crisp case. Brush over the outer edge with beaten egg, and place the oval ring of paste on top, to form a high case. If this is done while the pastry is hot the egg will make them stick together. Do not use too much egg or the appearance of the case will be spoilt. The case is then ready for filling up with any mixture desired, and should be heated through just before the hot mixture is piled up. Heat the covering also, and put on top of the filling just before serving.

1360 Meat Puffs

½ lb. cold roast beef
2 oz. ham or bacon
1 Bombay onion
pepper
salt
1 dessertspoon Worcester sauce
a little stock
short crust

To Prepare the Meat—Remove all skin and gristle from the meat and cut it into small dice. Prepare the ham or bacon in the same way and mix it with the meat. Add the onion chopped, season with pepper and salt and moisten with the sauce and a little stock.

To Make the Puffs—Roll out the pastry to a long strip five inches wide and about ⅙ of an inch in thickness and cut it across into oblong-shaped pieces three inches wide. Wet along both sides and one end of these pieces with white of egg and put a spoonful of the meat mixture in the centre of each. Double over first the dry end of the pastry, then the wetted one making one half overlap the other. Press down the edges and mark neatly with the back of a knife. Place the rolls on a floured baking tin, brush over the tops with beaten egg, and bake in a quick oven until the pastry is cooked and nicely browned.

1361 Mutton Rolls

Minced mutton (Recipe 157) **pastry** **beaten egg**

Roll out some pastry thinly, and cut it into squares of 4 or 4½ inches; damp the edges with white of egg, put a spoonful of minced mutton on each square, turn over one side and then the other to overlap it, press down the edges and mark neatly with the back of a knife. Place the rolls on a floured baking tin, brush over the tops with beaten egg, and bake in a moderate oven from 20 to 30 minutes.

1362 Patties

1 chicken*
2½ lb. mutton or beef*
1 lb. pork*
½ lb. ham or bacon*
1½ lb. billings†
½ lb. red onions
1 teaspoonful ground dry chillies
2-inch piece of rampa
¼ stem lemon-grass
a small sprig of curry-leaves
1 dessertspoonful chopped fennel
salt
powdered cinnamon
cloves and pepper
1 dessertspoonful dripping
1½ teacups thick coconut milk
10 hard-boiled eggs
dripping or oil for frying the patties

PASTRY:

3 lb. flour
6 oz. dripping
15 eggs
salt
stock or coconut milk

Remove all the flesh from the chicken and cut it up very finely together with the mutton, pork and ham, or pass through a mincing machine. Slice the billings and onions very finely. Heat the dripping in a saucepan and fry a dessertspoonful of the sliced onions, a small piece each of rampa and lemon-grass and a few curry-leaves. Then add the minced meat with which should be mixed the billings, the remainder of the onions, the fennel, chilli, saffron, rampa, lemon-grass, curry-leaves, and seasonings. Let it simmer gently for about 20 minutes, then add the coconut milk and boil until the gravy is almost absorbed; thicken with a little flour, if necessary. Take the curry off the fire and remember to remove all the leaves before filling the patties.

To Make the Pastry—Sieve the flour and keep aside about ½ lb. for rolling out the pastry. Mix the salt into the rest of the flour, and rub in the dripping lightly with the tips of the fingers. Then make a well in the centre of the flour and put in the eggs (only the yolks well beaten together) and a sufficient quantity of stock or coconut milk to form it into a nice stiff paste. Pour the stock in gradually rather than run the risk of making the paste too moist. Knead up the paste quickly and lightly, and when quite smooth roll it out rather thinly and cut into rounds of 3½ inches diameter. Wet the edges of the rounds with white of egg or cold water, place a little of the curry and a piece of hard-boiled egg in the centre of each, double over and press the edges well together. Fry in hot dripping or good coconut oil and drain well. This quantity of curry and pastry will be sufficient for about 200 patties.

**N.B.* The various meats used for the curry may be slightly boiled and then mixed, and instead of using so many different meats, beef and ham, or mutton alone may be used.

†If billings are not procurable, green tomatoes make a good substitute.

If liked, the patties can be baked instead of being fried.

1363 Chicken Patties

1 chicken
¼ lb. ham
1 tablespoonful grated bread
1 dessertspoonful finely chopped red onions
1 tablespoon Worcester sauce
powdered cinnamon
cloves and pepper
salt
1 egg
1 dessertspoonful dripping
about half a tea cup of stock
pastry

To Make the Mixture—Remove the flesh from the chicken and mince it finely or pass it through the mincing machine together with the ham. Season the meat with pepper, salt, cloves and cinnamon. Heat the dripping in a stewpan and fry the onions, then add the chicken mixture, pour in the stock, and let it simmer slowly for about 15 minutes. Take if off the fire and mix in the egg slightly beaten, the grated bread, and the sauce.

To Make the Patties—Make some pastry according to directions given in the previous recipe, and grease some patty tins. Roll out the pastry rather thinly, and cut out double the number of rounds there are of tins. Line the tins with the pastry, and fill them up with the chicken mixture. Wet round the edges of the pastry lining the tins, lay on the covers, and press the two edges well together. Cut narrow strips of pastry about ¼ inch wide, damp one side of it, and lay the strips round the edges of the tins and press down lightly. Pinch round with finger and thumb, or use a fancy pastry cutter in cutting out the strips. Brush the patties over with beaten egg just before putting into the oven. Bake in a quick oven from 20 to 30 minutes.

1364 Fish Patties

1 lb. boiled fish
¼ lb. Bombay onions
pepper
salt
a pinch of powdered dry chillies
1 dessertspoonful dripping
2 hard-boiled eggs
pastry
dripping or oil for frying the patties

Any good white fish can be used for these patties. Break the fish into flakes or small pieces and be careful to remove bones and any skin. Heat the dripping in a saucepan, put in the onions chopped and allow to cook for a few minutes without browning. Then add the fish and a little fish stock (the water in which the fish was boiled) and the seasonings and stir over the fire for a few minutes longer. Chop the eggs and add to the fish mixture when it has cooled a little.

Roll out the pastry rather thinly and cut into 4-inch squares. Put a little of the fish mixture in the centre of each square, wet the borders of the pastry with white of egg or cold water and fold each corner to the middle, making them meet and overlap slightly in the centre like envelopes. Press the joins well together. Fry in dripping or good coconut oil.

If liked, the patties can be baked instead of being fried. Brush the patties over with beaten egg before baking.

1365 Prawn Patties

2 teacupfuls minced prawns
1½ teacups sliced billings
2 tablespoonfuls sliced red onions
1 teaspoon or a little less of ground dry chillies
a pinch of ground saffron
1-inch piece rampa
¼ stem lemon-grass
a small sprig of curry-leaves
1 teaspoonful chopped fennel
powdered cloves
cinnamon
pepper and salt to taste
1 teaspoonful dripping
¾ teacup thick coconut milk
pastry
dripping or oil for frying

Shell the prawns and remove the heads and tails. Then mince them not too finely. Heat the dripping in a saucepan and fry a dessertspoonful of the sliced onions, a small piece each of the rampa and lemon-grass and a few curry-leaves. Then add the minced prawns, the billings, the remainder of the onions, the fennel, chillies, rampa, lemon-grass, curry leaves and seasoning. Let it simmer gently for about 10 minutes, then add the coconut milk and boil until the gravy is almost absorbed. Take the curry off the fire and remember to remove all the leaves before filling in the patties. Roll the pastry and make and fry the patties as directed in Recipe 1362.

1366 Sardine Patties

a small-sized tin of sardines
2 or 3 tablespoons anchovy sauce (Recipe 502)
a pinch of cayenne
1 teaspoonful chopped parsley
1 teaspoon lime juice
pastry (made as directed in Recipe 310)

Skin and bone the sardines and mince them. Heat the sauce in a saucepan and add to it the parsley, cayenne and lime juice. When thoroughly hot, put in the minced sardines and mix well together. Roll out the pastry rather thinly and cut out rounds with a fluted cutter about 2½ or 3 inches in diameter. Put a spoonful of the sardine mixture in the centre of each round, wet half way round the edges with white of egg or cold water, fold over and press the edges well together. Place the patties on a floured baking tin, brush them over with beaten egg, and bake in a moderate oven until the pastry is cooked and nicely browned.

1367 Chicken and Ham Pies

¼ lb. cooked chicken
¼ lb. cooked ham
1 teacup white sauce
1 dessertspoon Worcester sauce
pepper
salt
a grate of nutmeg
pastry

Weigh the chicken and ham free from bone and cut them in small pieces or chop them finely. Have ready a small teacup of good white sauce of a fairly thick consistency, mix the prepared meat with this and add the seasonings. Make thoroughly hot before using.

To Make the Pies—Grease some patty tins and roll out the pastry to about ⅛ inch in thickness. Cut out double the number of rounds there are of tins. Line the tins with the pastry and fill them up with the chicken and ham mixture. Wet round the edges of the pastry lining the tins, lay on the covers and press the edges well together. Cut out narrow strips of pastry about ¼ inch wide, damp one side of it and lay the strips round the edges of the tins and press down lightly. Pinch round with finger and thumb, or use a fancy pastry cutter in cutting out the strips. Brush the patties over with beaten egg just before putting into the oven. Bake in a quick oven from 20 to 30 minutes.

1368 Ham and Egg Pies

6 oz. cooked ham	**salt**
4 hard-boiled eggs	**mustard**
2 raw eggs	**a little stock**
pepper	**some good pastry**

To Prepare the Filling—Chop the ham and the boiled eggs finely and season with pepper, salt and a little mustard. Add the two raw eggs beaten and enough stock to moisten the mixture.

To Make the Pies—Grease some patty tins and roll out the pastry to about $\frac{1}{4}$ of an inch in thickness and cut out double the number of rounds there are of tins. Line the tins neatly with the pastry and fill them with the ham and egg mixture, piling it rather high in the centre. Then wet round the edges of the pastry lining the tins and press the other rounds on the top. Trim and mark round the edges neatly and brush them over with beaten egg or milk. Place them on a baking tin and bake in a hot oven. They should be nicely browned and the pastry well cooked. Should they become too brown before the pastry is cooked, cover with paper.

Sweet Dishes with Pastry

To Line and Decorate a Tart Dish with Pastry

Any kind of pastry may be used for this. Short Crust or Dripping Crust is perhaps the most suitable but any other kind of pastry may be used, if preferred. The tart can be made in two ways, the filling baked along with the pastry, or the pastry case made and baked and the jam or filling put into it afterwards. Sprinkle a flat pie-dish or tart dish with flour. Roll the pastry to the thickness of $\frac{1}{8}$ inch, line the dish with it and trim round the edges with a knife. Prick a few holes with a fork at the bottom of the pastry to prevent it rising and blistering, and put in the filling. Cut some narrow strips of pastry, twist them and lay them across the tart in a lattice-work pattern. Then wet the edges of the dish with white of egg, cut a band of pastry long enough and wide enough to cover the rim of the dish and lay the band round, joining it neatly. Mark this round with the back of a knife and flute round the edges with a pair of pincers. Brush the pastry over with beaten egg, or water and sugar, and bake in a good oven. If the case is to be baked before the filling is put into it—line the dish in the same way as above, trim round the edges and lay a band of pastry round it. Mark and decorate this prettily and brush over with beaten egg. Prick the pastry lining the bottom of the dish with a fork, line it with greased paper and fill it with raw-rice or put in some crusts of bread in order to keep the shape. Bake in a good oven until the pastry is nicely browned and well cooked. Then remove the rice or bread and the case is ready for the filling.

Roll out the trimmings of pastry and stamp out some leaves or stars or other fancy shapes. These should be baked separatley on a tin and used for decorating the tart.

For tarts with tinned fruit, see Apricot Tart (Recipe 1383).

To Line Patty Pans

Sweet Paste or Puff Pastry is the best to use for this. Roll out the pastry very thinly and stamp it out into rounds with a plain or fluted cutter. The rounds of pastry should be a little larger than the diameter of the tins to allow for shrinkage. Sprinkle the tins with flour and press the pastry well into the shape of the tin. The tins are now ready for the filling.

1381 Almond Tartlets

¼ lb. ground almonds	**3 eggs**
¼ lb. soft sugar	**rose flavouring**
2 oz. butter	**puff pastry**

Line some patty pans with puff pastry. Mix the almonds and sugar together, beat in the butter and add the eggs well beaten. Flavour to taste and fill the prepared tins with the almond mixture. Bake in a brisk oven for about 20 minutes.

1382 Apple Tart

½ lb. apples	**rind of half a lime**
½ oz. butter	**pastry**
3 oz. sugar	

Peel, core and slice the apples very thinly and put them into a stewpan with the butter, sugar, chopped lime rind and very little water. Stew slowly until quite soft and pulpy, stirring frequently with a wooden spoon. Then turn the mixture into a basin and allow to cool. Make an open tart according to the directions given on page 327, but do not bake it. Fill it with the apple mixture and bake in a moderate oven until the pastry is nicely browned and well cooked.

1383 Apricot Tart

tinned apricots	**2 whites of eggs**
sugar	**pastry**

Line and decorate a pie-dish with pastry as directed above and bake it a nice brown. Then fill the case with tinned apricots, which have been drained from their syrup, and sprinkle over with sugar. Beat up the whites of eggs to a very stiff froth, add to them 2 tablespoonfuls of sugar and pile it roughly over the apricots. Dredge with a little sugar and bake in a moderate oven until the meringue is crisp and becomes a golden brown. This may be served hot or cold.

N.B. **Other tinned fruit** may be used in the same way.

1384 Cheese Cakes

¼ lb. cheese
1 oz. butter
1 oz. soft sugar
1 oz. flour
1 oz. sultanas
lemon flavouring
1 egg
flaky pastry

Beat the butter and sugar together, add the yolks of eggs, flour, the cheese very finely grated, and the sultanas. Mix well, then add a few drops of lemon flavouring and, lastly, the white of egg beaten to a stiff froth. Line some patty pans with pastry and fill them up with the cheese mixture. Lay two thin strips of pastry across the top and bake in a moderate oven.

1385 Coconut Cheese Cakes

¼ lb. desiccated or finely ground coconut
½ lb. soft sugar
2 oz. butter
3 yolks of eggs
1 dessertspoon brandy
rose flavouring
nutmeg
pastry

Beat the butter and sugar together, then beat in the yolks of eggs and mix in the coconut, add the brandy and rose flavouring and a grate of nutmeg. Mix well together and pour into patty pans lined with pastry . Bake in a good oven until the pastry is cooked and the mixture sets.

1386 Lavinia Cheese Cakes

2 oz. flour
4 oz. powdered sugar
1 oz. butter
4 eggs
½ teaspoon baking powder
vanilla or almond flavouring
jam
pastry

Beat the butter and 2 oz. of the sugar to a cream and beat in the eggs leaving out the whites of two. Mix in the flour gradually and lastly the baking powder. Line some patty pans with pastry, put a little jam into each, fill up with the mixture and bake in a moderate oven for about 20 minutes. Take them out of the pans and let them cool. Then whip the two remaining whites of egg, to a stiff froth with the 2 oz. of sugar and spread smoothly over the tartlets. Place them in a cool oven just to set the icing.

1387 Picnic Cheese Cakes

1 egg, its weight in cake crumbs and butter
1 tablespoonful soft sugar
vanilla flavouring
candied peel
apricot jam, pastry

Beat the butter and sugar together and add the yolk of egg and the cake crumbs. Mix well, then add a little vanilla flavouring and, lastly, the white of egg beaten to a stiff froth. Line some patty pans with pastry, place a little jam at the bottom of each and fill up with the mixture. Lay a strip of candied peel on the top of each and bake in a brisk oven for about 20 minutes, or until the pastry is cooked and the mixture feels firm to the touch.

1388 Potato Cheese Cakes

½ lb. potatoes
½ lb. sugar
2 oz. currants
3 eggs
lemon flavouring
pastry

Boil the potatoes and mash them finely, then add the butter, sugar, currants, flavouring and the eggs well beaten. Mix all well together. Line some patty pans with pastry, three-quarters fill them with the mixture and bake in a moderate oven until nicely browned.

1389 Rice-flour Cheese Cakes

1 oz. roasted rice-flour
1 oz. soft sugar
1 oz. butter
½ oz. currants
2 eggs
¼ teaspoon baking powder
vanilla flavouring
pastry

Beat the butter to a cream and beat into it the eggs and the sugar. Mix in the flour gradually, then the currants picked and cleaned, and the flavouring, and lastly the baking powder. Line some patty pans with pastry, fill them with the mixture and bake in a moderate oven until the pastry is crisp and the mixture nicely browned.

1390 Rulang Cheese Cakes

¼ lb. rulang
½ lb. soft sugar
¼ lb. pumpkin preserve (Recipe 1121)
10 yolks of eggs
100 cadjunuts
½ wineglass rose-water
¼ teaspoon chopped lime rind
¼ teaspoon powdered cardamoms
pastry

Put the yolks of eggs into a basin, add the sugar and beat well together. Then add the rulang, the cadjunuts finely chopped, the pumpkin preserve, rose-water and spices and mix all well together. Line some patty pans with pastry, fill them with the mixture and lay two strips of pastry across the top. Bake in a hot oven for about 25 minutes.

1391 Chocolate Tartlets

2 oz. grated chocolate
4 oz. cake crumbs
2 oz. sugar
2 oz. butter
½ oz. corn-flour
3 eggs
vanilla flavouring
flaky pastry

Beat the butter and sugar together, then beat in the yolks of eggs, add the chocolate, cake crumbs, cornflour and flavouring and, lastly, the whites of eggs beaten to a stiff froth. Have ready some patty pans lined with pastry and fill them with the chocolate mixture. Bake in a moderate oven. When done dredge with sugar.

1392 Coconut Tart

2 oz. desiccated or finely ground coconut
1 oz. roasted and finely sifted rice-flour
2 oz. sugar
1 oz. butter
2 eggs
vanilla or rose flavouring
cadjunuts
pastry

Beat the butter and sugar together, then add the eggs well beaten, the rice flour and the coconut, flavour to taste and mix well together. Line a pie-dish with any kind of pastry preferred, but do not bake it. Fill up with the coconut mixture, sprinkle the top with sliced cadjunuts and bake in a moderate oven until the pastry is cooked and the mixture lightly browned.

1393 Custard Tartlets

1 pint milk
4 eggs
flavouring
1 tablespoonful sugar
sweet paste or short crust

Put the milk into a saucepan and heat it over the fire. Beat the eggs with the sugar and pour the hot milk on to them, stirring all the time. Flavour with any flavouring liked and stir the custard occasionally until cold. Have ready some patty pans lined with pastry. Fill them up with the custard and bake in a moderate oven until the pastry is cooked and the custard lightly browned.

1394 Fancy Cones

¼ lb. flour
½ lb. sugar
4 eggs
a pinch of salt
vanilla flavouring

Beat the sugar and eggs together for about 5 minutes. Then add the flour, salt and flavouring and mix very smooth. Have ready some flat baking tins well buttered. On these drop the batter in teaspoonfuls, some inches apart, and with the back of the spoon spread each little heap in 2 or 3 inch rounds. Bake in a moderate oven until nicely coloured and while still warm, twist each one into a cone. These may be filled with any nice jam whipped cream or any cheese cake filling.

1395 Fancy Tartlets

¼ lb. sultanas
¼ lb. cadjunuts
½ lb. sugar
¾ teacup water
flavouring
pastry

Wash the sultanas and remove the stalks: skin, and then chop the cadjunuts roughly. Put the sugar and water into a saucepan and stir over the fire until it forms a thick syrup. Add the sultanas and cadjunuts, stir well, take it off the fire and flavour with rose or any other flavouring preferred. Line some patty pans with pastry and put a little of the prepared mixture into each. Lay some narrow strips of pastry in a trellis work pattern across the top. Wet the edges with white of egg, and lay a narrow band of pastry round. Mark round the rim with the back of a knife and flute the edges. Brush over with beaten egg and bake in a brisk oven for about 20 minutes, or until the pastry is lightly browned.

1396 Jam Puffs

sweet paste	**jam**
egg	**sugar**

Roll out the pastry rather thinly and stamp out rounds 4 inches in diameter. Place a little jam in the centre of each, wet round the edges with white of egg and fold the paste over on three sides in the form of a triangle. Flute round the edges with a pair of pincers of a knife, brush them over with beaten egg and dredge with sugar. Place the puffs on a floured tin and bake in a hot oven until the pastry is lightly browned.

1397 Jam Tarts

short crust jam

Roll out the pastry to about ¼ inch in thickness and stamp out an equal number of rounds about 3 inches and 2 inches in diameter. Place the larger rounds on a floured baking tin and brush them over with beaten egg. Then with a smaller cutter stamp out the centres of the smaller rounds and place the rings upon those on the tin. Brush the tops with beaten egg and bake in a brisk oven. When baked fill the centres with any nice jam.

1398 Macaroon Tartlets

¼ lb. ground almonds	**almond flavouring**
½ lb. powdered sugar	**jam**
4 whites of eggs	**puff or flaky pastry**
a squeeze of lime juice	

Sieve the sugar into a basin, add the ground almonds to it, also the lime juice and a few drops of almond flavouring. Add the whites of eggs and beat the mixture well together. Line some patty pans with pastry, put a little jam into each and fill up with the almond mixture. Lay two thin strips of pastry across the top, dredge well with sugar and bake in a moderate oven until the pastry is nicely browned and the mixture firm to the touch.

1399 Mango Tart

mango jam	**4 yolks of eggs**
1 pint milk	**2 whites of eggs**
1 tablespoonful cornflour	**vanilla flavouring**
2 tablespoonfuls sugar	**pastry**

First prepare a custard. Mix the cornflour to a smooth paste with a little of the milk; put the remainder of the milk into a saucepan and heat it over the fire, mix in the cornflour and let it cook from 5 to 10 minutes stirring all the time. Then remove the saucepan from the fire and allow the contents to cool slightly. Beat the sugar and eggs together and add the flavouring. Mix this together with the contents in the saucepan and stir the custard occasionally until cold. Make an open tart according to the directions given on page 327 but do not bake it. Put a thick layer of jam at the bottom of the tart and cover with the custard. Bake in a moderate oven until the pastry is cooked and the custard lightly browned. Sprinkle with sugar and serve the tart either hot or cold.

1400 Mince Meat

½ lb. suet
½ lb. currants
½ lb. sultanas
½ lb. raisins
½ lb. ginger preserve
½ lb. mixed candied peel
½ lb. apples
¼ lb. shelled almonds
1 lb. sugar
2 tablespoonfuls marmalade
1 dessertspoonful mixed spice
1 teacup brandy

First prepare the ingredients. Chop the suet finely, wash, pick and dry the currants, wash and stem the sultanas, stone and chop the raisins, cut the ginger preserve in pieces, shred the peel finely, peel and core the apples and chop them, and blanch and chop the almonds. Put all these ingredients into a basin, add the sugar, marmalade and spices and mix thoroughly with the hand. Then add the brandy and mix again. Pack into jars or pots, cover closely and keep in a cool place for at least a fortnight before using.

1401 Mince Pies

puff pastry **mince meat**

Roll out the pastry to the thickness of ⅛ inch and cut out double the number of rounds there are of tins. Keep the best rounds of pastry for covering, and line the tins with the others. Fill them with mince meat, wet the edges of the pastry lining the tins with white of egg, lay on the covers and press the edges closely together. Ornament the edges to taste, brush them over with slightly beaten white of egg and dredge a coating of finely powdered sugar over them. Bake in a moderately hot oven from 25 to 30 minutes.

1402 Peach Tart

3 tinned peaches
2 tablespoonfuls cake crumbs
soft sugar
a teacup of peach syrup
2 eggs
a few drops of vanilla flavouring
juice of half a lime
pastry

Make a tart according to the directions given on page 327 and bake it before the filling is put in. Meanwhile prepare the filling. Cut the peaches in small pieces. Put the peach syrup into a saucepan, add the lime juice and a little sugar, bring to the boil and simmer for 10 minutes. Take the saucepan off the fire and stir in the yolks of eggs beaten.

Return the saucepan to the fire and stir very carefully until the custard thickens without boiling. Allow the custard to cool. Sprinkle the pastry case with the cake crumbs, then put in the pieces of peach and pour over the custard. Whip the whites of eggs to a stiff froth, add a little sugar and a few drops of vanilla flavouring and pile this rockily on the top of the tart. Dredge with a little more sugar and bake in a fairly cool oven until the meringue hardens and becomes a golden brown. Serve either hot or cold.

1403 Pineapple Tart

pineapple preserve pastry

Line a pie-dish with pastry as directed on page 327 but do not bake it.

Prick the pastry at the bottom of the dish with a fork and fill it with pineapple preserve. Cut some narrow strips of pastry, twist them and lay them across the tart forming a trellis-work. Then cut a band of pastry and lay it round the dish, mark the edges with the back of a knife, brush the pastry over with white of egg, and sugar, and bake in a good oven until the pastry is nicely browned.

1404 Pineapple Tartlets

pineapple preserve pastry

Line some patty pans with pastry, put a little pineapple preserve in the centre of each and wet round the edges of pastry with white of egg. Cut some narrow strips of pastry, twist them, and lay them in a trellis-work pattern over the top. Then cut a band of pastry about $\frac{1}{3}$ of an inch wide, using a fluted cutter, and lay it round the tart. Brush over with white of egg and sugar and bake in a brisk oven for about 20 minutes or until the pastry is lightly browned.

1405 Plantain Tart

sour plantains **whites of eggs**
dates **water**
sugar **pastry**

Make a tart according to directions given on page 327 and bake it before the filling is put in. Peel and cut the plantains in slices; stone and cut the dates in pieces. Arrange the two kinds of fruit in layers in the pastry case, sprinkle them with sugar and pour in just a *very* little water. Then make a meringue with whites of eggs and sugar and spread this on the tart to cover the fruit. Sprinkle with more sugar and place the tart in a very moderate oven until the meringue hardens and is lightly coloured. This may be served hot or cold.

1406 Pumpkin Tart

pumpkin preserve   pastry

Make an open tart as directed on page 327 and bake it before the filling is put in. Then fill the case with pumpkin preserve and decorate the top with a few leaves and stars which have been previously cut out of the trimmings of pastry and baked on a tin separately.

1407 Sweet Patties

jam   egg   pastry   sugar

Any kind of pastry may be used for these. Roll the pastry out thinly and cut it into rounds 4 inches in diameter. Wet half-way round the edges of them with white of egg, place a little jam in the centre of each round, double over and press the edges well together. Flute round the edges with a pair of pincers or a knife, brush them over with beaten egg and dredge well with sugar. Place them on a floured baking tin and bake in a brisk oven from 15 to 20 minutes.

Short Eats—Savouries—Sandwiches

Short Eats

The term "short eats" was originally used to describe the dainty sandwiches, dry cheese or other savoury biscuits, potato chips, and miniature sausages accompanying the drinks at sherry or cocktail parties, which usually began at six o'clock in the evening and lasted for a couple of hours at the most.

The popularity of these savoury morsels was such, however, that very soon their scope was extended, until now the term is so widely used that it includes every known variety of savoury "appetiser", while new kinds are constantly being introduced by inventive hostesses.

The time at which they may be served has also been extended, and short eats may now appear at all afternoon and evening functions, however informal or important these occasions may be. They have to some extent even come to take the place of *hors-d'oeuvres* before luncheon and dinner.

The chief requisite of short eats is that they should appeal to the eye as well as to the palate; but they must also be easy to eat—that is, small enough to be conveyed to the mouth with the fingers or, at the most, a small wooden pick.

The arrangements of short eats for serving may be as individual as the hostess pleases: some like to have each variety set out on its own plate or small dish, while others prefer to use a larger dish or tray with several varieties placed on it in defined lines or groups. Both ways are correct, and it is a matter of personal convenience which is chosen.

It is important to pay attention to details of colour, both in the food itself and in its garnishing. Even the most delicious and palate-intriguing foods can lose much of their appeal through being presented in a careless manner.

It has been the aim in this chapter to show some of the ways in which "left-overs" of meat, fish, vegetables, etc. may be utilized in making palatable and attractive short eats, although some recipes have been included to meet the demand for something more elaborate for use on special occasions.

Informal entertaining requires that simple short eats should be available at very short notice, and many of the recipes given indicate how time may be saved by keeping a small stock of such things as fried bread croutons, biscuits, etc. ready for use when occasion demands; while with the almost universal use of refrigerators in the homes of today, the preparation of these delicacies is still further simplified.

1421 Anchovy Circles

With a one-inch fluted pastry cutter stamp out rounds from quarter-inch thick slices of day-old bread, and from the centre of each cut out an inner round of a little less than half-an-inch diameter. Fry the circles of bread thus formed until crisp and golden brown in a pan of boiling coconut oil. Lift out carefully, and drain very well on kitchen paper.

Curl a thin strip of anchovy fillet all round the top of each circle of fried bread, and with a No. 5 icing tube pipe a decoration of anchovy butter over the fish. Leave in the refrigerator for the butter to harden.

Arrange neatly on a plate or dish, on which has been placed a paper d'oyley, and garnish with small tufts of fresh parsley.

1422 Asparagus Rolls

asparagus
½ pint milk
1 oz. butter
1 oz. flour
yolks of two eggs
pepper
salt
bread cases

Make the bread cases according to directions given in Recipe 1429.

To Make the Filling—Chop some asparagus tips. Heat the butter in a stewpan, stir in the flour, add the milk and stir until it boils. Then put in the asparagus and yolks of eggs, season with pepper and salt, and stir over the fire until the mixture thickens.

Fill the bread cases with the mixture, put on the lids and serve hot.

N.B. The quantities of the ingredients must be regulated according to the amount of asparagus.

1423 Aspic Jelly

2 calves' feet
5 pints cold water
a small sprig of parsley
2 small sticks of celery with some of the leaves
1 large Bombay onion
the white part of 1 leek
3 red onions
1 large carrot
1 dessertspoonful peppercorns
1 lime
2 tablespoonfuls each of malt and tarragon vinegar
the whites and shells of 2 eggs
a few drops of clear chilli vinegar
salt

Wash the feet and blanch them. Divide each into five or six pieces and wash again.

Put into a large stewpan with the cold water, and bring to the boil. Remove the scum carefully. Have ready all the vegetables peeled, washed, and cut into large pieces. Add these, with the parsley, peppercorns, and a heaped teaspoonful salt to the boiling liquid, and reduce the flame to allow the contents to simmer gently for about five hours. Lift out the pieces of calves' feet, and strain the stock into a basin. When cold, place in the refrigerator until the fat has risen to the surface and set into a hard sheet. Remove this very carefully, using metal spoons dipped in boiling water and quickly wiped dry. The clearness of the finished jelly depends on the removal of every particle of fat, and if it cannot all be taken off with the spoons it is advisable to wipe off the rest with a cloth wrung out of hot water. This must be done carefully, without breaking the jellied stock, below, or tiny particles of fat may seep through. The sides of the basin above the jelly must be wiped with a hot wet cloth to remove any splashes of fat which may have congealed there after pouring in.

Put the jellied stock into a perfectly clean saucepan and melt over a moderate flame, then add the strained juice and the very thinly-pared rind of lime, the whites and shells of the eggs, and whisk with a wire egg-whisk until the liquid is quite hot, then add all the vinegars and bring to the boil, whisking constantly. When the liquid boils up almost to the top of the pan stop whisking, reduce the flame, and leave to simmer slowly for about half an hour. Pour into a jelly bag and allow to strain undisturbed into a bowl placed underneath.

If liked, 1 gill of sherry may be added when the vinegar is put in. This improves the flavour.

1424 Beef Puffs I

Prepare the underdone beef in the same way as Beef Canapes (Recipe 9), adding a little horse-radish sauce to the mixture but keeping it fairly dry. Shape into small balls the size of a marble. Roll in beaten egg and then in fine browned breadcrumbs until well coated. Fry in oil, drain, and skewer each with a small wooden pick. Serve on a hot dish. In shaping the balls the hands may be lightly dusted with flour if the mixture seems sticky.

1425 Beef Puffs II

Prepare the beef mixture as directed above, then coat each ball in the manner described for Oyster Fritters I, using the same batter mixture, and making sure that each ball is well coated with it before dropping into the oil. Skewer as before, and serve hot.

1426 Cauliflower Canapes

boiled cauliflower
thick white sauce
grated cheese
seasoning of powdered mustard
white pepper
fried bread croutons

Cut out some of the sprigs of the cauliflower very carefully, to avoid breaking them up, and separate each little "flower" head as neatly as possible with a sharp pointed knife.

Season the white sauce very well with the mustard and pepper, add enough grated cheese to give a good flavour, and re-heat in a double saucepan, stirring well until the cheese dissolves. Leave to cool slightly, then mix in the prepared cauliflower. Cover the pan with a cloth wrung out of hot water, and leave to become cold. With a small teaspoon put a heap of the mixture in the centre of each crouton, cover with grated cheese, and place under a hot grill just long enough to brown the top lightly.

N.B. This method of preparing **Vegetable Savouries** may be adopted with almost any cooked vegetable, but asparagus, leeks, murunga, a mixture of peas with diced carrots and turnips, and cabbage are, perhaps, the most suitable.

1427 Cheese and Asparagus Boats

short crust
asparagus tips
melted butter
grated cheese
butter
cayenne pepper

Line small boat-shaped tins with the pastry, rolled out very thin. Prick the bottom of each in several places with a fork, and put a small piece of greaseproof paper in each with uncooked rice to fill the case. Bake in a quick oven, remove paper and rice, and cool on a wire rack.

Chop asparagus tips into very small pieces, mix with a little melted butter, and almost fill the cases with it. Mix the grated cheese to a soft paste with butter, season with cayenne, and spread over the asparagus. Put into a hot oven to heat through, then brown the top under a grill. Serve very hot.

1428 Cheese Puffs (Bouchees)

4 oz. finely-grated cheese
2 oz. sieved flour
2 eggs
salt and pepper to taste
oil for frying

Choose a rather dry piece of cheese, as it grates better than when quite fresh. Sieve the flour again with the salt and pepper, mix in the cheese and stir in the yolks of the eggs with a wooden spoon until all the ingredients are well mixed.

Have ready a deep pan three-fourths filled with boiling coconut oil or good dripping.

Whisk the whites of the eggs to a very stiff froth and stir into the cheese mixture lightly but thoroughly. As soon as it is well mixed take up small teaspoonfuls at a time and drop into the oil. The mixture will puff out at once, and the puffs should not be allowed to fry too long or they will become tough instead of being light and crisp. When just nicely coloured a golden brown lift out and drain at once on kitchen paper. Serve in a hot dish on a folded napkin.

For convenience, the puff mixture may be made some time before it is required; but once the whisked whites of eggs have been added frying must be begun immediately. They should also be served as soon as possible after being cooked.

Care must be taken to see that the oil is really boiling, otherwise the puffs absorb too much of it and become sodden. These remarks apply to all fried foods, but especially to those of the fritter variety. The best way of testing the oil for the correct heat is to drop in a small piece of bread. If it sizzles and rises to the surface at once, at the same time taking on a delicate golden tinge, then the temperature is about right.

1429 Chicken Rolls

bread cases **chicken mince**

To Make the Bread Cases.—Cut some stale bread into slices about 2 inches thick, and with a pastry cutter stamp them out into rounds about 2¼ inches in diameter, then with a smaller cutter, mark the centre about three fourths of the way through. Brown the rolls in the oven or fry them in dripping until a nice brown colour, drain well and carefully remove the centres. Keep a little lid for each case.

Prepare the same chicken mixture as for chicken patties (Recipe 1363). Fill the bread cases with this mixture, put on the lids, and serve hot.

1430 Cream Cheese Biscuits

small round or square cheese biscuits
cream cheese
horse-radish sauce
grated cheese
strips of gherkin
butter

Mix the cream cheese with just enough butter to make a pliable paste, and add horse-radish sauce to give a sharp flavour.

Spread the mixture on the biscuits, smoothing it over with a knife, dip each one into grated cheese to coat the top, and decorate with a thin strip of gherkin stuck through the centre.

1431 Egg Boats

3 hard-boiled eggs
about 2 rounded teaspoonfuls butter
2 dessertspoonfuls cream cheese
gherkin to garnish
ovals of bread and butter
white pepper
salt

Remove the shells from the eggs very carefully, cut into quarters, and put the yolks through a fine sieve to powder them. Wipe out the yolk-cavities with a damp cloth, and allow the egg cases to chill in a covered dish.

Mix the cheese and butter with the yolks until a very smooth paste is formed, season to taste. Cut the gherkin into long strips, very thin, and cut into angle-shaped pieces to form the "sails". Pipe a small round of the yolk mixture in the centre of each piece of bread, and fix the egg-quarters rounded side down, to look like small boats. Fill in the cavities with the piped mixture in a neat, very small pattern, carrying the decoration up to the two pointed ends of the egg. Press in the gherkin sails, and chill until wanted.

When cream cheese is not available use any soft cheese. Grate very finely, or press thin slices through a fine sieve, then pound to a smooth paste or mash against the sides of a basin with the back of a wooden spoon. If the cheese is not quite smooth, the mixture will stick in the icing tube, the grains of cheese creating a blockage.

1432 Egg Croutons

3 hard-boiled eggs
1 rounded tablespoonful butter
a dash of white pepper
anchovy sauce
12 pieces of bread quarter-inch thick cut with a fluted oval pastry-cutter measuring about $2\frac{1}{4} \times 1\frac{1}{4}$ inches
butter for spreading

Cut the eggs into halves lengthwise, remove the yolks carefully, and cut the whites again into halves—making four long-shaped quarters from each egg.

Pass the yolks through a fine sieve to powder them, then mix in the tablespoonful butter, pepper, and enough anchovy sauce (or essence, as it is sometimes called) to give a rich colour to the mixture. Butter the ovals of bread lightly.

Put the creamed yolk mixture into a forcing bag with a No. 5 icing tube, and pipe enough of it into the hollow of each slice of egg to fill it. Place the slices, hollow side down, on the pieces of bread, and very neatly pipe a line of the mixture all round the cut edges of the eggs, finishing off with a line of the same mixture piped down the centre of the curved top of each slice. This tube makes very tiny "flowers" which may be piped singly, set close together, or the tube may be waved slightly while piping to make a curly line. Both methods are very dainty when finished, and for colour-contrast a very tiny sprig of parsley, a small strip of pickled gherkin, or a thin slice of stuffed olive may be laid in the centre of each egg.

1433 Savoury Eggs

4 hard-boiled eggs
1 oz. butter
anchovy paste
pepper
salt
lettuce

Shell the eggs and cut them in halves crosswise. Remove the yolks and cut a little piece off each half of the white so that it will stand firmly. Put the yolks into a basin with the butter, pepper, salt, and a little anchovy paste and mix well together. Fill the hollow of each half-egg with this mixture, arrange the eggs on freshly washed lettuce leaves and serve.

N.B. This dish may be varied in many ways. Any nice savoury ingredient may be used for the stuffing instead of the anchovy, such as finely chopped ham, tongue or game, grated cheese, boned sardines, etc.

1434 Savoury Egg Croutons

1 gill clear stock, or marmite	**salt and pepper to taste**
2 small eggs and 1 extra yolk	**triangles of fried bread**

Beat the eggs, add the stock, and season with salt and pepper, if necessary. Marmite is rather strongly flavoured, and when this is used care must be taken not to over-season. Strain through a piece of fine muslin, letting this rest on the bottom of the basin and then drawing it up gently so that there are no bubbles of froth in the strained custard, or these will cause "holes" in it when baked. Pour carefully into a greased fireproof custard cup or bowl, and steam very slowly until it feels firm to the touch. The bowl must be covered with greased paper to prevent moisture getting into the custard.

Leave it in the bowl until cool, then turn out very carefully on to a pastry board and cut into thin slices, which must then be cut with a sharp knife into triangles to fit the croutons. Place in position carefully, and garnish with a thin slice of green chilli.

1435 Scotch Eggs

(See Recipe No. 377). For use as Short Eats, cut into quarters when cool. They may, if liked, be masked with a thick cheese sauce.

1436 Savoury Fish Croutons

The remains of any boiled white fish may be used for this. Remove skin and bones, and flake into small pieces. Prepare the tomato sauce as in the above recipe, and while hot turn the fish into it. Pile up on small squares or rounds of fried bread or butter toast, re-heat under the grill for a minute, and serve at once, with the parsley sprinkled over the top.

1437 Liver and Bacon Curls

short lenghts of streaky bacon cut very thin	**salt and pepper**
sheep's liver	**a little made mustard**
flour	**frying fat**

Put the liver into a basin and cover with boiling water. Leave to stand thus for ten minutes, then take out and wipe dry. Cut into short lengths, about 1½ inches and ½ inch thick, and dust very lightly with sieved flour seasoned with pepper and salt. Fry very quickly, in bacon fat if possible, and when sealed on all sides lift out and drain on kitchen paper. Place the lengths of bacon on a dish, and smear over with the mustard, then roll up a piece of liver in each slice of bacon, and fasten securely by winding coarse thread round each roll. Place in a baking tin in which a little bacon fat has been melted, bake in a hot oven until the bacon is crisp, then remove the thread. Skewer each with a wooden pick, and serve hot.

1438 Savoury Potato Rolls

½ lb. boiled potatoes
6 thin rashers of streaky bacon
4 red onions, finely-chopped
1 tablespoonful ghee
1 level teaspoonful minced parsley
1 heaped teaspoonful grated cheese
a little cold milk
2 small green chillies chopped into small pieces after the seeds have been removed
pepper and salt
beaten egg
fine browned crumbs
dripping for frying

Fry the rashers until very crisp then chop up into small pieces. Fry the onions and chillies in the ghee until cooked without being browned.

Mash the potatoes while hot, until free from lumps; mix to a thick, creamy consistency with some of the bacon fat left over from frying, and a little cold milk. Strain the fat, if necessary, and only add enough to give a flavour. Beat in the onions, chillies, and parsley with a fork until the mixture is light but firm, then add the bacon and beat again until well mixed. Shape into small sausage-shaped rolls, dip in egg and breadcrumbs, and fry to a golden brown colour. Drain on white paper, and serve very hot.

1439 Prawn and Olive Canapes

rounds of buttered bread not more than 1¼ inch in diameter
boiled prawns
thick mayonnaise sauce
chopped olives
cayenne pepper to season strongly
slices of stuffed olive

Keep aside as many of the smallest prawns as there are rounds of bread, and chop as many more as will be needed to top the rounds. Cut 1 slice of stuffed olive for each canape, and chop the bits left over into very small pieces—two good slices can be cut from each olive, and the top and bottom ends are sufficient for mixing. Stir the chopped prawns into some mayonnaise sauce, add the chopped olives and cayenne pepper. Pile up on the rounds of bread, and garnish the top of each with a small prawn and slice of olive.

1440 Savoury Prunes

prawns **mango chutney** **beef or mutton dripping**

Wash the prunes well, and soak for at least an hour to soften. Slit with a sharp knife and remove the stones. Fill up with chutney, and tie round with cotton to keep closed while cooking.

Place in a baking tin with enough melted dripping to be used for basting. Bake in a hot oven for about ten minutes, pouring the dripping over several times, and turning the prunes once, during cooking. Lift out, drain on white kitchen paper, and serve very hot. The best dripping to use is that collected after meat has been roasted, because this is well seasoned and improves the flavour considerably.

The prunes must, of course, be well dried after soaking.

1441 Devilled Roe Croutons

soft roes
1 small fried crouton for each person
butter
black pepper
salt
a squeeze of lime juice
mustard powder
a good pinch of cayenne
a little hot mango chutney

Fry the rounds of bread, measuring about 1¼ inches in diameter, in very hot oil, and spread while still hot, with enough of the liquid part of the chutney to cover each piece liberally. Put a sheet of white kitchen paper on the bottom of a baking-tin, place the prepared croutons on it, and keep hot in the oven with the door open.

The roes must be washed meanwhile, well dried, and cut up into small pieces, and all other ingredients should be ready for use. Melt a little butter in a pan, stir in the mustard and mix well, then drop in the roe and shake the pan over a moderate flame until lightly fried. Season highly with black pepper and cayenne, strain off the fat, and add strained lime juice and salt to taste.

Pile up on the croutons, and put a strip of the mango from the chutney on top. Return to the oven, close the door for two minutes, then serve at once.

1442 Sardine Toast, American

1 dozen medium-size sardines
2 level tablespoons thick tomato sauce
1 dessertspoonful grated cheese
1 red onion finely chopped
a small nut of butter
1 dozen finger-lengths of buttered toast or fried bread
a little finely-chopped parsley

Place the sardines on a plate, and pour over them enough hot water to remove the oil. If the plate is slanted over a basin while this is being done the water and oil run off quickly. Lift the fish out carefully and dry on a soft cloth, rubbing off the skin at the same time with a gentle movement to avoid spoiling the shape. Split open with a sharp pointed knife and remove the centre bone, then close together again.

For the sauce, fry the onion in the butter until just browned, turn in the tomato sauce and the cheese, and stir over a low flame for a few minutes. Remove, and leave to cool.

Place a sardine on each piece of toast, mask with the sauce, and heat under a red-hot grill for two or three minutes. Sprinkle each with a little parsley, and serve immediately.

1443 Savoury Rounds

small rounds of white bread
rounds of boiled ham the same size
hard boiled egg
mayonnaise sauce
parsley

Butter the rounds of bread, and cover with the ham. Chop the eggs into very small pieces, mix with mayonnaise to bind, and put a spoonful on top of the ham. Decorate each round with a tiny sprig of parsley.

For added flavour, chopped gherkin, olive, or pearl onions may be mixed in with the egg.

1444 Short-Biscuits

4 oz. sieved flour
4 oz. butter
1 level teaspoonful fine salt
1 mustardspoonful white pepper
a pinch of cayenne or powdered dried chillies, or a good pinch celery salt

Cream the butter in a basin, and when quite soft stir in the flour mixed with the salt and other seasonings used. Mix lightly to a smooth paste. Have ready very small paper cases, or buttered and floured boat-shaped tins or other small fancy tins. Put the mixture into a forcing bag with a fancy tube at the end, and pipe into the cases or tins. Bake in a quick oven for 8 minutes, then reduce the heat and allow to cook under the browning shelf until firm to the touch and very lightly tinged with colour on top: about 15 minutes in all, when very small tins or cases are used.

Lift out on to a wire rack to cool, when the biscuits will be crisp. They are, however, extremely brittle, and must be handled with care to avoid crumbling.

These biscuits are a good foundation for any savoury butter decoration, such as anchovy butter, or cheese and butter cream mixture; or they may be served plain.

Savouries

The savoury has become quite an important course, and is now served both at large and small dinner parties. Many persons do not care for sweets, so it is as well to include a savoury in every menu. Savouries may be served either hot or cold, and they are usually served after the sweets. It takes the place of the old-fashioned cheese course, and the flavour of cheese predominates in many of these dishes.

1461 Angels on Horseback

1 dozen oysters
a few thin slices of bacon
chopped parsley
strips of fried or toasted bread
lime juice
pepper and salt

Beard the oysters and season each one with pepper and lime juice. Then roll them in thin slices of bacon which must be cut in squares large enough to roll round an oyster. Fix the rolls with a tiny wooden skewer, and fry or grill them until the bacon is cooked a nice brown colour. Place one on each strip of fried or toasted bread, garnish with chopped parsley and slices of lime, and serve hot.

1462 Asparagus Cream

1 small tin asparagus tips
½ pint cream
2 scant tablespoonfuls mild grated cheese
white pepper and salt
a good pinch of cayenne pepper
3 leaves of gelatine (about ¼ oz.)
1 tablespoonful water

Drain the liquor from the tin, and dry the tips on a cloth. Cut the gelatine into small strips and rinse in cold water, put into a small saucepan with the cold water, and dissolve over gentle heat. Strain half of the asparagus liquor, add a little salt, and put in about a ½ teaspoonful of the dissolved gelatine. Stir until warm and well mixed then pour into the bottom of a small mould rinsed with iced water, and leave to set. When almost firm decorate with some of the flower-tips, cut off the spears of asparagus, and leave to set very firmly.

Stir the rest of the gelatine into the cream, add the cheese, and season to taste, stirring well until all streaks of gelatine disappear. Add all the remaining flower-tips from the asparagus spears, and small pieces cut from the upper, very tender, parts of the spears. Avoid any stringy bits. Stir very gently until evenly mixed, and let the mixture chill until almost ready to set, then pour into the mould and set firm.

This cream should be strongly seasoned with the two kinds of pepper but salt must be added according to the degree of saltiness in the cheese.

A small or picnic size tin usually contains about 18 spears.

1463 Asparagus Ice

1 tin asparagus tips
1 tin cream
3 tablespoonfuls of mild grated cheese
white pepper and salt to taste
thin wafers of cheese cut with a fancy pastry cutter into half-moon shapes

Drain the liquor from the tin of asparagus, and place each piece on a cloth to dry. With a very sharp knife cut off the flower-tip from each piece, and chill these thoroughly in a covered dish

Chop the rest of the asparagus into very small pieces, discarding any bits at the ends which may be stringy. Whip the cream until fairly stiff with a wire whisk, season with the pepper and salt, stir in the grated cheese and chopped asparagus, and freeze. Serve on flat ice-cream plates, decorating with the chilled flower-tips and two sections of the cheese wafers.

The liquor and any discarded pieces of asparagus may be utilized for seasoning plain cream soup—made with milk, cornflour, and a little cream, if available.

1464 Iced Asparagus with Sauce Vinaigrette

a tin of asparagus

Vinaigrette sauce (Recipe 491)

Ice the asparagus by placing the tin in the refrigerator or on ice. When wanted, take the asparagus out of the tin and arrange on an asparagus dish. Serve the sauce separately.

1465 Asparagus Souffle

1 oz. each butter and flour
1 gill milk
1 tablespoonful grated cheese
pepper and salt
the yolks of 2 large eggs and the whites of 3
1 small tin asparagus tips
a good pinch of powdered dried chillies
butter for greasing souffle mould or dish

Drain the liquor from the asparagus, and dry the spears on a folded cloth. Cut into very short lengths, discarding the coarse ends which are stringy. (These may be used for flavouring a plain cream soup). Melt the butter in a small saucepan, stir in the flour and cook for a few minutes, then add the milk in which the cheese has first been melted. Stir well, while adding, until the mixture is smooth, then stir over a low flame until it begins to leave the sides of the pan. Pass through a wire sieve, pressing down well with the back of a wooden spoon and removing any of the panada which clings underneath. To this add the yolks of the eggs, and beat in well, then add the prepared asparagus which must be quite dry or it will sink to the bottom during cooking. Season liberally with pepper, and salt to taste. Beat up the whites of the eggs to a very stiff froth, and fold them into the mixture as slightly as possible. Add the chilli powder, and turn into a well-buttered souffle dish. Bake in a hot oven until well risen and lightly browned on top. Serve immediately.

1466 Devilled Biscuits

plain biscuits, such as milk, thin captain, water, etc.
butter
cayenne
salt
anchovy or sardine paste

Butter the biscuits, sprinkle them with salt and cayenne, and spread with anchovy or sardine paste. Then toast them in the oven until brown and crisp or, if preferred, fry the biscuits in butter season with pepper and salt and while hot spread with the fish paste. Re-heat in the oven for a few minutes and serve very hot.

1467 Cauliflower and Cheese

cauliflower
white sauce (Recipe 534)
butter
salt
grated cheese
breadcrumbs

Boil the cauliflower (see Recipe 409), drain well and place it on a buttered pie-dish. Pour the sauce over it and sprinkle thickly with cheese and breadcrumbs. Place a few pieces of butter on the top, and brown in a quick oven.

1468 Cheese Ramequins

3 oz. mild grated cheese
1 oz. flour
¼ pint milk
1 egg
white pepper
salt and cayenne to taste
butter

Put the flour in a basin and add the milk very gradually until it is smooth, then beat with a rotary beater until it is full of air bubbles. Beat the egg well and stir in, add the cheese and flavour to taste. Beat up again for a few minutes, and put into well-buttered ramequin dishes. Bake in a hot oven until well risen and nicely browned.

1469 Cheese Souffle

1 oz. butter
3 oz. grated cheese
½ oz. flour
1 gill milk
3 eggs
a pinch of cayenne
pepper
salt

Melt the butter in a small enamelled saucepan, add the flour and mix well together. Pour in the milk and stir quickly until the mixture is very thick and will come away from the sides of the saucepan. Then remove the pan from the fire and add the yolk of the eggs, one at a time, beating each one in until thoroughly blended. Now stir in the cheese and seasoning, and lastly the whites of the eggs beaten to a stiff froth. Pour the mixture into a well-greased souffle dish or pie-dish, not more than half filling it, and bake in a quick oven until well risen, nicely browned and firm to the touch. Serve very hot.

1470 Cheese Straws

3 oz. flour
2 oz. grated cheese
2 oz. butter
1 yolk of egg
about 2 tablespoons cold water
a pinch of cayenne
salt to taste

Rub the butter into the flour and add the cheese and seasonings. Beat the yolk of egg with the water and add sufficient of this to bind the flour, etc. The pastry should be rather stiff. Turn on to a flavoured board and knead till smooth. Then roll it out into a strip about 4 inches wide and one-eighth inch thick. Trim the edges and cut most of the pastry into "straws" about quarter-inch wide. Cut out the remainder of the pastry into 6 or 8 rings. Place all on a greased baking tin and bake in rather a quick oven for about 10 minutes or until very lightly browned. Watch them carefully as they burn very easily. When ready, place 5 or 6 straws through each ring and arrange them on a dish. Serve either hot or cold.

1471 Cucumber Savoury

1 cucumber
1½ oz. grated cheese
1 oz. powdered breadcrumbs
chopped fennel or parsley
pepper and salt
1 egg
butter
cheese sauce

Choose a straight thick cucumber. Peel it, cut it in two lengthwise and scoop out the seeds. Sprinkle the inside with salt and turn it cut side down to drain. Meanwhile prepare the stuffing. Mix the cheese and breadcrumbs together, add a little chopped fennel or parsley, season with pepper and salt and moisten with the egg. Put the stuffing into the cucumber, place the halves together and bind it round with tape. Place the cucumber, on a baking dish, put a few pieces of butter on the top and bake for about half an hour, basting occasionally with the butter. When ready, lift the cucumber on to a dish and remove the tape. Serve hot with cheese sauce (Recipe 509) poured over it.

1472 Egg and Cheese Savoury

to every hard-boiled egg allow
1 oz. grated cheese
1 teaspoonful fine white breadcrumbs
pepper and salt to taste
a pinch of pounded dried chilli sieved
1 teaspoonful thick cream
a small nut of butter

For the COVERING:
browned breadcrumbs
a little more butter
1 tablespoonful each of cream and milk—for each egg

Cut the eggs in halves lengthwise, remove yolks and pass through a sieve. Mix all the first lot of ingredients together with the yolks, and fill the cavities of the eggs with the mixture, spreading it to the edge of each egg as thickly as the mixture will allow.

Butter a glass baking dish, sprinkle with a layer of the browned crumbs, and lay the eggs on it, curved side uppermost.

Pour the cream and milk over dust the top with a little more of the browned crumbs, and put a small piece of butter on top of each egg. Bake until heated through, and serve with strips of Melba toast.

1473 Herring Roes on Toast

tinned herring roes **anchovy paste** **hot buttered toast**

Spread some fingers of hot buttered toast with anchovy paste, lay the roe on them and place in the oven for a few minutes.

1474 Macaroni and Cheese

¼ lb. macaroni
2 oz. grated cheese
1 oz. butter
a litle made mustard
pepper and salt
breadcrumbs

Break the macaroni into short lengths and put it into a saucepan of rapidly boiling water slightly salted. Cook quickly with the lid off the pan and stir now and again to prevent the macaroni sticking to the pan. Boil until tender, then drain well. Melt the butter in a stewpan, add the macaroni, two-thirds of the cheese and the mustard, and season to taste with pepper and salt. Stir over the fire until thoroughly mixed. Then pour the mixture into a greased pie-dish, sprinkle the surface with breadcrumbs and the remainder of the cheese, place a few small pieces of butter on the top, and bake in hot oven until lightly browned.

1475 Potted Meat Toast

potted meat
butter
parsley
mustard
salt
grated cheese
hot toast

Take any nice potted meat and mix it with an equal quantity or a little less of butter, add a little mustard and salt and mix well. Then spread this mixture rather thickly on slices of hot toast, sprinkle the top with grated cheese and place under the gas grill until thoroughly hot. Garnish with parsley and serve immediately.

1476 Fried Sardines

sardines
egg and breadcrumbs
hot buttered toast
lime
parsley

Choose large sardines. Take them out of the tin and drain off as much of the oil as possible, then dip them in beaten egg, roll in very finely powdered breadcrumbs and fry a nice golden brown colour in boiling fat. Have ready some strips of hot buttered toast, upon each of which place a sardine, and garnish with thin slices of lime and small sprigs of parsley.

1477 Stuffed Tomatoes

1 lb. medium size tomatoes
2 oz. minced chicken and ham or tongue
1 tablespoonful chopped red onions
1 tablespoonful grated bread
1 dessertspoon Worcester sauce
1 teaspoonful chopped parsley or fennel
dripping
pepper and salt

The tomatoes should be round and as nearly of one size as possible. Wipe the tomatoes, remove the stalk, and cut a round piece neatly out of the top of each. With an egg-spoon scoop out a little of the pulp taking care not to spoil the shape of the fruit Take half of the pulp and mix with it the minced meat, grated bread, two thirds of the onions and the parsley, and season to taste with pepper and salt. Melt a little dripping in a saucepan put in the remainder of the onions, and when browned, put in the mixed ingredients and let it cook for a few minutes. Fill the tomatoes with this mixture and replace the tops. Arrange on a buttered pie-dish, put a small piece of dripping on each tomato, and bake for about 20 minutes.

1478 Tomato Toast

1 gill tomato puree
½ lb. grated cheese
2 tablespoons powdered bread-crumbs
1 teaspoon made mustard
a pinch of cayenne or finely powdered dry chillies
hot buttered toast

Make the tomato puree by rubbing some fresh or tinned tomatoes through a fine sieve. Add the other ingredients to the tomato puree and stir over the fire until hot but do not allow the mixture to boil. Have ready some squares of hot buttered toast, pour the tomato and cheese mixture over them and serve very hot.

1479 Welsh Rarebit

¼ lb. grated cheese
2 tablespoons milk
1 tablespoonful made mustard
1 dessertspoonful butter
yolks of 2 eggs
pepper
buttered toast

Put the cheese, milk, butter, mustard and pepper into a saucepan and stir over the fire, until the cheese is melted. Then add the eggs well beaten, and continue to stir until the egg begins to set. Pour the mixture on squares of hot buttered toast and serve at once.

Sandwiches

BREAD a day old is usually used for sandwiches, but fresh bread, though difficult to cut, make nicer sandwiches. Specially made sandwich loaves can be got from the baker. Slice the bread thinly and evenly and trim off all crust. Spread the slices with butter, place the filling between, and cut into triangles, small squares or finger lengths.

When ready, pile the sandwiches high on a plate covered with a pretty d'oyley or lace-edged paper. When different kinds of sandwiches are served at receptions they often have tiny flags or labels stuck on them denoting their variety.

Should the sandwiches not be required for some hours after they are made, put them into a plate, cover with another, taking care not to crush the sandwiches, and wrap in a damp towel.

1491 Anchovy Sandwiches

anchovy paste
bread and butter

Spread a layer of anchovy paste between thin slices of bread and butter, press lightly together, trim and cut into shape.

N.B. Milk biscuits may be used instead of bread and butter.

1492 Asparagus Sandwiches

asparagus tips **bread and butter**

Cut the asparagus tips in 2-inch lengths and split them in two or use them whole. Place each piece on a thin slice of well-buttered bread and then roll up.

N.B. If liked sprinkle a little grated cheese over the asparagus.

1493 Bacon Sandwiches

Make in the same way as Ham Sandwiches (Recipe 1504).

1494 Beef Sandwiches

cold roast beef **made mustard**
bread **butter**

Spread some slices of bread with butter, mixing the butter first with a little made mustard. Lay thin slices of roast beef between each two slices of bread, press well together, trim, and cut into neat sandwiches.

N.B. Cold **mutton, chicken, corned beef**, etc. can be made into sandwiches in the same way.

1495 Beetroot Sandwiches

boiled beetroot **made mustard**
grated cheese **pepper and salt**
butter **brown or white bread**

Spread some slices of brown or white bread with butter, mixing the butter first with a little made mustard. On half the number of slices put a layer of thinly sliced beetroot and sprinkle over with grated cheese, pepper and salt. Cover with the remaining slices of bread and press well together. Then trim and cut in shape.

1496 Cheese Sandwiches

3 tablespoonfuls grated cheese **1 teaspoonful made mustard**
1 tablespoonful butter **bread and butter**

Mix the cheese, butter, and mustard together, and spread the mixture between slices of bread and butter. Press lightly together, trim and cut into fingers.

N.B. Any plain biscuit may be used instead of bread and butter. And instead of grated cheese, slices of cheese may be used.

1497 Cheese and Chilli Sandwiches

grated cheese **green chillies (capsicum or curry chillies)**
bread and butter

Spread some slices of bread with butter, sprinkle grated cheese and a little chopped green chilli over half of them, cover with the remainder of the bread, press together, trim and cut into shape.

1498 Cheese and Egg Sandwiches

2 tablespoonfuls grated cheese
1 hard boiled egg
1 tablespoonful butter
pepper and salt
made mustard
bread

Chop the hard-boiled egg, mix it with the cheese and butter and season with pepper, salt and mustard. Half a teaspoon of sugar may be added, if liked. Spread a thickish layer of this mixture between two thin slices of bread. Press together, trim and cut into triangles.

1499 Chicken and Ham Sandwiches

roast chicken
boiled ham
made mustard
bread and butter

Cut some cold chicken and cold ham into very thin slices. Spread thin slices of bread with butter, mixing the butter first with a little made mustard. Place a slice of chicken and a slice of ham between each two slices of bread, press well together, trim and cut in shapes.

1500 Cucumber Sandwiches

cucumber
bread and butter
made mustard
pepper

Slice the cucumber thinly, and put the slices into salt water, let them remain a few minutes, then drain well and season with pepper and salt.

Lay the sliced cucumber between slices of bread and butter that have been lightly spread with mustard, press together, trim, and cut into neat shapes.

1501 Egg Sandwiches

2 eggs
1 oz. butter
pepper and salt
bread and butter

Break the eggs into a basin, beat them together and season with pepper and salt. Melt the butter in a saucepan, add the beaten egg and stir over the fire until the eggs just begin to set and the mixture is of a thick creamy consistency. Turn out on a plate and allow to cool. Spread a good layer of this between two slices of bread and butter, trim neatly and cut in shape.

N.B. A slice of cucumber or tomato placed between is an improvement to these sandwiches.

1502 Egg and Lettuce Sandwiches

2 hard-boiled eggs
bread and butter
lettuce
pepper and salt

Shell the eggs, slice them thinly and season with pepper and salt. Take the inside of a lettuce, wash it and dry lightly in a towel, and cut it in fine shreds. Prepare the slices of bread and butter, place the egg on half the number of slices, put a little of the shredded lettuce on the top, and cover with the remainder of the bread. Press together, trim and cut into shape.

N.B. Watercress may be used instead of lettuce.

1503 Foie Gras Sandwiches

Puree de Foie gras can be bought in tins or jars. Spread the paste between thin slices of bread and butter, press lightly together and cut into neat little sandwiches.

N.B. If liked, milk biscuits may be used instead of bread and butter.

1504 Ham Sandwiches

cooked ham | **1 teaspoonful made mustard**
bread | **1 tablespoonful butter**

Mix the butter and mustard together, and spread thin slices of bread with this mixture. Lay thin slices of ham between each two slices of bread, press well together and cut into triangles.

1505 Harlequin Sandwiches

bread and butter | **different fillings**

Spread the slices of bread with butter and then put together in 5 or 6 layers spreading each with a different filling, such as cream cheese, chopped beetroot (boiled), shredded lettuce, chopped hard-boiled egg, salmon paste, sliced cucumber, etc. Press well together and wrap in a damp cloth, and when ready to serve cut in slices.

1506 Lettuce Sandwiches

yolks of 3 hard-boiled eggs | **1 dessertspoonful butter**
chilli vinegar | **crisp lettuce**
salt | **bread**

Mash the yolks of eggs, season with salt and a little chilli vinegar and mix in the butter. Mix to a paste and spread on thin slices of bread. Place a crisp, fresh lettuce leaf between two slices of prepared bread, press together and cut into shape with a sharp knife.

1507 Lettuce and Corned Beef Sandwiches

cabbage lettuce | **bread and butter**
corned beef | **mayonnaise**
made mustard | **salt and pepper**

Wash the lettuce well in salt water, shake the leaves dry, and toss in mayonnaise dressing. Have the corned beef chilled and sliced, very thin. Season each slice of corned beef with pepper, salt, and a little mustard. Place a lettuce leaf on a slice of bread, cover with a slice of corned beef, then top with another slice of buttered bread. It is necessary to use the large sandwich loaves for these sandwiches.

1508 Mutton Sandwiches

cold roast mutton	**made mustard**
butter	**bread**

Spread some slices of bread with butter, mixing the butter first with a little made mustard. Lay thin slices of roast mutton between each two slices of bread, press well together and cut into neat sandwiches.

1509 Potted Meat Sandwiches

Potted meats which are sold in tins and jars will be found very convenient for making sandwiches. Spread the paste thinly between slices of buttered bread, press lightly together and cut into any fancy shape.

N.B. A little butter and mustard mixed with the paste is an improvement.

1510 Prawn Sandwiches

3 tablespoonfuls chopped prawns	**pickled gherkins**
Mayonnaise sauce	**pepper and salt**
anchovy essence	**bread and butter**

Take some boiled prawns, chop them or cut in small pieces. Put them into a basin and moisten with Mayonnaise sauce. Season with pepper and salt and add a few drops of anchovy essence. Butter some thin slices of bread, spread half of them with the prawn mixture, sprinkle over with a little chopped gherkin and cover with the remainder of the bread. Press together, trim and cut into shape.

1511 Prawn and Egg Sandwiches

a few boiled prawns	**a pinch of powdered dry chillies**
2 hard-boiled eggs	**a squeeze of lime juice**
1 oz. butter	**bread and butter**

Chop the prawns and add the eggs also chopped. Season to taste, add the butter and mix well together. Spread this paste between slices of bread and butter, press together, and cut into triangular shapes.

1512 Salmon Sandwiches

2 tablespoonfuls salmon	**lettuce**
1 dessertspoonful butter	**bread and butter**
seasonings	

Free the salmon from any skin and bone, put it into a small basin and break it up with a fork. Season to taste, add the butter and mix well. Place this paste on thin slices of bread and butter, place a fresh, crisp lettuce leaf between two slices of prepared bread, press together, trim and cut into fingers.

1513 Sardine Sandwiches I

3 tablespoonfuls boned sardines	**pepper**
1 dessertspoonful butter	**bread and butter**

Remove all skin and bone from the sardines and mix into a paste with the butter, and season with pepper. Spread the paste between slices of buttered bread, press together, and cut into neat sandwiches.

1514 Sardine Sandwiches II

sardines	**powdered dry chillies**
butter	**lime juice or vinegar**
mustard	**bread and butter**
salt	

Bone and skin the sardines and mix them to a paste with a little butter, and mustard, salt, a pinch of powdered dry chillies and a squeeze of lime or a little vinegar. Spread this paste between thin slices of bread and butter, trim neatly and cut in shape.

N.B. A thin slice of cucumber may be placed between, if liked.

1515 Sardine and Egg Sandwiches

6 sardines	**salt**
1 hard-boiled egg	**pepper**
1 tablespoon butter	**brown bread and butter**

Skin and bone the sardines and mix to a paste with the butter. Add the yolk of egg and season to taste with salt and pepper. Butter some slices of brown bread, spread half of them with the sardine mixture, sprinkle with finely chopped white of egg and cover with the remainder of the bread. Press together, trim and cut into shape.

1516 Tomato Sandwiches

1 or 2 tomatoes	**a pinch of powdered dry chillies**
1 teaspoon vinegar	**pepper and salt**
2 teaspoons salad oil	**bread and butter**

Choose nice, ripe tomatoes. Put them into a basin, pour boiling water over them and let them remain for a few minutes. Then lift them out and remove the skins. Put the tomatoes into a bowl, add the vinegar, salad oil, powdered chillies, pepper and salt, and mash all up together. Spread this paste between thin slices of bread and butter, press lightly and cut into fingers.

Ices

ICES have become so popular in recent years that no dinner or supper is considered complete without a frozen sweet. In hot weather especially they are very acceptable at afternoon "At Homes" and other receptions.

The simpler forms of ices, such as those given in the following recipes, are neither expensive nor difficult to make.

Cream Ices are followed by Water Ices.

The Freezing Outfit

There are a number of excellent ice machines on the market and they are not so very expensive. The freezing machine consists of a can in which the mixture to be frozen is placed, and this is contained in a wooden pail in which the freezing mixture (ice and coarse salt) is packed. The can is provided with a beater which, as the machine is turned, scrapes the frozen cream from the sides of the can and ensures, even freezing. Instructions for the working of the machine are given with each machine.

The Care of a Freezer—The freezer must always be kept clean. Once it is used all parts must be thoroughly washed and well dried before being stored away, otherwise it will get mouldy and rusty. Oil the machine from time to time, but use oil sparingly.

Directions for Freezing

First prepare the mixture to be frozen, as it is important that this should be cold or it will take a longer time to freeze and ice will be unnecessarily wasted. The ice should be crushed or broken into small pieces and mixed with coarse salt in the proportion of three parts ice to one of salt. Fix the can into the pail, pour in the mixture to be frozen (it should not be more than three-fourths full), adjust the cover and crank, and pack the mixture of ice and salt in the space between can and tub until within an inch of the top of the can. When packed and ready allow it to stand for about 5 minutes until the ice begins to melt and the mixture becomes chilled. Then begin by turning the crank slowly for the first 5 minutes, and gradually turning it faster but evenly until the mixture is of the stiffness wanted. As the freezing proceeds it will be found more difficult to turn the crank. The time required for freezing will depend on the make of the machine and the kind of mixture frozen. A little experience will soon teach you when the mixture is sufficiently frozen, and it is a matter of individual taste how hard the ices should be. Be very careful when opening and shutting the can so that none of the salt gets into it, for one grain will entirely spoil the mixture.

All ice creams should be prepared some time before they are required, for it takes time for the flavour to mature, as it were. When ready, wipe the top of the can to prevent salt water getting into it when opened, remove the beater, scrape off the cream from the sides of the can with a wooden spoon and press it down in the can to make it compact. Put on the lid, and plug the opening on the top of the cover with a cork. Re-pack the pail with ice and salt and cover with a piece of carpet or old blanket. If the cream is to be served within an hour, no more ice will be necessary, but if it is to be kept longer, the ice and salt will have to be replenished according to the length of time it is to be kept. It will not be necessary to drain off the water that accumulates in the pail as it will flow through the overflow hole which is on the side of the pail. See that this hole is always kept open.

Moulded Ice Cream

For a moulded ice pudding the mixture is prepared and frozen in the same way as for the ordinary ice cream, but it should not be frozen too hard. Take an ice pudding mould, rinse it out with cold water and fill the mould with the frozen mixture, heaping it a little over the brim. Cover the top with a sheet of buttered paper, butter side up, and put on the lid. Bind the seam with a strip of cloth dipped in hot suet—this will harden at once and make the mould perfectly water tight and prevent the salt and ice from leaking into it. Pack the mould in ice and salt, covering it completely, and cover the whole with a piece of carpet or blanket. Leave it from one to three hours according to the size of the pudding. The cream will keep hard for several hours if the ice and salt is replenished from time to time. When ready to serve, wash the mould with cold water, wipe it perfectly dry and then remove the lid and paper. Invert the mould on a dish and let the pudding slip out. If it doesn't turn out immediately, let it stand for a minute or two when the warmth of the air will melt the sides sufficiently for it to slide out on the dish.

N.B. If you have no ice pudding mould, the freezing can may be used.

Cream Ices

The word "cream" is used as a distinction from "water". Many so-called cream ices do not contain any cream at all, custard or milk being used in place of cream.

Ices require more sugar and stronger flavouring than other sweets.

1531 Almond Ice Cream

1 pint custard — **almond flavouring**
2 oz. almonds — **green colouring**

Make the custard according to either of the recipes given for cream ices. Flavour with almond flavouring and colour a pale green. Blanch and pound the almonds to a paste and add to the custard. Mix well and freeze.

1532 Apricot Ice Cream

1½ pints custard — **1 tablespoon lime juice**
1 lb. tinned apricots — **a few drops carmine**

Mash the apricots and rub through a fine sieve with the back of a wooden spoon. Then add some of the syrup from the tin and rub as much as possible through the sieve. Add the custard to the fruit pulp and strain in the lime juice. If necessary, brighten the colour by adding a few drops of carmine. Freeze as directed.

1533 Chocolate Ice Cream

1½ pints custard — **sugar to taste**
¼ lb. chocolate — **vanilla flavouring**
3 tablespoons water

Grate the chocolate and dissolve to a smooth paste with the water. Then stir it into the custard, sweeten to taste, and flavour with vanilla. Freeze in the usual way.

1534 Coffee Ice Cream

1½ pints custard — **sugar**
¾ pint strong coffee — **vanilla flavouring**

Mix the custard and coffee together, sweeten to taste, add the flavouring and freeze.

1535 Custard for Cream Ices I

1 pint milk — **4 yolks of eggs**
¼ lb. sugar — **2 whites of eggs**
flavouring

Beat the yolks of eggs and mix in the sugar. Bring the milk nearly to boiling point, take it off the fire and add to it the egg mixture stirring all the time. Return the saucepan to the fire and stir carefully until the mixture thickens but do not let it boil or the egg will curdle. When cold, flavour to taste and just before freezing stir in the whites of eggs beaten to a stiff froth. This custard forms the basis of many cream ices. You can make this plainer or richer by using less or more eggs. The cream can be named after the flavouring used.

1536 Custard for Cream Ices II

1 pint milk
1 dessertspoonful cornflour
¼ lb. sugar
2 eggs
flavouring

Mix the cornflour smoothly with a little of the milk. Put the remainder of the milk into a saucepan, add the sugar and beat it over the fire. Stir in the cornflour and cook from 5 to 10 minutes, stirring all the time. Then remove the saucepan from the fire and allow the contents to cool slightly. Beat the eggs and add it to the sauce; return the saucepan to the fire and cook again until the egg thickens. When cold, flavour to taste.

1537 Frozen Fruit Pudding

1½ pints custard
vanilla flavouring
½ lb. preserved fruit
2 tablespoons sherry or brandy

Make the custard according to Recipe 1535 or Recipe 1536 and flavour with vanilla. Pour the custard into the freezing pot and half freeze it, then add the preserved fruit such as cherries, apricots, etc., cut into small pieces, and the sherry or brandy. Freeze again until sufficiently stiff. Then remove the beater, pack down, and let it stand for about 2 hours to ripen. See directions at the beginning of the chapter.

1538 Ginger Ice Cream

½ pint custard
½ pint cream
3 oz. preserved ginger
½ teacup ginger syrup

Make in the same way as Vanilla Ice Cream (Recipe 1548) adding the ginger chopped fine and the syrup to the custard.

1539 Nougat Pudding

1½ pints custard
¼ lb. almonds
¼ lb. sugar
a squeeze of lime juice
1 tablespoon sherry or brandy

Blanch and chop the almonds coarsely and dry them in a cool oven until a pale brown colour. Put the sugar into a saucepan, add the lime juice and stir over the fire until it acquires a pale brown colour. Then add the prepared almonds, mix well, and pour the mixture into a flat buttered dish. When cold and hard, pound it finely and add to the custard. Stir in the sherry or brandy and freeze. Then mould as directed at beginning of chapter.

1540 Orange Ice Cream

1½ pints custard
rind of 2 oranges
juice of 3 oranges
3 oz. soft sugar
yellow colouring
carmine

Wipe two of the oranges and grate the rind off them very lightly and rub it into the sugar. Strain the orange juice and dissolve the flavoured sugar in it. Then make the custard according to directions given in Recipe 1535, let it cool, add the orange juice and a few drops of yellow colouring and carmine to produce an orange colour and freeze as directed.

1541 Papaw Ice Cream

1 pint thick custard
1 medium-sized ripe papaw
6 cubes crystallized ginger
strips of ginger for garnishing

Make the custard a little sweeter than usual and allow to cool. Cut the papaw into sections, and remove the seeds and inner skin. Pass pulp through a coarse sieve, and add the cubes of ginger chopped into small pieces. Stir into the custard and freeze. Decorate each serving with strips of the ginger.

1542 Peach Ice Cream

1 lb. tinned peaches
1½ pints custard
sugar to taste

Mash the peaches and rub through a sieve adding some of the syrup from the tin. Add the custard to the fruit pulp, sweeten to taste and freeze in the usual way.

1543 Peach Melba

tinned peaches
vanilla ice cream
raspberry syrup

Take the peaches out of the tin carefully, drain well and place them in the refrigerator or on ice until required. Then take some pretty sundae glasses and put a good spoonful of vanilla ice cream into each, place a half peach on the top, pour a little raspberry syrup over and serve very cold.

N.B. Raspberry or Strawberry jam (sieved) could be used instead of syrup.

1544 Raspberry Ice Cream

1½ pints custard
1 lb. raspberry jam
1 tablespoon lime juice
a few drops of carmine

Make the custard according to Recipe 1535 or Recipe 1536. Mix the custard and jam together, add the lime juice and a few drops of carmine and freeze in the usual way.

1545 Ratafia Cream Ice

½ pint thick custard
½ pint thin cream
¼ lb. ratafia biscuits
2 tablespoonfuls castor sugar
1 scant tablespoonful Noyeau or a few drops essence of almonds

Crush the biscuits until they resemble coarse breadcrumbs. Whisk the cream with the sugar until dissolved and add the cold custard. Flavour. Turn into an ice tray and freeze until firm but not hard, stirring occasionally meanwhile. Add the crushed biscuits and stir well to mix, then finish freezing. If liked, serve ratafia biscuits with the ice.

If a refrigerator is not available the mixture may be frozen in an ice cream freezer, and when moderately stiff the biscuits should be put in, and mixed in with the blade of a knife. Freeze again until firm.

1546 Rose Ice Cream

2 pints milk **rose flavouring**
½ lb. sugar **carmine**

Dissolve the sugar in the milk, add the flavouring and a few drops of carmine and freeze as directed.

N.B. Almond or Vanilla Ice Cream may be made according to this recipe by changing the flavouring and colouring.

1547 Sundaes

Sundaes, broadly speaking, consist of vanilla ice cream served in a glass with some fruit syrup poured over. But they can be varied. Either tinned or fresh fruit can be added and also whipped cream. For decoration chopped nuts and crystallized fruit are generally used.

1548 Vanilla Ice Cream

½ pint custard **sugar**
½ pint cream **vanilla flavouring**

Make the custard according to directions given in Recipe 1535 flavouring with vanilla, and sweeten to taste. Whip the cream, add it to the custard and freeze in the usual way.

N.B. A plainer ice may be made by using only custard instead of custard and cream.

Water Ices

The foundation of most water ices is a syrup of sugar and water to which is added fruit juice, jam, or fruit pulp made from fresh fruit or tinned fruit. If liked, the sugar can simply be dissolved in the fruit juice or water, but it is better boiled into a syrup.

1561 Aerated Water Ice

1 bottle lemonade **1 bottle kola** **3 tablespoonfuls sugar**

Add the sugar to the lemonade and kola, mix well, and freeze in the usual way.

1562 Apricot Water Ice

1 lb. tinned apricots **essence of almonds**
1½ pints syrup for ices **carmine**
1 tablespoon lime juice

Rub the apricots through a fine sieve adding some of the syrup from the tin. Add this fruit pulp to the syrup, make according to directions given in Recipe 1570. Strain in the lime juice and add the flavouring and enough carmine to make it a pretty pink colour. Freeze as directed.

1563 Mixed Fruit Ice

1 pint orange juice
rind of 2 oranges
1 pint syrup for ices
2 whites of eggs
½ lb. mixed fruit
sugar
1 glass sherry or liqueur

Take any kind of fruit in season such as pineapples, mangoes, plantains, and papaws, and cut them in dice. Sprinkle the fruits with sugar, pour the sherry or liqueur over and let it stand for half an hour. Make the Orange Water Ice according to directions given in Recipe 1566 and when it is partly frozen add the whites of eggs beaten to a stiff froth, and the prepared fruit. Then freeze again until sufficiently stiff.

1564 Granadilla Ice

1 granadilla
1 lb. sugar
1 wineglass brandy or port wine
a very small pinch of salt

Take a ripe granadilla, cut it in two lengthwise and scoop out all the juice and seeds into a bowl. Then pull out the tough skin in the fruit next to the seeds and scrape out the pulp from the fruit with a spoon. Mix the pulp with the juice and seeds, add the sugar, brandy and salt and sufficient water to make up 3 pints. Mix well and freeze in the usual way.

1565 Guava Water Ice

1 lb. China guavas
1 pint water
2 oz. sugar
1 dessertspoon lime juice
syrup for ices

Cut the tops and bottoms off the guavas, put them into a stewpan with the water and simmer gently until the fruit is boiled and the water reduced by half. Mash the fruit well in the liquid, then rub through a fine sieve, stir in the sugar and add the lime juice. To ½ pint of this fruit pulp add ½ pint Syrup for Ices (Recipe 1570). When cold, freeze in the usual way.

1566 Orange Water Ice

1 pint orange juice **rind of 2 oranges** **1 pint syrup for ices**

Peel the rind off the oranges thinly and put it into a basin. Pour the syrup boiling hot over the rind, cover the basin and let it stand until cold. Then add the orange juice, strain, and freeze in the usual way.

1567 Peach Water Ice

Make in the same way as Apricot Water Ice (Recipe 1562), substituting peaches for apricots.

1568 Pineapple Water Ice

1 large pineapple **syrup for ices**

Pare the pineapple taking out the eyes, cut it in quarters and remove the core. Chop the fruit finely, put it into a coarse cloth and squeeze out all the juice. Add a little water to the pulp and squeeze again. If there is any more juice left in the fruit, add more water and squeeze again until perfectly dry. Measure the juice and to every pint of juice allow 1 pint Syrup for Ices (Recipe 1570), and 1 tablespoonful lime juice. Freeze as directed.

N.B. Instead of using syrup for ices, sugar may be used dissolved in the fruit juice.

1569 Strawberry Water Ice

1 lb. strawberry jam **1 tablespoon lime juice**
1½ pints syrup for ices **a few drops carmine**

Make the syrup as directed in Recipe 1570. Rub the jam through a fine sieve and add it to the syrup, along with the lime juice, and deepen the colour with a few drops of carmine. Freeze as directed.

1570 Syrup for Water Ices

½ lb. sugar **1 pint water** **juice of 1 lime**

Put the sugar and water into a saucepan, bring to the boil and boil for 10 minutes. Remove any scum that rises. Add the lime juice, strain, and the syrup is ready for use as soon as it is quite cold.

1571 Woodapple Ice

Woodapples **sugar**

Break the shell and scoop out the inside of the fruit with a spoon. Put it into a basin, add a little water and squeeze the fruit well. Then rub it through a fine sieve or strain through coarse net. Return the pulpy mass left in the sieve into the basin, add more water, squeeze again and strain. If there is any more juice left in the fruit, add more water and squeeze again until nothing is left but the seeds. Measure the pulpy juice and to every pint allow ½ lb. sugar or a little more or less according to the acidity of the fruit. Mix well and freeze in the usual way.

Beverages

In this chapter are found some useful and simple recipes for home-made wines and various other drinks.

Cups and Drinks

1581 Aerated Water Drink

2 bottles ginger beer
2 bottles ginger ale
sugar to taste
crushed ice

Put the ginger beer and ginger ale into a jug, sweeten to taste, and just before serving add some crushed ice.

N.B. A dash of angostura bitters will improve the flavour.

1582 Burgundy Cup

Make in the same way as Claret Cup (Recipe 1584).

1583 Cider Cup

1 pint cider
1 oz. soft sugar
1 liqueur glass brandy
1 orange
1 bottle soda water

Put the sugar into a jug, add the orange thinly sliced, and the brandy and stir well; add the cider and stir till the sugar has dissolved. Cover the jug and chill it for about an hour. Strain off into another jug, and add the soda water also iced, at the last.

N.B. A few slices of pineapple may be added to the cup, if liked.

1584 Claret Cup

1 bottle claret
2 bottles soda water
¼ lb. soft sugar
1 wineglass brandy or sherry
1 orange
about 8 slices pineapples
6 thin slices cucumber
ice

Cut the orange in slices and put that and all the ingredients, except the soda water, into a large jug, stir until the sugar is dissolved and chill for about one hour. Then strain off into another jug and add the soda water, also iced, and a lump of ice.

N.B. Lemonade may be used instead of soda water, and the sugar lessened.

1585 Fruit Cocktail

Fruit drinks are both delicious and refreshing and are always welcome. Almost any combination of fruit (fresh or canned) and mixtures of fruit juices sweetened to taste and iced make excellent drinks. Fruit cocktails should be served in long-stemmed cocktail or sundae glasses.

1586 Mixed Fruit Cocktail

2 small ripe bananas
2 apples
2 Jaffna mangoes
12 glace cherries
12 peeled grapes
the juice of 2 sweet oranges
a dash of strained lime juice
2 or 3 tablespoonfuls passion-fruit syrup
1 tablespoonful strained pineapple juice
some crushed tender leaves of mint
1 teaspoonful curacao

Peel all the fresh fruit, quarter the grapes and cherries, and dice the rest. Mix the liquid ingredients with the mint leaves, and pour over the prepared fruit. Stir well, and cover, and allow to become thoroughly chilled. Serve in ice-cold cocktail glasses. The mint may be removed before serving, but this is not necessary unless the leaves look very ragged after crushing.

1587 Ginger Beer

½ lb. green ginger
2¼ lb. sugar
10 bottles water
½ pint sweet toddy
1 wineglass bees' honey
the whites and shells of 2 eggs
1 lime
the juice of 1 lime
1 nutmeg
2 inch piece cinnamon
a blade of mace

Soak the ginger overnight in cold water, scrape the skin out with a knife and slice it finely. Put the sugar into a large chatty, add a teacup of water and the whites and shells of the eggs and mix and beat up well with the hand for about 10 minutes. Then add the rest of the water, the sliced ginger, the nutmeg cut in small pieces, the cinnamon and the mace. Mix all together and boil for an hour without stirring the mixture at all. Cut the lime in thin slices and remove the seeds. Take the chatty off the fire and add the slices of lime and the lime juice, but do not stir the mixture. Set it aside to cool and when perfectly cold strain the ginger beer through a fine cloth into another vessel. Then add the toddy and the honey, mix well, and strain again. Bottle at once in champagne bottles, filling them three-quarters. Use new corks and tie the corks down securely with twine. It will be ready for use 24 hours after bottling and it cannot be kept longer than 36 hours. This quantity will make a dozen bottles of ginger beer.

1588 Ginger Syrup

½ green ginger
2 lb. sugar
juice of 2 oranges
1 inch piece cinnamon
4 or 5 cloves
rind of half a lime
2 bottles water

Soak the ginger overnight in cold water, scrape the skin out with a knife and slice it finely. Put all the ingredients, excepting the orange juice, into a saucepan and stir over the fire until the sugar dissolves. Put the lid on and boil until the ginger is cooked and the syrup thick. Take it off the fire and add the orange juice, then strain through muslin, and when cold bottle for use. A little of this syrup mixed with iced water or aerated water will make a delicious drink.

1589 Hock Cup

1 bottle hock
2 bottles soda water
soft sugar to taste
1 liqueur glass brandy
1 glass curacao or any other liqueur
rind of 1 lime
4 thin slices cucumber

Chill the wine and soda water for some time before making the cup. Have the rest of the ingredients (the sugar may be omitted) ready in a jug, pour in the wine, add the soda water and a few small pieces of ice and serve at once.

1590 Iced Coffee

1 pint strong clear coffee
1 pint milk
2 or 3 oz. sugar
vanilla flavouring

Mix the ingredients together in a jug, pour it into bottles, cork, and set deep in ice until wanted.

Preparation for Lemon Flavour

1591 Iced Tea (Creamed)

½ oz. or 6 teaspoonfuls of Ceylon Tea
Peel of one lime or a few drops of vanilla
9 teaspoons of Condensed Milk
Sugar to taste

Warm the teapot and infuser by pouring in hot water. Place the tea in the infuser and the peel in the pot and pour in six cups of fresh water that has been brought to boil. Remove infuser after five minutes and let the peel remain another ten minutes. Strain the tea into a jug and add the milk and sugar. Place the jug in cold water until the tea is cold; then, pour into bottles and cool on ice.

Preparation for Vanilla Flavour

Prepare as above without lemon peel and a few drops of vanilla.

1592 Iced Tea (Pineapple)

Make a mixture of pineapple juice and orange juice in the proportion of 2 to 1. Add two tablespoonfuls of this mixture to each glass prepared as in recipe 1593.

1593 Iced Tea (Plain)

Take two dessertspoonfuls of good quality Ceylon Tea and brew it in the usual manner (5 minutes) in six cups of boiling water. Strain the liquid carefully into three tall glasses and add sugar to taste. Fill each glass with cracked ice and four slices of lime.

1594 Lemonade

juice of half a lemon or 1 lime
½ pint water
¼ teaspoon carbonate of soda
sugar to taste

Put the strained lemon juice into a large glass with the water, add enough sugar to sweeten it, and stir in the carbonate of soda. This makes a nice effervescing drink.

1595 Lemon Syrup

½ lb. lemons or limes
2 oz. citric acid
2 lb. powdered sugar
1 pint boiling water

Peel the rind off the lemons as thinly as possible, and cut it in small pieces. Put all the ingredients into a jug, straining in the juice of the lemons, and stir occasionally until the sugar and the acid are dissolved. Then strain through muslin and bottle and cork tightly. One tablespoon of this in a tumblerful of iced water or soda water will make a refreshing drink.

1596 Lime Squash

juice of 1 large lime
soda water
1 tablespoonful sugar
1 or 2 small lumps of ice

Strain the lime juice into a tumbler, add the sugar and the ice, fill up with the soda water and serve.

1597 Orangeade

juice of 12 oranges
rind of 2 oranges
¼ lb. sugar
3 pints water
crushed ice

Put the sugar and a pint of water into a saucepan with the orange rind and stir over the fire until the sugar is dissolved. Bring to the boil and allow to cool. Then remove the rind and strain in the orange juice. When wanted, add the remainder of the water and some crushed ice.

1598 Orange Soda

juice of one orange
1 dessertspoon brandy
soda water
ice

Put some crushed ice into a tall glass and strain in the orange juice, add the brandy, and fill up with soda water.

1599 Pineapple Cocktail

FOR EACH PERSON:

1 inch thick slice of ripe juicy pineapple
1 teaspoonful castor sugar
1 eggspoonful curacao
1 tablespoonful strained orange juice
1 teaspoonful (scant) lime juice
3 or 4 fresh mint leaves
1 glace cherry
a few drops of Maraschino
1 dessertspoonful castor sugar

Cut the pineapple into very small cubes, and place in a bowl with the juice which runs out from it, the first lot of sugar, and the curacao. Cover, and chill thoroughly.

In another covered bowl put the fruit juices, sugar, crushed mint leaves, and Maraschino, and chill this.

Just before serving, remove the leaves and mix the syrup with the fruit. All the sugar should be dissolved before mixing. Serve in chilled glasses, with the cherry on top.

1600 Pineapple Sherbet

1 good-sized pineapple
1 lb. sugar
2 pints water
juice of 2 limes
ice

Peel and slice the pineapple and chop it coarsely. Make a syrup with the sugar and a pint of water and pour it boiling hot over the pineapple; add the lime juice, stir all together and let it stand covered for a couple of hours. Then add the remainder of the water, strain into a jug, and just before serving add a few pieces of ice.

1601 Raspberry Lemonade

1 tablespoon raspberry syrup
1 tablespoon lime juice
1 tablespoonful powdered sugar
soda water
ice

Put some finely broken ice into a soda water glass and strain in the lime juice. Add the raspberry syrup and sugar and fill up with soda water.

1602 Rhubarb Sherbet

½ lb. rhubarb
1½ pints water
thinly peeled rind of half an orange
sugar to taste
ice

The rhubarb should be red-stalked and young. Cut it into short lengths, add the water and the orange rind and boil for 20 minutes. Then strain, sweeten to taste and serve when cold with a little crushed ice.

1603 Tamarind Cordial

½ lb. fresh tamarind 1½ lb. sugar 4 pints water

Soak the tamarind in the water for about half an hour. Squeeze and remove the seeds etc. and strain. Then boil for 20 minutes, add the sugar and boil for 30 minutes longer. Strain again and bottle. This quantity will make a bottle of cordial. A little of this syrup mixed with iced water makes a delicious drink.

1604 Tamarind Punch

fresh tamarind
water
jaggery or sugar
salt

Put some tamarind into a bowl, add a little water and squeeze the fruit well. Remove the seeds etc. and strain through coarse net. Add jaggery (scraped) or sugar to taste and a little salt and stir well. If the punch is too thick, thin it down with water.

Wines

1611 Almond Liqueur

1 bottle arrack
½ bottle water
1½ lb. sugar
1 oz. essence of almonds
¼ pint orange juice
1 wineglass rose-water

Make the sugar and water into a thickish syrup and let it cool. Then mix all the ingredients together and strain into bottles through flannel bags or filter paper. Cork and seal the bottles.

1612 Burnt Sugar

¼ lb. sugar **1 tablespoon cold water** **1 teacup hot water**

Put the sugar into a small saucepan, add the cold water and let it boil without stirring until the sugar becomes a dark brown colour. Then add gently the hot water, stir for a couple of minutes, and it is ready for use.

N.B. This is a liquid used for colouring wines, etc.

1613 Ginger Wine

2 bottles arrack
1 bottle milk
½ bottle water
1¾ lb. sugar
¼ lb. dry ginger
¼ pint lime juice
1 teacup burnt sugar (**Recipe 1612**)

Powder the ginger and put it into a bottle with half a bottle of arrack; cork the bottle tightly and keep it for three days. Shake the bottle well every day. On the third day, empty the contents of the bottle into a big jug and add to it the rest of the arrack, the water, the sugar, lime juice, Burnt Sugar, and the milk which must be boiled and cooled. Stir well with a wooden spoon until the sugar is dissolved. Then strain into bottles through flannel bags or filter paper. Cork and seal the bottles.

1614 La Creme

3 bottles arrack
2 bottles milk
½ bottle water
3 lb. sugar
1 oz. essence of almonds
¼ oz. dry ginger
1 nutmeg
1 blade of mace
12 cardamoms
15 cloves
4-inch piece cinnamon
¼ pint lime juice
rind of 5 limes
carmine

Bruise lightly the cloves, the cardamoms (with the skins), mace and cinnamon; cut the nutmeg in small pieces. Put these spices together with the lime rind into half a bottle of arrack, cork the bottle and keep it for at least three days, shaking the bottle well every day. Then empty the contents into a big jug, add the rest of the arrack, the lime juice, the milk, which must be boiled and cooled, and the sugar and water boiled to a thick syrup and cooled. Stir well and strain into bottles through flannel bags or filter paper. Then add enough carmine to make it a pretty pink colour. Cork and seal the bottles.

1615 Milk Punch

2 bottles arrack
¾ bottle milk
½ bottle water
1½ lb. sugar
half a wineglass lime juice
half a mandarin or orange rind
rind of 2 limes
20 cloves
10 cardamoms
3-inch piece cinnamon
half blade of mace
1 teacup burnt sugar
1 nutmeg

Bruise lightly the cloves, the cardamoms with the skins, the mace and cinnamon; cut the nutmeg in small pieces and put these spices together with the lime and orange rinds into half a bottle of arrack. Cork the bottle and keep it for about three days, shaking the bottle well every day. Then empty the contents into a big jug, add the rest of the arrack and the sugar and stir with a wooden spoon until the sugar is quite dissolved. Boil the milk, and while it is still slightly warm add the lime juice to it. Let it cool, then add it to the rest of the ingredients together with the Burnt Sugar. Stir well, and strain into bottles through flannel bags or filter paper. Cork the bottles tightly and seal them.

1616 Noyeau

1 bottle brandy or gin
¼ bottle milk
1 lb. sugar
1 oz. bitter almonds
1 oz. sweet almonds
rind of one lime

Blanch and pound the almonds and put them and the lime rind cut in small pieces into a bottle, add ¼ bottle of the brandy or gin, cork the bottle tightly and keep it for a week. Then empty the contents into a jug and add the remainder of the spirits, the sugar and the milk which must be boiled and cooled. Stir with a wooden spoon until the sugar is dissolved, and let it remain covered for a couple of days, stirring it every day. Then filter and bottle.

1617 Orange Wine

2 bottles arrack
1½ lb. sugar
½ pint orange juice
rind of 2 oranges
1 teacup burnt sugar

Peel the rind off the oranges as thinly as possible, cut it in small pieces and put it into half a bottle of arrack. Cork the bottle and keep it for about three days, shaking the bottle well every day. Then empty the contents into a big jug and add the rest of the arrack, the sugar, orange juice and the Burnt Sugar. Stir well with a wooden spoon until the sugar is dissolved, then filter and bottle.

1618 Rose Wine

2 bottles arrack
1 bottle rose-water
½ bottle water
2 lb. sugar
½ wineglass lime juice
carmine

Put the sugar and water into a saucepan and stir over the fire until it forms a thick syrup; set it aside to cool. When quite cold, mix it with the arrack, add the lime juice and filter into bottles through flannel bags or filter paper. Then colour it a pretty pink with a few drops of carmine. Seal the corks down.

1619 Vanilla Liqueur

1 bottle brandy
½ bottle water
1 lb. sugar
4 vanilla beans

Cut the vanilla into pieces, add it to the brandy and let it infuse for 10 or 12 days, shaking the bottle well every day. Boil the sugar and water to a syrup and add it hot to the brandy. Stir well, and when cool filter and bottle.

Invalid & Convalescent Cookery

At one time or another we all have to do with invalids, so it is necessary that this branch of cookery should be carefully studied by every woman. There are several important points to be considered when catering for an invalid. The doctor's orders should always be strictly carried out. Particular care should be paid to cleanliness both in the preparation and the serving. The food should be varied and well cocked, and served in the daintiest manner possible. A pretty traycloth, a pair of dainty cups and saucers etc., all help to tempt a listless appetite. Serve the food punctually at the hour expected. There should never be too much: nothing destroys the appetite so much as large quantities of food. All dishes and remains of food should be removed from the sick-room as soon as finished with. Do not consult a patient about his (or her) meal, but try to find out what will be liked and let it come as a surprise.

1631 Albumen or Egg Water

Boil a teacup of water, adding to it a small piece of cinnamon and a clove. Let the water cool, then mix in the white of an egg lightly beaten, a pinch of salt, sugar to taste, and a squeeze of lime. Strain through muslin; if liked, a teaspoon of brandy may be added.

1632 Arrowroot with Milk

Prepare in the same way as Arrowroot Water using milk instead of water; if desired, a little sugar may be added.

1633 Arrowroot Biscuits

½ lb. arrowroot	**2 oz. butter**
¼ lb. dough	**the yolk of 1 egg**
¼ lb. soft sugar	**a pinch of salt**

Beat the egg into the dough, add the butter, sugar and salt, and mix well. Then add the arrowroot (sifted), and knead all together with the hand until the ingredients are all well blended. Take small portions of the mixture and form into fancy shapes, using a little flour to prevent them sticking to the hands. Place them on a floured baking tin and bake in a moderate oven from 20 to 25 minutes. This quantity is sufficient for 3 dozen little biscuits.

1634 Arrowroot Pudding

1 teaspoonful arrowroot
½ pint milk
1 teaspoonful sugar
2 eggs
a pinch of salt
a little flavouring

Mix the arrowroot to a smooth paste with a little of the milk and put the remainder of the milk into a saucepan and heat it. When hot mix the arrowroot into it, stirring well, and continue stirring until the mixture boils and thickens. Then take it off the fire, and when cold, stir in the sugar and the yolks of the eggs lightly beaten, and flavour with lemon or any other flavouring preferred. Lastly, stir in the whites beaten to a stiff froth with a pinch of salt. Pour the mixture into a greased pie-dish and bake in a moderate oven until nicely browned.

1635 Arrowroot Water

1 teaspoonful arrowroot
salt
½ pint boiling water

Put the arrowroot into a dry saucepan, (aluminium or tin) and roast it over the fire for a few minutes, stirring all the time. Then take the saucepan off the fire, and when the arrowroot has cooled, mix it into a paste with a little cold water, and pour over it the boiling water, stirring all the time. Return the saucepan to the fire and boil for 5 minutes. Add salt to taste, and, if liked, a little sugar.

1636 Barley and Milk

Prepare in the same way as Barley Water (Recipe 1637), adding milk and omitting the lime juice.

1637 Barley Water

2 tablespoons pearl barley
sugar
2 breakfastcups of cold water
lime juice

Wash the barley and soak it in cold water for about half an hour, then drain and put the barley into a saucepan with a little water. Let it boil 5 minutes, pour off the water, and put the barley on again with two breakfastcups of fresh water. Boil slowly from 1½ to 2 hours, adding more water if necessary. Then strain and add lime juice to taste, and a little sugar, if liked, or omit both lime juice and sugar and add only salt.

1638 Barley Water from "Patent Barley"

1 heaped dessertspoonful Robinson's patent barley
sugar to taste
2 teacups boiling water
lime juice

Mix the barley to a smooth paste with a little cold water. Pour this into a saucepan containing the two teacups of boiling water, and boil for 5 minutes, stirring all the time. Add lime juice to taste, and a little sugar, if wished. Strain and serve.

N.B. If a more nourishing drink is required, a larger quantity of barley should be used, and it may be mixed with milk—the lime juice in this case being omitted.

1639 Beef Juice

Wash the meat, remove all fat and skin from it, and shred it down very finely with a knife. Put the meat into a towel and squeeze out all the juice. Add a pinch of salt and serve it at once as it does not keep.

1640 Beef Tea

½ lb. beef **½ pint cold water** **salt**

Choose a fresh, lean and juicy piece of meat. Wash it, and shred it very finely. Put the shredded meat into a jar, add the water and a little salt, cover the jar and let it stand for half an hour. Stir well before putting it on to cook. Then place the jar, closely covered, in a saucepan with cold water to reach three-quarter way up the sides. Bring to the boil, and let it simmer slowly from 1½ to 2 hours. When sufficiently cooked, remove the jar from the saucepan, stir the beef tea well and strain.

1641 Beef Tea Custard

1 teacup beef tea **1 egg**

Break the egg into a cup, remove the speck, and beat it up. Then add the beef tea and more seasoning, if necessary. Mix well together, pour into a greased cup and steam very gently until set. Let it stand for a minute or two, turn out and serve hot or cold.

N.B. A good meat stock—beef, chicken or mutton—may be used instead of beef tea, and the custard may be baked instead of being steamed.

1642 Savoury Beef Tea

½ lb. beef
1 pint cold water
3 or 4 red onions
2 cloves
12 peppercorns
a small piece of cinnamon
salt

Cut the meat into small dice, removing every particle of fat and skin. Put it into a saucepan, add the water, and, if time permits let it soak for quarter of an hour. Then add the onions, cloves, peppercorns and cinnamon. Place on the fire, bring slowly to boiling point, and then simmer very gently for 1½ hours. Strain, season with salt and serve.

N.B. If liked, a piece of celery may be used for flavouring.

1643 Raw Beef Sandwiches

2 oz. lean juicy beef **bread and butter**

Wipe the meat with a damp cloth, and with a sharp knife shred it down very finely. Add any seasoning that may be allowed and spread between thin slices of bread and butter. Cut into neat strips and serve.

1644 Invalid Blancmange

1 dessertspoonful cornflour
1 teacup milk
sugar
orange juice

Mix the cornflour to a smooth paste with a little of the milk. Put the remainder of the milk into a saucepan and bring to the boil. Remove from the fire, and add to it the mixed cornflour, stirring well. Return to the fire and boil for 5 minutes stirring all the time. Pour the mixture into a mould that has been rinsed out with cold water, and set aside until cold. When wanted turn out on a plate, pour over it a wineglass of strained orange juice, sprinkle over with sugar and serve.

1645 Bread and Milk

a thick slice of stale bread **½ pint milk a little sugar**

Remove the crust from the bread and cut it into 3 or 4 pieces. Bring the milk to boiling point, pour over the bread, cover, and let it stand for 5 minutes. Serve very hot with a little sugar or golden syrup.

1646 Calf's Foot Jelly

2 calf's feet
5 or 6 pints cold water
a glass of sherry, or ½ a wineglass brandy
6 oz. sugar
4 cloves
2-inch piece cinnamon
1 blade mace
rind of 2 limes
juice of 2 oranges
white and shells of 2 eggs

Wash the feet thoroughly (you can buy them cleaned), and divide them into 3 or 4 pieces, cutting away any discoloured parts. Put the pieces into a lined saucepan with cold water to cover them. Bring quickly to boiling point and throw the water away. Rinse out the saucepan, return the pieces to it and cover again with cold water—from 3 to 6 pints. Put the lid on the pan and cook slowly from 7 to 8 hours—until the stock is reduced to about a pint. Strain through a coarse towel, and allow the stock to stand until it is quite cold. Then remove every particle of fat from the top and put the stock into the saucepan. Add the sugar, spices, lime rind, orange juice, the egg shells which should be washed and crushed, and the whites of the eggs lightly beaten. The pan should not be more than half-full or the jelly will boil over. Whisk over the fire, until it just begins to boil, then allow to boil up as high as it will without boiling over. Take it off the fire, and allow to stand for about 20 minutes, then strain through a coarse towel. First pour some boiling water through the towel and then pour the jelly. It will not be clear the first time, so strain it 2 or 3 times until it runs through perfectly clear. Add the wine or brandy to it, after it has been strained. Pour into a wet mould and set it in a cool place or on ice.

N.B. This jelly will take 2 days to make. Prepare the stock the first day and make the jelly on the second.

1647 Chicken Broth

1 chicken
cold water
4 small red onions
1 clove
12 peppercorns
a small piece of cinnamon
salt

Skin the chicken and cut it in small pieces. Wash thoroughly, and put into a saucepan with sufficient water to cover it. Add the onions, clove, pepper and cinnamon, and let it simmer gently for 2 hours, adding more water, if necessary. When cooked, strain and add salt to taste.

N.B. If a stronger broth is wanted the chicken must not be skinned, and the bones may be broken up, so as to draw out all the goodness. If liked, the broth may be thickened with a teaspoonful of sago or tapioca.

1648 Essence of Chicken

Cut the chicken into joints, wash well, and cut all the flesh from the bones. Break up the bones and cut the meat in small pieces. Put the meat, bones and skin into a jar without any water. Cover the jar closely and place it in a saucepan with cold water to reach half-way up the sides. Cover with the lid, and simmer slowly from 4 to 5 hours. If the water boils down more must be added. When cooked, remove the jar from the saucepan and strain all the liquid away from the chicken. Season to taste and serve in small quantities.

1649 Chicken Mince

¼ lb. uncooked chicken
½ oz. butter
½ teaspoon flour
1 gill milk
pepper and salt
hot buttered toast

Mince the chicken very finely. Melt the butter in a saucepan, put in the minced chicken and cook on the fire for a few minutes without allowing to brown. Sprinkle in the flour and add the milk gradually. Season to taste with pepper and salt. Cover the saucepan and let it simmer slowly until the chicken is tender. Cut some toast into neat pieces, butter it while hot and pile some of the chicken mince on each piece.

1650 Steamed Custard Pudding

1 egg
1 teacup milk
a little sugar
flavouring

Boil the milk, add sugar to taste and pour it boiling hot on the egg lightly beaten. Mix well together and flavour the custard with nutmeg, grated lime peel, or anything which may be preferred. Pour it into a greased cup and steam very slowly until set. Turn out carefully and serve.

1651 Egg Flip

Break an egg into a teacup. Remove the speck, add a teaspoonful or more of sugar and a grate of nutmeg, and beat it together until quite frothy. Then fill up the cup with boiling milk or coffee. Stir briskly when pouring in the milk. If liked, a teaspoon of brandy may be added.

1652 Egg Poached in Milk

1 fresh egg
1 teacup milk
salt
1 teaspoon butter
a round of buttered toast

Melt the butter in a small saucepan, put in the milk, add a pinch of salt and bring it to the boil. Break the egg into a cup and carefully slip it into the boiling milk. Poach very gently for 3 minutes or until the white is nicely set without being hard. Place it on a round of buttered toast and pour some of the milk round it.

1653 Fish Custard

1 tablespoonful boiled fish
1 egg
2 tablespoons milk
pepper and salt

Seer or any white fish will do for this. Break the fish in flakes and season with pepper and salt. Break the egg into a cup, remove the speck, and beat up with the milk. Add the fish to it and pour into a greased cup. Steam gently until set. Turn out when ready and serve either hot or cold.

1654 Ginger Tea

1 tablespoonful coriander seed
12 slices green ginger
2-inch piece cinnamon
sugar to taste
2 teacups water

Wash the coriander well and put it into a saucepan with the ginger cut in small pieces and the cinnamon. Add the water and boil gently until the quantity is reduced by half. Then strain, sweeten to taste and serve very hot.

1655 Kohila Conjee

Take three or four pieces of kohila yam from a bundle and cut into small pieces. Wash and pound with about a tablespoonful of scraped coconut. Squeeze out the juice adding a little water and strain the juice. Make a small quantity of thick conjee with country rice and add the prepared juice. Bring the mixture to the boil. Add salt to taste. Sweeten if desired with jaggery or sugar.

1656 Kohila Conjee With Sago

Cook a little sago conjee and add kohila juice prepared as for Kohila Conjee. Bring to the boil.

1657 Kohila With Custard Powder or Cornflour

Pound the kohila yam and coconut and add enough water to make about ¾ cup of juice. Bring this to the boil. Take 1 level teaspoon of custard powder or cornflour and mix into a smooth cream with a little cold water. Add this to the kohila juice and keep stirring this over the fire for two or three minutes. Add salt and sugar or jaggery if desired.

1658 Mace Water

a blade of mace **8 cloves** **a teacup of boiling water**

Put the mace and cloves into a cup, pour over the boiling water, cover the cup closely and let it stand until cold. Then strain and it is ready.

1659 Milk Toast

a thick slice of stale bread
½ pint milk
a teaspoon of butter
a little sugar
a grate of nutmeg

Remove the crust from the bread and toast it a pale brown. Put the milk, butter and sugar into a saucepan, bring to boiling point, add the nutmeg and pour over the toast.

1660 Mutton Broth

½ lb. mutton
1 tablespoonful pearl barley
1 pint cold water
4 red onions
12 peppercorns
a small piece of cinnamon
1 clove
salt

Remove all fat, cut the mutton into small pieces, and put into a saucepan with the water, the barley (which should be soaked overnight in cold water), the onions, clove, pepper, and cinnamon; bring to the boil and skim well. Simmer slowly for 2 hours then strain and let it stand till cold. When cold remove the fat from the surface, return the broth to a clean saucepan, re-heat, season to taste and serve.

1661 Invalid Mutton Chop

1 mutton chop — **salt**
pepper — **butter**

Trim the chop neatly, removing most of the fat, and sprinkle with a little pepper and salt. Place the chop on a buttered deep plate, put a few pieces of butter on the top, and cover over with another plate. Have ready a saucepan half full of boiling water, place the plates on it and cook from 15 to 20 minutes. Then turn the chop and cook about the same length of time on the other side. The water must be kept boiling all the time and if it boils away more boiling water must be added. Serve the chop as soon as it is ready, along with any juice that has run from it.

1662 Mutton Tea

Prepare in the same way as Beef Tea (Recipe 1640).

1663 Rice Water

¼ measure muttusamba rice — **2 pints cold water** — **salt**

Wash the rice well and put it into a saucepan with the water. Simmer slowly for half an hour or until the rice is boiled; then strain, add salt to taste, and it is ready for use.

1664 Roasted Rice Water

1 dessertspoonful rice — **2 teacups cold water** — **salt**

Put the rice into a dry saucepan (aluminium or tin), and roast it over the fire until the rice is browned, stirring all the time. Then add the water, and simmer slowly for half an hour or until the water is reduced by half, stirring occasionally. Strain, add salt to taste and serve.

1665 Sago Gruel

1 dessertspoonful sago — **sugar to taste**
1 teacup cold water — **a pinch of salt**
1 teacup milk

Wash the sago and soak it in the water for about half an hour. Then boil gently until clear, stirring occasionally. Add the milk and a pinch of salt, sweeten to taste and serve.

1666 Sago Pudding

1 tablespoonful sago — **1 egg**
1 teacup milk — **a pinch of salt**
1½ dessertspoons sugar — **essence of lemon or chopped lime peel**

Wash the sago, put it into a small saucepan with the milk and boil until it is very thick, stirring all the time. Then add the sugar, salt and flavouring. Remove the saucepan from the fire, and when the contents have cooled a little, stir in the egg well beaten. Pour the mixture into a buttered mould, and steam from 20 to 30 minutes.

1667 Soda, Milk and Egg

1 egg
1 teaspoonful sugar
1 teacup milk
1 split soda

Beat the egg and sugar together, add the milk, stir well and add the soda water. Serve at once.

N.B. Less soda water might be used. If liked, a teaspoonful of sherry may be added.

1668 Stewed Spaghetti

2 oz. spaghetti
a breakfast cup of chicken broth
½ oz. butter
1 oz. cheese
pepper

Break the spaghetti in pieces and put it into a saucepan, add the broth and seasoning and simmer slowly until the spaghetti is tender and the stock is nearly all absorbed. Then add the butter and cheese. Serve hot.

1669 Tapioca Pudding

Make in the same way as Sago Pudding (Recipe 1663).

1670 Toast Water

Toast a slice of stale bread to a very dark brown colour. Put it into a jug, add 2 cloves and pour in a pint of boiling water. Cover the jug closely and let it remain until cold, then strain and use.

1671 Vegetable Broth

1 tablespoonful dhall
2 carrots
2 leeks
1 turnip
1 Bombay onion
2 stripes celery
salt, pepper
3 pints water

Wash the dhall well in several waters removing discoloured ones which float on top of the water. Put the dhall into a saucepan, add the 3 pints of water and bring to the boil. Skim well and let it simmer for half an hour. Then add the vegetables prepared and cut in small pieces. Simmer slowly for about 2 hours or until the vegetables are quite soft, stirring occasionally. Season with salt and pepper. The broth could be sieved, if liked.

1672 Whey

1 teacup milk **1 tablespoonful lime juice** **a little sugar**

Put the milk into a saucepan with sugar to taste and bring it to the boil. Add the lime juice to the boiling milk, let it stand for a while until the milk curdles, then strain through muslin.

Index

THE numbers given are the numbers of Recipes.

The Recipes in each Chapter and Section in the book are arranged in alphabetical order.

In the Index, Chapters and Sections are arranged in alphabetical order and the Recipes arranged alphabetically under each, with helpful additional items from other parts of the book thrown in.

Certain recipes are also repeated in their place in alphabetical order.

For GENERAL HINTS, please see beginnings of Chapters and Sections.

No. of Recipe

Invalid & Convalescent Cookery—*Contd.*

Jams & Preserves

Meat

(Including Recipes under Meat, Beef & Veal, Lamb & Mutton, Pork, Poultry & Game)

Please see first under MEAT for your needs.

PRINTED BY LAKE HOUSE PRINTERS & PUBLISHERS LTD